Against Capitalism

Against Capitalism

David Schweickart

Westview Press
A Member of the Perseus Books Group

Copyright © 1996 by Westview Press, A Member of the Perseus Books Group

Published in 1996 in the United States of America by Westview Press, Inc., 5500 Central Avenue, Boulder, Colorado 80301-2877, and in the United Kingdom by Westview Press, 12 Hid's Copse Road, Cumnor Hill, Oxford OX2 9JJ

Library of Congress Cataloging-in-Publication Data
Schweickart, David.
Against capitalism / David Schweickart.
    p. cm.
  Rev. ed. of: Capitalism or worker control? 1980.
  Includes bibliographical references and index.
  ISBN 0-8133-3113-7
  1. Comparative economics.   2. Capitalism.   3. Socialism.
I. Schweickart, David. Capitalism or worker control?   II. Title.
III. Series.
HB90.S38   1996
330.12'2—dc20   92-47480
                                                                              CIP

The paper used in this publication meets the requirements of the American National Standard for Permanence of Paper for Printed Library Materials Z39.48-1984.

10   9   8   7   6   5

For Patsy

But there was in store a still greater victory of the political economy of labor over the political economy of property. We speak of the co-operative movement, especially the co-operative factories raised by the unassisted efforts of a few bold hands. The value of these great social experiments cannot be over-rated. By deed, instead of by argument, they have shown that production on a large scale, and in accord with the behests of modern science, may be carried on without the existence of a class of masters employing a class of hands; that to bear fruit, the means of labor need not be monopolized as a means of domination over, and of extortion against, the laboring man himself; and that, like slave labor, like serf labor, hired labor is but a transitory and inferior form destined to disappear before associated labor plying its toil with a willing hand, a ready mind, and a joyous heart. . . . At the same time, the experience of the period . . . has proved beyond doubt that, however excellent in principle, and however useful in practice, co-operative labor, if kept within the narrow circle of the casual efforts of private workmen, will never be able to arrest the growth in geometrical progression of monopoly, to free the masses, nor even to perceptibly lighten the burden of their miseries. . . . To save the industrious masses, co-operative labor ought to be developed to national dimensions, and consequently, to be fostered by national means. Yet, the lords of land and the lords of capital will always use their political privileges for the defense and perpetration of their economic monopolies. So far from promoting, they will continue to lay every possible impediment in the way of the emancipation of labor. . . . To conquer political power has therefore become the duty of the working classes.

– Karl Marx, "Inaugural Address of the Working
Men's International Association" (1864)

Contents

Preface

It hardly needs to be said that this book swims against the tide. Everyone knows that socialism is dead, that communism is dead. We have all read the obituaries. Here's Richard Rorty, famous philosopher and recipient of a MacArthur "genius" grant:

It is going to take a long period of readjustment for us Western leftist intellectuals to comprehend that the word "socialism" has been drained of force – as have been all other words that drew their force from the idea that an alternative to capitalism was available. [We are] going to have to stop using the term "capitalist economy" as if we knew what a functioning non-capitalist economy looked like.[1]

The obituaries may be premature. This book will argue that Rorty is quite wrong: We *can* say what a functioning noncapitalist economy would look like. The collapse of Communist rule in Eastern Europe and the Soviet Union, though hardly irrelevant to this matter, does not prove what Rorty and so many others think it does.

This book advances an even stronger thesis: Because there exists an alternative to capitalism that is not merely viable but plainly superior, capitalism no longer has a valid justification, either economical or ethical. If this is right, then intellectuals (Western ex-leftists and all others) should stop pretending that capitalism has any claim to our moral allegiance. We should admit that we cannot get beyond capitalism at this moment not because there exists no viable, desirable "beyond" but because those who most profit from the present order are too powerful. Simply that. In the face of such power, one may decide to cultivate one's garden, or to work to ameliorate the harsher aspects of "actually existing capitalism," or to struggle for radical transformation. A case might be made for any of these as an honorable option. What cannot be maintained, if the argument herein is sound, is that "you need capitalism to ensure a reliable supply of goods and services, and to ensure that there will be enough taxable surplus left over to finance social welfare."[2]

Needless to say, so strong a thesis as this book advances cannot be established with the certainty of a mathematical proof or a scientific discovery. The conclusion cannot be deduced by means of logic alone from self-evident axioms, nor is there a country to which one can point

[1] Rorty (1992, p. 16).   [2] Ibid.

and say, "There you have it." The argument has more the form of a court proceeding: When the defendant pleads not guilty, the prosecutor must amass the evidence, bit by bit, and fit it together, block by block, until a case is made "beyond a reasonable doubt." That will be my strategy here, with capitalism in the dock, the reader as the jury.

The court analogy does not carry through completely. In a criminal court it is sufficient to convince the jury that the defendant has committed a serious crime. In the arena of political philosophy it is not sufficient simply to document the deficiencies of capitalism. Most of these are well known. But the powerful rejoinder to such criticisms is a thunderous "What's your alternative?" The Churchillian defense of democracy is transposed to capitalism: "It's the worst possible system, except for all the others." This work will confront this challenge squarely. An alternative will be presented, to be called "Economic Democracy." Its structures will be elaborated in some detail, and its economic viability defended. It will be compared with various models of capitalism along a variety of economic and ethical parameters and will be shown to be strongly preferable.

A second disanalogy with a court proceeding concerns rhetoric. Lawyers, notoriously, use whatever rhetorical tricks they can muster so as to influence a jury. My formal training is in mathematics and philosophy, not law. I am committed to a *reasoned* defense of the book's thesis. I want to be scrupulously fair in presenting the arguments in favor of capitalism and in acknowledging the possible weaknesses of Economic Democracy. I shall try to be explicit regarding the values to which the arguments appeal, and how acceptable these values are likely to be to people of goodwill, be they conservative, liberal, or Left. Not every argument presented here will be acceptable to everyone, because some, as will be demonstrated, rest on disputed values. I hope, however, that when all is said, even the most conservative reader will be rationally persuaded, not on all points but on enough to reach a final verdict: Capitalism no longer has a valid justification.

This book has had a protracted gestation. Twenty-two years ago I resigned my position as an assistant professor of mathematics to study philosophy, convinced that there was something deeply amiss with our society. I came to identify an important part of that "something" as capitalism, and undertook a dissertation to establish a proof. In working out the argument, it became clear to me that I could not avoid a fundamental question: Can there exist an economically viable socialism that does not tend, as the Soviet model clearly does, toward an antidemocratic concentration of power? So I plunged into the study of economics and emerged, first, with a dissertation and then, some years later, with a book: *Capitalism or Worker Control?: An Ethical and Economic Appraisal.*[3]

In the fall of 1990 I decided to do a revision of that book. Initially I thought of this as a minor undertaking – update a few statistics, polish a few arguments, add a few footnotes. But as I reread my work, it became obvious that a book on socialism to be published in the 1990s would have to be very different from one published in 1980. The political climate is different now, after twelve years of Reaganesque rule in the United States. Moreover, since 1980 there has been an explosion of theoretical and practical research on a topic I had made central to my alternative to capitalism: workplace democracy. Mathematical models have proliferated, as have case studies of producer cooperatives and of participatory workplaces. The world situation has also changed drastically. The Japanese and German economies suddenly loom large in much economic thinking. International trade and international competitiveness have become major concerns. That was not so a decade ago.

Of course, the most dramatic changes have occurred in Eastern Europe: the momentous events of 1989, soon followed by the breakup of the Soviet Union, then the savage bloodletting in what was once Yugoslavia. I had to question seriously, as I began to reread my work, whether the arguments set out there would hold up. Or would they now seem laughably naive? (Yugoslavia, after all, had been an important inspiration.)

I must say that they did seem to hold up rather well, even though it became clear as I read that there is now much more to be said on certain topics, and there are additional topics that must be addressed. A reader of my earlier book will notice that the basic structure of that book has been preserved in this volume. In Chapter 1, I evaluate a series of noncomparative justifications for capitalism (more this time than before); then in Chapters 2–5, I engage in an extended comparison of a model of socialism (this time called Economic Democracy) with an idealized version of capitalism. As before, I set out the comparison in terms of efficiency, growth, and noneconomic values. In Chapter 6, I turn to two quite distinct "liberal" modifications of what is basically the "conservative" ideal, to see how they fare.

The argument from Chapter 1 through the middle of Chapter 6 follows my earlier book, although everything has been rewritten, and much new material has been incorporated. Beginning with the second section of Chapter 6, the material is almost all new. As the second liberal alternative, I substitute Lester Thurow's "new liberalism" for John Kenneth Galbraith's post-Keynesian "ideal industrial state," because new liberalism has

---

[3] Schweickart (1980).

emerged as the main liberal alternative to Keynesian liberalism.[4] This substitution requires that the issue of international trade be addressed, a topic wholly neglected the first time around.

Chapters 7 and 8 treat questions given only cursory attention before – questions, respectively, of transition and of other forms of socialism. The prospects and lessons of Eastern Europe figure prominently in both chapters. Chapter 7 also discusses the relevance of Economic Democracy to the Third World.

Chapter 9 concludes the book on a somewhat personal note. There I address an issue tangential to the main topic of the book, but of particular interest to me, given my self-identification: the relation of Economic Democracy to Marxism. I trust that this will be of some interest to others also.

Because this book is deeply interdisciplinary, it is bound to annoy various experts. I am writing for both philosophers and economists, so I have tried to avoid appealing to the specialized knowledge of either discipline without first providing careful explanations. This strategy should make the book accessible to any intelligent lay reader, though perhaps at the cost of appearing to specialists insufficiently rigorous at various points. I don't know any way around this dilemma.

The book is meant to be accessible to a wide range of readers, but I must add this warning: The book is low on rhetoric and rather densely argued, with many footnotes, and so it will not be an easy read. I know from experience that students often find the material in Chapter 1 especially rough going. Readers who are impatient to find out what Economic Democracy is all about can jump ahead to Chapter 2 – although I think something is lost in doing so.

The ideas and arguments of this book, which have preoccupied me through most of my academic life, have been enriched by many people – students, colleagues, radical economists (many of whom I met while serving for several years on the editorial board of the *Review of Radical Political Economics*), Left philosophers, personal friends, and family. I cannot begin to thank each of them here individually, but a number who have been particularly important should be mentioned. Over the years I have discussed many of these ideas at length with Frank Thompson and Drew Christie, and all of them with Patsy Schweickart (who contributed

---

[4] These terms will be clarified in Chapters 2 and 6. To oversimplify somewhat: Keynesian liberalism is the economic vision of the "traditional" Democratic Party in the United States, whereas what I am calling "new liberalism" is the vision of many of the younger economists now advising the party. Keynesian liberals emphasize full employment and welfare; new liberals want structural changes that will enhance both equity and international competitiveness.

some revisions to Chapter 9). While working on this book, I also bene-
fited from exchanges with Tom Sheehan (who kept feeding me relevant
news clippings), David Ingram, Tom Weisskopf, Milton Fisk, Sandra
Bartky, Justin Schwartz, Mike Howard, Bob Stone, Larry Udell, Holly
Graff, Charles Mills, Femi Taiwo, Paul Gomberg, Tom Carson, Sharryn
Kasmir, Diane Suter, Carol Araullo, and Gilles LeCompagnon. I must
thank my daughter Anita for her work as my research assistant one
summer, my daughter Karen for similar help another summer, and Ann
Dolinko for research assistance during the academic year 1991–2. Special
thanks must be extended to Jaroslav Vanek and John Roemer. When I
was debating with myself whether to undertake this project or to write
a book on a different subject, both argued, in the end persuasively, that
the topic at hand was the more important one. Special thanks, too, to
a special class at the Loyola Rome Center, whose fresh enthusiasm
rekindled my own.

One final note: The manuscript for this book was completed in September 1992, two months before the election of Bill Clinton to the U.S.
presidency. Although I could have made changes before publication so
as to reflect this event, it has not been necessary to do so. Had the book
been written after the election, the tone might have been slightly different in certain places, but the overall argument would have been the
same. I must say that I am pleased (and rather surprised) that the new
liberalism that I analyze in Chapter 6 has moved so quickly to center
stage.

1. Noncomparative justifications

Capitalism – can it be justified? To situate the question, let us ask first, How has it been justified?

As capitalism emerged from a dying feudalism, the concept of self-interest became the focus of attention. Proponents of the rising order were divided as to the intrinsic morality of this "fundamental human passion," but all agreed that it could be immensely useful to society when suitably harnessed to a free market.[1]

Their arguments – or, in any event, capitalism – carried the day. But soon trouble was brewing in another pot. Using the economic categories of Adam Smith and David Ricardo (specifically, the labor theory of value), Karl Marx argued that capitalism is inherently exploitative. Even without monopolies (Smith's concern) or landowners (Ricardo's bête noire), free, competitive capitalism exploits the working class, for workers are the source of all value, and yet they are excluded from the economic surplus. Capital, said Marx, is not a *thing* possessing mysterious productive power but, rather, a *social relationship* among human beings, a relationship of power. The free market masks the fact that capitalist society is formally homologous to a feudal or even slave society: A ruling class controls the means of production while a dominated class does the work.

The Marxian challenge, particularly when backed by an increasingly militant working class, placed capitalism on the defensive. But the Marxian argument had a theoretical vulnerability: its underlying value theory. Soon, throughout Europe and America, a new economics came into being. Jevons in England, Walras in Switzerland, Menger, Böhm-Bawerk, and Wieser in Austria, and John Bates Clark in the United States proclaimed the obsolescence of the labor theory of value. "Classical" analysis gave way to "marginalist" analysis. Neoclassical economics was born.[2]

The intellectual victory of neoclassical economics did not prevent the

---

[1] See Hirschman (1977) for a good account of this debate.

[2] I do not mean to suggest that neoclassical economics is in fact superior to Marxian economics. I am persuaded that the standard critiques of the labor theory of value fail against more sophisticated versions of the theory (Schweickart, 1988, 1989). I am also persuaded that Marxian analysis, with or without the labor theory of value, is more useful to understanding the way the world works than is neoclassical theory. Many of the arguments in this book are derived from Marx, even though they are not expressed in Marxian terminology.

Russian Revolution. Socialism descended from the ideal to the real. For a decade or so, various neoclassical economists tried to prove the economic impossibility of socialism,[3] but soon the profession took a different turn. The fact–value distinction was invoked, and economists declared themselves independent (qua economists) of ethical concerns.[4] Henceforth, justification of capitalism would be left to philosophers, politicians, and economists qua citizens. Economic arguments, of course, remained important: that capitalism is more efficient than socialism or more conducive to economic growth. Human-nature arguments asserting the natural link between innate egoism and free enterprise were still invoked, although with decreasing frequency as socialism spread throughout the world. But another argument became increasingly prominent. With the Russian Revolution deteriorating into Stalinism, vigorous attempts were made to reaffirm the causal connection between capitalism and freedom or, rather, because fascist and other ruthlessly authoritarian capitalist regimes made that causal linkage implausible, the connection was affirmed between socialism and totalitarianism. "Socialism," declaimed Friedrich von Hayek, "is the road to serfdom."[5]

How do things stand today? Not altogether settled. Since 1989, the Western media have declared the death of socialism. Francis Fukuyama proclaims the end of history, with liberal capitalism as the telos.[6] Robert Heilbroner, a prominent economist long sympathetic to the Left, asserts that "less than seventy-five years after it officially began, the contest between capitalism and socialism is over: capitalism has won."[7]

And yet, deep doubts persist. We look at the world around us. We see so much pain, so much despair. Is this really the fate of the human species? Is this really the best we can do? If *this* is the end of history, why are we celebrating?

Not only at the level of popular consciousness but also at the theoretical level there is uneasiness, a lack of consensus. Among economists the neoclassical paradigm still reigns. It was disrupted for a while by Keynes (and the Great Depression), but the pieces were reassembled with much

---

[3] Ludwig von Mises was the most prominent figure. More on this in Chapter 3.

[4] See Robbins (1932) for a famous statement of this position. The separation actually began toward the end of the nineteenth century with the realization, by Pareto, that marginalist analysis did not require the assumption that utility be of cardinal magnitude. By 1947, when Paul Samuelson published his classic *Foundations of Economic Analysis*, the split was complete: "Today it is customary to make a distinction between the pure analysis [of an economist] qua economist and his propaganda, condemnations, recommendations qua citizen. In practice, if pushed to extremes, this somewhat schizophrenic rule becomes difficult to adhere to and leads to rather tedious circumlocutions. But in essence, Robbins is undoubtedly correct. Wishful thinking is a powerful deterrent to good analysis and description, and ethical conclusions cannot be determined in the same way that scientific hypotheses are inferred or verified" (Samuelson, 1965, p. 219).

[5] Hayek (1944).   [6] Fukuyama (1992).   [7] Heilbroner (1989, p. 98).

Keynesian economics incorporated.[8] This revised neoclassicism, however, has been under fierce attack since the 1960s. Marxists, neo-Marxists, institutionalists, neo-Ricardians, and neo-Keynesians all reject the neoclassical model; all are suspicious of marginalist categories.[9] Many, though not all, are critical of capitalism itself.

The turmoil of the 1960s shook political philosophy as well as economics. As a deep-seated questioning of "the system" by angry young people spread, two Harvard philosophers came to capitalism's defense. John Rawls argued that certain forms of capitalism can be just. (He allowed that certain forms of socialism might also be.) Robert Nozick, critical of Rawls's liberal, redistributive ethic and of all concessions to socialism, defended a more conservative, "libertarian" version of capitalism.[10] But not all political philosophers have been so sympathetic to capitalism. Paradoxically, given the political tenor of the times, Left political philosophy in the English-speaking world flourished in the 1980s and continues to do so. Although by no means a majority, critics of capitalism are prominent in almost all academic disciplines.

The purpose of a work such as this is not to count hands but to evaluate arguments. If we look at the arguments that have been advanced in defense of capitalism, we see that they fall into two basic categories: comparative arguments and noncomparative arguments. By "comparative" I mean an argument of the form "In light of the viable alternatives, capitalism is best." The utilitarian argument belongs in this category, as do many liberty-based defenses. Noncomparative arguments assert that capitalism is just, because it satisfies a particular standard of justice. Those who advance such arguments usually claim also that socialism fails to meet the standard, but such a claim is not essential. A noncomparative argument takes the form "X satisfies standard J," whereas a comparative argument claims that "X better satisfies, or is more likely to satisfy, standard J than does any viable Y."

It is my view that the comparative arguments for capitalism are by far the more important. They will be the focus of the greater part of this work. Certain noncomparative arguments, however, are also significant,

---

[8] Joan Robinson liked to call the contemporary version "neo-neoclassicism," or, more bluntly, "bastard Keynesianism." See Robinson (1976, p. 5).

[9] Many of these tendencies, particularly the less radical, are coalescing into a rival "post-Keynesian" paradigm, which will be discussed more fully in Chapters 2 and 6. For a philosophically sophisticated critique of neoclassical theory from a post-Keynesian point of view, see Hodgson (1988).

[10] Rawls (1971); Nozick (1974). It should be said that the primary intent of Rawls's enormously influential treatise was to articulate a theory of justice, not to defend capitalism. But it does present, as an application of the theory, a model of "fair capitalism," which we shall examine in Chapter 6.

both historically and because they are still frequently invoked, if more often obliquely than directly. They deserve careful attention, not so much because they are difficult to refute (which they are not) but because they are often sources of serious misconceptions that continue to haunt the more sophisticated comparative arguments.

In this chapter we shall analyze several noncomparative arguments. All defend "entitlement" claims. To the Marxian charge that profit is derived from unpaid labor, all reply that the charge is false. All assert that the capitalist is entitled to that profit. On what grounds? "Productive contribution," say many. "Risk," say some. "Sacrifice," say a few. "Liberty," says Nozick. We shall examine these responses.

Before beginning, some words about the key term. What is this "capitalism" we shall be interrogating? Let us understand capitalism to be a socioeconomic system characterized by three features. First, the means of production are, for the most part, privately owned, either by individuals directly or through the mediation of corporations. Second, the bulk of economic activity is directed toward the production of goods and services for sale on a free market – "free market" meaning that prices are determined largely by supply and demand, without government interference. Third, labor power is a commodity. That is, a large percentage of the work force sells its capacity to labor to those who can provide it with tools, raw materials, and a place to work.

To be capitalist, a society must feature all three sets of institutions: private property,[11] a free market, and wage labor. Many past societies, as well as current ones have exhibited one or two of these characteristics, but not all three. For example, a feudal society consisting of self-sufficient estates worked by serfs had private property but neither a free market nor wage labor. A society of small farmers and artisans (colonial New England, say) is not capitalist, for despite the presence of private property and a market, there is little wage labor. On the other hand, all Western industrial nations today *are* capitalist. The presence of an elaborate welfare apparatus, a number of nationalized industries, or a ruling party self-labeled as "socialist" does not render a society noncapitalist. So long as the bulk of its enterprises are privately owned, are worked by hired labor, and produce goods for sale at largely unregulated prices, a society is capitalist.

With this characterization in mind, let us now consider how such societies have been (noncomparatively) justified.

---

[11] I am using "private property" in the Marxian sense, which distinguishes private property (factories, farmland, productive machinery) from personal property (consumer goods purchased for their own sake, not for the sake of making money).

Marginal product as contribution

John Bates Clark was an early exponent of the claim that capitalist distribution accords with the ethical standard of *productive contribution*, that is, of the claim that capitalism is just because it returns to each individual the value he produces. "The indictment that hangs over society," Clark writes, "is that of 'exploited labor'." But the charge is false, for it can be shown that "the natural effect of competition is . . . to give to each producer the amount of wealth that he specifically brings into existence."[12] Hayek agrees. For Hayek, the fundamental issue is "whether it is desirable that people should enjoy advantages *in proportion to the benefits which their fellows derive from their activity* or whether the distribution of advantages should be based on other men's views of their merit." The first alternative, he insists, is that of a free (capitalist) society.[13] Nozick disagrees, citing "inheritance, gifts for arbitrary reasons and charity" as countervailing considerations, but he allows that "distribution according to benefit is a major patterned strand in a free capitalist society."[14]

But is it? That is what we shall investigate in this and the next three sections of this chapter. Specifically, we wish to inquire whether or not property income – income derived from ownership of the means of production – can be legitimized by the canon that "justice consists in the treatment of people according to their actual contribution to their group."[15]

According to Milton Friedman and most other neoclassical economists, the essential principle of capitalist distribution is "to each according to what he and the instruments he owns produces."[16] But this principle presents a problem. Because it is characteristic of capitalism that the owners of the means of production often are distinct from those who operate those means, Friedman's claim presupposes that one can distinguish, in a precise, quantitative manner, between the contribution of the instrument and that of the operator. How might this be done? Notice that we cannot simply *define* the contribution of each to be what the market returns to each, for that begs the question. We know what the market returns. What we want to know is whether or not such returns really reflect contributions.

Marx provides one way of thinking about the problem. For Marx, the value of the instrument is simply passed on to the final product, while new value is created by living labor. If a $100 machine produces 1,000 items during its normal lifetime, it contributes ten cents to the value of

[12] Clark (1956, pp. 4–5).   [13] Hayek (1960, p. 94); emphasis added.
[14] Nozick (1974, p. 158).
[15] Rescher (1966, p. 78). This canon is called variously the canon of "productivity," "social contribution," "productive contribution," or simply "contribution."
[16] Friedman (1962, p. 161). This is the *essential* principle. Contemporary neoclassical distribution theory has added refinements that need not concerns us here.

each item. Because the machine itself is the product of labor, that ten cents – and all the rest of the commodity's value – is ultimately reducible to labor.

This answer is unacceptable to the neoclassical tradition, which much prefers Clark's alternative. The modern version of Clark's solution begins with a concept, adds a couple of definitions, and then invokes a mathematical theorem – a simple theorem, but perhaps the most ideologically significant mathematical result in history. The basic concept is that of a *production function*, a technical function that specifies for a given technology the maximum productive output for each and every combination of relevant technical inputs. Suppose, for example, that corn is the joint product of labor and land, the units of each being homogeneous in quality.[17] The production function can be represented as $z = P(x, y)$, where z is the maximum number of bushels of corn that can be produced by x laborers working y acres of land (using the specified technology). Now the question is this: Given that both labor and land are required for the production of corn, what is the distinct productive contribution of each factor?

The key to the answer is the notion of *marginal product*. The marginal product of a particular technical input is defined to be the extra output that resulted from the addition of *the last unit* of that input, all other inputs held constant. For example, the marginal product of labor, given ten workers and five acres of land, is the difference between what ten workers and nine workers would produce on those five acres, that is, $P(10, 5) - P(9, 5)$. The marginal product of land in the same case is $P(10, 5) - P(10, 4)$.

It is a standard result of elementary calculus that when a function $P(x, y)$ is differentiable and x and y are large, $P(x, y) - P(x - 1, y)$ is closely approximated by $P_x(x, y)$ (the partial derivative of P with respect to x), and $P(x, y) - P(x, y - 1)$ by $P_y(x, y)$ (the partial derivative of P with respect to y).[18] Applying this result to our economic model, we can say that the marginal product of a technical input is closely approximated by the partial derivative of the production function with respect to that input (when the quantities involved are large).

So far, nothing has been proved. We have merely defined some terms. But now consider a curious mathematical result first demonstrated by

---

[17] For the sake of simplicity we shall carry through our analysis in terms of a two-variable function instead of the more traditional three-variable function (land, labor, and capital). We shall ignore the "Cambridge controversy" surrounding the neoclassical treatment of capital as a factor of production on par with land and labor, and simply identify capital with land. The Cambridge (England) critique of the neoclassical argument is independent of the one given here. For the elegant philosophical overview of the Cambridge controversy, see Hausman (1981, pp. 65–84).

[18] $P_x(x, y)$ and $P_y(x, y)$ are both functions of x and y derived from $P(x, y)$ by standard mathematical procedures.

the great eighteenth-century mathematician Leonhard Euler. If $P(x, y)$ is a "well-behaved" function,[19] then $P(x, y) = xP_x(x, y) + yP_y(x, y)$. This equation, interpreted to our context, states that the output of x laborers working y acres of land is equal to the sum of two quantities, the first being the number of laborers multiplied by the marginal product of labor, and the second being the number of acres multiplied by the marginal product of land. Thus, if we *define* the contribution of each worker to be the marginal product of labor [i.e., $P_x(x, y)$], and if we *define* the contribution of each acre to be the marginal product of land [i.e., $P_y(x, y)$], then the total contribution of labor, $xP_x(x, y)$, plus the total contribution of land, $yP_y(x, y)$, is precisely equal to the total output, $P(x, y)$. This gives us a "natural" division of the total output into the contribution of labor and the contribution of land, computed from purely technical information. No reference has been made to private property, wage labor, or the market. No questions have been begged.

Equipped with a systems-neutral definition of "contribution," the neo-classical economist can now ask whether or not capitalism distributes its total output accordingly. The answer is a reassuring "not always." Adam Smith's distrust of monopoly is vindicated: Monopolies distort distribution. However, in a state of "perfect competition," where uniform goods and services command uniform prices, and where no monopolistic collusions exist, the distribution resulting from each individual striving to maximize her own well-being will be precisely that proposed by Euler's theorem. In a society of x equally skilled laborers working y acres of uniformly fertile land, the wage rate (per worker) will be $P_x(x, y)$, and the ground rent (per acre) will be $P_y(x, y)$. Given enough assumptions, this can be rigorously demonstrated.[20]

These results are nontrivial, but what exactly has been proved? Has it been established that perfectly competitive capitalism distributes in accordance with the canon of contribution? Is it true that each person receives in proportion to what he produces? Clark has no doubts:

If each productive factor is paid according to the amount of its [marginal] product, then each man gets what he himself produces. If he works, he gets what he creates by working; if he also provides capital, he gets what his capital produces, and if further, he renders services by coordinating labor and capital, he gets the

[19] It is sufficient that $P(x, y)$ be smooth and homogeneous of order 1. The first condition requires that a smooth variation in input factors produce a smooth variation in output. The homogeneity condition, in mathematical terms that $P(ax, ay) = aP(x, y)$ for all a, translates into the economic condition that increasing all the production factors by $a\%$ results in an $a\%$ increase in the total output.

[20] Essentially, the argument is this: Wages will be at least as high as the marginal product of the last laborer, for if they were lower, each landowner would try to entice laborers away from his neighbors; wages will not be any higher than that, for that would involve paying the last person more than he yields. See Pen (1971, pp. 76–87) for more details.

product that can be traced separately to that function. Only in one of these three ways can a man produce anything. If he receives all that he brings into existence through any of these three functions, he receives all that he creates at all.[21]

For Clark, this conclusion has enormous ethical and political import:

The welfare of the laboring class depends on whether they get much or little; but their attitude toward other classes – and therefore the stability of society – depends chiefly on the question whether the amount they get, be it large or small, is what they produce. If they create a small amount of wealth and get the whole of it, they may not seek to revolutionize society; but if it were to appear that they produce an ample amount and get only a part of it, many of them would become revolutionists and all would have the right to do so.[22]

But the marginalist argument, for all its ingenuity, is unsound. It lacks a crucial premise. If "contribution" means what it means in the ethical canon (and in ordinary English), Clark has *not* shown that perfectly competitive capitalism distributes according to contribution. He has shown that one can define a partition of the total product without reference to the market mechanism and that "well-behaved" capitalism distributes according to this partition. No mean accomplishment, that, but it remains to be argued that his definition of "contribution" is *ethically* appropriate.

To decide this question, we must consider Clark's analysis more closely. Why is a laborer said to receive exactly what he has produced? The neoclassical answer: If he ceases to work, the total product will decline by precisely the value of his wage. [His wage, $P_x(x, y)$, is approximately $P(x, y) - P(x - 1, y)$.] True enough, but here's the problem: If two workers quit together, the total output will not decline by the sum of their wages. The total product will decline by more than that, for the wage each worker receives under conditions of perfect competition is the marginal product of the *last* laborer – and the neoclassical argument presumes a declining marginal productivity; that is, the marginal product of the tenth laborer is assumed to be less than that of the ninth, that of the ninth is assumed to be less than that of the eighth, and so forth. This decline is not due to declining skills, because all laborers are presumed equally skilled, but to a diminishing-returns assumption. It is assumed that x laborers on a fixed piece of land (when x is sufficiently large) will produce more than $x - 1$ laborers, but that the average production of each will then be slightly less.

Perhaps an example with a picture will add some clarity. (See the accompanying graphs.) Assume that we have ten laborers working five acres of land. On the top graph we plot the marginal product of the first

[21] Clark (1956, p. 7).   [22] Ibid., p. 4.

Marginalist Calculation of the Contribution of Labor and Land

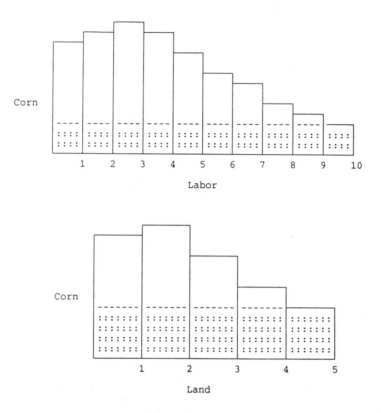

laborer, the marginal product of the second, the marginal product of the third, and so on through the tenth. The area under the first rectangle on the left is the marginal product of the first worker – what he could produce on five acres if he worked alone. The area under the second rectangle is the marginal product of the second worker, the difference between what the two workers could produce together on the five acres and what one could produce alone. In this case, because of the advantages of cooperation, the total output (the sum of both rectangles) has increased more than twofold. These advantages continue to dominate when a third worker is added, but for the fourth and subsequent workers, diminishing returns have set in, overriding the advantages of cooperation. Each new worker adds something to the total, but now less than the previous worker. (This is due, remember, not to declining skill, for all are assumed equally skilled, but to the fact that more and more laborers are cultivating the same fixed amount of land.)

Because each rectangle represents what a given worker adds to the output, the total output of corn produced by the ten workers is the total area beneath the step curve. According to the marginalist definition, the *contribution of labor* is the dotted area, the number of workers multiplied by the marginal product of the last worker. Because of declining marginal productivity, the contribution of labor is less than the total product. The difference, by Euler's theorem, is precisely the contribution of the land. That is to say, if we do a similar calculation holding labor constant and varying the acres of land (as in the lower graph), the dotted area in that case, by definition the contribution of the land, will equal the non-dotted area of the upper graph (and vice versa).[23]

But what exactly is this latter contribution, this "contribution" of the land? Mathematically, it is the marginal product of the fifth acre of land multiplied by the number of acres. But what is its physical significance? It is not the quantity of corn that would have been produced on the land without any laborers. Without any laborers there would be *no* corn. Nor is it the amount that could have been produced had the landlords themselves tilled the soil.[24] Nor does it bear any relation to that portion of the social product that must be saved for seed, or plowed back in to replenish fertility. In physical terms, the marginal product of the land is simply the amount by which production would decline if one acre were taken out of cultivation. It does not reflect any *productive activity* whatsoever on the part of the owner of the land. *It does not, therefore, measure his productive contribution.*

Let me repeat this argument in a slightly different form, to highlight how the neoclassical terminology obscures the important issue. Clark claims that a person can create wealth in one of three ways: by working, by providing capital, or by coordinating labor and capital. If we regard "coordinating labor and capital" as a managerial activity directly related to the productive process,[25] then both working and coordinating labor and capital are productive activities in a perfectly straightforward sense: Should laborers and managers cease their mental and physical work, the

---

[23] The areas are not precisely equal in the example described. Euler's theorem applies only when the quantities of inputs are large enough that the production function can be represented by a smooth graph.

[24] That would be $P(n, 5)$, where n is the number of landowners. $P(n, 5)$ bears no relation to $5P_y(10, 5)$.

[25] This is not quite how Clark conceives of it. For Clark, this coordination is meant to characterize the entrepreneur, the person who borrows money from the capitalist to hire laborers. But because this activity is tied definitionally to capitalism, I shall reinterpret "coordinating labor and capital" to make it less problematic as a universal wealth-creating activity.

production of wealth would likewise cease. The economy would grind to a halt.

"Providing capital," however, is something quite different. In Clark's perfectly competitive world, the technology is given and the physical capital already exists. So "providing capital" means nothing more than "allowing it to be used." But an act of granting permission, in and of itself, is not a productive activity.[26] If laborers cease to labor, production ceases in any society. But if owners cease to grant permission, production is affected only if their *authority* over the means of production is respected. If it is not, then production need not diminish at all. Workers can continue doing exactly what they were doing before – producing the corn and bread and steel and machine tools and all the other commodities required by their society. Whatever it is that owners are doing when they grant permission for their assets to be used, it should not be called "productive activity."

The inappropriateness of the neoclassical notion of "contribution" becomes even more apparent if we try to apply it to other forms of society to ascertain who creates what, and whether or not distribution accords with this creation. Consider a feudal lord. If he owns far more land than his peasants can till, then he creates, in "providing land," no wealth at all, because the marginal product of his last acre is zero. Subtracting an acre would not diminish production. But as his peasant population increases, and with it the marginal product of that last acre, his "contribution" also increases. The tribute once unjustly extracted becomes fair, even philanthropic, as the share of the wealth "he creates" expands.

To jump forward in time, instead of back: Suppose a government suddenly nationalizes the means of production, then does nothing else but charge workers a use tax. We wouldn't say, would we, that the government is engaging in productive activity, or that the tax is a return for the government's productive contribution? Not even if the tax rate is exactly equal to the marginal product of the productive factor.

Because providing capital is not a productive activity (at least not within the static, perfectly competitive model that has been presupposed), then income derived from this function can hardly be justified as being proportional to one's productive contribution to the group. Clark's normative argument collapses.

In fairness to contemporary neoclassical economists, it should be noted

[26] To borrow G. A. Cohen's formulation, one could say that an activity is productive (of use values) "if and only if it is required because of the material nature of production, rather than because of its social form" (Cohen, 1983, p. 320). See Cohen (1978, ch. IV) for a defense of the material/social distinction upon which this definition rests.

that few who think seriously about such things accept Clark's normative analysis. But it must also be said that the neoclassical categories seem to impede clear thinking. H. G. Johnson is representative:

The positive theory that factors derive their incomes from their contributions to the productive process should be sharply distinguished from the question of whether the owners of the factors are ethically entitled to own them, or whether their returns would be different if ownership or preferences were different.[27]

This might seem to be an improvement over Clark, but really it is not. Johnson has distanced himself from Clark's ethical claim, but not from the notion that providing capital is a productive activity. His comment well illustrates the tendency of neoclassical analysis to mislead normative thought.

Notice that what Johnson says is ambiguous: "factors derive their incomes from their contributions." If by "factors" he means land, labor, and capital, then what he says is plainly false. Land, labor, and capital do not receive income; owners of factors do. If by "factors" he means the owners, then he is claiming that these owners do make a contribution, which suggests that they are engaging in productive activity – which they are not. This formulation also suggests that the ethical issue at stake is either the legitimacy of ownership claims, in virtue of which the owners make their contribution, or the appropriateness of the ethical canon itself (that income should accord with contribution). In other words, the neoclassical formulation, "factors derive income from productive contributions," shifts one's attention away from an examination of the more important question, the problematic nature of that peculiar "activity" that is supposed to constitute a capitalist's contribution: providing capital.

At the risk of repetition, let me summarize my discontent with the neoclassical argument. The essential flaw in the neoclassical justification of capitalist distribution is neither that it rests on a questionable ethical canon nor that it presumes the legitimacy of the existing distribution of property. Most economists are aware of the normative nature of these issues and so are content to leave them to philosophers and politicians. The flaw is the assumption that providing capital is a productive activity, a notion that appears as virtually a truism when mediated by neoclassical categories. In defining the "contribution" of a productive factor in such a way as to yield a "natural" division of the product into the "contributions" of these factors, what could seem more natural than to call the "contribution" of the factor the "contribution" of the owner, particularly when it is precisely this "contribution" that the free market

[27] H. Johnson (1973, p. 37).

returns to each owner? And if each owner "contributes" to the final product, what could seem more natural than to regard him as engaging in productive activity? What could be more natural? And yet a sleight of hand has been performed, for, as we have seen, in the static, perfectly competitive neoclassical world we have been considering, the owner has not engaged in anything that might be called "productive activity," and hence he cannot appeal to the ethical canon that justifies reward on the basis of productive contribution. Even if the owner had a perfectly valid claim to his property, and even if this canon were perfectly sound, he could not justify the income he receives from his property by appealing to this canon.

We must conclude that the marginal-product definition of "contribution" is inadequate to the task of showing that capitalist distribution accords with the ethical canon of contribution. It provides a criterion for judging the assertion that "X percent of the product is the contribution of labor; Y percent is the contribution of land," and so on, but it does so at the cost of severing the "contribution" of a factor owner from anything but a legal relation to the factor itself. In a technologically fixed, perfectly competitive world, capitalists qua capitalists take no risks, do not innovate, do not sacrifice, do not engage in anything that could be called productive activity. The abstraction from individual activity that allows one to define the contribution of a factor in a precise mathematical manner also removes from consideration any reason one might give for claiming that the "contribution" of the factor is, in any ethically relevant sense, a measure of the productive activity of the owner. If one is to defend capitalism, one must either redefine "capitalist contribution" or abandon the contribution canon as its justification. However elegant mathematically marginal-product theory may be, it fails as the basis for an ethical argument.

Capitalist contribution as entrepreneurial activity

The marginalist definition of "contribution" fails to agree with ordinary ethical usage because it abstracts completely from all characteristic activities of property owners. An alternative definition is suggested by Joseph Schumpeter's well-known critique of the neoclassical model we have been considering:

The essential point to grasp is that in dealing with capitalism we are dealing with an evolutionary process. It may seem strange that anyone can fail to see so obvious a fact, which moreover was long ago emphasized by Karl Marx. Yet that fragmentary analysis which yields the bulk of our propositions about the functioning of modern capitalism persistently neglects it. . . . The fundamental impulse that sets and keeps the capitalist engine in motion comes from the new consumer goods, the new markets, the new forms of industrial organization that capitalist enterprise creates.[28]

If it is true, as Schumpeter and Marx propose, that the fundamental feature of capitalism is its dynamism, then it would seem more appropriate in determining the respective contributions of capitalists and laborers to compare society at different points in time, rather than to look at hypothetical variations of capital and labor, given a fixed technology at a particular point in time (as was done in the marginalist analysis in the preceding section). Insofar as a particular increase in output over time can be attributed to the activities of a capitalist, perhaps we can define his contribution to be that increase. A simple model illustrates this idea.

Suppose a capitalist-landowner employs ten people to grow corn. Working in the usual fashion these workers could produce, let us say, 1,500 bushels of corn. But suppose our capitalist-landowner reorganizes production, innovates, with the result that his workers now produce 2,000 bushels. The extra 500 bushels is *his* contribution.

This notion appears promising, but a difficulty surfaces at once. This concept of contribution will not serve to justify our capitalist's income, because he will receive more than 500 bushels at the end of the year, more, that is, than his contribution. Unless he was paying his workers the full 1,500 bushels before his innovation (in which case he would not be a capitalist), he will receive 500 bushels plus the profit he usually receives.

Perhaps we can avoid this difficulty by considering a newly arrived capitalist. When we look at a representative capitalist, it appears that a portion of his income derives solely from his ownership of the means of production. But appearances might be misleading. What appears to be a reward for mere ownership might in fact be a reward for prior activity. To consider this case, let us modify our model. Suppose that land is plentiful and free and that a person, working independently, can produce 150 bushels of corn per year. Suppose an entrepreneur appears. Eating little and thinking a lot, he accumulates 1,500 bushels of corn and a new idea: an innovative concept for a new kind of plow. He hires, with his "capital," ten workers, at a wage of 150 bushels each, and sets them to work, first at making the plow and then at using it. Suppose the result is a 2,000-bushel harvest. Surely we can call 500 bushels the capitalist's

---

[28] Schumpeter (1962, p. 83). Schumpeter does not advance the ethical argument we are about to consider. Like so many of his colleagues, he eschews ethics for "science." For a contemporary ethical defense of capitalism along Schumpeterian lines, see Kirzner (1989). Kirzner identifies his overall position as closer to that of Mises and Hayek than to Schumpeter's, but the differences are not relevant to the argument of this section. Kirzner's distinctive "ethics of finders-keepers" does not address, let along overcome, the difficulties I shall raise with the Schumpeterian defense.

contribution. After all, the workers could have produced only 1,500 without him.

This notion of "contribution" seems both unambiguous and straightforwardly ethical. The contribution of the capitalist appears well defined and linked to a specific productive activity, namely, innovation.[29] But a complication arises if we continue our model into the second year. The process just described can now repeat itself, with one important difference: No new innovation is required for a 2,000-bushel harvest. The blueprint for the plow and the reorganization scheme are now in existence. Suppose the laborers work the second year as they did the previous year, first making a plow, then using it. Another 2,000-bushel harvest is recorded. Who, we now ask, contributed this 2,000 bushels? In one sense the capitalist has contributed 500, because the increase, measured from the original base point, is 500 and is due to his innovation. In another sense he has contributed nothing, for if we take the base point to be the preceding year, then there has been no increase, and hence no capitalist contribution. The capitalist introduced no new technology this year. Which sense of capitalist contribution do we intend when we define it to be the increase in production that can be attributed to his entrepreneurial activities?

Surely the second sense will not do, for that depends on a completely arbitrary specification of the time interval. To measure the increase from the preceding year might seem natural in the case of corn, which has an annual growing season, but it seems hardly so natural in the case of steel production or bread baking. We might just as well specify two years or ten years or six months or six weeks. There is no "natural" time interval beyond which the contribution ceases to be that of the capitalist and becomes that of his workers.[30]

So we cannot specify a time limit. But this means that we have a definition of "contribution" that entails that certain contributions are perpetual, whereas others are only transitory. The capitalist and his laborers both expend mental and physical energy during the first year, and each makes a "contribution." However (by our selected definition), the contribution of the capitalist continues into the next year, and into the next. If he innovates anew, he will be entitled (by the canon of

---

[29] Nothing turns on the specific innovation being a technical invention. Any exercise of creative intelligence that leads to an increase in production would suffice – what Kirzner would call "discovery."

[30] The lifetime of the innovator might seem tempting, particularly to advocates of confiscatory inheritance taxes, but that cannot be right. We cannot define the quantitative contribution of an innovation in terms of the longevity of the innovator. How much one contributes depends on what one does, not on how long one stays alive. If Edison had survived in an advanced state of senility a decade beyond his actual eighty-four years, his contribution would not have been greater.

contribution) to the increase brought on by his new innovation as well, but his original contribution never ceases. In pointed contrast, the contribution of a laborer ends with her labor. Each year she must "contribute" anew.

The reader has perhaps become uneasy with the direction this argument has taken. My model is vastly oversimplified as a version of capitalist reality; there is no competition, no risk, no obsolescence of technology. Do we really need the concept of "perpetual contribution" to justify capitalism? Have not our simplifications led us astray?

We can approach these questions by looking at the problem from a different perspective – the opposite end, so to speak. To justify capitalism in terms of the contribution canon, one needs, first of all, a definition of "contribution," then a demonstration of its ethical significance, and finally an argument that capitalism does in fact reward according to that definition. We have defined "contribution" to be the increase effected over time, and then, using a simplified model, we have uncovered "perpetual contribution," a rather disturbing concept. Let us look up from our simple model for a moment and consider contemporary capitalist reality. To see if we need the concept "perpetual contribution," we must ask whether or not there really are "perpetual rewards" under capitalism.

But of course there are. In all capitalist societies there are institutions that reward individuals irrespective of their current activities. An accumulation of money, however acquired, may be invested as an individual sees fit. He may put it in a savings account, or buy government or corporate bonds. If he does, he collects interest until the account is closed, the bond is sold, or the institution goes under (i.e., indefinitely). If he purchases stock instead, he receives an annual dividend, again indefinitely. Such income is quite independent of an original innovation (if there was one) to which the initial accumulation is traceable. To be sure, the reward is not eternal as a matter of logical necessity. We live in a contingent world, where businesses fail, as do banks (though deposits these days, as we know only too well, are usually taxpayer-insured). But the point is that the reward is not tied either legally or in practice to the continued performance of any productive activity on the part of the investor. As John Kenneth Galbraith has observed,

No grant of feudal privilege has ever equalled, for effortless return, that of the grandparent who bought and endowed his descendants with a thousand shares of General Motors or General Electric. The beneficiaries of this foresight have become and remain rich by no exercise or intelligence beyond the decision to do nothing, embracing as it did the decision not to sell.[31]

[31] Galbraith (1967, p. 394).

I think it must be granted that our model is not irrelevant to reality. Capitalism does reward some individuals perpetually. Thus, if it is to be justified by the canon of contribution, one must defend the claim that some contributions are indeed eternal.

Perhaps this can be done. Certain innovations, even when superseded, have served as the basis for new technologies. Did not Einstein stand on Newton's shoulders? Surely there is nothing objectionable ethically about rewarding lasting contributions lastingly.

Perhaps not, but this line of argument will not justify capitalism. To see why, let us return to our entrepreneur and his innovative plow. What exactly was the nature of his "contribution" that qualified it as perpetual? The seemingly obvious answer that he created a new kind of productive instrument and reorganized production in a more efficient manner will not do, for he need not have done these things himself. He could have hired an engineer to design his plow and a management consultant to reorganize his enterprise. Such people are regularly employed under capitalism. Nor will it do to say that the idea to construct the plow was his, for the idea itself could have originated with his research-and-development division. Ideas and their execution regularly come from such places. A perpetual reward may follow from an idea, but it need not go to its originator.

It is tempting to say that the capitalist *supplies the money*; he *provides the capital*. This is certainly his distinctive "service" qua capitalist. But we are back to the problem encountered in the neoclassical argument. And our conclusion is the same: *Providing capital is not a productive activity*. It is no more a productive activity in a dynamic setting than in a static one.

Let us dwell on this point, for it is as important to understanding our world as it is counterintuitive to our culture. Objections cry out to be heard. Is not capital vital to growth? Is supplying it not a productive endeavor nonpareil? Do not all countries, especially underdeveloped ones, strive mightily to acquire capital? Do they not offer investment incentives and tax credits to attract it? Such policies are not irrational, are they?

In fact they may be. Such is the contention of some (usually radical) development economists, who point to the unhappy consequences of such strategies.[32] We shall not join the "development of underdevelopment" controversy here, because that would take us too far from the argument at hand, but we do need to look carefully at the notion of "providing capital." Its analysis is as important to the ethical issue with which we are concerned as it is to questions of development strategy.

At the heart of the matter is the concept of capital itself. What is "capital"? Marx said that it is a social relation, but few contemporary

---

[32] See, for example, Amin (1976), especially Chapter 4. For an influential, if simpleminded, statement of the conventional view, see Rostow (1960).

economists think in such terms. Capital, for most, is one of two things, or, rather, both at once: physical things (equipment and material) and money for investment.[33] Now it cannot be denied that capital, as the existing material means of production, is necessary for production. Without the means of production, nothing can be produced. But "providing" this sort of capital – an existing material thing – is simply "allowing it to be used," the nonproductive activity analyzed in the preceding section.

Capital as investment funds would seem to be another matter. Investment funds generate growth, do they not? Is that not an axiom of economic theory? Let us think for a moment. Consider a person with a chest full of cash, eager to invest. How he acquired it need not concern us. We want to understand how his disposal of it will increase production. To produce something, there must be brought together equipment, raw materials, and laborers. Let our investor lend his money to an entrepreneur who purchases these necessaries. The laborers are set to work with the machinery on the raw materials, and soon goods are produced. It is all quite simple.

But notice, this case is also a matter of granting permission. The workers, raw materials, and machinery already exist. The workers could begin production themselves (perhaps at the instigation of their entrepreneurial comrade), except that property rights intervene. They cannot gain access to the machinery and raw materials, for these things are the property of others. To use them, one must have permission, which the entrepreneur secures by means of her borrowed capital.

What if the machinery were not already in existence? Suppose our entrepreneur used her borrowed capital to place an order. Would that not bring a machine into being? Yes, but she (or the workers) could have placed that order without borrowing money. In either case human beings exist who could produce the desired machine. Would they do so? With borrowed money the entrepreneur can pay them in advance, or on delivery. But if the machinist to whom our entrepreneur advances a sum can buy food with it, then that food already exists. So the farmer, say, could advance that food. And the things the farmer would buy already exist, so they could be advanced. Farmers, machinists, and laborers (including entrepreneurial laborers) are all necessary for production and for growth – but not people to "provide capital."[34]

[33] Joan Robinson never tired of arguing that these two aspects of capital are hopelessly confused and logically irreconcilable within the framework of neoclassical theory. See Robinson (1970) for details. I think she is right, but that issue, which concerns the viability of the neoclassical paradigm, is not our interest here.

[34] We are not addressing here questions of motivation and incentive. How best to motivate people to interact in socially desirable ways is a mater for comparative analysis; that will come later. Here I am simply arguing that the material nature of production does not necessitate a class of people whose function it is to "provide capital."

Two arguments are sometimes better than one. Let us look at the matter from another angle. Suppose, instead of relying on our friend with the chest full of money, the government simply rolled its presses to produce the same quantity of crisp bills and gave them to our entrepreneur. Exactly the same production would result. But would we want to call the printing of money a productive activity? That would surely be misleading, perhaps dangerously so, tempting officials to believe that rolling the presses longer and longer would miraculously generate wealth. It is equally dangerous – at least to clear thinking about the ethical issues – to speak of providing capital, when done by a private individual, as a productive activity.

To bolster our arguments with an appeal to authority, we could do worse than to cite Keynes:

It is much preferable to speak of capital as having a yield over the course of its life in excess of its original cost, than as being *productive*. For the only reason why an asset offers a prospect of yielding during its life services having an aggregate value greater than its initial supply price is because it is *scarce*. . . . If capital becomes less scarce, the excess yield will diminish, without its having become less productive – at least not in the physical sense.

I sympathize, therefore, with the pre-classical doctrine that everything is *produced* by *labour*, aided by what used to be called art and is now called technique, by natural resources . . . and by the results of past labour, embodied in assets, which also command a price according to their scarcity or abundance. It is preferable to regard labour, including, of course, the personal services of the entrepreneur and his assistants, as the sole factor of production, operating in a given environment of technique, natural resources, capital equipment and effective demand.[35]

Let us be clear about the preceding arguments. I have not argued that the government ought to take control of investment, much less that investment should be financed by printing money. I have made no claims as to the relative efficiency or innovativeness of alternative structures. These are crucial issues, but they belong to a comparative analysis of capitalism and socialism. Questions concerning efficiency, innovativeness, and even risk are irrelevant to our present concern, which is whether or not capitalism can be justified by the principle that individuals should receive in proportion to their productive contributions to society. Such a justification requires that we identify a productive activity engaged in exclusively by capitalists that merits not merely a reward but (as we have seen) a perpetual reward. This we have not been able to do. Innovative activity seemed the best candidate, but this "entrepreneurial" definition has not survived analysis. The only distinctive activity of a

---

[35] Keynes (1936, pp. 213–14). Keynes's proposal, notice, is more stringent than mine. He does not even want to call capital productive, whereas I have drawn the line at calling providing capital a productive activity. He is probably right. The slope from capital as productive to providing it as a productive activity is slippery indeed.

capitalist is providing capital, and that, we see once again, is not a productive activity at all.

The neoclassical definition of "contribution" considered in the first section fails for lack of ethical content; the entrepreneurial definition of this section rectifies that problem, but it cannot serve in the defense of capitalism because the class of entrepreneurs is not coextensive with the class of capitalists. Such coextension might once have been roughly the case, but not so today. Nor is there anything in the structure of capitalism to keep the classes from diverging. Indeed, the capitalist-entrepreneur, as Schumpeter observed, declines in functional importance as capitalism develops. His words, uttered nearly half a century ago, still have the ring of (heretical) truth:

> To act with confidence beyond the range of familiar beacons and to overcome that resistance to change requires aptitudes that are present in only a small fraction of the population, and that define the entrepreneurial type as well as the entrepreneurial function. . . .
> This social function is already losing importance and is bound to lose it at an accelerating rate in the future even if the economic process itself of which entrepreneurship was the prime mover went on unabated. For, on the one hand, it is much easier now than it has been in the past to do things that lie outside the familiar routine – innovation itself is being reduced to routine. Technological progress is increasingly becoming the business of trained specialists who turn out what is required of them and make it work in predictable ways. . . .
> On the other hand, personality and will power must count for less in environments which have become accustomed to change – best instanced by an incessant stream of new customers' and producers' goods – and which instead of resisting accepts it as a matter of course. The resistance which comes from interests threatened by innovations in the productive process is not likely to die out as long as the capitalist order persists. . . . But every other kind of resistance – the resistance in particular of consumers and producers to a kind of thing because it is new – has well-nigh vanished already.[36]

Interest as time preference

The basic problem in trying to justify capitalism by an appeal to "contribution" is the problem of identifying an activity or set of activities, engaged in by all capitalists and only by capitalists, that can be called (preserving the ethical connotations of the word) "contribution." It is true that some capitalists innovate, reorganize, and manage, but it is also true that many do not. This fact, if not its ethical implications, is acknowledged by most economists; it is reflected, for example, in the

---

[36] Schumpeter (1962, p. 83). In endorsing this quotation, I do not mean to suggest that the entrepreneurial spirit is no longer important. But as Schumpeter points out, this spirit has become increasingly more collective. As we shall see, it can be wholly detached from capitalism.

standard distinction between interest and profit. Interest is the return to capital, the reward for owning a productive asset. Profit is the residual accruing to the entrepreneur after wage, rental, and interest accounts have been paid. It is his reward for risk and innovative achievement. Samuelson's treatment exemplifies this distinction:

The market rate of interest is that percentage of return per year which has to be paid on any safe loan of money, which has to be yielded on any safe bond or other security, and which has to be earned on the value of any capital asset (such as a machine, a hotel building, a patent right) in any competitive market where there are no risks or where all the risk factors have already been taken care of by special premium payments to protect against any risks.[37]

The basic problem for one trying to justify capitalism (noncomparatively) is precisely this category: interest, a return that requires neither risk nor entrepreneurial activity on the part of the recipient. The basic problem is not profit, as many on the Left too hastily conclude. The real problem is interest.

Let me put the issue starkly. If I put $100 in the bank, why should I get back $110? My account is federally insured, so I take no risk. I can withdraw my money whenever I want, so I am not inconvenienced. I have not the slightest idea what is done with my deposit, so I can hardly claim to be exercising some socially useful entrepreneurial judgment. How can I argue, without language abuse or bad faith, that I have engaged in a productive activity? Common sense (if undistorted by prevailing ideology) would seem to argue for the opposite conclusion – that the bank is doing me a service, providing me with a safe, convenient repository for my excess wealth. I should be paying the bank interest, not the bank me.[38]

Frankly, I don't think the commonsense argument can be refuted. However, not many economists or political philosophers are deterred by common sense when that common sense conflicts with the reigning ideology. Things cannot be so simple, scholars say. It ought to be possible to concoct a theory that would yield more palatable conclusions.

Marginalist theory is one such attempt. As we have seen, it fails. So does the appeal to entrepreneurial activity. A third attempt is "time-preference theory," a theory associated with the Austrian neoclassicals, especially Eugen Böhm-Bawerk.

Böhm-Bawerk would seem to agree with the conclusions we have reached thus far. Interest income, he writes,

---

[37] Samuelson (1980, p. 560).

[38] Lest anyone think that interest income is too trivial to merit attention, it is worth noting that U.S. personal income from interest exceeded $500 billion in 1987, a figure three times larger than total after-tax corporate profits that year, and twenty times larger than net rental income (*Economic Report of the President*, 1988, p. 273).

arises independently of any personal act of the capitalist. It accrues to him even though he has not moved any finger in creating it. . . . And it flows without ever exhausting the capital from which it arises, and therefore without any necessary limit to its continuance. It is, if one may use such an expression in mundane matters, capable of everlasting life.[39]

If interest "arises independently of any personal act of the capitalist," a justification that appeals to "contribution" would appear difficult indeed, but not everyone is put off. A recent defense of interest based on time-preference theory is provided by the philosopher N. Scott Arnold.[40] Arnold offers two distinct arguments in support of the legitimacy of interest.[41]

The first is this: Transactions involving interest payments are not relevantly distinct from other forms of exchange. Hence, "only if one regards all forms of exchange as exploitative would interest be necessarily exploitative."[42]

We note that this identification of moneylending with other forms of exchange is sharply at variance with Aristotle's view. Aristotle is quite blunt on the subject: "The most hated sort of wealth getting and with greatest reason, is usury, which makes a gain out of money itself and not from the natural object of it. For money was intended to be used in exchange and not to increase at interest."[43] For Aristotle, the "unnaturalness" of usury lies in the fact that, unlike other exchanges, moneylending involves the exchange of goods that are qualitatively identical. It is this notion that time-preference theory disputes. "The basic point," says Arnold, "is that money now and money later are different goods."[44]

It is difficult to resist the impression that linguistic chicanery is afoot here. The jacket I wear today is the same jacket I shall wear next week. So long as it has not been altered or damaged, it is not a different jacket simply because the time index is different. But we must be careful. Because the "use value" of money is its *purchasing power*, it might be argued that the time index is significant for money as it is not for other goods.

---

[39] Böhm-Bawerk (1959, vol. 1, p. 1). The three volumes included in this edition were originally published in 1884, 1889, and 1909.

[40] See Arnold (1985). For a shorter version of this defense, see Arnold (1990, pp. 101–8). It should be noted that Böhm-Bawerk does not conceive of this theory as a normative justification. Like Schumpeter, he thinks of economics as value-free "science."

[41] These two arguments correspond to what Daniel Hausman identifies as the two fundamental "laws" of Austrian theory: that individuals prefer present consumption to future consumption, and that storing up the current services of land and labor increases their productivity at a decreasing rate (Hausman, 1981, p. 55).

[42] Arnold (1985, p. 96).

[43] Aristotle, *Politics*, 1258 b 2–5. Aquinas is not much gentler: "It is by its very nature unlawful to take payment for the use of money lent, which payment is known as usury; and just as a man is bound to restore other ill-gotten goods, so is he bound to restore the money which he has taken in usury" (*Summa Theologica*, Question 78).

[44] Arnold (1985, p. 96).

After all, inflation affects the use value of money, if not the use value of my jacket.

This argument doesn't bite, for what I am attacking, and what time-preference theory wishes to defend, is *real interest*, not *nominal interest* – the former defined as the nominal (empirical) rate minus the rate of inflation. Time-preference theory is intended to explain and justify interest in the absence of inflation.

If there is chicanery afoot in calling "money now" a different good from "money later," it is by no means harmless, for the intended effect is to subsume moneylending under the normative rubric of exchange, thus vindicating the claim that a person is doing the same thing (from a moral point of view) when he trades his apples for your oranges as when he lends you $100 on the condition that you repay him $110.

But are these cases sufficiently analogous to warrant this conclusion? Common sense would say no. There are obvious differences. In the first case, two commodities are involved; in the second, only one (and a quasi commodity at that). In the first case, both parties have something; in the second, he has something, but you don't. In the first case, the situation is one of equality; in the second, inequality dominates the relationship: He has more than you have now, and he will get back more than he gives.[45]

Time-preference theory is set up to respond to these observations. Granted, the time-preference theorist replies, there are differences between commodity exchange and moneylending, but the essential natures of the two transactions are the same. In each case the parties to the exchange have different, complementary preferences. The essence of exchange is precisely the voluntary mutual satisfaction of these complementary desires.

The complementary desires operative in ordinary exchange are obvious. I prefer your oranges to my apples; you prefer my apples to your oranges. The complementary preferences operative in money lending are less transparent. This is where theory comes in. The time-preference theorist offers the following accounts:

People have different *time preferences* with respect to consumption. Some prefer to consume now rather than later. They have a "high time preference." Some are more inclined to defer consumption. They have a "low time preference." Most people are in the former category. In Arnold's words, "people generally prefer present goods to (comparable) future goods."[46] For many, this preference is so strong that they are willing to

---

[45] I am pointing to the prima facie relationships that govern the exchange. Obviously, if the exchange is embedded in a larger context, such claims need not be true.

[46] Arnold (1985, p. 95). As to why this is so, Arnold offers that "since humans are not immortal, time is both valuable and scarce." That is to say, most people prefer to

consume relatively less later if they can consume more now. Others, however, are willing to defer consumption now provided that they can consume more later. It follows from these facts about human beings that unless specifically prohibited, an interest rate will emerge that will allow preferences to be satisfied to everyone's satisfaction. It follows, further, that if interest is prohibited, the situation will not be Pareto-optimal, for there will be individuals who would like to consume more now even if that would mean consuming less later, as well as individuals who would be happy to defer consumption if they could be suitably rewarded. The satisfaction of all parties concerned is blocked by fiat.[47]

This account has a certain rough plausibility, especially if we picture the transaction as between relative equals (as indeed the story language inclines us to do). If you and I have about the same income and pretty much spend what we make, there seems to be nothing wrong with me giving you $500 (so that you can have a new stereo system now) in return for a repayment of $550 a year from now. It seems plausible to describe this situation as me preferring to consume less now in return for more consumption later, and you preferring to consume more now in return for less consumption later. Surely only an unsophisticated premodern (or a godless Communist) would cry foul.

Notice, however, how the description fares if we picture the parties as they would more likely be pictured by Aristotle – say an impoverished artisan and a rich merchant. The poor man does not choose between more consumption now/less later and less consumption now/more later. If there is no consumption now, there won't be a "later." The choice is between consuming now and starving now. How one will manage the "later" will have to be dealt with later (probably by more borrowing and by servitude).

For his part, the merchant might see his choice along time-preference lines (as between consuming more now/less later and consuming less now/more later). More likely, however, he sees his choice as between keeping his excess savings under the mattress, where its magnitude will remain constant, and loaning it out and having it grow. His preference is not more consumption in the future rather than more consumption now; it is between a given consumption now and either X in the future or $(X + n)$. It follows that, in what would likely seem to Aristotle to be the paradigmatic case, the time-preference description fails utterly, even at the level of explanation, to say nothing of justification. It explains

buy now and pay later, because later they may be dead. British economist Roy Harrod is less generous than Arnold. Harrod sees "pure time-preference" as "a polite expression for rapacity and the conquest of reason by passion" – quoted by Sen (1984, p. 117).

47 The concept of Pareto optimality will be examined in more detail in Chapter 3.

neither artisan's nor the merchant's motivation, nor does it justify the practice of usury.[48]

It might be objected that it is unfair to burden the time-preference theorist with a case that perhaps may once have been paradigmatic, but no longer is. There is a validity to this objection, though I cannot resist pointing out that the theorists themselves tend to make sweeping claims for their account.[49] Still, it must be granted that even a good theory will have trouble with certain cases, especially anachronistic ones.

What must surely give us pause, however, is that the theory also founders on the essential test case for *capitalist* interest: the providing of funds to an entrepreneur. According to time-preference theory, the parties to the exchange have opposite preferences, the lender having a low time preference (i.e., a disposition to consume later), and the borrower having a high time preference (a disposition to consume now). But the entrepreneur has no such penchant for consumption. He does not borrow to consume, but to purchase equipment and to hire workers. He, too, must defer consumption. Neither he nor the capitalist will be able to consume until sufficient time passes, until (and unless) the investment pays off. The entrepreneur borrows so that he will have something in the future rather than nothing. Time preference enters not at all into the explanation of his behavior. As Joan Robinson observes,

Present purchasing power is valuable partly because under the capitalist rules of the game, it permits its owner . . . to employ labor and undertake production that will yield a surplus of receipts over costs. . . . This has nothing whatsoever to do with the subjective *rate of discount of the future* of the individual concerned.[50]

Time preference need not enter into the explanation of the capitalist's behavior any more than the entrepreneur's. If Marx and Weber are right, the motivational structure for the paradigmatic capitalist is accumulation, not consumption. Moneymaking becomes an end in itself. The capitalist qua capitalist invests now not to have more to consume later but to have more to invest later. As Marx puts it, "Accumulate, accumulate. That is Moses and the prophets."[51]

As with the case of the artisan and the merchant, we find that time-preference theory provides no insight into the behavior of the agents involved. As an "explanation" of capitalist interest – let alone a

---

[48] Differential risk might be an explanatory or justificatory factor here, because the $X is likely safer under the mattress than loaned out, but that is quite a different matter from preferring present consumption to future consumption. (Risk will be discussed in a subsequent section.)

[49] Arnold (1985, p. 96) sees the theory as explaining consumer loans, business loans, fixed capital pricing, and "all forms of capital formation, even in a moneyless economy."

[50] Robinson (1966, p. 395); emphasis in original.

[51] Marx (1967, p. 595). This behavior, as Marx notes, is not irrational, because having more to invest later in no way precludes more consumption also.

justification – it fails. Or at least one of its arguments fails. The claim we have been examining is the claim that "only if one regards all forms of exchange as exploitative would interest be necessarily exploitative." This claim, that moneylending is morally indistinguishable from commodity exchange, is the one to which Aristotle would most strongly object. I have argued that common sense is on his side, as is often the case with Aristotle.[52]

There is a second argument associated with time preference that goes beyond the claim that moneylending is merely a form of exchange like any other. If we look at it closely, we see that it has nothing to do with the "voluntary" nature of the transaction, nor, for that matter, with preference. It has much to do, however, with time.

It looks specifically at the capitalist qua capitalist and appeals to the principle to which the arguments of the first two sections of this chapter appealed, the *canon of contribution*. To my charge that the capitalist qua capitalist makes no contribution, because he need not labor, need not manage, need not innovate, the time-preference theorist objects. According to Arnold, "the capitalist *qua* capitalist makes an essential contribution to production. [He is] the supplier of time."[53]

We should let these words sink in for a moment. "The capitalist *qua* capitalist [is a] supplier of time." Is this credible? Or is it (to invoke Bentham) "nonsense on stilts"? After all, time is not something one supplies, like coal or oil or apples or oranges. One might say that a worker "supplies time," although such a phrase is clearly metaphorical, a substitute for saying that the worker supplies her labor – or, more directly, that the worker works. (If she merely "supplies her time," she won't work for long.) What could time-preference theory possibly mean by the assertion that the capitalist supplies time?

Again the theorist has a theory, that is, a story to tell. The classic story is the tale of (cheap) grape juice becoming (valuable) wine.[54] The updated version goes something like this: Production takes time. More effective production normally requires the introduction of capital goods, the production of which takes time that might otherwise be devoted to the immediate production of consumer goods. Because it is the capitalist who, instead of consuming what he is entitled to consume, supplies the

---

[52] Needless to say, I do not deny that moneylending and commodity exchange have certain features in common. In particular, both are voluntary transactions. But if time-preference theory is merely an elaborate way of saying that interest payments are voluntary, then it has by no means resolved the ethical problem, for nobody but the most single-minded advocate of laissez faire thinks that all voluntary transactions are just. Instead, it has occluded precisely what needs to be clarified, namely, the specific nature of interest. (A critique of single-minded advocacy of laissez faire will be offered in the later section on Nozick.)

[53] Arnold (1985, p. 99).   [54] See Hausman (1981, pp. 40–4).

money with which these new capital goods are purchased, he may be regarded as the supplier of that commodity without which productivity would not increase: time itself.

Nonsense on stilts? I confess, I still think so. Let us think carefully about what is being asserted: that the capitalist, in abstaining for a period from consumption, is contributing the time that makes increased production possible. To avoid being misled by linguistic formulations, let us think about what really happens when a capitalist "defers consumption." A simple model is illuminating.

Consider a steady-state economy consisting of two sectors, a consumption-goods sector producing corn and a capital-goods sector producing plows and cultivators. Let us assume that these implements need to be replaced each year. Suppose the labor force of this economy consists of 100 workers, employed by a single capitalist; 10 workers make the plows and cultivators, and 90 workers, using the implements produced the preceding year, grow corn. Let us assume that an average harvest is 1,000 bushels and that each worker receives 9 bushels, leaving the capitalist with a profit of 100 bushels.

Suppose our capitalist chooses to defer consumption so that productivity might increase. How can his aim be accomplished? It can be accomplished by making production more "capital-intensive" (more "roundabout," the Austrian theorists would say). This means producing more capital goods (i.e., more plows and cultivators). So our capitalist can use a portion of what he is entitled to consume to entice certain workers to shift from the growing of corn to the production of farm implements. Suppose he does this, thus doubling the labor force in the capital-goods sector to 20, and hence reducing the labor force in the consumption-goods sector to 80.

What happens? During the period following his decision there will be less corn produced, say 900 bushels, because the work force in agriculture will have declined, and the extra plows and cultivators will not yet have come on-line. When they do come on-line, however, corn production will increase, let us say to 1,100 bushels. A transition will have been made to higher productivity. Corn production will have moved from 1,000 to 1,100 bushels through a temporary trough of 900 bushels.

The elements of our second time-preference tale would seem to be in place. Our capitalist, in deferring consumption, has made production more roundabout, more time-intensive, with the result that productivity has increased. But notice, there is nothing in this story that might reasonably be called "supplying time." What was necessary for production to become more capital-intensive was a reallocation of the work force. In this instance it was done by the capitalist supplying an immediate material enticement. But this reallocation could have taken place by other means. A governmental authority could have ordered more workers into capital-goods production. The workers might have decided democratically to shift. The capitalist himself could simply have required them to switch, on pain of being fired, rather than by offering an inducement. In all these cases production would have become more capital-intensive (i.e., time-intensive). In none of these cases, no more than in the original case, does the initiating agent supply that time.

Recall that the claim that prompted this model was that the capitalist, in abstaining for a period from consumption, was supplying the time that would make increased productivity possible. We can now see what is really going on. Our initial commonsense reaction was right: The capitalist is not a supplier of that mysterious metaphysical entity "time." He is not supplying anything. What he is doing is using a portion of the social surplus that he is entitled to consume to *influence the allocation of the work force*. It is this reallocation of labor – not the injection of more "time" – that ultimately increases production.

In our model, the linkages between "deferring consumption" (i.e., saving) and increased productivity are direct and transparent. In reality they are often obscure and much mediated – and less certain to hold. For example, when I put my $100 in the bank, I authorize the bank to lend it out. Consider three possibilities. Suppose it is not lent out. Then aggregate demand deceases, and the economy slackens. That is to say, production decreases, with no guarantee that it will pick up again. Suppose the loan officer makes a consumer loan. In this case there is no direct effect on capital formation. The positive social effect of the loan is to counteract the negative effect on aggregate demand occasioned by my decision to save. Production need not decline, but it need not increase either. It is only in the third case, when a loan is made to an entrepreneur of a certain sort, that capital intensity will increase. The loan gives an entrepreneur the authority to direct the employment of workers. In general, new capital formation will occur if and only if the net effect of the entrepreneur's exercise of this authority is a shifting of labor from the consumer-goods sector of the economy (or from the ranks of the unemployed) to the producer-goods sector. If the entrepreneur uses his loan to authorize the construction of new physical plant or to place orders for new equipment, this will occur; if he simply buys out an existing concern, it will not.

Because new capital formation is so tenuously connected to my savings, it is evident that I am not, by my decision to defer consumption, supplying anything intrinsic to production. I am not engaged in a productive activity. I am not making a "productive contribution."[55] The second time-preference argument comes up short.

---

[55] Notice that I collect my interest whatever the loan officer does with my money, whether or not productivity is ultimately increased, which is a nice arrangement for those of us who can afford to save, and a marvelous arrangement for those who can save a lot. .

One final counterargument merits attention: "You grant that I do something when I decide to save. I transfer authority over my funds to someone else. I select a bank or a bond issue or a financial advisor. But doesn't that involve deliberation and judgment that ultimately benefit society, and hence entitle me to a reward?"

First, so long as federally insured, risk-free options are available, the only exercise of intelligence required to guarantee reward is to find an insured institution (or several institutions, if one's surplus exceeds the limit insurable by any one institution). A quick walk through the Yellow Pages should suffice. That this exercise may have consequences that are far from socially beneficial – consequences that will not, however, impinge on one's reward – is evidenced by the current savings-and-loan debacle.

Moreover, if this sort of deliberative activity is to justify one's reward (via the canon of contribution), one must be able to argue that in general the reward is proportional to the deliberation. That is, it must be the case that a person with $500 to invest tends to deliberate five times longer or more intensively or more astutely than a person with $100 to invest. (One with $5 million must deliberate 50,000 times longer or more intensively or more astutely.) I trust that no one thinks that an empirical investigation of the proportionality claim would validate it.

To conclude, let me offer a clarification. It might be thought that I am claiming that the production of new capital goods in no sense requires a sacrifice of possible consumption. That is not my claim. It is often the case that an increase in capital goods requires that some members of society consume less for a period *than they could if the deployment of society's labor and other resources were unchanged*. Workers must be shifted from the consumer-goods sector to the capital-goods sector. This is quite different from saying that certain members must consume less *than they are entitled to consume*. Time-preference theory gets its prima facie plausibility from a conflation of these two senses of deferred consumption. When these senses are distinguished, it becomes evident that the capitalist qua capitalist contributes no more as a supplier of time than he does as a supplier of marginal product or as a supplier of entrepreneurial skill. The contribution defense fails once more.

Interest as reward for waiting

We have not been able to come up with a viable defense of capitalist distribution based on the canon of contribution. Perhaps another ethical principle will fare better.

If interest, the key stumbling block, cannot be justified by an appeal to productive contribution, what other justification might it have? Alfred Marshall, the enormously influential British pre-Keynesian, responds with a different neoclassical answer: Interest is the *reward for waiting*.[56] Like Clark, Marshall confronts the Marxian critique.

It is not true that the spinning of yarn in a factory, after allowance has been made for the wear and tear of the machinery, is the product of the labor of the operatives. It is the product of their labor, together with that of the employer and subordinate managers, and of the capital employed; and that capital itself is the product of labor and waiting. If we admit it is the product of labor alone, and not of labor and waiting, we can no doubt be compelled by an inexorable logic to admit that there is no justification of interest, the reward of waiting; for the conclusion is implied in the premises. . . .

To put the same thing in other words, if it be true that the postponement of gratification involves *in general* a sacrifice on the part of him who postpones, just as additional effort does on the part of him who labors, and if it be true that this postponement enables man to use methods of production of which the first cost is great but by which the aggregate enjoyment is increased, as certainly as it would be by an increase of labor, then it cannot be true that the value of the thing depends simply on the amount of labor spent on it. Every attempt to establish this premise has necessarily assumed implicitly that the service performed by capital is a "free good," rendered without sacrifice, and therefore needing no interest as a reward for its continuance.[57]

We notice at once that Marshall, in true neoclassical fashion, conflates production factors with their owners. This is striking in the last sentence. The assumption that Marshall is bent on refuting – that the service performed by capital is a free good rendered without sacrifice and therefore needing no reward for its continuance – is plainly true. A field does not sacrifice in growing corn; a spinning wheel needs no reward for turning cotton into yarn. Their owners are another matter.

What about these owners? Marshall has introduced a new element into the neoclassical story; his appeal is not to productive contribution, but to *sacrifice*. A different ethical canon has been invoked.

Sacrifice arguments have always appeared ludicrous to critics of capitalism. (Does the mine owner really sacrifice more than a miner? A stockholder in General Motors more than an autoworker?) Marshall himself is not unaware of this objection; hence his stress on the "in general" qualification.[58] But as we shall see, this qualification cannot save what really is at bottom an impossible defense. The sacrifice argument is worth analyzing, however, because some not-so-obvious misconceptions that underlie it often persist even when the ethical argument itself is rejected.

Any demonstration that capitalist distribution accords with the ethical canon of sacrifice must involve three steps: first, a specification of the

---

[56] This answer bears obvious resemblance to the time-preference theory just discussed, but there is a significant difference at the normative level. Time-preference theory appeals to the moneylender's contribution; Marshall, as we shall see, appeals to something else.
[57] Marshall (1948, p. 587).   [58] Ibid., p. 233.

nature of an economic agent's sacrifice; second, an identification of some quantitative measure of that sacrifice; third, a demonstration that capitalism (in general) distributes according to the sacrifice so defined and measured. (A complete argument would also require a justification of the canon itself and a proof that the defined sacrifice is appropriate to the canon, but these steps will not concern us. The argument fails before it gets that far.)

The first step seems straightforward enough, at least for workers. All sacrifice their leisure; many also undergo mental and physical discomfort. As for capitalists, Marshall answers that they wait, that is, they postpone gratification. When a person has to choose between consuming at once and deferring consumption, she normally finds it painful to postpone gratification, and this pain is not fully compensated by later consumption of an equal amount. (Note the difference between this account and time-preference theory, which makes no reference to pain.)

The second step of the argument involves quantification. How does one measure the pain one feels in postponing consumption? An obvious answer suggests itself (at least to one schooled in neoclassical theory): by the amount of money it would take to persuade one to make that sacrifice, just as one measures the discomfort of a job by the amount one must pay to get someone to do it.

Do we have any reason to think that capitalism will compensate a person with exactly that amount? For an affirmative answer, Marshall brings the neoclassical categories to bear on *interest rates*. These rates, he claims, are determined by the money market, which places entrepreneurs in search of capital in contact with households tempted to save. When the market is in equilibrium, interest rates are such as to call forth exactly as much savings as entrepreneurs are desirous of borrowing. If the market is in equilibrium at 6 percent, say, this indicates that savers find a 6 percent premium to be sufficient compensation for the pain they feel, while at the same time entrepreneurs are willing to pay that much, because they expect to be able to increase productivity enough with the money they borrow to pay this premium and still have sufficient excess to compensate themselves for risk and entrepreneurial skills. Thus the quantitative connection between pain and reward.

Common sense suggests that something is amiss here. Analysis reveals some difficulties. Even if we assume the general validity of the neoclassical account of interest-rate formation, the argument does not show that capitalism rewards in accordance with sacrifice. In fact, the neoclassical account, taken seriously, demonstrates that it does not, for the 6 percent premium is not what the average saver (or savers "in general") will require as an inducement to save; it is what the most reluctant saver will require, the saver at the margin. It is the premium that will be required to entice the last few dollars from the last few households to bring total savings into line with total investments. Unless it were the case that nobody would save without 6 percent compensation (scarcely a plausible assumption, nor one compatible with neoclassical sensibilities), some people would have saved at 4 percent, though presumably fewer, some at 2 percent, and so forth. These people, according to the neoclassical tale, would have evaluated their pain of deferred gratification at less than 6 percent, and so these people would be overcompensated by the market. Indeed, for some it is extremely convenient that there are social institutions that will pay for the use of accumulated wealth. Beyond a certain point, personal consumption might prove difficult, and alternative arrangements expensive (storage facilities, guards, and the like). One's "pain of abstinence" in such cases might well be negative. One would pay not to consume. One's "pain" would be pleasure. Now, plainly, a system that rewards pleasure – or that rewards generally in excess of a saver's pain – cannot be justified by the canon of sacrifice.[59]

An alternative, more straightforward critique of Marshall's argument is to deny that his paradigm applies to reality. The plausibility of Marshall's analysis, with its "in general" clause, rests on the assumption that the typical saving unit is a small- or medium-income household. For such a household, "waiting" might plausibly involve pain comparable to a laborer's discomfort. But in contemporary capitalist societies, such households are not the source of most savings; the bulk of the interest payments do not go to them. As Simon Kuznets has noted, "only the upper income groups save; the total savings of groups below the top decile are fairly close to zero."[60]

But if the significant savers are not the small- or medium income households, but rather the wealthy, then the plausibility of comparing the "sacrifice" of postponement with the sacrifice of labor evaporates. Marx makes the obvious point: "The more, therefore, capital increases by successive accumulations, the more does the sum of value increase which is divided into consumption-fund and accumulation-fund. The capitalist can, therefore, live a more jolly life and at the same time practice more 'abstinence.'"[61]

Marshall's analysis, as an ethical argument appealing to the canon of sacrifice, is plainly fallacious. This we have just seen. But there remain

[59] An analogous argument shows that workers, too, are overpaid, because the wage rate is what it takes to coax the most reluctant worker away from her leisure. I would caution against concluding that because everyone gets more than he deserves, capitalism is indeed the best of all possible worlds. The reader is invite to find the flaw in this not uncommon sort of neoclassical reasoning.

[60] Kuznets (1965, p. 263). This observation refers, of course, to net savings, the difference between a household's gross savings and its debt.

[61] Marx (1967, p. 667).

elements of Marshall's case that deserve further attention. For Marshall, "waiting" is the postponement of gratification that leads to increased productivity. His basic assertion is that capital is the product of labor and such waiting. Is it? Is this "waiting" identical with the "saving" people do under capitalism when they put money in the bank or buy a bond or share of stock? Does production *require* such saving? Political philosophers often take these neoclassical assumptions for granted. Nozick, for example, repeats the standard litany: "The total product is produced by individuals laboring, *using means of production others have saved to being into existence*, by people organizing production or creating means to produce new things or things in a new way."[62]

The fact of the matter is that all of the foregoing questions should be answered in the negative: Capital is not the product of waiting; waiting is not identical with capitalist saving; neither waiting nor saving is necessary for production. Nozick is wrong to think that savers bring means of production into being.

To be sure, there is an economic truth underlying Marshall's thought, but his formulation of that truth is inaccurate and unfortunate. There is a sense in which "waiting" is a condition for capital *increase*, though not for capital per se. We can see this, and understand the answers to the foregoing questions, by returning briefly to the corn-plow model of the preceding section.

Recall our 100 workers, employed by a capitalist, 10 workers making plows and cultivators, and 90 growing corn. If the workers in the capital-goods sector produce just enough implements to replace those that wear out, and those in the consumer-goods sector produce enough corn to feed everyone, the society can persist indefinitely. In such an economy, new means of production are constantly being produced (as replacements), and yet there is nothing resembling Marshall's "waiting": a "postponement [that] enables man to use methods of production of which the first cost is great but by which the aggregate enjoyment is increased." Capital goods here are not the product of waiting.[63]

Of course, if this society wishes to increase its stock of capital goods, it may have to postpone some gratification. If we assume full employment of people and resources, then, as we noted in the preceding section, a capital-goods increase requires a shifting of a part of the work force from the consumer-goods sector to the capital-goods sector.[64] This shift

---

[62] Nozick (1974, p. 152); emphasis added.

[63] It might be objected that waiting was necessary *in the beginning* to get the process started, to produce the original plows and cultivators. That may be true – the original implements may have required deferred gratification – but they have long since been replaced. Those that are now produced, year after year, require no such postponement.

[64] Notice that the full-employment assumption is necessary for there to be *any* correlation between capital and waiting. If unemployed people are set to work on idle resources to

will allow the "aggregate enjoyment" to be increased at a later date, as the increased output of capital goods makes its way to the consumer-goods sector, thereby increasing productivity; but in the meantime, actual consumption must be cut back from what is technically possible. (Recall our model: Corn production increases from 1,000 bushels to 1,100 through a one-year trough of 900.) Society must wait, but its waiting will pay a social dividend. This is the valid core of Marshall's doctrine.

It is significant, and perhaps surprising, to notice that this sort of waiting has nothing whatsoever to do with one quite ordinary sense of "saving" – the setting aside of a portion of the total output so as to meet future contingencies. Virtually all societies (and many individuals) save in this sense. Grain reserves are maintained; cans of tomatoes are stored in the basement. This saving may be regarded as "deferred consumption," but it is quite different from Marshall's "waiting." This saving has no connection with bringing means of production into being, or, rather, it has a negative effect: The more the work force must produce emergency reserves, the less it can produce means of production or goods for current consumption.

Now, of course, in some societies a different sort of saving occurs: Not things are saved, but money (*entitlement* to things), and the money is not stashed in a mattress, but put in a bank, where it "grows." It is this sort of saving Nozick has in mind when he writes of saving as "bringing means of production into being."

It is unfortunate that one word refers to two quite distinct practices. Conflating the universal practice of holding in reserve with a practice that is institutionally specific can be deeply misleading. For one thing, it suggests that the act of saving is some sort of universal, wealth-creating, productive activity. It is not. As was demonstrated in the preceding section, the capitalist's decision not to consume was neither a necessary condition nor a sufficient condition for an increase in corn production. (Recall that workers could have shifted to plow production without being enticed by the corn the capitalist was entitled to consume.)

The conflation also suggests that when the capitalist decides to defer consumption, he alone consumes less, and so he alone is entitled to a reward for his waiting. That the antecedent clause is false can also be seen from our model. In the first period, the capitalist uses a part of the 100 bushels to which he is entitled to entice some workers from corn production to farm-implement production. Thus, he does not consume all to which he is entitled. As a result, corn production declines in the

produce material means of production, then the capital stock of society is increased without any deferred consumption. As Hyman Minsky (1986, p. 61) notes, "every economist since Richard Kahn and Maynard Keynes has known that in a world with unemployment more investment is not only compatible with but leads to more consumption."

next period (to 900 bushels). Because the capitalist is entitled to a portion of that also, worker consumption, previously 9 bushels apiece, necessarily declines. (In the real world, where transactions are mediated by money, this decline is effected by higher prices, the supply of consumer goods having temporarily contracted.) So we see that both capitalist and workers forgo consumption, but with two significant differences: First, the capitalist, but not his workers, chose to consume less; second, the capitalist, but not his workers, is entitled to a reward for his waiting.

In fairness to capitalism, we should continue the story. Workers necessarily consume less during period two, because output has contracted. In the third and subsequent periods, output rises above what it had been initially. Although it is the case that the capitalist is legally entitled to the whole of the increase, some of it may trickle down. And in fact (the historical record is clear here), most (though not all) workers do share in the productivity gains. So workers as well as capitalist are rewarded for their "postponement." The differences, however, remain: (1) Capitalists choose to "wait," whereas the decline in worker consumption follows from these choices. (2) Capitalists are legally entitled to a reward for their waiting, whereas worker gains must trickle down.

It seems clear that much confusion can be avoided if we shun the kinds of locutions to which neoclassical analysis is prone, locutions that suggest that the act of saving (in a capitalist society) is a productive activity. It is more properly regarded as an element of a complex decision-making procedure. When an individual (in a capitalist society) saves his money rather than spends it, his "act" of postponement reduces aggregate demand for consumer goods. A signal is sent (in the form of unsold goods) for the market to contract. He "votes" for less production. If that money is placed in a bank (or otherwise made available for investment), and if an investor borrows it and then spends it, a countersignal is given. Because the investor's expenditures are likely to be at least in part for capital goods, the net effect of the two signals is to shift workers from the consumer-goods sector of the economy to the capital-goods sector. Thus a societal decision to "wait" is registered.

There are various possible complications that could be added to the foregoing scenario, but we shall not pursue them here.[65] The important point to be made is that the institutional arrangements that allow investment funds to be generated by private monetary savings should be regarded as part of the societal apparatus for deciding on the contours of

---

[65] One was suggested in the preceding section. If the act of saving is not offset by investment, then that private act, far from bringing means of production into existence, can have the opposite effect. It is the well-known (Keynesian) story: Saving reduces aggregate demand; this reduction, in turn, forces workers from their jobs and idles factories. It is a curious system, is it not, that rewards such antisocial acts?

production, not as part of society's productive apparatus. The act of saving is no more an act of production than is purchasing a commodity. Buying a share of Chrysler Corporation is no more an act of production than is voting to build a new highway. All of these actions will influence future production, but they are quite distinct from production itself.[66]

The institutional arrangements covered by the notion of "saving" under capitalism are but one set among many for arriving at decisions regarding postponement of social consumption and a rechanneling of workers. Workers can be ordered by political authorities; they can be enticed by economic incentives; they can decide democratically to move from one sector of the economy to another. Investment funds can be generated by private savings, by taxation, or by printing presses. Which of these (or other) methods are to be preferred is a matter we shall consider in detail later. Utilitarian and libertarian considerations will have to be brought to bear. But in such analyses we must keep clearly in mind that societal "waiting" and private saving are quite distinct notions, complexly related. Above all, we must avoid simplistic assumptions about the causal link between such saving and increased production.

Profit as reward for risk

If neither "contribution" nor "sacrifice" will do as a justification for capitalist income, what about *risk*? In popular consciousness this is perhaps the most common justification of all. The capitalist risks his money. So he deserves a reward.

The argument is flawed, but it is not without a reasonable core. There would seem to be nothing a priori objectionable about rewarding people who take risks, if such risk taking is socially beneficial. But the matter is not so simple as it may appear.

We have already noted that the risk defense has no force against what I have called the real problem with capitalism: risk-free *interest*. But let us set aside this objection for now. Let us suppose our capitalism to be completely laissez-faire, lacking all risk-free alternatives. In this setting, if banks or corporations fail, you lose your holdings. No governmental bailouts.

The first thing we observe is that we cannot invoke the risk principle as a justification of capitalism in the same way that we invoked the

---

[66] Implicit here is yet another argument against justifying interest (and hence capitalism) by appealing to the canon of contribution. Clearly, the reward for voting is one's vote – the influence one exerts. Similarly, the reward for purchasing a commodity is that commodity. By analogy, the reward for saving should be not interest but one's savings – the ability to consume at a later date.

canon of contribution or sacrifice. We cannot propose, even tentatively, that capitalism rewards in accordance with risk. One might make such a claim with respect to labor, on the grounds that, ceteris paribus, riskier, more dangerous jobs tend to pay more, but nothing of the sort holds for capital. We cannot say that riskier investments pay more. We can only say that riskier investments, *if they succeed*, tend to pay more. If they do not succeed – and the riskier they are the more likely it is that they will not – the investment will not pay at all. By the same token, it is wrong to say that the capitalist who risks his money *deserves* a return on his investment. If such risk entailed entitlement, then a failed investor would have grounds for complaint, which clearly he does not. Unlike a worker in a hazardous occupation, a bankrupt investor cannot say, "I have taken the risk, so I am entitled to reward."

We cannot analyze risk in the same fashion as contribution or sacrifice. We cannot look for a quantitative measure of risk, and then see whether or not capitalism rewards accordingly. A more appropriate normative standard would seem to be that of "pure procedural justice," a notion deriving from the concept of a "fair game." The principle invoked in a pure-procedural defense is that if one plays by the rules and the rules are fair, then the reward is just no matter how much (or how little) it is.[67]

To conceive of a pure-procedural defense of capitalism is to think of capitalist investment as a game. The question to be asked is, Are the rules fair? An objection comes at once to mind: Not everyone can play. One can play the game only if one has something to invest. That's one of the rules.

One might protest that no one is legally excluded from the game. No laws restrict investment opportunities to a particular class. But two points must be borne in mind. First of all, the obvious point: Whatever the law may say, large numbers of people simply do not have any discretionary funds to invest. (Samuelson observes that, talk of "people's capitalism" notwithstanding, "only about 25 million out of 225 million Americans own any appreciable amount of stocks, and that is a generous estimate.")[68]

The second point is less obvious. Consider this simplest of games: You and I flip a fair coin; we each bet a dollar per round; heads I get your dollar, tails you get mine. The game is "fair" in the sense that we both face the same odds at any toss of the coin. However, a complication arises when we look at the game over time and in light of initial conditions. If I enter the game with $20, and you with $10, you are twice as likely to go bust as I. If you do go broke, and another player enters with $10, he

---

[67] See Rawls (1971, p. 86): "Pure procedural justice obtains [when] there is a correct or fair procedure such that the outcome is likewise correct or fair, whatever it is, provided that the procedure has been properly followed."

[68] Samuelson (1980, p. 66).

will be three times more likely to be cleaned out than will I (because my initial stake has been supplemented by your losings). As a limit case: If my stake is infinite, yours is finite, and the game is endless, I cannot lose, and you cannot win – despite the "fairness" of the procedures.

So the large investor, although he has more to lose, is less likely to lose than is the small investor. Add to this fact the further consideration that wealth gives one access to information, expert advice, and opportunities for diversification that the small investor often lacks, and we see that the balance between magnitude of loss and likelihood of loss tilts toward the wealthy.

Because the rules of the capitalist investment game not only exclude many potential players but also discriminate among the actual players in favor of the wealthy, we would seem to have good grounds for questioning the "fairness" of even clean capitalism. But an objection demands to be heard. The small investor has no grounds for complaint, it is urged, because she freely chooses to enter the game. She doesn't have to. She can spend her money, or she can put it in a shoe box. Unless one is committed to so strong a paternalism as to allow the government to prohibit adult investors from risking the money they want to risk, one has no moral grounds for objecting to the capitalist rules.

This objection, it seems to me, has strong prima facie force. Small investors (who are, after all, mostly from the upper middle class) would hardly seem to be such a benighted lot as to require paternalistic intervention. In fact, the argument is strengthened by the fact that the capitalist investment game is a *positive-sum game*. The small investor, although disadvantaged vis-à-vis the large investor, is still likely to make money. (The stock market may not be a magic-carpet ride, but neither is it a scam.) To prohibit small investors from playing would be to block them from pursuing not merely their desires but also their rational self-interests.

Let us think more carefully about the game-theoretic concept just introduced. A game is positive-sum if the total expected gain from playing, computed probabilistically, is positive.[69] More simply put, a positive-sum game is one in which more money is won than is lost. If a game is zero-sum (i.e., if gains and losses match), then one is not disadvantaged by being excluded, because the expected gain from playing is zero. On balance, one is no better off playing than not playing. If the game is negative-sum, as is, for example, any gambling game where the house gets a cut, one's expected gain (when the game is pure chance) is negative.

---

[69] To compute a player's "expected gain," one multiplies each possible outcome by the probability that that outcome will occur, then adds these products. For example, if I were to make $2 when a fair coin turned up heads and lose $1 when it turned up tails, my expected gain for one toss of the coin would be $2(0.5) - 1(0.5) = \$0.50$. A game is positive-sum if adding up the expected gains of all the players yields a positive total.

If monetary gain is one's only reason for playing, one is better off sitting it out.

I have claimed that capitalist investment is a positive-sum game. If this is so, then people who are excluded are disadvantaged. As we have already noted, many people are indeed excluded. They lack the resources to play. If capitalist investment were a zero-sum game, such people would have no grounds for complaint. If the investment game were negative-sum (like a state lottery), such people could count themselves lucky for being kept out. But the capitalist investment game is not zero-sum, nor negative-sum. It is positive-sum.

Is it really? A case is sometimes made that net profit is zero. Frank Knight, the economist most closely associated with the risk theory of profit, has ventured that it is no greater than zero, and quite likely negative. People enjoy risk taking, he claims, and are willing to pay for the privilege of doing so.[70] Knight may be right about net profit, but only because he uses the term "profit" in a strict, technical sense. Like Samuelson, he distinguishes profit from "the returns to the productive services of capital" (i.e., from "interest").[71] What a businessman calls "profit," Knight separates into an interest component (which he regards as generated by the capital itself) and a residual (pure) profit, positive or negative (which he attributes to risk).

This theoretical distinction is important in certain contexts (as we have already seen), but not here. The capitalist investment game pays out not only "pure" profit, but interest and dividends as well, and this total is decidedly positive.[72] If Knight's empirical conjecture is right, the overall rate of return on stocks, bonds, and other uninsured investments will be somewhat lower than the going interest rate, but this is irrelevant to the issue at hand. The fact remains, those who play the investment game usually gain by doing so, for they are playing a game where the net gain (interest, dividends, pure profit) is positive.

This analysis of the objection to my charge that the capitalist game is unfair to small investors has led to a deeper critique. Small investors are indeed disadvantaged vis-à-vis larger ones, but all participate in a game in which they are likely to benefit at the expense of those excluded. One is tempted to say that in the current era of Lotto capitalism there are two

---

[70] Knight (1921, p. 368). I should note that Knight would prefer his theory to be called "uncertainty theory" rather than "risk theory," because he distinguishes the two concepts. For Knight, "risk" is calculable (e.g., by insurance actuaries), whereas "uncertainty" is not. Because this distinction does not bear on my argument, I shall use "risk" for both concepts.

[71] Knight (1921, p. 18).

[72] Perhaps the best proxy for investment income is what shows up in the national accounts as "property income." This figure usually is about one-quarter of the gross national product (GNP). It is never negative. See Samuelson (1980, p. 502).

games in town: an (unfair) positive-sum game for the rich and upper middle classes (the financial markets), and a (fair) negative-sum game for the rest (the state lotteries).

The careful reader may well have lingering doubts. How is it possible for the investment game to be positive-sum? What is the warrant for the claim just made that those who invest benefit at the expense of those who do not?

These are important questions, the answers to which will take us near to the heart of capitalism. Let me address them by first detouring through another question. What is the point of the capitalist investment game? That is to say, what is the purpose of stock markets, bond markets, savings banks, and other institutions that allow those with surplus money to risk it in the hope of seeing it grow? What is the point for society? (Individual motivation for playing a positive-sum game is hardly mysterious.)

Clearly, the point is not to reward risk per se. People take countless risks that go unrewarded, even when successful. Every time I dodge my way across Sheridan Road, I take a risk. Every time I leave aside my seat belt, I take a risk. There are no social institutions in place to reward me monetarily for my success at survival, nor can we imagine any such being advocated. The risks we want to reward are those that, when run successfully, are socially beneficial.

The point of the investment game is to encourage socially beneficial behavior of two quite distinct sorts. The primary goal is to foster entrepreneurial activity: actions by talented people that lead to new products, new techniques of production, and so forth. But in order to implement a new idea, an entrepreneur needs the labor of other people. The past labor of other people (in the form of equipment and raw materials) must be combined with the present labor of other people so as to give material substance to the entrepreneur's vision. At bottom, what an entrepreneur needs is *authority*, the authority to command the labor of others. How does one acquire such authority? In a capitalist society, by having the money with which to purchase it. And where does the entrepreneur lay hold of such money? In a capitalist society, partly from one's own savings, but for the most part from individuals who have money to spare. Thus we have the secondary goal of the capitalist investment game: to encourage those with money to spare to make it available to those who can put it to good use.

Thinking now about the primary goal, we notice something rather striking. If we make the functional distinction between entrepreneur (the person actually undertaking the productive action) and investor (the person advancing the capital), we see that the entrepreneur (qua entrepreneur) takes no risks. Leaving aside whatever funds of her own she may have put up, which are, strictly speaking, inessential to her role as entrepreneur, we find that she has nothing to lose. If the project fails, her backers lose their investment. If the project fails, her workers lose their jobs. If the project fails, society loses the material and intellectual resources that could have been employed elsewhere. But the entrepreneur, apart from her reputation, is no worse off than when she began.[73] So the (pure) profit she receives if the project is successful (what is left after wages, material costs, interest, and dividends have been paid) is not a reward for risk at all. It is a reward for her productive activity. It is the investor, not the entrepreneur, who is rewarded for risk.

We are now situated to understand how it is that the investment game is positive-sum, and why it is that the overall gain is (largely) at the expense of the nonplayers. The basic insight is Marx's. "Use values," that is, goods and services utilized by human beings, are the products of human beings shaping nonhuman nature to human ends. Use values are the products of labor and nature.[74] Use values are produced by those human beings, entrepreneurs included, who engage in productive activity.[75] Recall now the basic result we have gone to such lengths in previous sections of this chapter to establish: Providing capital is not a productive activity. Putting money in a bank, buying stock, investing in a money-market fund – these activities, which form the core of the capitalist investment game, entitle people to a share of society's produced use values, but these people do not contribute in any direct, material way to their production.

How is the positive-sum investment game possible? One gets something for nothing only when someone else gets nothing for something. Investment income – the reward to those who have risked their money in bank accounts, stock shares, real-estate trusts, venture capital, and the like – is possible only because those who produce the goods and services of society are entitled to less than their productive contributions. If capitalist distribution did indeed accord with the canon of contribution (which, as we have seen, is often claimed), then the capitalists would get nothing.

[73] I don't mean to pretend that the psychological pain attendant on failure is nothing. But in strictly monetary terms, she is no worse off than before.

[74] "We see, then, that labour is not the only source of material wealth, of use-values produced by labour. As William Petty puts it, labour is its father and the earth its mother" (Marx, 1967, p. 43). Contrary to what is often alleged, Marx did not ignore the role of nature in the production of wealth.

[75] Use values are not restricted to material things. The people (mostly women) who perform the enormous labor of caring for the young and the old are engaged in productive activity, as are (I would argue) poets, priests, performers – anyone who, by an expenditure of mental or physical energy, produces a good or a service desired by human beings. (The question of productive labor versus reproductive or nonproductive labor may be relevant to some issues, but not to the one at hand.)

Let me be clear about what I am asserting and what I am not. I am trying to explain how it is possible that the capitalist investment game (whole and usually in its parts) is positive-sum. In most years, more money is made on the stock market than is lost. How is this possible? I claim that this is possible only because those who engage in productive activity receive less than that to which they would be entitled were the cannon of productive contribution governing distribution. The reward to risk derives from this discrepancy.

I am not asserting (yet) that rewarding risk in this manner is wrong. The entrepreneur engages in productive activity of an important nature. In a capitalist society an entrepreneur must have access to funds to enact her vision. These funds come from investors. But the entrepreneur's gamble poses a risk to an investor. Because he can lose, he must be enticed to take the risk. This, remember, is the secondary function of the capitalist investment game. I have argued that this part of the game is unfair, that it is a positive-sum game from which many are excluded, a game that favors those who have much over those who have little. Still (it could be argued), unless the secondary goal of the investment game is met, the primary goal – encouragement of entrepreneurial activity – will be thwarted. The game may not be fair, but it serves a socially useful function. All things considered, the game is justified.

Unless, that is, there are alternative, superior, mechanisms for providing authority to entrepreneurs. Do such alternatives exist? It may be doubted that such superior mechanisms existed during the early days of capitalism. Given the political and technical configurations that obtained during the first centuries of capitalism, it is unlikely that a more effective mechanism could have existed for encouraging entrepreneurial talent than permitting private individuals to "provide capital" for promising ventures in return for a cut of the proceeds. But is this still the case?

We need not continue this line of investigation here, for we have moved onto the terrain of the comparative argument. It should be apparent at this point that the only risk defense of capitalist profit that might succeed is a *comparative defense*. If the capitalist investment game were unambiguously fair, a noncomparative defense might work, but as we have seen, it is not. Because the game is tainted, we must evaluate it not in and of itself but in comparison with other institutional arrangements that might accomplish the same purpose. Such arrangements do in fact exist. We shall soon turn to their comparative evalutation.

Capitalism as just because it is just

A harbinger of the resurgent conservatism just over the horizon was the appearance in 1974 of a defense of capitalism by Harvard philosopher Robert Nozick. His is a noncomparative defense, purporting to show that a certain form of capitalism – quite different from the then-prevailing liberal ideal – fits the correct conception of justice.[76]

In preceding sections I have defended the thesis that capitalism cannot be justified by appealing to the ethical canon of contribution, sacrifice, or risk. Nozick agrees, but his reasons are different from mine. These are *patterned* principles, he says, and liberty upsets all patterns. A "patterned principle" is one requiring that distribution vary according to some one or several natural dimensions, such as contribution or sacrifice or labor or need. No such pattern is acceptable, however, because none "can be continuously realized without continuous interference with people's lives."[77] The same charge is leveled against utilitarian and Rawlsian principles of distribution.[78]

The appropriate theory for evaluating socioeconomic systems, according to Nozick, is his *entitlement theory* of justice. Its cornerstone is a procedural principle similar to the one invoked by the risk defense. For Nozick, *whatever arises from a just situation by just steps is just.* Thus, if original holdings were justly acquired, and if all subsequent transfers are just, then the resulting distribution is just, whatever it may be. It need not correlate with contribution, sacrifice, risk, the greatest happiness for the greatest number, or anything else.

What counts as a just transfer or a just original holding? For Nozick, a *just transfer* is any voluntary exchange; a *just original acquisition* is a taking of something that has not been claimed by anyone else, which satisfies the "Lockean proviso" that this not materially worsen the positions of others no longer at liberty to acquire that particular holding.[79]

Such a theory of justice might seem wholly inapplicable to modern capitalist reality. In the United States, a native population was nearly exterminated, and millions more human beings were stolen from their homelands and brought here in chains. In Britain, enclosure movements trampled long-standing peasant rights and forced great numbers of people off the land. Throughout the world, Western colonizers rampaged. It would be difficult to dispute Marx's indictment:

> The discovery of gold and silver in America, the extirpation, enslavement and entombment in mines of the aboriginal population, the beginning of the conquest and looting of the East Indies, the turning of Africa into a warren for the commercial hunting of black-skins, signalized the rosy dawn of the era of capitalist production.[80]

[76] Nozick also argues that socialism cannot be just, but that is a separate matter that does not concern us now. His antisocialist arguments will be dealt with in later chapters.
[77] Nozick (1974, p. 165).
[78] The utilitarian principle requires that distribution provide the greatest happiness for the greatest number. Rawls's conception of justice will be discussed in Chapter 6.
[79] Nozick (1974, pp. 151, 178ff.).   [80] Marx (1967, p. 751).

Nozick is not unaware of this difficulty. He supplements his procedural principle and his two principles of just holdings (transfer and original acquisition) with a *principle of rectification*. Although he admits that he knows of "no thorough or theoretically sophisticated treatment of such issues,"[81] the basic conception is simple: If injustices have occurred, then transfers are justifiable in order to bring the current distribution into line with what would have been the case had injustices not occurred. How current societies might be altered by such a rectification cannot be said, though Nozick is confident that "socialism as the punishment for our sins would be to go too far."[82]

Nozick has taken aim at both socialists and liberals. Not any form of capitalism is just – only an untrammeled capitalism with a *minimal* state. In particular, no redistribution of wealth is justifiable, apart from rectification. Taxation is theft, unless to compensate for the protective services rendered by the minimal state or to redress past injustices. Not surprisingly, Nozick's *Anarchy, State and Utopia* has drawn heavy return fire. Much of it, in my view, has been accurate and deadly.[83] Nonetheless, we should not dismiss entitlement theory too quickly.

It would be easy to write off entitlement theory on the grounds that its core theory is so far removed from reality that its (quite undeveloped) principle of rectification cannot save it. But to do so, by us at any rate, would be too facile, for Nozick has a point to make. It is my thesis that capitalism is unjust. Not merely U.S. capitalism or British capitalism, but capitalism as such. Nozick's challenge to my thesis is this: "What if a radical rectification of wealth were to occur in our society? Ignore the practical problems in effecting such a redistribution; a theoretical point is being made. If holdings were rectified and the system continued, would that capitalism not be just? If so, then your objection cannot be to capitalism as such, but to a particular form of capitalism. Your general thesis collapses."

To respond to Nozick, we must abandon this world for one in which rectification has been made. Better, let us go to the beginning of the story, to Nozick's "state of nature," to see if and how a just capitalism might arise. Whether or not a just capitalism did arise is not our concern. We want to see if one *could* arise.

It will be recalled that by "capitalism" we mean a commodity-producing society in which the majority of the population gain access to the means of production by selling their labor power to those who own the means of production. If capitalism is to be justified by entitlement theory,

[81] Nozick (1974, p. 152).   [82] Ibid., p. 231.
[83] For two early liberal critiques, see Nagel (1975) and Scanlon (1976). For views from further left, see Ryan (1977) and Cohen (1977). More critiques and some defenses of Nozick can be found in Paul (1981).

a plausible account must be given to show how this state of affairs might come about without violating anybody's rights. There is, of course, the classic tale so ridiculed by Marx:

In times long gone by there were two sorts of people; one the diligent, intelligent and above all frugal elite; the other, lazy rascals, spending their substance, and more, in riotous living. . . . Thus it came to pass that the former sort accumulated wealth, and the latter sort had at last nothing to sell except their skins. And from this original sin dates the poverty of the great majority that, despite all its labor, has up to now nothing to sell but itself, and the wealth of the few that increases constantly although they have long ceased to work.[84]

Nozick seems to have some such picture in mind. He attacks the Marxian claim that workers are forced to deal with capitalists, asking, rhetorically, "Where did the means of production come from? Who earlier forwent current consumption then in order to gain or produce them? Who now forgoes current consumption in paying wage and factor prices . . . ? Whose entrepreneurial alertness operated throughout?"[85] For Marx, this is the "insipid childishness . . . everyday preached at us in defense of property."[86] It is certainly a one-sided account of the actual development of capitalism. But, as I have pointed out, Nozick need not refer to the actual genesis of capitalism, only to its possible genesis.

It cannot be denied that it is logically possible for a capitalist society to emerge as in the classic fable. But it is important to note that this account and the brutal reality of original acquisition are not the only scenarios. A quite different account can be given, one less sanguine than Nozick's vision, but fully in accordance with his principles of justice. Nozick advocates an unregulated free-market system. In such a system an alert entrepreneur might well increase production. Many have. Who benefits? The entrepreneur, of course, and also the consumers. But not his competitors. They may go to the wall.

This observation is obvious, yet its significance is often overlooked. The impacts of productivity changes operating through a free market can be and have been momentous. Millions of native weavers starved when British textiles poured into India. Community structures in the United States and Western Europe were ruptured and transformed when agricultural mechanization drove small farmers and peasants from the land. No force was used (or at least it need not have been). The free market, unregulated and coupled with private ownership, is an invisible hand – one that can quite effectively strip the means of production from individuals and compel them to search for employers. There is no force, no fraud, no infringement of liberty. There is no "injustice."

[84] Marx (1967, p. 713).
[85] Nozick (1974, p. 254). Notice how the neoclassical categories shape Nozick's thinking.
[86] Marx (1967, p. 713).

I am not suggesting that the market mechanism is wholly pernicious. I shall argue, in fact, that it has an important role to play in a well-ordered socialist society. There are significant advantages to be had in utilizing the market. But there are also significant disadvantages, especially when the market is accompanied by private property and wage labor. Any serious discussion of the capitalism–socialism controversy must confront these issues. An unregulated capitalist market can, as the foregoing examples show, lead to massive social dislocation and produce enormous pain and suffering. It might be the case that the advantages of such a system are sufficient to counterbalance the risk and reality of such pain, but that is scarcely self-evident.

It is precisely this question that cannot even be debated if entitlement theory is valid. The advantages of capitalism can be elaborated. Nozick appeals to the "familiar social considerations favoring private property" to support his claim that the Lockean proviso regarding original acquisition is not violated by capitalism, even when all the "original" property has been taken.[87] The advantages of capitalism can be discussed, but not the disadvantages. What a clever theory! The disadvantages need not be considered, for, as we realize when we look closely, the legitimacy of the defining institutions of capitalism – private property, the market, and wage labor – is *presumed* throughout. To put the point more precisely, if one accepts (1) Nozick's procedural principle that whatever emerges from a just situation by just steps is just, (2) his principle concerning the justice of voluntary transfers, and (3) the legitimacy of the original acquisition of property, then one must grant the legitimacy of capitalism, no matter what or how serious its disadvantages.

The basic institutions of capitalism are built into the theory: If a private individual can legitimately claim ownership to the natural resources of the earth and to the products of his labor (as Nozick's theory posits), then private ownership of the means of production is legitimate. If it is legitimate to make whatever property transfers one wants so long as personal coercion is avoided (as Nozick's theory posits), then the free market is legitimate. And because what may be "voluntarily transferred" includes one's own labor power (as Nozick's theory posits), wage labor is legitimate. The legitimacy of the basic institutions of capitalism follows at once from Nozick's presumptions. There is no space within which to insert an objection.

Of course, if the presumptions themselves are self-evident or solidly grounded, then one must accept their implications. But are they? Consider

---

[87] Nozick (1974, p. 177). The idea is this: Because of productivity increases due to capitalism, a person now can make more working for another than he could in the past working on his own; hence, he is not materially worse off because all the "original property" has already been appropriated.

the principle that private appropriation of natural resources and means of production (with or without a Lockean proviso) is morally legitimate. Neither the original inhabitants of the Americas nor the major socialist traditions (to name but two classes of dissenters) have found this self-evident. Consider the principle that all voluntary transfers are just. Notice what is to count as "voluntary":

Z is faced with working [for an owner of capital] or starving; the choices and actions of all other persons do not add up to providing Z with some other option. . . . Does Z choose to work voluntarily? . . . Z does choose voluntarily if the other individuals A through Y each acted voluntarily and within their rights.[88]

It seems not unreasonable to say that if "voluntary" need not imply any wider choice than working for a capitalist or starving, then the voluntary-transfer principle is problematic.[89] So, too, is the procedural principle itself, which provides the foundation of entitlement theory. It is hardly self-evident that one should accept as just a socially disastrous outcome that results from a series of seemingly innocuous decisions.

My criticism of Nozick comes to this: Entitlement theory does indeed justify capitalism. The justice of the basic capitalistic institutions follows immediately from the theory's (barely defended) premises. The market mechanism is taken as the paradigm of voluntary exchange: private property is presumed just, and wage labor is regarded as nonproblematic. Hence the fundamental issues that have traditionally exercised liberal and socialist critics of laissez-faire capitalism – the destructive social consequences of an untrammeled free market – are simply excluded from debate. For Nozick, capitalism is just, whatever the social consequences, because . . . well, because it is just.

[88] Nozick (1974, pp. 262–3).
[89] Nozick's example can be taken a step further. What if, as a result of A through Y acting voluntarily and within their rights, nobody wants to hire Z? Does Z "choose voluntarily" to starve? It seems that Nozick must either assent to this assertion or maintain that involuntary, preventable starvation does not render a society unjust, or else claim that involuntary unemployment is impossible – not an enviable "choice" for a moral theorist.

2. Terms of comparison

We have disposed of the main noncomparative arguments purporting to justify capitalism. Capitalism cannot be justified by appealing to "contribution," because providing capital (or "time") is not a productive activity. Capitalism cannot be justified by appealing to "sacrifice," because many who profit do not sacrifice. Nor can one appeal to "risk," because the capitalist investment game is rigged. A justification does follow (immediately) from Nozick's entitlement theory, but that ethical theory begs so many questions that the conclusions derived from it have no force.

The noncomparative arguments are out of the way, but the game is far from over. The arguments we have considered all suffer from having an overly restricted ethical base. Each, having grounded its case on one specific ethical value, can be refuted by showing that capitalism does not adhere to that value, or that the value itself is inappropriate or insufficient to the issue at hand. That was the strategy of Chapter 1, but it was almost too easy. We can imagine an impatient Clark objecting: "But to distribute at variance with marginalist contribution will lead to inefficiency!" Or a Schumpeterean proclaiming that "without capitalist incentives, a dynamic entrepreneurial class will not develop." Or Marshall: "Without interest, insufficient savings will be forthcoming to finance needed investment." Or Knight: "Without profit, socially desirable risks will not be taken." Or Nozick: "Give up capitalism and we lose our liberty."

These objections cannot be made within the ethical framework of Chapter 1. They are irrelevant to the claim that capitalism satisfies the ethical standard J, where J is a specific value (contribution, sacrifice, risk, or liberty). Each appeals (implicitly) to an ethical theory that permits the weighing of advantages and disadvantages and the comparison of alternative institutional structures. They are *comparative claims*. As such, they constitute capitalism's strongest line of defense. The essential claim, which subsumes the foregoing (and much more), is simply put: Given the strengths and weaknesses of various economic systems, capitalism yields the greatest balance of good effects over bad. Or – a variation of the preceding claim – of all the alternatives, capitalism is most likely to yield the greatest balance.

These claims are formidable. They would be difficult to establish, to be sure, but they would also be difficult to refute. To pick holes in specific arguments purporting to prove that capitalism yields the best of all possible worlds is not hard, but it is quite another matter to prove that the claim itself is false. To do that, it is not sufficient – though of course it is necessary – to identify specific weaknesses in capitalism. One must also make explicit one's values (to make clear what one is counting as "good" or "bad"), and above all, one must provide a concrete alternative that does not suffer from those weaknesses or other more serious ones. This latter move is the crucial, difficult one.

It is a move that many critics of capitalism have been reluctant to make. Marx himself assiduously avoided "utopian" speculation, confident that a victorious working class would construct an appropriate set of alternative institutions. Such reticence may once have been appropriate, but no longer.

There are important reasons for facing the question of alternatives. First of all, too many socialist experiments in this century have turned out badly. Some have been horrific. It is a sobering, indeed chilling, fact that not a single country that abolished private ownership of the means of production retained or instituted free and open elections, and not one retained or instituted civil liberties as extensive as those found in many Western capitalist countries. Certainly there are historical factors to be taken into account, and it is certainly true that capitalist "democracy" is something other than what the high-school civics texts describe. Still and all, the historical record cannot but give pause to anyone who examines it honestly. One can no longer believe that the abolition of private property will automatically usher in a just society.

There is a second important reason for discussing alternatives. We now know more than Marx or Engels did when they polemicized against "utopian socialism."[1] This century has witnessed unprecedented social experimentation: laissez-faire capitalism, fascism, welfare-state capitalism, centrally planned socialism, socialism with markets, capitalism with planning, collectivized farms, worker cooperatives, and on and on. And such experimentation has undergone unprecedented analysis. We can see more clearly now what works and what does not; we can understand better why certain projects succeed and others fail. There is much we do not know, of course, but we can speak with far greater confidence now than would have been warranted a century ago. Reticence now looks less like openness to the future, more like avoidance of hard questions.

---

[1] See Engels (1935). In fairness to Marx and Engels, it should be noted that often they were quite appreciative of those (such as Owen, Fourier, and Saint-Simon) they labeled "utopian." Their essential objection to the "utopians" was not to their ultimate vision but to their conviction that this vision would come to pass through ethical argumentation and communal experiment divorced from concrete political struggle – a still-relevant issue, as we shall see in Chapters 7 and 8.

A third reason for proposing alternatives is that they are needed – I am inclined to say desperately needed. Capitalism may claim to have succeeded in the "First World," but few would advance that claim for those portions of our planet designated "Third World," wherein reside the majority of humankind. And, of course, the "Second World" of Communist and ex-Communist countries is in a state of momentous flux, with economic restructuring everywhere under way. Knowing that they no longer want what they have had, a few in these countries want a reformed socialism; many more are pinning their hopes on some sort of capitalism. In either case, major structural changes must be decided upon, and then implemented. But what is the range of choices? What are the likely consequences of specific reforms? I do not think these questions can be adequately addressed in the absence of a cogent model of viable, desirable, democratic socialism.[2]

Before turning to socialism, we need to look more closely at capitalism. We have defined capitalism as a free-market economy in which the means of production are largely privately owned, and the majority of the population are engaged in wage labor. This definition is adequate for marking off capitalist societies from noncapitalist societies, but it does not capture the *ideal* defended by proponents of capitalism. We must become clearer about this ideal. Many, perhaps most, proponents of capitalism are unhappy with "actually existing capitalism" – certainly in the United States, where the signs and trends are so foreboding. Many, perhaps most, would like reform. To avoid what would be an unfair procedure – comparing an ideal-world socialism with real-world capitalism – we must address the capitalist *vision* – not what capitalism as currently constituted is, but what, properly constituted, it could be.

In fact, we must consider several visions, for advocates of capitalism are by no means unanimous. We cannot consider all possible variations, but we can do justice to capitalism's defenders by examining certain key, contrasting models. Most proponents of capitalism think of themselves as either conservative or liberal. (We shall ignore that peculiar, incoherent creature, the American "moderate.") To the conservative position belongs a certain idealized vision of capitalism, internally consistent (more or less), but much at variance with the liberal ideal – or, rather, at variance with the liberal ideals, for modern liberalism is currently rent by two conflicting conceptualizations of capitalism, each suggesting a distinct model as its goal.

Before sketching the differences, let me clarify some terminology. The terms "conservative" and "liberal" are both problematic. "Liberalism" is

---

[2] It is fashionable now in many Eastern European circles to dismiss all consideration of socialism, however reformed, on the grounds that people are tired of experiments – as if the rapid dismantling of existing structures and their replacement by privatized property and an unregulated market were not a high-risk experiment of the first order.

especially ambiguous. The term is sometimes used to designate the intellectual and political tradition that emphasizes liberty and laissez faire,
two key ingredients of contemporary conservatism; sometimes it is used
to designate the nonsocialist welfare-oriented tradition opposed to precisely this conservatism; at other times it is used to refer to the features
common to both these traditions.[3]

"Conservative" is also ambiguous. The term connotes resistance to
change, and yet many "conservative" theorists have advocated (and do
advocate) change – sometimes drastic change (e.g., the Reagan "revolution"). For this reason, many such theorists (more in the past than now)
have hesitated to call themselves "conservative." This was especially the
case during the long period of Democratic Party hegemony in the United
States stretching from Franklin Roosevelt through Lyndon Johnson, during which time "conservative" suggested someone rather far from the
mainstream. During that period, "conservative" theorists often made the
case that their legitimate title had been usurped by their opponents,
arguing that they, not their opponents, were the true heirs of Locke,
Adam Smith, Tocqueville, and other great "liberals" of the past.[4] During
those glory days for the Democratic Party, such theorists preferred the
label "classical liberal" to "conservative." Today, with "conservative" a
respectable title again, the term is not so contentious; so in what follows
we shall use the terms "conservative" and "classical liberal" interchange-
ably.[5] We shall call the nonsocialist opposition to this tradition "modern
liberal."

Contemporary conservatives (classical liberals) are indeed the heirs of
Adam Smith. Their fundamental commitment is to a capitalist economy
as free as possible from governmental interference, as close as possible
to Adam Smith's laissez-faire ideal. Conservatives tend to be critical of
governmental welfare programs, labor unions, and Keynesian deficit
spending. The basic problems of contemporary capitalism are held to
be rooted in excessive governmental regulation of the economy. ("Government is not the solution," Ronald Reagan was ever fond of saying,

---

[3] To compound the ambiguities, it has become common in recent years (at least in the
United States) for politicians of all stripes to distance themselves from the term "liberal,"
which has been twisted into almost a curse. But whatever difficulties it has in speaking
its name, "liberalism" remains the touchstone of the Western political tradition.

[4] See, for example, Hayek (1960), "Postscript," or Friedman (1962), "Introduction."

[5] In doing so, I am using "conservative" to designate contemporary *economic conservatism*,
which is something different from the *social conservatism* with which it has formed, over
the past decade and a half, a sometimes-strained political alliance. The latter, most stri-
dently represented by Right religious fundamentalism, has no qualms about using the
power of the state to impose its moral vision on dissenters, whereas the former is deeply
suspicious of all encroachments by the state on individual liberty. Because social conservatives lack the ideological commitment to the specific economic vision that animates
the economic conservatives, and because we are centrally concerned here with economic
alternatives, it is economic conservatism that will concern us in this work.

"government is the problem.") If the role of government were drastically curtailed, conservatives maintain, the free market would generate liberty and prosperity for all.

The economists in the conservative camp are all indissolubly wedded to the neoclassical paradigm. Two of them, Friedrich Hayek and Milton Friedman, are Nobel laureates, the latter "by far the most influential economist of the [mid-1960s to mid-1980s] period."[6] Both will be recurring objects of our attention.[7]

Among contemporary philosophers linked to the conservative tradition, Robert Nozick is the most prominent. The values stressed in his work are those of classical liberalism: a strong commitment to liberty and individualism, a suspicion of equality, an aversion to governmental control, whether democratic or not. The opening sentences of Nozick's major work exemplify the classical-liberal ethos: "Individuals have rights, and there are things no person or group may do to them (without violating their rights). So strong and far-reaching are these rights that they raise the question of what, if anything, the state and its officials may do."[8]

Modern liberalism stands in opposition to classical liberalism, but it must be further subdivided if we are to do justice to the question of economic ideals. Within modern liberalism, opinion is deeply divided concerning the fruitfulness of neoclassical economics. Classical liberalism embraces the neoclassical heritage without reservation. A large number of modern liberals do so also, or rather they embrace a neoclassical economics that features certain Keynesian addenda. This segment, comprising the "old-fashioned liberals" of the Roosevelt-Johnson mode, we shall call "Keynesian liberalism." The opposition segment, which is highly critical of neoclassical economics, we shall label "post-Keynesian liberalism." Within post-Keynesianism one can distinguish two versions, an earlier post-Keynesianism and a more recent "new liberal" variant, the latter being the form with which we shall be most concerned.[9]

---

[6] This assessment from Robert Heilbroner, a nonsympathetic commentator (Heilbroner, 1990, p. 1106).

[7] Each represents a school of economics associated with classical liberalism. Hayek derives from the "Austrian school," which goes back through Ludwig von Mises to the nineteenth-century marginalists Böhm-Bawerk, von Wieser, and Menger. Friedman represents the "Chicago school," a group of economists centered at the University of Chicago, whose characteristic tenor was set during the interwar years by Henry Simons and especially Frank Knight. Hayek, in fact, is associated with both schools; he left his native Austria prior to the outbreak of World War II and joined the faculty at the University of Chicago in 1950, where he remained for twelve years. Friedman transferred to Stanford University's Hoover Institute on War, Revolution and Peace in 1977, although he remained on the faculty at the University of Chicago until 1982.

[8] Nozick (1974, p. ix). In recent years Nozick has distanced himself from his more extreme earlier views (Nozick, 1989, pp. 286–7).

[9] I am using the term "new liberal" here, rather than "neo-liberal," even though the latter term is sometimes used to designate this ideal. But in the arena of international economics,

From the time of the Great Depression until the early 1970s, classical liberalism gave ground to Keynesian liberalism. By the 1960s, Keynesian liberalism commanded the heights of the economics profession. Enclaves of conservative thought persisted (most notably at the University of Chicago), and a few Left dissidents raised their voices now and then, but the "new economics" ruled with an untroubled conscience. Those were the halcyon days of Keynesian liberalism. But in the 1970s Keynesian liberal policies ran into trouble, and rebellion broke out on both the Left and Right. Keynesian liberalism remains a powerful intellectual tradition, but its self-confidence has certainly been shaken.

Keynesian liberalism, like classical liberalism, holds to the main tenets and techniques of neoclassical analysis, though the Keynesians have been freer with supplements. They support a free-market economy, but one in which the government plays an active role in mitigating the harsher effects of laissez faire. Historically, the dominant concern of the Keynesians has been unemployment (Keynes's major work, *The General Theory of Employment, Interest and Money*, appeared in 1936, during the depths of the Great Depression), but they have also been supportive of labor unions, government regulatory agencies, and public-welfare programs. In general, Keynesian liberals back a host of measures condemned by classical liberals. Consider the questions that Paul Samuelson, a Keynesian-liberal Nobel laureate, puts to Friedman:

Can a human being today seriously be against social security? Against flood relief? Farm legislation? Pure food and drug regulation? Compulsory licensing and qualifying of doctors? And of auto drivers? Be against foreign aid? Against public utility and SEC regulation? Against the post office monopoly? Minimum wages? The draft? Price and wage controls? Anticyclical fiscal and monetary policies? Auto-safety standards? Compulsory and free public schooling? Prohibition of heroin sales? Stricter federal and state housing standards for migrant workers? Maximum interest rate ceilings on usurious lenders? Truth-in-lending laws? Government planning? Can a man of good will oppose Pope Paul VI's encyclical naming central economic planning as the key to development?[10]

If we look from economists to philosophers, we find the Keynesian–post-Keynesian distinction more difficult to draw. Most philosophers who work in the areas of social and political philosophy are modern liberals,

particularly that part concerned with the Third World, "neo-liberal" is commonly used to describe the policies pushed by the Reagan and Thatcher administrations and the International Monetary Fund, policies that prescribe privatization, the cutting of social services, and the opening up of the economy to free trade. "Neo-liberalism" in this sense is quite different from (indeed, it is virtually the opposite of) the post-Keynesian "new liberalism" that will be a focus of our attention. (Neo-liberalism in this sense is really indistinguishable from what we are calling "classical liberalism." There is really nothing "neo" about it.)

[10] Samuelson (1980, p. 791). Although many conservatives would hesitate to push their principles quite so far as Friedman, who has written against all these things, they would oppose far more of these items than would Samuelson or other (Keynesian) liberals.

as opposed to classical liberals. They do not subscribe to the laissez-faire ideal, and they are critical of the classical-liberal absolute priority (or, perhaps more correctly, the classical-liberal concept) of liberty.[11] Modern liberals value liberty, but they also give significant weight to equality. In stark contrast to classical liberals, they regard as legitimate many governmental measures intended to effect some redistribution of wealth from top to bottom. Unlike socialists, however, they do not believe it necessary to radically restructure the basic institutions of capitalism.

One contemporary philosopher who is clearly a Keynesian liberal is John Rawls. Unlike most philosophers, he ventures frequently onto the terrain of economics, and when he does so his analysis leans heavily on the neoclassical paradigm. We shall pay particular attention to Rawls later on in this work, for his model of "fair capitalism" may be taken as a representative example of the Keynesian-liberal ideal.

Post-Keynesianism is a reaction to the Keynesian-neoclassical theoretical synthesis. Post-Keynesians are sympathetic to much of Keynes's work, but they disagree strongly with his suggestion that neoclassical theory comes into its own again once the government acts to secure full employment.[12] Post-Keynesianism, which emerged as a self-conscious movement in the mid-1970s, comes in two distinct forms, what one might think of as an earlier version and a later version.[13]

In the early version, the large corporation is given the preeminent role. Early post-Keynesians argued that large corporations, together with organized labor and big government, have rendered the reality of modern capitalism so different from the neoclassical "perfect-competition" parable that the neoclassical categories are useless. They are worse than useless, it is said. They are positively detrimental to a clear comprehension of contemporary economic and social difficulties. The best-known representative of early post-Keynesianism is John Kenneth Galbraith, past-president of the American Economics Association, John Kennedy's ambassador to India, an innovative thinker whose economic treatises have often been best-sellers.[14]

---

[11] See Dworkin (1978, pp. 113–43).   [12] See Keynes (1936, p. 378).

[13] The first major statement of the new movement was by Kregel and Eichner (1975). The *Journal of Post-Keynesian Economics* appeared in 1978 under the editorship of Paul Davidson and Sidney Weintraub. Post-Keynesianism usually traces its origins to Joan Robinson and her younger colleagues at Cambridge for their relentless attacks on the foundations of neoclassical economics, and to Kalecki, Sraffa, and Keynes himself.

[14] For an analysis of Galbraith's alternative vision, see Schweickart (1980, pp. 192–205). I am omitting a discussion of Galbraith from this work. For all the considerable insight he brought to bear on the functioning of modern American capitalism, his overall evaluation now appears much too sanguine, neglecting, as it does, the impact of international competition on our once-vaunted economy. New liberalism retains most of the Galbraithian analyses that have proved fruitful, while recasting his vision so as to accommodate the perceived urgency of coming to grips with the decline of the U.S. economy in the international arena.

During the 1980s, early post-Keynesian liberalism mutated into "new liberalism." The attitude toward neoclassical economics that defines post-Keynesianism – the conviction that neoclassical categories impede rather than enhance an understanding of the world – has persisted,[15] but the focus of concern has shifted dramatically: from the domestic arena to the international, from a concern that our large corporations are no longer disciplined by the market to a concern that they are being defeated in the market. It was suddenly perceived in the 1980s that Japanese (and Western European and South Korean and Taiwanese) goods were flooding into the country, that American jobs were moving abroad, that we were being "deindustrialized" – and that the neoclassical prescriptions (loudly proclaimed and sometimes followed by the Reagan administration) were doing little to reverse these trends. New liberalism insists that to revitalize our economy, to build a world-class economy, we must have a new vision and new policies.[16]

One of the most persistent, articulate, imaginative theorists of this second version of post-Keynesianism is Lester Thurow – economist at the Massachusetts Institute of Technology (MIT), economic advisor to Democratic Party presidential aspirants (most recently, Paul Tsongas), currently the head of MIT's Sloan School of Management. The new liberal ideal, as articulated by Thurow, will be investigated in Chapter 6.

Modern liberalism, both the "standard" and "new" versions, will be analyzed in detail later, with Rawls and Thurow serving respectively as representatives. But the major portion of this work will involve a comparison of a form of socialism – what I shall call "Economic Democracy" – with classical liberalism's laissez-faire ideal. Laissez faire is the purest form of capitalism, the one that most clearly exhibits capitalism's underlying structure. It is also the form out of which, by way of reaction, the other ideals have emerged. It is essential to understand this model – its structure and dynamic, its strengths and weaknesses – in order to comprehend adequately the other forms of capitalism, or, for that matter, certain features of Economic Democracy. We shall return to alternative conceptions of capitalism later, but it is this basic form that we must now examine.

Capitalism: Laissez Faire

Apart from a few libertarian anarchists, no classical-liberal theorist advocates complete laissez faire. All recognize that government must engage

---

[15] See Thurow (1983).

[16] It should be noted that the terminology I am using here has not yet become standard. Those whom I call "post-Keynesian" or "new liberal" do not always identify themselves as such.

in certain economic activities, from defining property rights and enforcing contracts to checking monopolistic power. Nevertheless, laissez faire lies close to the heart of classical liberalism. However much its advocates may disagree on secondary matters, they are united on this basic point: As much as possible, the economy should run itself.

But how can an economy run itself? How can millions of individuals produce, distribute, and consume millions upon millions of products unless guided by some central authority or some rigid tradition? The answer was formulated two centuries ago by Adam Smith:

> As every individual, therefore, endeavors as much as he can both to employ his capital in the support of domestic industry and so to direct that industry that its produce may be of the greatest value, every individual necessarily labours to render the grand revenue of the society as great as he can. He generally, indeed, neither intends to promote the public interest, nor knows how much he is promoting it. . . . He intends his own gain, and he is in this, as in many other cases, led by an invisible hand to promote an end which is no part of his intention. . . . By pursuing his own interest he frequently promotes that of society more effectually than when he really intends to promote it.[17]

The essential elements of this rather remarkable process are by now well known. Individual greed is held in check by competition. The "invisible hand" directs via that mighty law: supply and demand. If society wants more boots than are being supplied, and fewer sandals, then bootmakers can raise their prices, and sandalmakers must lower theirs. With bootmaking now more profitable, people and resources shift from sandalmaking to the boot business. Thus the supply of boots increases, and that of sandals declines – in accordance with society's desires, but without any central command.

This simple supply–demand paradigm is overwhelmingly important, for in an ideal laissez-faire economy it governs not only the movement of boots and sandals but also a vast array of other economic phenomena: all consumer goods and services, capital goods, land usage, the labor market, saving and investment, the stock market, foreign-exchange rates, international trade, and more. In view of its importance, it is appropriate to ask, how well does it work? What are the strengths and weaknesses of an economy based on the competitive pursuit of self-interest? What values does it promote or retard?

Classical liberalism and laissez faire have long been associated with liberty. Classical liberalism rose to prominence in the seventeenth and eighteenth centuries as a philosophy opposed to aristocratic privilege, to the unlimited authority of monarchs, to all forms of governmental tyranny, including (by the nineteenth century) "tyranny of the majority." Government, to the classical liberal, is by its very nature coercive, and

---

[17] Smith [1976, p. 456 (IV. ii. 9)].

coercion is opposed to liberty. Because "that government is best which governs least," it follows that a society that organizes its economic activity without government intervention is most desirable.

Laissez faire is alleged to have other strengths. It not only promotes liberty but also turns out goods and services efficiently. Adam Smith laid the basis for this argument, but the neoclassicals have refined it enormously. They have carefully defined the concept of efficiency; they have specified the requisite conditions; they have proved theorems.

It is worth examining briefly one of their basic results. In it, the actors in the neoclassical drama stand forth clearly, and the ways in which they are held to interact come into focus. Self-interest and competition remain the fundamental elements, but, as we shall see, they are more finely elaborated.

In the neoclassical version of laissez faire, the consumer is king. Consumers express their preferences by purchasing goods and services on the market, and this sets the economy into motion. The consumer is king in this ideal world, and his prime minister is the entrepreneur. Consumers express their desires; entrepreneurs hasten to satisfy them. Consumers, faced with the array of goods, concretize their desires by selective buying. The interaction of these expressed demands with the available supplies determines prices.

Entrepreneurs now respond. Those goods that are most profitable are produced in greater numbers; those that are less profitable are cut back. To produce, the entrepreneur must employ the factors of production (land, labor, and capital) and must organize them (if he is to be successful) as efficiently as possible.

Individuals under laissez faire are not merely consumers. They wear two hats. They are also owners, owners of factors of production. Thus, the entrepreneur, to produce, must pay rent to the owners of land, interest to the owners of capital, and wages to the owners of labor, with all rates being determined by the ubiquitous law of supply and demand. The money received by these owners may now be spent on consumer goods again, or (and here the individual dons a third hat) a portion of it may be saved. These savings may be lent out to an entrepreneur, at a rate again determined by supply and demand, this time operating in the money market.

The actors are now in place for another round. Goods have been produced, individuals have been supplied with funds with which to express their preferences, and a fresh store of capital has been set aside. The process may continue – by itself, automatically, with no need for government intervention.

I have described how laissez faire is seen to operate, but I have not demonstrated its efficiency. Here the analysis begins in earnest. The first thing needed is a precise notion of efficiency. Economists once thought in terms of utilitarian optimality – the greatest happiness for the greatest number – but that concept was discarded long ago as "unscientific." What is settled on instead is *Pareto optimality*. A state of affairs is Pareto-optimal if and only if every alternative state that would make some people better off would also render others worse off. That is, there is no possible change that would make no one worse off than before and someone better off. (Cutting a cake with a sharp knife results in a Pareto-optimal distribution, no matter how unequal the slices, so long as the entire cake is consumed. Bludgeoning it apart with a baseball bat would not be Pareto-optimal.)

Armed with this concept of efficiency, the neoclassical theorist can now proceed to his theorem. But first some assumptions are necessary, for laissez faire is not always efficient. The most important assumption concerns monopoly. There must not be any. Competition must be "perfect." This means that no individual or collection of individuals can take into account the effects on price levels of their own decisions to buy or sell. Everyone is a "pricetaker." There are no "pricemakers," neither firms nor labor unions. No one can drive prices up by withholding supplies, nor drive them down by refusing to buy.

Additional assumptions are necessary, although they need not concern us here. (They will be taken up later.) What we wish to do now is understand the basic result, the first fundamental theorem of welfare economics: A perfectly competitive laissez-faire economy, when all markets are in equilibrium, is in a state of Pareto optimality. That is, no output that would be unambiguously more satisfying can be produced from the given input. No one could be made happier without making someone else unhappier. In essence, there is no deadweight inefficiency in the system that would allow production or consumption to expand in some area without contracting in another.

This conclusion does not hold if the system contains a monopolist. One might think that a monopolistic system would also be Pareto-optimal (because making a monopolistic system competitive would surely make the monopolist unhappy), but this is not so, for if the monopolist were to produce as much as he would under conditions of perfect competition, then there would be sufficient excess created to make him as well off as before, and some people even better off. This is not to say that if he produced that much, he would in fact be better off. Not at all. His restraint is not stupid. It pays to be a monopolist. The situation is not Pareto-optimal because if he had acted as a perfect competitor, and if some redistribution had been effected, then others could have been made better off without making him worse off.

We can say even more. There is the second fundamental theorem of welfare economics (less significant to our purpose, but interesting in its own right), which demonstrates (again given suitable assumptions) that every Pareto-optimal allocation of benefits is the competitive equilibrium of some initial distribution of assets. That is to say, if the system discussed earlier had begun with a somewhat different initial distribution of existing resources, it would have been possible to reach a perfectly competitive equilibrium in which everyone – including the ex-monopolist – would receive as much as before, and some people more.

An example may clarify these results. Suppose an initial distribution of resources of 5 units each to A and B would yield, under perfect competition, a resultant distribution of 10 to A and 10 to B. If A were to behave as a monopolist, however, he might be able to secure 12 for himself, though B's return might fall to 6. The second situation is not Pareto-optimal, because, in the first case, 2 could have been redistributed from B to A to make A as happy as he would be in the second case, and B happier. Or, by the second fundamental theorem of welfare economics, some other initial distribution (perhaps 6 to A and 4 to B) would have produced a perfectly competitive equilibrium giving 12 to A and 8 to B. A's monopolizing, in effect, not only steals a slice of B's share of the cake, but beats a portion of the cake to useless crumbs.

The conclusion that a perfectly competitive laissez-faire economy in equilibrium will be Pareto-optimal is a nontrivial result. Its proof is by no means obvious.[18] The significance of the result, however, is a matter of debate, some elements of which we shall review later. For now, we are content to understand the claim and the essential structure of the system about which the claim is made.

So far, we have noted two basic claims in support of laissez faire. It is said to be the system most in accordance with liberty. It is said to be an optimally efficient system. A third claim is also often made. Laissez faire is said to give maximal range to human initiative, and thus to best promote optimal growth.[19] The lure of great reward stimulates talented in-

[18] A familiar version of the standard neoclassical argument can be found in the work of Lerner (1944, ch. 2, 5, and 6). A far more sophisticated mathematical treatment – which proves rather than assumes the existence of equilibrium prices – is given by Debreau (1959). For a philosophically acute assessment of the Debreau approach – what is now called "general-equilibrium theory" and sometimes is alleged to be one of the intellectual triumphs of the century – see Hausman (1981, ch. 5–7).

[19] At its inception, when neoclassical theory called the labor theory of value into question, growth arguments gave ground to efficiency arguments as the focus of academic attention. Mainstream theory did not really return to growth questions until after World War II. [Harrod (1939) provided the initial stimulus, though growth theory did not really revive until after the war.] Historical factors no doubt played a role. Soviet productivity surged during the interwar years, while capitalism foundered in the Great Depression. With the postwar boom, however, growth arguments again gained prominence, in academia and in popular consciousness. The race with the Russians was on, and the

dividuals to take the risks so essential to path-breaking innovation. The relentless pressure of competition spurs the more reluctant to follow suit.

Few thinkers have ever denied the dynamic nature of capitalism. Not even Marx doubted this aspect. Indeed, an extract from the *Communist Manifesto* reads like a paean:

The bourgeoisie, during its rule of scarce one hundred years, has created more massive and more colossal productive forces than have all preceding generations together. Subjection of nature's forces to man, machinery, application of chemistry to industry and agriculture, steam navigation, railways, electric telegraphs, clearing of whole continents for cultivation, canalization of rivers, whole populations conjured out of the ground – what earlier century had even a presentiment that such productive forces slumbered in the lap of social labor.[20]

The outline of the grand comparative argument for capitalism is now in view. The argument consists of subarguments purporting to establish three propositions: (1) that capitalism is more compatible with liberty than is socialism, (2) that capitalism is more efficient in the allocation of existing resources than is socialism, and (3) that capitalism is more innovative and dynamic than is socialism.

Each of these claims is of fundamental importance; each must be analyzed in detail. But before doing so, we need the comparative term – a vision of socialism to set beside the basic capitalist ideal.[21]

Socialism: Economic Democracy

The model to be elaborated here and defended in subsequent chapters does not spring whole from political or economic theory, nor is it a stylized economic structure of some particular country or region. The model is a synthesis of theory and practice, a "dialectical synthesis," I like to think. To be more specific, what I shall call "Economic Democracy" is a model whose form has been shaped by the theoretical debates on alternative economic organizations that have proliferated over the past twenty years, by the empirical evidence on modes of workplace organization, and by the historical record of various post–World War II large-scale "experiments." From these experiments there are negative lessons to be learned, notably from the failure of central planning in the

West was winning. The general fascination with growth was clouded somewhat in the 1970s by environmental concerns, but growth still figures importantly (if more anxiously) in capitalism's defense repertoire.

[20] Marx and Engels (1948, pp. 13–14). Marx and Engels criticize bourgeois society not for its lack of productivity but for its basis in structures "too narrow to comprise the wealth created" (Ibid., p. 34).

[21] As we shall see, it will be necessary to render the "perfectly competitive" model of laissez faire more realistic, in order for the comparison to be fair. This will be done in Chapter 3.

Soviet Union and Eastern Europe, but there are positive lessons also, deriving especially from three central cases.

Let us begin with a socialist "failure." In the early 1950s, a small Eastern European country with "two alphabets, three religions, four languages, five nations, six federal states called republics, seven neighbors and eight national banks"[22] embarked on a remarkable course. In 1948 Stalin accused Yugoslavia of antisovietism. By 1949 all trade between Yugoslavia and other Communist countries had been halted, and an economic boycott imposed. Pressed by events, Yugoslavia began a highly original construction: a decentralized socialist economy featuring worker self-management of factories. Milovan Djilas recounts the decision:

Soon after the outbreak of the quarrel with Stalin, in 1949, as far as I remember, I began to reread Marx's *Capital*, this time with much greater care, to see if I could find the answer to the riddle of why, to put it in simplistic terms, Stalinism was bad and Yugoslavia was good. I discovered many new ideas and, most interesting of all, ideas about a future society in which the immediate producers, through free association, would themselves make the decisions regarding production and distribution – would in effect, run their own lives and their own future. . . . It occurred to me that we Yugoslav Communists were now in a position to start creating Marx's free association of producers. The factories should be left in their hands, with the sole proviso that they should pay a tax for military and other state needs.[23]

Kardelj and Djilas pressed Tito, who was initially skeptical.

The most important part of our case was that this would be the beginning of democracy, something that socialism had not yet achieved; further, it could be plainly seen by the world and the international workers' movement as a radical departure from Stalinism. Tito paced up and down, as though completely wrapped in his own thoughts. Suddenly he stopped and exclaimed: "Factories belonging to the workers – something that has never yet been achieved!"[24]

The system thus born (imposed top-down, it should be noted, and without the benefit of any economic theory) underwent many modifications during the succeeding decades, but the basic structure of worker self-management persisted and was combined with ever greater reliance on the market. For a long while the results were impressive. Between 1952 and 1960 the Yugoslav economy recorded the highest growth rate of any country in the world. From 1960 to 1980, Yugoslavia, among the low- and middle-income nations, ranked third in growth per capita.[25]

[22] Horvat (1976, p. 3).   [23] Djilas (1969, pp. 220–1).   [24] Ibid., pp. 222–3.
[25] See Horvat (1976, p. 12) and Sen (1984, p. 490). There is a large literature on Yugoslavia. For a short discussion relevant to our purposes, see Nove (1983, pp. 133–41). For more detail, see, in addition to Horvat (1976), Comisso (1979), Tyson (1980), Estrin (1983), and Lydall (1984). For a highly critical but quite useful appraisal of the Yugoslav experiment in light of recent difficulties, see Lydall (1989).

These statistics reflect a real transformation in the quality of life for millions. In 1950 Yugoslavia was – as it had been since its creation in 1918 – a poor, underdeveloped country, with three-quarters of the population rural peasants. By 1975, rural peasantry composed only 30 percent of the population, and Yugoslavia had attained a standard of living approximately two-thirds that of Italy. Even Harold Lydall, a major critic of the Yugoslav experiment, concedes that "it is clear that Yugoslavia, under its system of 'socialist self-management,' has achieved a high rate of economic growth of both output and consumption. The average standard of living has changed all out of recognition in the past thirty-five years."[26] Moreover, though the pendulum swung back and forth between liberalization and repression, Yugoslavia was without doubt the freest of any Communist state, freer also than most non-Communist low- and middle-income countries. To cite but one indicator: After 1967, the people of Yugoslavia enjoyed almost complete freedom to travel outside its borders, a freedom widely used.

But during the 1980s the Yugoslav economy collapsed.

The real social product . . . has fallen by 6 percent from 1979 to 1985 and even further since then. . . . Labor productivity in the social sector fell in the same period by about 20 percent, and the real personal incomes of social sector workers by about 25 percent. The standard of education, health and housing services has also fallen. . . . Despite a vast amount of overmanning, both in industry and government . . . there are more than a million persons registered as seeking work, four-fifths of whom are young people.[27]

In addition, ethnic antagonisms, long in abeyance, revived with new intensity. In the early 1990s the country fractured into warring factions and hostile states.

What happened? Why did the Yugoslav economy fall apart? What lessons are to be learned? Should we conclude, with Oxford's Lydall, that the Yugoslav experiment was fatally flawed from the beginning, or agree with Cornell's Jaroslav Vanek that any country that tries the Yugoslav path, while avoiding the now-evident design flaws, "has the best chance to move forward out of the universal crisis of the late twentieth century"?[28] Let us set these questions aside for now and move from socialist "failure" to capitalist "success."

In 1945, General Douglas MacArthur looked out over a devastated Japan and instituted five basic reforms: female suffrage, the right of labor to organize, liberal education, abolition of autocratic government, and democratization of the economy. The elements of this last reform included

---

[26] Lydall (1984, p. 183). The comparison of Yugoslavia and Italy comes from Kravis's careful analysis, cited by Lydall (p. 185).
[27] Lydall (1989, pp. 4–5).   [28] Vanek (1990, p. 182).

breaking up the *zaibatsu* (huge capitalist conglomerates), the imposition of a stiff wealth tax, and major land reform. The goal was to create a competitive capitalist country that might be relatively poor, but democratic and egalitarian.

But with the Chinese Communists victorious in 1948 and the outbreak of the Korean War in 1950, that goal changed dramatically. According to Michio Morishima:

Abandoning the original policy aim of building a democratic country based on the free enterprise system, whose actions would be restrained and peaceloving, there was a shift to measures such as would rebuild Japan into a powerful country equipped with the military and economic strength appropriate to an advance base of the "free" (anti-communist) camp. As a result of this shift Japanese capitalism re-emerged like a phoenix in a form almost identical to that of the prewar period.[29]

Today it is rather often forgotten that the Japanese economic "miracle" did not begin only after World War II. Following the Meiji Revolution (1867–8), Japan deliberately set out to build a modern industrial economy. In 1905 Japan's victory in the Russo-Japanese War stunned Western consciousness: For the first time since the onset of Western imperialism, nonwhite had triumphed over white. The Japanese economy surged ahead. By the end of World War I, Japan had become one of the world's five great powers, and although hit hard by the Great Depression, Japan's economy, fueled by military expenditures, recovered more quickly than those in the West.[30] It was that economy that, in Morishima's words, "re-emerged like a phoenix" in the 1950s.

The structural features of the Japanese economy contrast sharply with those of Western capitalism, and even more sharply with the laissez-faire ideal. Its central features include the following:

1. Large-scale state intervention, particularly regarding investment decisions.[31]
2. A dual economy, one half dominated by a handful of competing conglomerates (*keiretsu*, successors to the prewar *zaibatsu*), the other half consisting of thousands of smaller firms, often linked hierarchically via subcontracting arrangements to one another and to a *keiretsu*.[32]
3. Workplace relations (in the *keiretsu* sector) characterized by lifetime employment guarantees, wages tied tightly to seniority, substantial bonuses linked to company earnings, and considerable worker participation in decision making.[33]

---

[29] Morishima (1982, pp. 161–2). My account here draws heavily on Morishima.
[30] Johnson (1982, p. 6) points out that in 1937 the phrase "Japanese miracle" was used to describe the 81.5 percent increase in industrial output from 1931 to 1934.
[31] See Johnson (1982) for a detailed discussion of this aspect.
[32] See Gerlack (1989) and Sakai (1990).
[33] There is a large literature on this topic. See, for example, Leibenstein (1987, pp. 177–219) and Hashimoto (1990).

It hardly need be said that in material terms the Japanese economy has been astoundingly successful. Between 1946 and 1976, Japan's economy increased 55-fold. A country the size of California, devoid of significant natural resources, Japan now accounts for 10 percent of the world's economic production.[34] (The United States accounts for 20 percent.) But a price has been paid for these accomplishments: very little class or occupational mobility, a system that gives a young person who finishes school only *one* chance of signing on with a good company, an educational system that compels Japanese teenagers to study thirteen to fifteen hours per day. All this has resulted in a highly productive and disciplined labor force, but, says Morishima, "it must not be forgotten that it has also resulted in the annihilation of their own selves."[35] There would seem to be lessons to be learned here. But what lessons?

Let us consider a third case, this one, in my judgment, an unambiguous success (no scare quotes needed). At about the same time that the Yugoslav nation was beginning its novel restructuring and the Japanese economy was coming up to speed under the stimulus of Korean War procurements, another experiment, far humbler in scope, was getting under way in a small, depressed town in the Basque region of Spain. In 1943 a school for working-class boys was established in Mondragon, at the instigation of Don José Maria Arizmendi, a local priest who had narrowly escaped execution by Franco's forces during the Civil War.[36] The "Red priest," as he was called in conservative circles, was a man with a vision.[37] Believing that God gives almost all people the same intellectual potential but that unequal relations of power block the realization of this potential for most, and dismayed that not a single working-class youth from Mondragon had ever attended a university, Father Arizmendi structured his school to promote technical education, but also "social and spiritual" education. Eleven members of his first class of twenty students went on to become professional engineers. In 1956, five of those former students and eighteen other workers set up, at

[34] Johnson (1982, p. 6). Certain physical indices are also revealing. Between 1946 and 1978, iron and steel production increased 110-fold, chemical production 94-fold, and machinery production 164-fold. If we set aside wartime destruction and measure from 1940, the figures are 15-fold for both iron/steel and chemicals, and 35-fold for machinery. Ratios calculated from Johnson's table (1982, pp. 4–5).

[35] Morishima (1982, p. 183).

[36] I shall follow a common precedent here and use the short form of Don José's surname. The long form is Arizmendiarrieta.

[37] Arizmendi's vision is often said to have derived from Catholic social doctrine, in opposition to Marxism, but this interpretation has been called into question by recent scholarship. Certain Left Catholic thinkers were important to him (Maritain and Mounier), but so also was Marx. Likewise important was an example set earlier in Mondragon. In 1920, as a result of a long strike, workers pooled their resources (supplemented by union funds) and set up their own factory (producing firearms), which survived until the Civil War. See Whyte and Whyte (1988, pp. 19–20, ch. 18).

the priest's urging, a cooperative factory to make small cookers and stoves. In 1958 a second cooperative was formed, to make machine tools. In 1959, again at Father Arizmendi's instigation, a cooperative bank was established.

The movement took off. Thirty-four industrial cooperatives were added to the group during the 1960s. Expansion was even more rapid in the 1970s. By the late 1980s the Mondragon Group comprised nearly 20,000 workers in more than 180 cooperatives. In addition to industrial cooperatives making home appliances, agricultural equipment, machine tools, motor coaches, electrical equipment, boilers, generators, numerical control systems, thermoplastics, medical equipment, home and office furniture, and much more, there are agricultural cooperatives, construction cooperatives, education cooperatives, a consumer cooperative, a women's cooperative, a social-security cooperative, and a research-and-development cooperative. The cooperative bank has expanded to nearly a hundred branches throughout the Basque region and is now the fourteenth largest bank in Spain.[38]

By all accounts the experiment has been astonishingly successful. The productivity of Mondragon firms has been found to exceed that for comparable capitalist firms.[39] The failure rate for new Mondragon cooperatives is nearly zero. The group's success in confronting economic hard times has been exceptional. (The Basque region was hit hard by the recession of the late seventies and early eighties; between 1975 and 1983 the Basque economy lost 20 percent of its jobs. But during that same period the Mondragon group – though undergoing some painful readjustments – suffered virtually no unemployment.)[40]

The outstanding structural feature of a Mondragon firm is its democratic nature. Workers meet at least once a year in a General Assembly. They elect (one person, one vote) a Supervisory Council that appoints the firm's management; they also elect a Social Council that has jurisdiction over matters directly affecting workers' well-being, and a Watchdog Council to monitor, collect, and verify information for the General Assembly.

The outstanding structural innovation of the Mondragon Group is its creation of a network of support institutions – above all, the Caja Laboral Popular, the "working people's bank," which interacts with the produc-

---

[38] As of 1987, the Mondragon Cooperative Group consisted of 94 industrial cooperatives, 26 agricultural cooperatives, 44 educational cooperatives, 17 housing cooperatives, 7 service cooperatives, and a consumer cooperative; figures from Caja Laboral Popular, cited by Meek and Woodworth (1990, p. 518). See Morrison (1991, app. 1-1) for a complete listing.

[39] "It makes little difference whether the Mondragon group is compared with the largest 500 companies, or with small- and medium-scale industries; in both comparisons the Mondragon group is more productive and more profitable" (Thomas, 1982, p. 149). See also Thomas and Logan (1982).

[40] Bradley and Gelb (1987).

tive enterprises in various ways: providing capital for expansion, providing technical and financial advice, assisting in the transfer of workers from one enterprise to another, assisting in the creation of new firms. The Caja also looks to the long-range interests of the region, plans new development, and works to harmonize conflicting interests. That its self-image is quite different from that of an ordinary bank can be seen from one of its recent documents. The Caja Laboral Popular, it proclaims:

– stands irrevocably for respect for human liberty, to which end it will dedicate all its economic and human resources. . . .
– will promote freedom of expression and of opinion, the achievement of democratic freedom and of a just distribution of income. . . .
– will dedicate its efforts to strengthening the economy which it serves, with the firm purpose of improving the quality of life of its citizens [through] technological perfection [and] a balanced sectoral distribution . . . which will redress ecological and high-density imbalance.[41]

Another support structure deserves special mention. The Mondragon Group has established a network of educational cooperatives, among which is one of Spain's most prestigious technical colleges, as well as a business school and a student-run enterprise offering both technical courses and (paid) cooperative work experience. This investment in an educational system emphasizing technical and business competence, together with democratic, cooperative values, appears to have been an important element of the group's success.[42]

The socialist model of economic democracy to be defended in this work has features in common with Yugoslav socialism, Japanese capitalism, and Mondragon cooperativism, but it is not a stylized version of any of these. Our model differs from each of these experiments in various crucial respects (which will become clear as we proceed), but these experiments, their successes as well as failures, constitute empirical evidence highly relevant to our analysis.

Before sketching this model, let me make some terminological specifications, for the terms I shall be employing can be variously understood. I shall call "socialist" any economic system that does not feature (extensive) private ownership of the means of production. This usage is not wholly rigorous, because a primitive hunter-gatherer society is not really "socialist," nor is it noncontroversial. (Some would reserve "socialist" for those societies embodying certain ideals.) It should suffice, however, for our purposes.

The particular socialist model that I shall defend will be designated "Economic Democracy."[43] Economic Democracy, as I use the term here

---

[41] Whyte and Whyte (1988, pp. 90–1).   [42] See Meek and Woodworth (1990).
[43] Earlier (Schweickart, 1980) I designated a similar model "worker control." I have decided to use a different term here, partly to underscore the democratic nature of the

(capitalized to indicate the specific model), means something more than general control of an economy by the citizenry, and it means something different from that feature common to both the Yugoslav and Mondragon systems whereby workers in a given firm democratically control the operation of that firm. This latter feature, which will be an element of Economic Democracy, I designate as "worker self-management." Thus, Economic Democracy is a form of socialism featuring (among other things) worker self-management.

Like Yugoslov socialism (in theory, if less so in practice), Economic Democracy is a worker-managed market socialism.[44] Unlike the pre-1989 Yugoslav variety, Economic Democracy presupposes political democracy. I leave open the political particulars, but I assume a constitutional government that guarantees civil liberties to all; I assume a representative government, with democratically elected bodies at the community, regional, and national levels.[45] Of course, it has been argued that such a structure is incompatible with socialism, and that argument cannot be neglected, but for now I shall assume that political democracy is not contradictory to the economic structure I propose.[46] If this assumption is correct (and I shall argue later that it is), then our model will be more democratic than either Yugoslav socialism or Western capitalism. In its classical form, Yugoslav socialism was (in theory) democratic at the workplace, but it had a one-party, authoritarian state; contemporary Western capitalism is (in theory) politically democratic, but it is authoritarian at the workplace. Our model will be democratic in both spheres.[47]

The economic structure of the model I propose has three basic features:

---

model, but also because this model gives weight to three distinct roles each person assumes: worker, to be sure, but also consumer and citizen.

[44] In a Yugoslav enterprise the director was chosen by a workers' council from among those nominated by a selection committee (one-third of its members representing the firm, one-third the trade union, and one-third the government, usually the local commune). Because these latter two groups were dominated by the party, and because often only one nominee was presented, worker control was quite restricted – as was the working of the market, given widespread price controls. Both effective workplace democracy and the market were undermined further by the major "reforms" of 1974. See Lydall (1984), especially pages 92–100 and 110–23.

[45] I am glossing an important issue. The focus of this work is on the economic structure of a viable, desirable socialism. But Marx is surely right that political, educational, cultural, and other social structures cannot be divorced from a society's economy. It follows that an economy different from capitalism should have a politics and culture also different. The economic model I propose is not so different as to suggest political (or educational or cultural) structures completely different from those we now have, but one would expect some changes. For a recent, philosophically sophisticated attempt at drawing the contours of a socialist society with an economic structure similar to what I am advocating, see Gould (1988).

[46] The incompatibility argument will be taken up in Chapter 5.

[47] Many recent works have advocated, in more or less detail, an economic structure similar to the one I am articulating. To list but a few: Horvat (1982), Nove (1983), Bowles and Gintis (1986), Cunningham (1987), Gould (1988), and Miller (1989).

1. Each productive enterprise is managed democratically by its workers.
2. The day-to-day economy is a market economy: Raw materials and consumer goods are bought and sold at prices determined by the forces of supply and demand.
3. New investment is socially controlled: The investment fund is generated by taxation and is dispensed according to democratic, market-conforming plan.

Let me elaborate on each of these elements:[48]

1. Each productive enterprise is managed by those who work there. Workers are responsible for the operation of the facility: organization of the workplace, factory discipline, techniques of production, what and how much to produce, how the net proceeds are to be distributed.[49] Decisions concerning these matters are made democratically: one person, one vote. Of course, in a firm of significant size, some delegation of authority will doubtless be necessary. A workers' council or general manager (or both) may be empowered to make certain kinds of decisions.[50]

---

[48] Theoretical models of economywide worker self-management did not appear in the economic literature until rather recently. The first formal model was presented by Ward (1958). The second important paper on the subject was by Domar (1966). In the early 1970s, Jaroslav Vanek emerged as the chief American theoretician of worker self-management. Vanek (1970) offers an extensive technical analysis of a basic model in terms of the standard neoclassical categories. A less technical treatment can be found in his companion piece (Vanek, 1971). The 1980s witnessed a vast increase in the formal modeling of alternative systems; among the many practitioners were Nobel laureate James Meade (1986) and general-equilibrium theorist Jacques Drèze (1989).

My treatment of worker control is less technical than those of the economists. I avoid the neoclassical categories and give a straightforward analysis. I make fewer simplifications than are required to prove theorems. I try to take into account various difficulties suggested by certain technical models, without presuming that a tendency suggested by a theoretical model will necessarily be important in practice. Whenever a tendency derived from a formal model is posited, it must be evaluated in terms of concrete institutions and reasonable suppositions about motivations, to determine its significance.

[49] It might be decided, by the community, by the region, or even at the national level, to impose certain restrictions on income distribution. It might be insisted that the income differential between the highest-paid and lowest-paid employees in any firm not exceed a certain ratio. (In Mondragon the ratio was, for many years, 3 : 1, but it has recently been raised to 6 : 1 to keep its best people from being lured away by capitalist firms.) It probably should be insisted that no one's income drop below a certain minimum. It might be advisable to have an official wage structure reflecting equal pay for comparable skills, with supplementary bonuses based on the firm's profitability. [This would be akin to the Mondragon practice of paying wages at rates comparable to capitalist wages in the area, then apportioning a share of the firm's profits to each member's "capital account" (Thomas and Logan, 1982, ch. VI), and to the Japanese practice of paying a firm's workers sizable semiannual bonuses based on the firm's success.] These and other details I leave unspecified, in part so as to keep the essential structure in view, in part because it is not yet clear what the optimal set of restrictions might be.

[50] The Mondragon system of indirect election probably is optimal for most enterprises – an elected workers' council that appoints the management. What is to be optimized is the balance between accountability and authority. Managers need enough autonomy to allow them to manage effectively, but not so much that they can exploit the work force to their own advantage. (Both of these factors are very important. Democratic socialists should not minimize the importance of structures and attitudes that will allow managerial

But these officials are elected by the workers. They are not appointed by the state, nor elected by the community at large.

Although workers manage the workplace, they do not own the means of production. These are the collective property of the society. Societal ownership manifests itself in an insistence (backed by law) that the value of the capital stock of a firm be kept intact. A depreciation fund must be maintained to this end; money from this fund may be spent on whatever capital replacements or improvements the firm deems fit, but it may not be used to supplement worker incomes. If an enterprise finds itself in economic difficulty, workers are free to reorganize the facility, or to leave and seek work elsewhere. They are not free, however, to sell off their capital stocks without replacing them with others of equal value – not without explicit authorization from the relevant community authority (the bank with which it is affiliated, to be discussed shortly). If a firm is unable to generate even the minimum per-capita income, then it must declare bankruptcy. Movable capital will be sold off to pay creditors. Any excess must be returned to the investment fund, while fixed capital reverts to the community – both processes mediated by the affiliated bank. Workers must seek employment elsewhere.[51]

2. Worker self-management is the first basic feature of our model; the market is the second. Our socialist economy is a market economy, at least insofar as the allocation of existing consumer and capital goods is concerned. The alternative to market allocation is central planning, and central planning (as theory predicts and the historical record confirms) is conducive to an authoritarian concentration of power, as well as inefficient.

A decade ago the claim that central planning is fundamentally flawed was hotly contested by many socialists. This is much less the case today. The arguments for central planning will be discussed in more detail in a later chapter, but it is now recognized by most socialists that without a price mechanism sensitive to supply and demand, it is extremely difficult for a producer or planner to know what and how much and what variety to produce; it is extremely difficult to know which means are the most efficient. It is also widely recognized that without a market, it is difficult to bring into sufficient alignment personal and societal interests so as not to tax excessively non-self-oriented motivations. The market, as we have seen, resolves these problems (to a significant, if incomplete, degree) in a nonauthoritarian, nonbureaucratic fashion. That is no mean achievement.

skills to flourish. A justifiable concern for technocratic elitism should not blind one to the real frustrations and inefficiencies that attend excessive restriction of managerial prerogatives.)

[51] The unemployment problem and other efficiency concerns will be discussed in the next chapter.

Our socialist economy is a market economy. Firms buy raw materials and machinery from other firms and sell their products to other enterprises or consumers. Prices are largely unregulated, except by supply and demand, although in some cases price controls or price supports may be in order (the former in industries that exhibit monopolistic concentrations, the latter in agriculture to dampen the uncertainty due to weather variations, and perhaps to preserve a way of life that might otherwise disappear). Our socialist society has no overriding commitment to laissez faire. Like modern liberalism, it is willing to permit government intervention when the market malfunctions. Unlike Nozick, our socialist society does not view the market as an absolute good, the paradigm of free human interaction. As we shall see, the market may be regarded as a form of democracy embodying a particular conception of freedom. But it is only one form of democracy embodying only one conception of freedom; there are other forms and other conceptions that must be given their due. It is better to think of the market as a useful instrument for accomplishing certain societal goals. It has certain strengths (as we have seen), but also inherent defects (to be discussed later). The trick is to employ this instrument appropriately.

Because enterprises in our economy buy and sell on the market, they strive to make a "profit." Here, however, "profit" is not the same as capitalist profit. Firms strive to maximize the difference between total sales and total *nonlabor* costs. In Economic Democracy, labor is not another "factor of production" technically on par with land and capital. Labor is not a commodity at all, for a worker, on joining a firm, becomes a voting member and is entitled to a specific share of the net revenue.

These shares need not be equal for all members. The workers themselves must decide how to distribute the revenue. They may opt for equality, or they may decide to remunerate the more difficult tasks more highly; they may find it in their interest to offer special premiums for scarce skills, to attract and hold the talent they need. Such decisions are made democratically.[52]

3. The third fundamental feature of Economic Democracy is a feature that, paradoxically, is more evident in capitalist Japan and cooperativist

---

[52] As mentioned earlier, society might want to set a minimum income below which no worker may fall; it might couple this with job-security provisions that would prohibit dismissal of a worker without cause when there is sufficient revenue available to pay this minimum. Such provisions might interfere somewhat with allocational efficiency: If a business began to decline and these egalitarian constraints came into force, skilled people in the firm might be tempted to leave, and other skilled people who might be able to revive the firm's declining fortunes might not be readily attracted. Such "institutionalized solidarity," however, would prevent those who were better off from making those worse off bear the brunt of an economic downturn.

Mondragon than in socialist Yugoslavia: social control of investment.[53] It is a crucial feature. Worker self-management aims at breaking the commodity character of labor power and the attendant alienation. The market is a check to overcentralization and bureaucracy. Social control of new investment is the counterfoil to the market, designed to alleviate the "anarchy" of capitalist production.

Under capitalism, the market serves two distinct functions: It allocates existing goods and resources, and it determines the course and rate of future development. In our model these two functions are separated. There is no "money market" bringing together private savers and private investors, whose interaction determines an interest rate. Development is not the unplanned outcome of private decisions.

In our model, investment funds are generated and dispensed via democratically mediated processes. They are generated not by offering the enticement of interest to savers but by *taxing capital assets*. This tax serves two important purposes. It encourages the efficient use of capital goods,[54] and it constitutes the funds for new investment. This "capital tax" is the surrogate of interest in a capitalist economy, which serves the same double function. In fact, because taxation is the source of the investment fund, there is no reason at all to pay individuals interest on their personal savings, nor, for that matter, is there a need to charge interest on personal loans. The ancient proscription on "usury" returns under Economic Democracy.[55]

---

[53] See Horvat (1976, pp. 218ff.) for an account of the various investment policies attempted in Yugoslavia over the years. In the early phase of its transition to a full market economy, the Yugoslav government did control investments, but that policy was abandoned in a climate of general opposition to all forms of government interference. By the early seventies one could say that "in many important respects . . . Yugoslavia bears more resemblance to the type of liberal market economy envisaged by Adam Smith than is the case in any country in western Europe" (Granick, 1975, p. 25). By way of contrast, most investment in Japan is mediated by government agencies (notably the Ministry of Finance and the Ministry of Industry and Trade), and in Mondragon investments are carefully supervised and planned by the Caja Laboral Popular. In both cases, goals other than profit maximization are given priority.

[54] Because enterprises must pay a value tax on their capital assets, they will want to economize on their use.

[55] Recall Aristotle's remark, quoted earlier, that "the most hated sort of wealth getting and with greatest reason, is usury." Economic Democracy can agree. Institutions might exist to keep an individual's savings safe (for a service charge, perhaps, and indexed to the rate of inflation) and to make personal loans (again for a service charge, and with repayment indexed), but with saving separated from investment, there is no need for interest.

There is one area of the economy, however, in which interest charges (surrogate or otherwise) likely are appropriate, namely, the private housing sector. Because it makes little sense to require people to save up the entire purchase price before buying a house, it is reasonable to charge those who borrow for that purpose a use tax (interest) on their mortgage – and to direct their interest payments to the investment fund, earmarking

Investment funds are generated by taxation. How are they to be dispensed? Although the society is democratic, it would not be feasible to attempt a popular vote on each investment project. The sheer number of projects would render such a proposal unworkable; moreover, such a procedure would negate a major benefit of socialized investment: the conscious adoption of a reasonably coordinated, coherent investment plan.

But how, exactly, should an investment plan be formulated and implemented? Here it should be emphasized that there is a range of options, no one of which is likely to be optimal for all countries at all times. At one extreme would be a set of institutions modeled on those of Japan: An elite bureaucracy draws up a plan, generates a consensus, passes it through the national legislative body, and then implements it rigorously – not by compulsion, but by using its wide discretionary powers over access to finance in order to cut back some firms and entice others to develop in desired directions.[56] At the other extreme would be a "plan" that would mimic the free-market outcome, while avoiding the capitalist middleman, a sort of "socialist laissez faire." In this case the investment fund is apportioned to a network of national, regional, and local banks, which make their grants using exactly the same criteria as a capitalist bank. The national legislature sets the use tax (interest rate), adjusting it yearly so as to bring the supply of investment funds into line with demand. The banks themselves are charged this rate. They are permitted to charge a higher rate on grants they make, and so, in trying to maximize their own profit, they weigh risk against projected profitability in exactly the same fashion as does a capitalist bank. Under such socialist laissez faire, there is no planning of the qualitative makeup of investment, no attempt to encourage or discourage any particular line of production, nor even any conscious control over the quantity of investment.

In constructing a specific model of socialism to set against various models of capitalism, we need to make a choice here. Let us select an investment mechanism that lies more or less midway between the extremes just posed. It will be more democratic and decentralized than that of the Japanese model; it will give society more positive control over investment than does socialist laissez-faire. In order to demonstrate that this mechanism is indeed superior to the capitalist mechanism on many

them for housing-construction loans. This arrangement would not involve the payment of interest to private individuals, and so should satisfy Aristotle.

I should add, though, that I am inclined to doubt that allowing moderate interest payments to private individuals under Economic Democracy would be a serious source of inequality (the essential ethical objection). Although other arrangements, theoretically more satisfying, are possible, consumer loans and the housing sector might be well served by regulated savings-and-loan cooperatives that would pay moderate interest on private savings that were lent out at a somewhat higher rate.

[56] See Johnson (1982, pp. 315–19) for an outline of institutions that would, in his view, enable an economy to approximate Japanese planning.

counts and does not possess any overriding, countervailing defect, it must be spelled out in some detail.

It should be noted that the planning I propose is not for the whole economy; the planning is only for the new investment to be undertaken, that is, investment not financed from depreciation set-asides. Although substantial money is involved, it constitutes but a fraction of the total economic activity of the nation. Some figures on the U.S. economy may help put this in perspective. Gross capital formation in the United States for the years 1970–84 averaged 26.2 percent of gross national product (GNP). Gross capital formation includes purchase or construction of nonmilitary structures by business firms, governments, and households, and nonmilitary durable equipment by businesses and governments. It also includes all expenditures on education and all expenditures on research and development (R&D).[57] Because the new investment to be financed from the investment fund under Economic Democracy will be for business and government capital expenditures only, one will subtract from this figure spending on residential housing, the noncapital portions of education and R&D expenditures, and all investments financed by depreciation set-asides. It seems reasonable to think of the investment fund as constituting 10–15 percent of GNP.[58]

It should also be noted that individual firms already operating will be unaffected by this planning unless they want to make changes in their operations that cannot be financed from their depreciation funds.[59]

[57] Lipsey and Kravis (1987, p. 32). The average for twelve other advanced capitalist countries with which Lipsey and Kravis compare the United States is 29.9 percent.

[58] The 26.2 percent figure calculated by Lipsey and Kravis decomposes into "conventional capital formation" (18.1), education (6.1), and R&D (2.0). One-quarter of the conventional capital formation is residential housing. If we allow that half of the remaining 13.5 percent conventional capital formation is depreciation, and that half of the educational expenditures are capital expenditures (both figures quite high estimates), the investment fund will be 12.5 percent of the GNP.

[59] In this model the depreciation set-asides are mandated by law, but controlled by the enterprises. They may be spent on any capital improvement that is desired by the firm, and when so spent are considered "ongoing" investment. Such spending is distinguished from "new" investment, which is bank-financed – and hence subject to whatever conditions have been negotiated. This distinction between new investment and ongoing investment is a somewhat arbitrary way of giving firms some autonomous control over their investment policies, but not so much as to give rise to macroeconomic instability. Whether firms should have such autonomy (and, if so, how much) is a matter of some dispute. Vanek, for one, urges that all depreciation funds be incorporated into the investment fund and that all (after-tax) profits be returned to the workers, thus allowing firms no unmediated access to investment funds (Vanek, 1970, p. 60). In sharp contrast, Mondragon firms require that a certain portion of the net profit be allocated to the reserve fund and that the remaining profit be distributed to the individual "capital accounts" of the members, where it remains, under the control of the firm, until the member leaves. Hence the firm has access to a large share of the profit – the reserve fund and net individual capital accounts – for purposes of autonomous investment. [For a defense of the Mondragon model, as against the one proposed by Vanek, see Gui (1984).]

A flat tax on the capital assets of each enterprise in the economy will generate a supply of funds for investment. Social control of these funds, suitably democratized and decentralized, will be achieved by means of interconnected plans and banks. Let us begin with the plans.

We should distinguish between three sorts of investments society might like to make: (1) those that enterprises will undertake spontaneously because they are profitable, (2) those investments intended to be money-making, but which because of positive consumption or production externalities, are more valuable to society than their profitability indicates,[60] and (3) those capital investments related to the provision of free goods and services, such as infrastructure, possibly schools, hospitals, urban mass transit, basic research facilities, and the like. Categories (2) and (3), comprise those endeavors that planning must promote.[61]

Two issues arise with respect to these latter sorts of endeavors: deciding which projects to promote, and allocating funds for those projects. The decisions themselves should be made democratically by the elected legislatures at the appropriate levels. Investment hearings should be held (as budget hearings are currently held); expert and popular testimony should be sought. The legislature should then decide the amount and nature of capital spending on public goods, as well as which areas of the cooperative sector it wishes to encourage.

The allocation of the investment fund will now proceed as follows: First, the national legislature decides, in accordance with the democratic procedures described earlier, on public capital spending for projects that are national in scope (e.g., an upgrading of rail transport). Funds for these projects are allocated to the appropriate governmental agency (e.g., the Department of Transportation). (These funds are for capital expenditures only, not for operating expenses. The operating expenses of all governmental agencies should be financed separately, presumably from an income or consumption tax.)[62] The national legislature may also decide that certain types of projects should be encouraged and, accordingly,

---

[60] The externality issue will be discussed in detail in Chapter 4.

[61] I shall not discuss negative measures here, because they are not particularly problematic or unfamiliar. If the nation (or region or community) wishes to prohibit or discourage the production or use of specific products, or if it wishes to set standards governing the use of certain technologies, the appropriate bills are introduced in the appropriate legislature, public hearings are held, and a vote is taken. If the legislature is unresponsive, referenda may be held. It seems clear that a democratic socialist society should avail itself of the full panoply of political mechanisms currently available, modifying them and supplementing them so as to make the political process more responsive to popular input.

[62] If all government revenues were to come from the capital-assets tax, the tax would be so high as to discourage new investment. Moreover, such an arrangement would occlude what this model makes clear – the flow of new investment funds. Clarity is important here, if democratic decisions about investment priorities are to be coherent and effective.

will specify the amount of funding to be made available and the tax rate for such projects.[63] The rest of the investment fund is distributed to the regions (states, provinces) on a per-capita basis (i.e., if region A has X percent of the nation's population, it gets X percent of the investment fund).[64]

Regional legislatures now make similar decisions: on regional spending of public capital and on "encouragement projects." Funds for the former are transferred to the requisite regional authorities; the remainder is allocated, per capita, to the communities, which then make decisions about local public investment and their own encouragement grants.

Democratic decisions having been made at the national, regional, and local levels, the communities now allocate their funds to their own banks. These banks, I propose, should be structured along the lines of Mondragon's Caja Laboral Popular. Each enterprise in the area affiliates with the bank of its choice, which holds its depreciation reserve and sales income, and provides it with working capital and perhaps other technical and financial services. It is to this bank that the enterprise normally looks for new investment capital, although it is free to apply elsewhere. Each bank is run as a "second-degree cooperative," the Mondragon term for a cooperative whose governing council includes representation from sectors other than the cooperative's workers. The governing council of a community bank should include representatives of the community planning agency, representatives of the cooperative's work force, and representatives of the firms that do business with the bank.[65] Each bank receives from the community a share of the investment funds allocated to the community, a share determined by the size and number of firms affiliated with the bank, by the bank's prior success at making profitable

[63] If the government had perfect knowledge, it could simply set the appropriate tax rate, and the desired amount of investment would be forthcoming. [See Ortuño-Ortin, Roemer, and Silvestre (1990) for a formal proof.] I am assuming, more realistically, that the government is less certain as to exactly how much it wants to invest in a particular project, so it sets a limit as to total amount and offers an incentive to firms to undertake such investments. Amounts and incentives can be readjusted the following year, depending on results.

[64] I am proposing here an egalitarian distribution. A less egalitarian alternative would be to return to each region that portion of the investment fund (less national deductions) collected from that region. This alternative would tend to exacerbate, rather than mitigate, regional disparities. Another alternative, perhaps the most attractive economically and ethically, would be to apportion the funds according to "need," as determined from a balance of income levels, enterprise needs, and national priorities. In my model I shall stick with the egalitarian distribution, above all for simplicity. I suspect that, in practice, a democratically decided distribution would be less egalitarian than I propose, but more egalitarian than in proportion to contribution.

[65] The Caja Laboral Popular has a governing board of twelve, four representatives of its workers, and eight representing the more than 100 cooperatives linked to the bank. Because the Caja's funds do not come from taxation, there is no perceived need to include community representatives.

grants (including lower-rate encouragement grants), and by its success in creating new employment.[66] The bank's income, to be distributed among its workers, comes from general tax revenues (because these are public employees) according to a formula linking income to the bank's success in making profitable grants and creating employment.

If a community is unable to find sufficient viable investment opportunities to absorb the funds allocated to it, the excess must be returned to the center, to be reallocated to where investment funds are more in demand.[67] Communities thus have an incentive to seek out new investment opportunities, so as to keep the allocated funds at home. Banks, too, have a similar incentive, so it is reasonable to expect that communities and their banks will set up entrepreneurial divisions, agencies that will monitor new business opportunities and provide technical and financial expertise to existing firms seeking new opportunities and to individuals interested in starting new cooperatives, helping them with market surveys, grant applications, and the like. These agencies might go so far as to recruit prospective managers and workers for new enterprises. (Mondragon's Caja Laboral Popular has just such a division – another of its successful innovations.)[68]

The basic framework for the social control of investment is now in view. To review briefly: We have the tax revenues from capital assets, collected by the central government, dispersed throughout society to a network of local banks; the banks dispense these funds (some specially earmarked so as to encourage democratically approved projects) to their affiliated firms and to newly created enterprises; banks use as their criteria projected profitability and employment creation. Thus we have a network of Mondragons (or mini-*keiretsu*, if you prefer) that receive their funds for new investment from the public investment fund. The bank at the center of each can make grants as it sees fit, charging the standard use tax on most, but allowing a reduced rate on encouragement projects. These grants, once received, are not repaid, but they add to the capital assets of the firm, and hence to its tax base.[69] Associated with most banks are

[66] This is not to suggest that employment should be created by making investments in areas that will not be profitable at all. Banks will be penalized for making bad grants. But profit maximization should not be the sole criterion either. That the two goals – profitability and employment creation – are not hopelessly contradictory should be clear from the success of the Caja Laboral Popular, which has had employment creation as one of its central goals from the beginning.

[67] A simple incentive structure to ensure compliance would be to charge communities a use fee for their allocated funds, from which would be deducted the tax revenues to the investment fund derived from their distribution to area firms. Thus a community would be penalized for holding onto funds or making unproductive grants.

[68] See Whyte and Whyte (1988, pp. 71–5) and Morrison (1991, pp. 111–34) for details.

[69] Economically, use tax–interest is a distinction without a difference, but the socio-psychological associations are not the same in the two cases. It seems to me that seeing the payment as a use tax that goes to the investment fund, instead of as interest,

entrepreneurial divisions that attempt to foster the expansion of existing firms and the creation of new firms.[70]

We now have before us the basic structure of Economic Democracy. We are in position to consider the dynamics of the system and compare it with a different, also simplified, model – that of competitive laissez faire. This system based on worker self-management, a somewhat restricted market, and socialized investment will be compared with a system that features private ownership of the means of production, a totally free market, and wage labor. Now the argument begins in earnest.

makes it more transparent that one is paying to gain access to property created by others, and that the payment is being recycled to allow others similar access. Apart from this consideration – which may in fact be minor – I see no principled objection to the use tax being called "interest."

[70] Economic Democracy provides for, indeed requires, "socialist entrepreneurs" – individuals or collectives willing to innovate, take risks, in the hope of providing new goods or new services or old ones in new ways. How these entrepreneurs compare with their capitalist counterparts will be discussed in Chapter 4.

3. Capitalism or socialism?: efficiency

In a sense, the efficiency question is the first question for any society. Unless a society is reasonably efficient in marshaling its resources, it cannot expect much innovative growth. And of course liberty, equality, and democracy are hollow concepts when people are hungry. As Brecht put it, "Erst kommt das Fressen, dann kommt die Morale."[1]

Economists are inclined to treat economic efficiency as an ethically neutral concept, but of course it is not. Economic efficiency is as much a value as liberty or equality. To be sure, the word "efficiency" can be taken in a neutral, instrumental sense to mean simply "productive of a desired effect," but *economic efficiency* means more than that. In ordinary usage, the effect of economic efficiency is presumed to be material goods and services, and its accomplishment is presumed to be with minimal expenditure of labor and resources. Thus, embedded in a commitment to economic efficiency are several value judgments: that material goods are indeed good, that scarce resources ought not be wasted, and that it is better to labor less than more. None of these judgments can plausibly be regarded as absolute. (Not all material goods are good; some labor is intrinsically satisfying; etc.) This not to say that a commitment to economic efficiency is inappropriate, but it should be borne in mind that such a commitment is a commitment to certain values. It is not normatively innocent.

Mainstream economists might protest that the notion of efficiency sanctioned by the profession is not that of ordinary usage. Their notion (as we have seen) is that of Pareto optimality: a state of affairs in which no movement from that state is possible that would make some people better off and no one worse off. But even this notion of efficiency embodies a major value judgment, namely, that the welfare of each individual is important. If one were unconcerned about the welfare of a certain segment of the population, one would have little interest in the society's being Pareto-optimal. So what if some are made worse off, so long as those who count are made better off?

This technical notion of efficiency, at least as it is commonly employed, embodies a second value judgment. When one attempts to apply the Pareto principle, a question arises concerning the criteria for individual welfare. Who determines when an individual is better off than before?

---

[1] Roughly, "Grub first, and then morality" (Brecht, 1967, p. 458).

The profession speaks with virtually one voice: the individual. A situation is Pareto-optimal when no one can be made better off *in terms of his own preferences* without making another worse off. Thus the judgment is made that individuals should be the ultimate judges of their own welfare. This is a highly significant value judgment. Plato, for one, would be appalled.

Before we proceed further, some remarks are in order about values in general, and about the basic ethical commitments to which the subsequent analysis will appeal. The arguments to be considered in this and the next several chapters are *normative arguments*. To choose between capitalism and socialism is to make an ethical choice. This is not to say that considerations of practicality, economic efficiency, and the like are irrelevant. Far from it. But any argument, at whatever level of concreteness or abstractness, that purports to demonstrate that one set of institutions is better than another appeals, explicitly or implicitly, to *values*. It aims to persuade by appealing to something presumed to be *good*, be it liberty, equality, economic efficiency, or whatever. Thus it situates itself, consciously or not, within a normative framework.

Fortunately, there is no need to specify a full-blown ethical theory before debating moral questions. Philosophers are far from agreeing as to what the correct theory might be. There is, however, widespread agreement concerning the basic values that an acceptable theory must explain. Philosophers today disagree as to the nature of moral utterances, the source of moral values, and the structure of value hierarchies, but few philosophers (or ordinary citizens, for that matter) would claim that torture, despotism, or grinding poverty is good. Virtually all (in this and most other cultures) would assign a positive value to happiness, to material well-being, to democracy.

Despite the fact that many values are relatively noncontroversial, it is useful in a work such as this to lay out clearly the specific values to which the arguments will appeal. For one thing, although there is much agreement concerning the relevant values, agreement is not universal. (In capitalist societies, the value of equality, as we shall see, is frequently challenged; in socialist societies, liberty has been given short shrift.) More importantly, I wish to make it clear that the case for Economic Democracy does not rest on esoteric values alien to our culture. What I intend to show is that anyone who shares a certain set of relatively noncontroversial values ought to prefer at least one form of socialism to any form of capitalism.

One further clarification, to head off a possible misunderstanding: When I appeal to a certain value, say material well-being, I am not claiming it to be an *absolute* good, one that can never be sacrificed. I am simply saying that anything (any social structure) that promotes this value has a prima facie claim to our allegiance. So long as the structure does not conflict with any of the other values we deem good, it requires no further justification. A structure that deviates from that value does require justification, justification in terms of other values to which we adhere. To say, for example, that material well-being is good is not to imply that the government should guarantee everyone a comfortable living. It might be the case that such a governmental commitment would conflict with other values we hold – economic efficiency, perhaps, or liberty. To maintain that material well-being is good is to hold a much more modest proposition: If one socioeconomic system provides a higher per-capita material standard of living than another, and if the first system does at least as well by our other values, then the first system is preferable to the second. In short, the value commitments upon which my argument is based are "weak." One need not have an absolute commitment to any of the values to which the argument appeals to find the argument compelling.

We have noted that economic efficiency, in both its ordinary sense and its technical sense, is not a value-neutral concept; it presupposes certain value commitments. Let us follow this track just a bit further. The underlying value to which almost all our arguments appeal is human happiness. Because we are evaluating economic structures, we are concerned with human happiness as it relates to the production, distribution, and consumption of material goods and services.

Our commitment to human happiness (which is itself a prima facie commitment, because human happiness might conflict with certain other values) devolves in this chapter into several more specific value commitments, also to be understood in the weak sense just described. We shall presume that material well-being is a prima facie good, and that, prima facie, a society should not squander scarce resources, nor require people to perform unnecessary labor. We shall assume that if no one would be made worse off by a shift from A to B, and some people better off (all in terms of their own preferences), then, prima facie, the shift should be made. If there is conflict or tension among these specific values in a specific argument, we shall adjudicate by referring to human happiness.

The basic question to be dealt with in this chapter is the efficiency of laissez-faire capitalism as compared with Economic Democracy. We have distinguished between the ordinary sense of economic efficiency (the production of material goods with minimal expenditure of labor and resources) and the more technical sense of Pareto optimality. The two concepts are not identical, but we shall not worry much about their differences in what follows, because our evaluations of the models at hand will not depend on which of these concepts we employ.[2]

---

[2] One can construct special cases that will satisfy one criterion but not the other. A society that is efficient in the ordinary sense of not wasting resources is not Pareto-optimal if people there would prefer to consume a bit less in exchange for working a bit less. A

Some other sorts of efficiency distinctions, however, will prove useful. Among the various forms of economic inefficiencies, one can distinguish what we shall call *allocative inefficiencies, Keynesian inefficiencies,* and *X-inefficiencies.* "Allocative" (or "allocational") inefficiencies are diminutions of overall welfare resulting from those market imperfections that cause prices to deviate from what they would be under conditions of perfect competition. These inefficiencies will be familiar to anyone who has taken freshman economics – essentially those caused by monopolies and "externalities." To isolate these types of inefficiencies for purposes of study, we assume that (1) the economy's technology is fixed (i.e., there are no innovations), (2) there is full employment of human and material resources in the society at large, and (3) each firm can readily transform its inputs into output in accordance with its goals (i.e., no waste occurs *within* the firm). "Keynesian inefficiencies" are those deviations from optimality that occur when human and material resources are not fully employed. "X-inefficiencies" are those assumed away by assumption 3, namely, inefficiencies that occur within the firm because of the firm's internal structure.[3] In this chapter we shall consider, in addition to allocative and Keynesian inefficiencies, those forms of X-inefficiencies associated with nonoptimal managerial and worker motivation under conditions of technological fixity. (We shall set aside questions of innovation and growth until Chapter 4.)

The relative orders of magnitude of these three forms of inefficiency should be noted. Vanek refers to allocational, Keynesian, and X-inefficiencies as "fleas, rabbits and elephants," respectively.[4] Leibenstein's survey of the empirical evidence finds allocational inefficiencies to be quite small, on the order of 0.1 percent of GNPs, whereas X-inefficiencies within firms often exceed 50 percent. While granting methodological problems with the comparisons, he notes that allocational inefficiencies almost have to be small, because prices higher than "right" prices in one area of the economy will be offset by prices lower than "right" prices in other areas.[5] Given the obvious seriousness of the unemployment that continually plagues capitalist economies, Vanek's metaphor does not seem ill-chosen.[6]

society in which people take great pleasure in wasting resources might be Pareto-optimal, but it is not economically efficient in the ordinary sense.

[3] The term "X-efficiency" was coined by Leibenstein (1966). His ideas were further developed later (Leibenstein, 1976, 1987). For an extended review of the empirical evidence and replies to various neoclassical critics of the concept, see Frantz (1988).

[4] Vanek (1989, p. 93).

[5] See Leibenstein (1976, pp. 29–44). As an emphatic demonstration of his point, Leibenstein shows that if half the firms in an economy are monopolies charging 20 percent higher prices than they should, then (under the reasonable assumption that demand elasticity is 1.5) the overall diminution in GNP due to allocational inefficiency is a mere 1.5 percent.

[6] When we reflect that the amounts of attention that economists have given to these various kinds of inefficiency seem to correlate inversely with these magnitudes, we might

We can now formulate the basic question to be addressed in this chapter: Given a fixed technology and known resources, which society is more likely to yield for its members the greater material well-being, where "material well-being" is the ratio of consumption satisfaction to costs – costs comprising human labor and scarce material resources? We shall assume that the evaluation of material well-being should be in terms of the preferences of the individuals themselves, although we leave open, at this point, the matter of exactly how these preferences are formed and expressed.

We restrict our attention to a fixed technology and to known resources in order to separate the efficiency issue from questions of innovation and growth. We focus on material satisfactions and costs, deferring until later a consideration of noneconomic costs and benefits. Our formulation lacks the formal precision usually found in welfare economics, but it is clear enough for our purposes and leads quickly to the substantive issues.

The efficiency strengths of Laissez Faire

In Chapter 2 we looked at the perfect-competition model and the associated efficiency theorem: Under appropriate conditions, a perfectly competitive laissez-faire economy in equilibrium is in a state of Pareto optimality. We observed that this theorem is not devoid of content. Its significance, however, is a matter of controversy.

Let me take a stand on this issue. I find the efficiency theorem to be, at best, irrelevant to the capitalism–socialism debate; if anything, it obscures comprehension of the real issues. It is irrelevant for the reason most critics cite: The assumptions necessary to prove Pareto optimality are miles from reality.

The most basic assumption is perfect competition itself, the case in which all are "pricetakers," and none are "pricemakers." As Tibor Scitovsky notes, it is difficult to visualize such a situation:

Many people in our economy regard price as given to them, but they do so, in most instances, because the price is set, either by the other party or by a third person. The difficulty lies in visualizing a price that everybody on both sides of the market regards as given, and that is determined by the "impersonal forces of the market."[7]

Scitovsky lists four conditions that must be satisfied for perfect competition to obtain:

sympathize with Horvat's irritation that "the authors exploring efficiency collectively use, figuratively speaking, 99 percent of their brain power to cope with 1 percent efficiency loss and only the remaining 1 per cent of their intellectual capacity to discover possible improvements of the order of 10 or 20 percent." He notes, sarcastically, that "the enormous allocational inefficiency of such endeavors is obvious" (Horvat, 1986, p. 15).

[7] Scitovsky (1971, p. 15).

a) customers of the seller must be able to withdraw their custom from him without inconvenience to themselves;
b) each seller's sales must be small compared to the market's total turnover;
c) all the buyers must be experts, in the strictest sense of the term, in the appraisal of the goods they buy;
d) all the buyers must know about the existence of alternative offers and all of them should be prepared to shift all their custom in response to even the smallest change in price.[8]

Obviously, these conditions hold in few, if any, real-world markets. More important for my argument, they could not be expected to hold for any plausible reform of capitalism. And these conditions merely establish perfect competition. Many more assumptions must be made for the efficiency theorem to follow: The economy must be in equilibrium, an assumption that abstracts from two of capitalism's most characteristic features: its relentless innovativeness and its cyclical fluctuations. Firms in the economy must face rising marginal costs – this assumption in the face of "the belief generally held by businessmen in competitive industries that they are operating under decreasing cost conditions, that is, that they could lower per-unit costs if only they could sell a larger output."[9] The list goes on, but we have carried it far enough. Scitovsky's *Welfare and Competition*, a work solidly within the neoclassical tradition, scrupulously details a great many more. Post-Keynesian critics have long lists of their own.[10]

One might well wonder at this point why there is even a controversy. Why are economists interested at all in a model with such counterfactual presuppositions? I would posit four factors. One is ideological: It is reassuring to capitalism's supporters that at least some form of capitalism is optimally efficient. Another involves professional virtuosity: To formulate a model and to prove interesting theorems about it require ingenuity and mathematical acuity, sometimes of the highest order. A third factor relates to the profession's positivism: It matters not what the assumptions are, so long as the conclusions are useful in making correct predictions.[11] The fourth is the Platonic consideration: An ideal standard allows us to see how far, and why, we fall short in practice.

Only these latter two reasons need concern us, and they need not concern us much. The positivist rationale is irrelevant to the specific question we are addressing, because the perfect-competition theorem makes no falsifiable predictions whatsoever.[12] The Platonic reason is

[8] Ibid., p. 16.   [9] Ibid., p. 389.
[10] Any post-Keynesian reference I have cited will contain examples, as will virtually anything written by Joan Robinson.
[11] Friedman's *Essays on Positive Economics* (1953) is the locus classicus of this widely held view.
[12] For a justification of this strong statement, see Hollis and Nell (1975, ch. 1).

unconvincing, for it is by no means clear that the insights into the real efficiency problems suggested by the neoclassical apparatus are not as easily obtained by less "rigorous" means (although they might seem less impressive divested of their undeniably elegant mathematical garb). I have yet to see a good example.[13]

These remarks are not meant to imply that the efficiency claims of Laissez Faire have no basis whatsoever. The perfect-competition theorem may not be admissible as evidence for the defense, but other arguments, resting on more realistic assumptions, can be marshaled. These we must consider.

Let us leave our perfect-competition fairyland and consider a more plausible laissez-faire ideal. If we cannot have perfect competition, let us at least have vigorous competition. We know that monopolies pose a problem for capitalism. Let us rule them out. Let us consider a capitalist economy free of government interference and also free of monopolies: Businesses will not conspire to set prices or to keep new firms from entering their fields; workers will not be compelled to join unions as a condition for work. The government will involve itself only minimally in the economy, essentially to enforce property rights, contracts, and the antitrust and right-to-work laws. This more realistic model we shall henceforth designate as Laissez Faire (capitalized to indicate that the referent is this specific model).

What are the strengths of this system – the true classical-liberal ideal – with respect to the question of economic efficiency? Three aspects would seem to be the most significant. Laissez Faire possesses

1. An effective mechanism for determining and responding to consumer preferences
2. Powerful incentives for minimizing material waste and for using appropriate technology
3. Effective procedures for allocating and using labor.

None of these strengths is unconditional, but all are important.

The mechanism whereby Laissez Faire deals with consumer preferences is the price mechanism. Goods and services are bought and sold. The only alternative to buying and selling, under conditions of scarcity, is physical rationing. Coupons would have to be issued (or some analogous device employed) that would entitle their bearers to specific quantities of specific items. One might imagine such rationing for certain basic goods – loaves of bread or gallons of gasoline – but it is staggering to

---

[13] It is noteworthy that Scitovsky, one of the foremost practitioners of the neoclassical game and a former proponent of the Platonic rationale, abandoned that framework in his later work (Scitovsky, 1971, 1976). This book will also keep its distance from the neoclassical categories. I am convinced that it pays to try to see things without the neoclassical spectacles – which are sometimes helpful, but more often distorting.

contemplate rationing all the items in an advanced industrial society. An enormous bureaucracy would be a necessity, and serious problems of inequities would have to be dealt with, but most serious of all, those distributing goods would have no effective means of gauging what people really want.[14] Imagine for a moment filling out a questionnaire in which you would specify which of the available consumer goods you would like next month, and in what quantities, and the relative strengths of your preferences. (This latter condition is necessary, because you could not expect to get everything you would want.) How many rolls of cellophane tape will you need, and of what width, and how important are they compared with the number of vacuum-cleaner bags? How many cans of what type of soup, and are these more or less important than two or three blank VCR tapes? When the economy can produce a great variety of items, and yet not everything that everyone wants, and when desires fluctuate, then there is no feasible alternative to pricing.[15]

In allowing people to purchase items as they please, the quantities desired and people's relative preferences are automatically registered. In addition, producers are provided with precise quantitative information on what can be produced at a profit. If prices are allowed to move freely in response to market conditions, producers, given their desire for profit, will adjust their production in accordance with consumer preferences.

The alternative to *free-market pricing* is government pricing, but the case for such price control – under nonmonopolistic conditions (an important qualification) – is slight. Holding down prices (to help consumers) will simply cause supplies to contract, unless subsidies are supplied to producers, a desirable procedure only in exceptional circumstances. Raising prices above what the market price would be (so as to discourage consumption) will reduce demand, but unless this is done via an excise tax (again desirable only in exceptional circumstances), this will generate windfall profits and encourage more production. Moreover, to give a government agency discretionary power over all (or most) prices would seem to invite a concentration of power and attendant corruption, not to mention bureaucratic and other inefficiencies.

Notice that the case for market pricing does not rest on the assumption that producers will raise prices when demand goes up (which they

---

[14] There is a certain vision of socialism that would dispute this and various other claims I make on behalf of the market. A model exemplifying this vision will be evaluated (quite critically) in Chapter 8.

[15] It is sometimes suggested that with supermarkets and other retail stores sufficiently computerized, preferences could easily be determined by monitoring what is being selected by consumers. But notice that because not everyone can have everything, how much one can have must be rationed. If a person is allowed a certain number of points, say, then goods must also be marked in points, so that the shopper can know how to select. But this is just a price system under another guise.

generally do) or cut them when demand declines (which they often do not). This assumption, especially the latter half, is too simple. When business declines, producers often take a gamble and raise prices, hoping that the per-item revenue increase will offset the decline in volume.[16] Price raising must be done cautiously, however, because higher prices will cut demand, and higher profits will attract competitors. So there are checks on producer greed. Moreover, and this is the important point, production (if not prices) moves in the desired direction. Production goes up when demand goes up, and falls when demand falls.

The major objection to allocating goods via free-market prices is the observation that the preferences registered are exclusively dollar-backed preferences. The market may be thought of as a form of democracy, in which purchases, in addition to satisfying immediate desires, are votes, votes for increased production of the purchased products. But if the market is a democracy, it is a democracy not of "one person, one vote" but of "one dollar, one vote." The more dollars, the more votes. No dollars, no votes.

This observation is undeniably correct, but as an objection to market allocation it derives its force from the assumption that these dollar votes are unfairly distributed. The question of income distribution is extremely important (and will be investigated in Chapter 5), but for now, let us simply observe that if the distribution of income is fair, then the free-market mechanism has much to recommend it, and the alternatives (rationing, surveys, centralized price setting) very little.[17]

The second strength of Laissez Faire concerns technology and material resources. Because firms aim to make a profit, and because profit is the difference between gross revenue and costs, there are strong incentives to utilize resources and technology effectively. Both the positive attraction of personal gain and the negative fear of competitive loss are ever present. A firm cannot afford material waste or obsolete technology.

If profit considerations do not dictate resource usage and production techniques, then central direction must do so. If profit is not the goal of a productive organization, then physical output (use values) must be.[18] Here the familiar problems surface. Even if the output quotas accurately

---

[16] See Wild (1978) for an insider's account of business practices and their variance from the perfect-competition assumptions.

[17] Nothing has been said here about what kinds of goods are suitable for market transactions. Drugs? Education? Sex? For a good discussion of this issue, see Anderson (1990). I am presuming here that most goods, though of course not all, are suitable.

[18] The word "profit" is to be understood here loosely for any market-based economic incentive relevant to enterprises. It is sometimes argued (correctly, in my view) that firms, in reality, seldom aim at profit maximization, usually preferring other goals – an increasing market share, for example, or the firm's growth. These distinctions are irrelevant to the issue at hand.

reflect consumer preferences, a firm may have insufficient information to properly select its technology and input the necessary resources. To produce fine pogo sticks, one would like to use the finest tools, even though these high-quality instruments embody much valuable labor and material that might be better employed elsewhere. How does the firm judge which tools are most appropriate? How does it decide among steel, aluminum, and fiberglass for the handles if they all meet the technical specifications? How does it decide how much time and effort to put into decorative elaborations?

Because the firm has neither the information nor the motivation to economize on inputs or technology, a central-planning authority must make the decisions. Once again the quantities involved quickly get out of hand, making efficient allocation impossible. (Alec Nove has noted that in the Soviet Union there were some 50,000 industrial establishments, making some 12 million identifiably different products.)[19] Unless a firm strives to find the right compromise between quality and cost (and to do so, both knowledge of the costs and incentives to minimize them are needed), the resources of the society will not be efficiently allocated. Granted, there can be abuses in a market system (e.g., shoddy merchandise deceptively packaged), but physical planning is not an attractive alternative.

The third major strength of Laissez Faire is the one that requires the most qualification: the allocation and use of labor. Workers are free to seek work where they will and to negotiate the highest price they can for their services. Thus the worker has an incentive to develop her useful skills, and the employer has an incentive to employ those skills as effectively as possible. Moreover, when demand for a product rises, the producing firm is motivated to expand production, and because this generally requires more labor, the firm seeks to attract workers, thus effecting a labor shift commensurate with consumer preferences. (The employer is encouraged to other, less desirable behaviors as well, as is the employee, but this will be considered later.)

The alternative to free labor mobility is assigned labor; the alternative to unregulated wages is wage regulation. Both alternatives have their drawbacks, overcentralization being the foremost (leaving aside the noneconomic issue of freedom). Planners must decide how many people of what capabilities must be employed where. They must decide which skills to encourage (through differential wages or other means) and which to deemphasize. As always with a centralized alternative, the problems of bureaucratic inefficiency loom large: how to collect the requisite

---

[19] Nove (1983, p. 33).

information, how to motivate socially useful behavior, how to mediate the conflicting claims of talent, effort, and need.

We have discussed the strengths of Laissez Faire: its efficiency in allocating consumer goods, resources and technology, and labor. There are also weaknesses of major proportions. But before examining them, we need to shift our attention to our competing model, for if it proves to be hopelessly inefficient, our investigation need go no further.[20]

How efficient is Economic Democracy?

In 1920, Ludwig von Mises fired the opening salvo in an academic skirmish that was to extend over several decades. Socialism, he declared, is impossible: Without private ownership of the means of production, there cannot be a competitive market for production goods;[21] without a market for production goods, it is impossible to determine their values; without these values, economic rationality is impossible.

Hence in a socialist state wherein the pursuit of economic calculation is impossible, there can be – in our sense of the term – no economy whatsoever. In trivial and secondary matters rational conduct might still be possible, but in general it would be impossible to speak of rational production anymore.[22]

The economic crises of the 1980s in the Soviet Union and Eastern Europe might seem to provide von Mises's definitive vindication. It is certainly fashionable these days to read the collapse of European Communism as proof positive that socialism cannot work. But let us proceed a bit more cautiously.

It has long been recognized that von Mises's argument is logically defective. Even without a market in production goods, their monetary values can be determined. In response to von Mises, a number of economists pointed out that Pareto's disciple, Enrico Barone, had already,

---

[20] Buchanan (1985) has argued that an efficiency comparison of radically different systems is a priori "shaky if not impossible." Efficiency comparisons, he argues, involve ascertaining degrees of preference satisfaction, but if the individuals are different in the two systems, their satisfactions cannot be compared, and if they are the same (one system having been transformed into another), the preferences themselves will likely have changed.

Buchanan's argument assumes that an intersystemic efficiency comparison is an end-state comparison, but that is not the sort of comparison we shall be making. Instead, we shall focus on the structural tendencies of the systems: those that promote efficient resource allocation and those that do the opposite. I argue that a clear judgment can be made as to which system has the better combination. (Notice that if Buchanan were correct, it would be impossible to say that Soviet central planning was less efficient than, say, Japanese capitalism.)

[21] By "production goods," von Mises means goods produced to serve as further means of production. He allows that a socialist society might utilize a market to allocate consumer goods.

[22] See von Mises (1935, p. 92).

thirteen years earlier, demonstrated the theoretical possibility of a "market-simulated" socialism.[23]

Of course, the market-simulated socialism of Barone and others is very different from the Soviet "command-economy" model, which does not permit a free market in either production or consumption goods and does not even try to mimic market behavior. Has not von Mises been proved correct, at least with respect to this model?

I think we should be fair here. Even command economies, which have recently come to such grief, have not been without substantial accomplishments. Between 1928 and 1980 the Soviet economy grew at an annual rate of 4.4 percent, its annual output moving from about one-quarter that of the United States to three-quarters. In the space of a generation, China (now with more than 1 billion people) succeeded in removing itself from the long list of countries still plagued by hunger. Since its inception in 1959, Cuban socialism has provided its citizens with a level of economic well-being that is tragically rare in Latin America beyond the upper classes.[24] As for Eastern Europe, we might attend to the West German poet-essayist Hans Magnus Enzenberger, reflecting (in 1985) on a recent visit to Hungary:

Hardly anyone remembered that before the Second World War there had been millions of agrarian proletarians in Hungary living below subsistence level, without land or rights. Many emigrated to find salvation; hundreds of thousands wound up as beggars. . . . After bitter conflicts and endless argument, the Kádár regime has definitively closed the gap between town and country and made possible an agricultural specialization that achieves large surpluses. The silence of the villages conceals the fact that here, behind the drowsy fences, where only a dog sometimes disturbs the noonday peace, Hungarian socialism has put an end to misery and servitude and achieved its most revolutionary successes.[25]

Let me be clear: To acknowledge that a market-simulated socialism is theoretically possible and that command economies are not without significant accomplishments is not to advocate either of these forms of

---

[23] Barone (1935). The principal attack on von Mises came from Fred Taylor and Oscar Lange. (For a collection of their principal papers, see Lippincott, 1938.) His major defender was Hayek, who shifted the question from theoretical impossibility to whether or not the theoretical solution could be approximated in practice. Lavoie (1985) has recently argued that Hayek's shift was not really a retreat and that the Taylor-Lange rejoinder was not definitive, because their theoretical models were excessively static. The model I shall be defending is far from static, and it should prove, even to those enamored of Austrian economics, that von Mises was wrong in asserting that "a socialist system with a market and market prices is as self-contradictory as is the notion of a triangular square" (von Mises, 1949, p. 706).

[24] On the Soviet Union, see Gregory and Stuart (1990); on China, see Drèze and Sen (1989); on Cuba, see Zimbalist and Brundenius (1989). More will be said about these matters in Chapter 8.

[25] Enzenberger (1989, pp. 114, 116).

socialism. But it is important that we set aside the simplistic proposition that socialism is impossible. Economic crises do not salvage logically defective arguments, nor do they negate historical accomplishments. Socialism can "work." The question is, how well?

It is equally important that we make distinctions. What I am advocating is a decentralized market socialism with worker self-management. This is something quite different from the theoretical models of market socialism debated earlier in this century, and quite different from Soviet-style command economies. Right now, the model before us is Economic Democracy, and the claim is that this model is not only "possible" (i.e., economically viable) but also desirable – for various reasons, including economic efficiency. The proposition to be defended in this chapter is that Economic Democracy, if implemented, would be more efficient than Laissez Faire.

It should come as no surprise that our model shares some of Laissez Faire's efficiency strengths. Economic Democracy is also a market economy. Like its profit-seeking capitalist counterpart, a self-managed firm is motivated to seek out and satisfy consumer preferences and to utilize its raw materials and technology cost-effectively. However, the attentive reader may be troubled. Profit under Economic Democracy is not the same as profit under capitalism. Labor counts as a cost under the latter, but not under the former. Might not this difference have efficiency consequences for the economy as a whole?

This is the issue – above all, the question of allocational efficiency – over which the bulk of the theoretical ink has been spilled in recent years.[26] I am inclined to agree with Leibenstein, Vanek, and Horvat that this debate has been mostly sound and fury signifying very little, given the relative magnitudes of allocational inefficiencies as compared with Keynesian and X-inefficiencies.[27] However, the early critics of worker self-management do point to something important, something that should not be lightly dismissed. There are good reasons (if not quite the reasons

---

[26] Formal models of worker self-management, using standard neoclassical categories, have become a growth industry over the past decade or so. (See Bonin and Putterman, 1987, for an extensive survey.) Responding to the early analyses of Ward and Domar, Vanek (1970) advanced the debate to a new level, providing a careful proof that, given suitable assumptions, a worker-managed economy is Pareto-optimal. Since then, various neoclassical economists have labored to show that such an economy cannot be efficient, whereas others have concocted models to show the opposite. At the abstract level, the issue now seems settled. Drèze (1989, p. 25) provided a general-equilibrium analysis that "establishes unequivocally the compatibility of labour management with economic efficiency.... To repeat, we have established precisely that economic efficiency is not a ground for objection to self-management, in the abstract context where competitive capitalism is efficient." Although such a conclusion is gratifying to a proponent of Economic Democracy, it cannot be asked to bear too much practical weight, given the restrictive assumptions that lie behind all such general-equilibrium theorems.

[27] See Leibenstein (1976, pp. 29–44), Vanek (1989, pp. 93–103), and Horvat (1986, p. 15).

the critics have put forth) for thinking that a worker-managed firm will not behave like a capitalist firm in certain significant circumstances.

Let us consider the standard version of the early criticism. A capitalist firm, it is said, attempts to maximize its *total profit* (profit being the difference between sales and both labor and nonlabor costs). A worker-managed firm, by contrast, will attempt to maximize *profit per worker* (profit here being the difference between sales and only nonlabor costs). But this seemingly insignificant difference has momentous implications, for if we couple these behavioral assumptions with the standard neoclassical assumptions about declining marginal productivity, it can be demonstrated that a worker-managed firm will react to market fluctuations as perversely as can be imagined: It will cut production and lay off people when demand increases; it will take on more workers and increase production when demand falls.[28] This is allocative inefficiency with a vengeance.

Defenders of worker self-management have taken two tacks in response to this argument. The first is to argue that in a fully competitive economy these perversions would be unstable and hence, presumably, would not occur. (A firm that cut its production in the face of higher demand would find itself with so high a rate of per-worker profit that new firms would quickly move into the area.) That is to say, long-term equilibrium trumps short-term perversity.[29]

The other tack is to appeal to empirical reality and common sense. Vanek, for example, asks the following:

How can one reasonably expect that a working collective will mutilate itself (discharging, say, one-tenth of its membership), if it has already realized a significant gain from a price increase, say 10 percent of income, for the sake of gaining an extra, say, one percent? Indeed, this sounds like an extract from a book of rules of capitalist conduct.[30]

---

[28] Ward (1958) provided the first proof of this much-discussed result. The argument for this counterintuitive result is not easy to grasp, but the logic is unassailable. Essentially, the reasoning is this: If we assume declining marginal productivity, then each additional worker added to a firm will diminish gross income per worker; hence, the profit per worker should be maximal when the firm employs one worker – except for the fact that fixed costs per worker also decline when additional workers are added, because these costs are spread among the work force. So employment stabilizes at a higher level than unity. Now consider the last worker to join the firm (the worker at the margin). Her addition dropped the average physical output by x (assuming declining marginal productivity) and hence the average gross income by px, where p is the price per unit of the output. This loss, however, was offset by the reduction she brought in the cost per worker of the fixed capital. In equilibrium, these exactly balance. But notice that a price increase makes the per-worker loss due to the last employee greater, without affecting the fixed-cost reduction – so she will be laid off. On the other hand, if prices fall, the per-worker loss is less, relative to the reduction in fixed capital costs, and so another worker will be taken on.

[29] This is essentially the strategy of Vanek (1970) and Drèze (1989).

[30] Vanek (1977, p. 20).

The empirical evidence supports Vanek. There has been no tendency for workers to lay off co-workers when times are good, neither in Mondragon nor in Yugoslavia. Even in bad times, layoffs are rare. Janez Prasnikar, having surveyed forty Slovene enterprises, stated flatly that "the self-managed firm, which is run by a work community, does not fire its laborers." In Mondragon, major efforts are made during recessionary times to avoid discharging workers.[31]

These various responses to the "perversity problem" are sufficient to demonstrate that the most prominent argument against worker self-management fails. But there is still a problem. If we grant (as we must) that a worker-managed firm will not lay off workers and cut production when demand increases, we are compelled to admit that worker-managed firms do not maximize profit per worker.[32] But if they do not maximize per-worker profits, what do they do? Are the factors that motivate the production decisions in a worker-managed firm the same as those that motivate a capitalist firm, or are they significantly different? If the latter, what are the efficiency (and other) consequences?

We can come up with a satisfactory answer to the question of motivation if we attend to experience and common sense. In practice, both capitalist firms and worker collectives separate those decisions having long-range, far-reaching import (above all, decisions about major investments) from decisions concerning demand fluctuation. We can suppose that in a worker-managed firm, minor changes in demand will be met, first, by compensating changes in inventories, then by adjustments to the workday – overtime when demand is up, some cutback when demand is slack.[33] If an increase looks permanent, new workers will be taken on. In general, firms do not like to turn away customers, do not like to lose market share to competitors. New workers reduce the per-capita fixed costs that the other workers bear, while bringing in new revenue, so their "cost" to existing workers, if any, is small.[34] If demand continues to grow,

---

[31] Prasnikar (1980, p. 27). See also Whyte and Whyte (1988, ch. 13). In 1985, at a time when the Basque region was suffering an unemployment rate of nearly 20 percent, only 104 of the 17,000 cooperative workers had been removed from enterprise payrolls – and these were receiving benefits from the cooperative social-security institution (Whyte and Whyte, 1988, pp. 155–6).

[32] For a theoretical critique of the profit-per-worker assumption, see Dow (1986). Horvat (1986) also takes exception to this assumption, making the telling observation that if we are going to assume the maximization of profit per worker for a worker-managed firm, we ought to assume the maximization of profit per unit of invested capital (i.e., the profit rate, not total profit) for a capitalist firm. But with this assumption, the capitalist firm displays exactly the same perverse behavior as the worker-managed firm. In reality, neither of these assumptions holds.

[33] The account in this paragraph is based largely on Horvat (1986). Horvat, in addition to his expertise in technical economics, draws on his experience as a manager and as a member of a workers' council.

[34] This, observe, is the commonsense response to the theoretical argument that taking on new workers is irrational. Under ordinary conditions of rising demand, the cost of adding new workers will be perceived (correctly) as small or nonexistent, whereas the risk

however, a long-run decision will have to be made concerning output capacity.

Thus we see that in the short run, a worker-managed firm responds in much the same fashion as a capitalist firm. Supply adjusts properly to demand. How do things fare in the long run?

Here we encounter another set of theoretical objections to worker self-management, distinct from the short-run perversity problem just discussed. Three arguments show up repeatedly in the literature. It is often argued that worker-managed firms will invest too little, either (1) because members are unable to protect themselves sufficiently against risk by diversifying their portfolios or (2) because they are unable to reap the full benefits of capital investment. The opposite objection is sometimes raised: that worker-managed firms will overinvest in capital relative to labor, given their reluctance to take on new members.[35] Let us look closer at these claims.

The issue of risk is more properly considered in the context of innovation and growth, so we shall defer discussion of that until the next chapter. The other insufficient-investment argument is essentially that workers, unlike capitalists, cannot reap the full benefits of their investments forever, because they will lose all income rights when they retire or leave the firm to work elsewhere. Their reward for deferring consumption will be less, and so they will invest less.

I must confess to a certain impatience with this sort of argument, which purports to derive a highly significant conclusion (i.e., the inherent inefficiency of worker self-management) from highly abstract and unrealistic formal assumptions (particularly because we know that another set of highly abstract and formal assumptions shows perfect efficiency). Common sense tells us that long-range investment decisions – by their very nature full of uncertainty – are not based on considerations of infinite time horizons or on the ability to calculate precisely one's eventual income. Opportunities present themselves. Financing may or may not be available. In our model, both the firm and the bank will assess the risks and the likely gains, then gamble. Under capitalism, entrepreneurs and investors assess the risks and the likely gains, then gamble. Technical arguments about finite versus infinite time horizons give us no real reason to think that the assessments in the two systems will significantly and systematically differ.[36]

---

of losing valued customers is palpable. In the theoretical model, it is assumed that precise marginalist calculations can be made, while such intangibles as customer loyalty are assumed away.

[35] The first argument usually is associated with Meade (1972), the second with Furubotyn and Pejovich (1974a), and the third with the early Ward-Domar analysis.

[36] It is worth quoting Keynes in this context, because he has such an acute sense of the deviations between capitalism in reality and capitalism in theory: "Enterprise only pretends to itself to be mainly actuated by the statements in its own prospectus, however

Not surprisingly, the empirical evidence indicates no systematic bias. Yugoslavia had been a high-investment economy, as is Mondragon. In a study of some five hundred French producer cooperatives (PCs), Saul Estrin and Derek Jones reported as their principal finding that "investment in French PCs is determined by the same factors as those determining investment in conventional firms, such as expected product demand and cash flow. For French PCs the variables stressed by labor–management theorists do *not* inhibit investment."[37]

If self-management does not inhibit investment, perhaps it promotes investment too much. This is the first of the three arguments mentioned earlier concerning the inefficiency of investment under worker self-management. The idea here is that a worker-managed firm will prefer capital-intensive investment to investment that is more labor-intensive, even when the latter is more productive, because worker-managed firms do not like to take on new workers. This objection is not wholly groundless. All else equal, worker-managed firms are less inclined to expand their work force. (More on this shortly.) But in this instance, all else is not equal, because under Economic Democracy the banks will use employment creation as an explicit criterion in giving out investment grants. That is to say, the firm seeking investment funds will have a special incentive to include employment expansion in its grant application. Because funds for new investment are public funds, and because employment creation is a public concern, there would seem to be little reason to worry that enterprises will become excessively capital-intensive at the expense of the unemployed.[38]

There remains one final argument against the allocational efficiency of worker self-management that merits consideration. It has to do with neither short-term supply–demand perversity nor long-term investment inefficiency. The essential claim is that a worker-managed economy will be less likely than a capitalist one to reward equal skills equally.[39] The workers in an innovative firm will be better off than those in a more sluggish firm. The workers in a dynamic industry will be better off than those in a stable or declining industry. This happens under capitalism as well, but under capitalism there is an important countervailing tendency

candid and sincere. Only a little more than an expedition to the South Pole, is it based on an exact calculation of benefits to come" (Keynes, 1936, pp. 161–2).

[37] Estrin and Jones (1989, p. 1); emphasis in original.

[38] Notice that the only real concern here is unemployment, a topic to be discussed in a later section of this chapter. If unemployment is not a problem, then Horvat surely has a point: "If it turned out that worker-managed firms were more capital-intensive, or more precisely, more mechanized, I would welcome it. Since capital can be produced and workers cannot, and since a higher machine–worker ratio means a higher per capita output, national output, with full employment, will be higher and so will be the rate of growth" (Horvat, 1986, p. 19).

[39] See Estrin (1982) for a statement of the argument and an empirical test.

that is lacking in a worker-managed economy. Under capitalism, workers compete for good jobs. In a truly competitive capitalist economy (such as the model we are considering), an employer will replace a highly paid skilled worker with an equally skilled worker who will work for less, and so wages for given skills will tend to equalize. A self-managed firm, by way of contrast, cannot be expected to replace some of its own members by new workers who will work for less pay.

The predicted result that a worker-managed economy will exhibit significant deviations from equal pay for equal work is not without empirical confirmation. Estrin's analysis of intersectoral and intrasectoral inequalities in Yugoslavia found them quite pronounced.[40]

A reader who is not an economist may be puzzled at this point. What does this have to do with allocational inefficiency? Equal pay for equal work would seem to be about justice, not efficiency. One can, however, draw efficiency conclusions from such inequality premises, given the requisite neoclassical assumptions. If equal skills are not remunerated equally, prices will not reflect real costs (labor being such a cost), and when prices do not reflect real costs, there is allocational inefficiency. Suppose, for example, that it takes the same quantity and quality of labor and other inputs to grow an apple as it takes to grow an orange, but that workers in the orange groves make twice as much as those in the apple orchards. In this case, when supply and demand are in balance, the price of oranges will be higher than the price of apples. This price difference indicates that, given the quantities produced, society values oranges more than apples. Hence, there would be an overall gain in utility if a few more oranges were produced at the expense of a few apples, provided this could be done at no increase in real costs. By hypothesis, that is the case. The quantity and quality of the labor and other inputs are the same for each. Ergo, Pareto nonoptimality.

It seems to me that honest reflection on this argument should convince the reader that the initial puzzlement was not unwarranted. The allocational inefficiencies associated with unequal pay for equal work are so indirect, so tentative, so likely to be nonexistent or small, that the real issue here is justice, and not efficiency.[41] I think we may safely say that the question of unequal pay for equal work belongs more properly with the equality comparisons between capitalism and Economic Democracy, and so may be deferred to Chapter 5.

[40] Estrin (1982, pp. 38–51). Estrin argues that these inequalities increased substantially following the mid-1960s reforms that allowed greater scope for self-management and the market.
[41] It should be pointed out that Estrin's empirical findings concern inequality, not allocational inefficiency (which is notoriously difficult to measure). It should also be noted that these inequalities may well have been due to the peculiarities of the Yugoslav investment mechanism that were independent of worker self-management.

Let us take stock. I have argued that self-managed firms will not respond perversely to fluctuations in demand and will not be seriously biased toward nonoptimal labor intensiveness or capital intensiveness. I have noted that because a self-managed firm is not likely to replace skilled members by equally skilled workers willing to work for less, there might be an inequality tendency here that is more pronounced than that under capitalism, but I have argued that the allocational effects of this are not likely to be significant.

It might be tempting to conclude at this point that for all intents and purposes, capitalist firms and worker-managed firms will react in the same way to competitive stimuli. Such an inference would be false. Worker-managed firms differ from capitalist firms in one crucial respect that has far-reaching consequences: *Worker-managed firms, as compared with their capitalist counterparts, do not have the same self-generated tendency to expand.* Under certain rather normal conditions (specifically, under conditions of more or less constant returns to scale and/or declining costs), worker-managed firms are not so inclined to grow, nor, when they do grow, are they inclined to grow by qualitative leaps.

Let me elaborate on this important claim. Consider a simple example. When costs per item are constant, a capitalist enterprise can increase its net profit by enlarging the scale of its operation, and this increase accrues to the owner of the enterprise. If a hamburger stand employing twenty people nets $20,000, a second stand doing similar business will net another $20,000. So the owner has an almost irresistible incentive to expand. Under worker self-management, by contrast, doubling the size of the enterprise may double the net profit, but it will also double the number of workers who must share that profit. Two hamburger stands run by forty people will generate precisely the same per-worker income as one stand run by twenty. Thus, the first stand, even if successful, has no incentive to open up another, or even to take on more workers, unless increasing returns to scale make a larger operation more efficient. (I am assuming, here, that there is no shift in demand and that all workers are paid equally.)

The enterprises contrast similarly when a cost-cutting innovation is introduced. The owner of a capitalist hamburger stand is strongly motivated, particularly if the cost reduction is dramatic, to cut prices and expand quickly. He hopes to get the jump on his competitors, perhaps to drive them to the wall or take them over, or at the minimum to enlarge his market share.[42] What about our cooperative hamburger stand? It seems

---

[42] To be sure, capitalist firms are not altogether keen on price competition, frequently spending large sums to cultivate slight or imagined product differences so as to mitigate such competition, frequently colluding (formally or informally, legally or illegally) to avoid such competition altogether. At the same time, aggressive price competition remains a real threat.

reasonable to assume that the members, having introduced a cost-cutting innovation, will be content to reap the expanded profit, feeling no compulsion to cut prices or expand production. An enterprise cuts prices so as to sell more. But if the innovation cuts capital costs or input materials, but is not labor-saving, then why sell more, since that would require working longer hours or bringing in new members? If the innovation is labor-saving, then the collective might want to cut prices and sell more, but they might prefer instead to keep prices and production constant and simply work less.

All things considered, it seems clear that the worker-managed enterprise has a significantly weaker internal motivation toward expansion than does a capitalist firm. The competitive impulses of a self-managed enterprise are more defensive than offensive. The firm's workers do not want to lose customers, nor lose market share, but they have less to gain from an expansion, particularly a large, aggressive one.

It might appear that I am appealing here to precisely the assumptions that I rejected earlier, namely, that a capitalist firm maximizes total profits, whereas a worker-managed firm maximizes profits per worker. Indeed, the resemblance here is strong. But notice that there is no appeal here to maximization. I want to insist that we think about enterprise decision making realistically. In the real world, fraught as it is with imponderables, decision-makers attempt to increase sales and decrease others costs. They may project target estimates, but they make no pretenses about maximizing anything. "Maximizing" is a theoretical construct, useful for proving theorems about highly simplified models, but it should not be confused with actual behavior.

My claim is that given realistic assumptions about economic motives and conditions, it follows that worker-managed firms are less inclined than capitalist firms to expand in certain important ways and under certain important conditions. Both will expand in response to an evident increase in demand. Both will expand if there are significantly increasing returns to scale. But a capitalist firm, much more so than a worker-managed firm, is motivated to expand when returns to scale are constant and/or costs decline. Capitalist firms are also more inclined to expand in large increments. As we shall see, these differences in expansionary inclinations will have important implications for our comparative evaluation of Economic Democracy and capitalism. Their efficiency implications, however, have little to do with the standard allocational arguments, although they will bear on two large topics to be considered separately in the last two sections of this chapter, namely, unemployment and the sales effort.

Before proceeding in that direction, let me note one consequence that should be kept in mind throughout. Because self-managed firms are less expansionary than capitalist firms, they will tend to be smaller. They will tend to expand so as to capture economies of scale, but not beyond that.[43] The experience of Mondragon (though not Yugoslavia) bears out this theoretical prediction. In 1974, following an internal dispute at its largest cooperative (which employed some 3,200 workers at the time), a decision was made to keep the member firms relatively small. When firms begin to get large, divisions are often spun off as independent entities.[44] The fact that relative smallness has not impeded efficiency tends to confirm the frequently asserted, though not unchallenged, view that capitalist firms often grow much larger than technical efficiency requires.[45] As for Yugoslavia, the very large sizes of many firms (30,000 workers and more) would seem to be best explained by government investment policies.[46]

We have surveyed the main arguments purporting to establish the allocative inefficiencies of a labor-managed economy and have found them wanting. We have also uncovered three tendential differences between Economic Democracy and Laissez Faire: In the former, equal skills will be less likely to be rewarded equally, the firms themselves will be smaller, and they will be less expansionary. These do not appear to have significant allocational implications.

At this stage of our analysis it looks as if Economic Democracy and Laissez Faire are comparably efficient. Both are market economies. The price mechanism is in effect, so both economies allow consumer preferences to be expressed effectively. The economies are competitive, with individual firms having concrete incentives to produce with the appropriate technology and with minimal waste of resources. Laissez Faire may have an edge in rewarding equal skills equally, but the efficiency implications of this would seem small.

It is time now to move from defense to offense. If Economic Democracy suffers no major efficiency weaknesses in comparison with Laissez Faire, does it exhibit any efficiency strengths? Can the case be made that Economic Democracy will be more efficient than Laissez Faire? It is to this matter that we now turn.

A comparison: X-efficiency

The economic model I am proposing extends democracy to the workplace. I have argued that a democratically run firm in a market environment has the same incentives as a capitalist firm to satisfy its customers and to utilize its technology and resources effectively. But, it will surely be asked, can a self-managed firm do that as well as a capitalist firm? Are

[43] For more on this theoretical argument, see Vanek (1970, pp. 287–8).
[44] See Thomas and Logan (1982, pp. 34–5).
[45] See Du Boff (1990).   [46] See Sacks (1983).

workers competent to make complicated technical and financial decisions? Are they sufficiently competent even to elect representatives who will appoint effective managers? I cannot deny that these are fair questions, but neither can I resist remarking on how odd it is that these questions are so quickly raised (as, in my experience, they always are) in a society that prides itself on its democratic commitment. We deem ordinary people competent to select mayors, governors, even presidents. We regard ordinary people as capable of selecting representatives who will decide their taxes, who will make the laws that, if violated, will consign them to prison, who might even send them off to kill and die. Should we really ask if ordinary people are competent to elect their bosses?[47]

But we have to ask this question. Rhetorical flourish cannot pass for argument on so crucial an issue. After all, workers in democratic, capitalist societies do not elect their bosses. Why not? Perhaps workers are indeed so ill-qualified that economic chaos would result, or if not chaos, at least a precipitous decline in efficiency.

Are ordinary people competent to elect their bosses and to participate in the management of their enterprises? We have to ask this question. The amazing thing is that we can answer it – as unambiguously as one would dare hope, given the complexity and significance of the issue. It is hard to imagine a more important ethicoeconomic question that can be so decisively settled. To a degree rare in the social sciences, the empirical evidence is clear.

Let us proceed here with some care, because much is at stake. The basic issue before us now is the efficiency of Economic Democracy. This issue, we have noted, breaks into three parts: the allocational and Keynesian efficiencies of the system as a whole, and the X-efficiency of worker–managed firms. The question of worker competence for selecting managers and otherwise participating in enterprise decision making is about the latter. It is not necessary, for our purposes, to try to isolate the X-efficiency effects of various elements of worker self-management: democratic selection of management, profit sharing, participatory options, and so forth. What we need to show is that these elements, taken together, are unlikely to lead to inefficiency within the firm.

Various theorists have raised questions about the X-efficiency of workplace democracy, pointing to such things as the reluctance of managers to exert themselves fully because they must share profits with workers, the reluctance of elected managers to discipline workers suffi-

---

[47] It probably will come as no surprise that Soviet managers were as resistant to the idea of workplace democracy as are capitalist owners and managers. Leonid Gordon (1991, p. 28) reported the widespread view among Soviet managers: "The only way to organize our economy efficiently is to make us the owners."

ciently, and the waste of time and effort associated with democratic decision making.[48]

Theorists have raised these objections, but the empirical evidence is overwhelming against them. The evidence is strong that both worker participation in management and profit sharing tend to enhance productivity and that worker-run enterprises often are more productive than their capitalist counterparts.

As to the efficiency effects of greater worker participation, there is the Department of Health, Education, and Welfare study of 1973, which concluded that "in no instance of which we have evidence has a major effort to increase employee participation resulted in a long-term decline in productivity."[49] Nine years later, surveying their collection of empirical studies, Derek Jones and Jan Svejnar reported that "there is apparently consistent support for the view that worker participation in management causes higher productivity. This result is supported by a variety of methodological approaches, using diverse data and for disparate time periods."[50] In 1990, a collection of research papers edited by Princeton economist Alan Blinder extended the data set much further and reached the same conclusion. David Levine and Laura Tyson, for example, have summarized their analysis of some forty-three separate studies:

> Our overall assessment of the empirical literature from economics, industrial relations, organizational behavior and other social sciences is that participation usually leads to small, short-run improvements in performance, and sometimes leads to significant long-lasting improvements. . . . There is almost never a negative effect.[51]

They have drawn a further conclusion: Participation is most conducive to enhancing productivity when combined with (1) profit sharing, (2) guaranteed long-range employment, (3) relatively narrow wage differentials, and (4) guaranteed worker rights (such as dismissal only for just cause).[52] Enterprises in Economic Democracy will tend to fulfill all these conditions.

As to the viability of complete workplace democracy, we note that workers in the plywood cooperatives in the Pacific Northwest have been

---

[48] The first objection was raised by Alchian and Demsetz (1972). For a sustained theoretical attack on models such as ours, see Jensen and Meckling (1979).

[49] U.S. Department of Health, Education, and Welfare (1973, p. 112).

[50] Jones and Svejnar (1982, p. 11).

[51] Levine and Tyson (1990, pp. 203–4). The case for profit sharing is equally strong. Blinder (1990, p. 7); commenting on an analysis by Weitzman and Kruse that examined sixteen studies using forty-two different data samples, observed that "the consistency of the disparate results is striking. Of the 218 estimated profit-sharing coefficients, only 6 percent are negative, and none significantly so. By contrast, 60 percent of all the regression coefficients are significantly positive. . . . This, I believe, is the strongest evidence to date that profit sharing boosts productivity."

[52] Levine and Tyson (1990, pp. 205–14).

electing their managers since the 1940s, and workers in Mondragon since the 1960s. We note that as of 1981 there were some 20,000 producer cooperatives in Italy, composing one of the most vibrant sectors of the economy.[53] Needless to say, not all self-management ventures have been successful, but I know of no empirical study that even purports to demonstrate that worker-elected managers are less competent than their capitalist counterparts. Most comparisons have suggested the opposite. Most have found worker-managed firms more productive than similarly situated capitalist firms. For example, Thomas on Mondragon:

> Productivity and profitability are higher for cooperatives than for capitalist firms. It makes little difference whether the Mondragon group is compared with the largest 500 companies, or with small- or medium-scale industries; in both comparisons the Mondragon group is more productive and more profitable.[54]

Or consider Berman commenting on the plywood cooperatives:

> The major basis for co-operative success, and for survival of capitalistically unprofitable plants, has been superior labour productivity. Studies comparing square-foot output have repeatedly shown higher physical volume of output per hour, and others ... show higher quality of product and also economy of material use.[55]

There is also the recent example of Weirton Steel, the largest worker-owned enterprise in the United States. In 1982, following a mediocre year and facing bleaker prospects, National Steel offered to sell its Weirton, West Virginia, plant to its 7,000 workers. The deal was completed in 1984. Weirton proceeded to post eighteen consecutive profitable quarters – at a time when many steel firms were suffering severe losses, including two of Weirton's competitors, who were forced into bankruptcy. "Weirton is the success story of the steel companies," said analyst John Tumazos of Oppenheimer and Company. "From a production and cost standpoint, Weirton is better than its competitors."[56]

The negative example of Yugoslavia? Not even Harold Lydall, perhaps the severest procapitalist critic of the Yugoslav economic system, argues that worker incompetence in selecting managers was the problem. As we

---

[53] References to the case of Mondragon were given in Chapter 2. On the plywood cooperatives, see Berman (1982, pp. 74–98), Gunn (1984, ch. 4), and Greenberg (1986). On the Italian cooperatives, see Earle (1986) and Estrin, Jones, and Svejnar (1987).

[54] Thomas (1982, p. 149).

[55] Berman (1982, p. 80). On the difficulty of making such comparisons, see Levin (1982).

[56] For an account of the structuring of the Weirton deal (from a rather critical Left perspective), see Prude (1984). For performance, see Greenhouse (1985, p. 4F), Serrin (1986, p. 1), and Beazley (1988, p. 43). It should be pointed out that during the first four years after taking over the plant, Weirton employees, though owning the plant, had only three of the twelve seats on the board of directors, the others being held by representatives of financial agencies, who had to be assured, before lending the buy-out capital, that the company would be run "responsibly." Full control devolved to the workers in 1989.

have seen, Lydall acknowledges that for most of the period from 1950 to 1979 Yugoslavia not only survived, but prospered. Things changed, much for the worse, in the 1980s. How does he account for this precipitous decline?

It is evident that the principal cause of failure was the unwillingness of the Yugoslav Party and government to implement a policy of macroscopic restriction – especially restriction of the money supply – in combination with a microeconomic policy designed to expand opportunities and incentives for enterprise and efficient work. What was needed was *more freedom for independent decision-making by genuinely self-managed enterprises* within a free market, combined with tight controls on the supply of domestic currency.[57]

The problem in Yugoslavia does not appear to have been an excess of workplace democracy. In the judgment of one Belgrade newspaper (as summarized by Lydall), "The most convincing explanation for the present social crisis is the reduction of the self-management rights of workers."[58]

If one thinks about it, it is not surprising that worker-managed enterprises should be X-efficient. Because workers' incomes are tied directly to the financial health of the enterprise, all have an interest in selecting good managers. Because bad management is not difficult to detect by those near at hand, who observe at close range the nature of that management and feel its effects rather quickly, it is unlikely that incompetence will long be tolerated. Moreover, each individual has an interest in seeing to it that co-workers work effectively, as well as an interest in not appearing to be a slacker oneself, and so less supervision is necessary.

To these considerations we might add the observations of Henry Levin, based on his seven years of field study:

There exist both personal and collective incentives in cooperatives that are likely to lead to higher productivity. The specific consequences of these incentives are that the workers in cooperatives will tend to work harder and in a more flexible manner than those in capitalist firms; they will have a lower turnover rate and absenteeism; and they will take better care of plant and equipment. In addition, producer cooperatives function with relatively few unskilled workers and middle managers, experience fewer bottlenecks in production and have more efficient training programs than do capitalist firms.[59]

It is not my intention to suggest here that workplace democracy is the miracle cure for economic malaise. Efficiency gains are not always dramatic. Not all cooperatives succeed. Failure is always painful, as is the

---

[57] Lydall (1989, p. 69); emphasis added. Lydall (p. 112) argues that the reforms of the mid-seventies constituted a "counter-reformation" to weaken the power of managers and give more power to the party politicians. In Yugoslavia, "while the official doctrine is that the workers, through their representatives on the workers' council, choose their director, in practice most directors, especially those of large or medium-sized enterprises, are chosen by local politicians."

[58] Lydall (1989, p. 96).   [59] Levin (1984, p. 28).

failure of a capitalist firm (and not only for the owners). But it seems to me that the evidence is overwhelming that worker-managed firms are at least as internally efficient as capitalist firms. In fact, the published findings establish more than this minimal conclusion. I do not see how there can be honest doubt on the part of anyone who reviews the literature with an open mind that, all else equal, worker-managed firms are likely to be more X-efficient than their capitalist counterparts.[60]

Trouble for Laissez Faire: unemployment

In our society, it is murder, psychologically, to deprive a man of a job or an income. You are in substance saying to that man that he has no right to exist.
                                                            – Martin Luther King, Jr.

It had long been a postulate of neoclassical theory that a free, competitive, capitalist economy would inevitably gravitate toward full employment.[61] It was granted that "frictional" unemployment might exist – unemployment due to people leaving one job in search of another, or due to temporary imbalances between openings and skills as a result of individual miscalculation or unforeseen changes in demand. But it was generally denied that "involuntary" unemployment was possible when the economy was in equilibrium. It was held to be impossible that an equilibrium situation could exist in which unemployed people would be willing to work for the prevailing wage, or even less, but employers would be unwilling to hire them.

John Maynard Keynes's monumentally influential *General Theory of Employment, Interest and Money* is a relentless attack on precisely this full-employment postulate. The volume of employment generated by an economy, he argues, is determined by the relationship between the "propensity to consume" and the rate of investment, and that volume need not correspond to anything like full employment. Equilibrium might be established at any level of unemployment.[62]

It might seem contrary to common sense, especially to common sense

[60] It should be noted that when cooperatives compete in a capitalist economy, all else is not equal (access to finance, support structures, etc.). We shall take up this matter in a later chapter when we address this important question: If self-managed firms are more efficient than capitalist firms, why have they not become the predominant form of economic organization?

[61] In this section, the term "neoclassical" will designate the pre-Keynesian version of the theory. This version is still adhered to by most conservatives in its more or less original form, or as (slightly) amended by the "New Classical Economics," which began its sustained attack on liberal Keynesianism in the mid-1970s. (The "New Classical Economics" is "Slightly Revised Chicago Economics," its most illustrious practitioner being Robert Lucas, Milton Friedman's successor at Chicago.) For a good (if partisan) account of the differences between contemporary Keynesians and the New Classicals, see Blinder (1989), especially his articles "Keynes after Lucas" and "Keynes, Lucas, and Scientific Progress."

[62] See Keynes (1936, pp. 27–32) for a summary of his employment theory.

gleaned during the decade-long Great Depression, that anyone could maintain that full employment is inevitable under free-market laissez faire. But the economists had an answer – the only possible answer, given the assumptions of their theory: Because a free market cannot have unemployment, the depressed capitalist economies must not be free. Labor unions, in particular, were singled out for blame. These "coercive," monopolistic organizations were charged with blocking the movement of the economy toward full employment by forcing wages above their appropriate levels.

This pre-Keynesian position is still maintained by many conservatives, among them Hayek: "Unions that had no power to coerce outsiders would thus not be strong enough to force up wages above the level at which all seeking work could be employed, that is, the level that would establish itself in a truly free market for labor in general."[63]

Hayek, of course, is not unaware of the Keynesian argument, but he is unpersuaded:

The development of Lord Keynes's theory started from the correct insight that the regular cause of extensive unemployment is real wages that are too high. The next step consisted in the proposition that a direct lowering of money wages could be brought about only by a struggle so painful and prolonged that it could not be contemplated. Hence he concluded that real wages must be lowered by the process of lowering the value of money. This is really the reasoning underlying the whole "full-employment" policy now so widely accepted. If labor insists on a level of money wages too high to allow full-employment, the supply of money must be so increased as to raise prices to a level where the real value of the prevailing money wage is no longer greater than the productivity of the workers seeking employment.[64]

This, it must be said, is a serious distortion of Keynes's argument. First, Keynes does not hold that increasing the money supply so as to depress real wages will increase employment, for he does not believe that the level of real wages determines the level of employment. This latter point he repeats relentlessly.[65] Second (and one would be tempted to call this distortion outrageous were it not so common), Keynes does not maintain that it is labor's insistence on too high a money wage that causes unemployment. The whole of the *General Theory*'s Chapter 2 is a critique of precisely this presumption:

It is not very plausible to assert that unemployment in the United States in 1932 was due to labor obstinately refusing to accept a reduction in money-wages or

---

[63] Hayek (1960, pp. 270–1).   [64] Ibid., p. 280.

[65] "Thus the volume of employment is not determined by the marginal disutility of labor measured in terms of real wages. . . . If the propensity to consume and the rate of new investment result in a deficient effective demand, the actual level of employment with fall short of the supply of labor potentially available at the existing real wage" (Keynes, 1936, p. 30).

to its obstinately demanding a real wage beyond what the productivity of the economic machine was capable of furnishing. Wide variations are experienced in the volume of employment without any apparent change either in the minimum real demands of labor or its productivity. Labor is not more truculent in the depression than in the boom – far from it. Nor is its physical productivity less.[66]

Keynes maintains, as Hayek surely must know, that the level of employment is not determined by the wage bargain struck between employees (unionized or not) and employers, but by other basic forces in the economy, the most critical being the level of investment and the quantity of savings – variables far removed from labor's control.

Of course, Keynes's saying it is so does not make it so, and Hayek's misrepresentation of Keynes does not in itself invalidate his own contention that Laissez Faire tends to full employment. What we need to examine are the arguments.

The neoclassical argument, though not often stated explicitly, is not difficult to reconstruct. Suppose there are unemployed workers desirous of work. If they are allowed to compete freely with the rest of the work force, they will force wages down, thus reducing production costs. According to neoclassical theory, a firm adjusts its production to bring the marginal cost of its product (the cost of producing one more item) into equality with the product's market-given price. Hence, a drop in costs signals an expansion in production, and this expansion provides jobs for the "temporarily" unemployed, moving the economy toward full-employment equilibrium.

This argument, we observe, depends on three crucial suppositions: that the firm can expand production, that the firm will expand production if wages decline, and that, if it does so, it will be able to sell its increased output. Let us examine each of these in turn.

We note, as a preliminary observation, that it is always possible for a firm to take on more workers, because the existing volume of work can always be spread around by reducing the hours of those already employed. But such actions will not be taken under Laissez Faire, because neither the employer nor the current employees will stand to benefit. So a firm will hire additional workers only if hiring them will increase production. But increasing production requires more than just labor. Tools, raw materials, and work space are needed as well. If production goods and production facilities are not available, then employment will not be increased, no matter how low competitive bidding forces wages. The economy cannot expand production.

In neoclassical theory, such a situation is impossible. The theory assumes that it is always possible to add more labor to the existing stock of capital to increase output. Such an assumption is plainly unrealistic as

[66] Keynes (1936, p. 9).

a general assumption (e.g., for underdeveloped countries), but it does not seem inappropriate to an economy operating at less than full capacity or to one capable of expanding its productive capacity with relative ease, as is usually the case with industrialized capitalist economies. So the first assumption, so long as we are referring to developed economies, is acceptable.

What about the second assumption? Will firms expand production when labor costs decline? This is a basic assumption of the perfect-competition model, but does it hold in reality? Under perfect competition, a firm assumes that it can sell at the going price all that it can produce; so when costs drop, it always expands production. In the real world, firms are less sanguine about sales. Certainly employers will be delighted to talk to workers willing to work for less, but they may simply replace current employees with cheaper ones, or use the threat of doing so to drive down wages. If this happens, neither production nor employment will increase. In the long run, production and employment might even decline.

For goods produced must be sold. Our third assumption says they will. But when wages decline, so does worker purchasing power, and if this is not offset by an increase in spending elsewhere, total demand will decline. The traditional argument invoked Say's law at this point: Investment spending will increase, because lower costs will mean greater profits, greater profits will mean greater savings, and greater savings will mean greater investment.

But neither the first nor third clause necessarily obtains. Lower costs will mean greater profits only if the products are sold, which they might not be if demand is adversely affected. Moreover, Keynes is surely right that the forces and motivations governing saving are quite distinct from those governing investment. There is no reason to assume that these quantities will always coincide.[67] It follows that firms that have reduced wages may find themselves unable to sell as much as they did before, let alone more, and so they react by cutting production and further reducing employment.

In short, a competitive economy might respond to an increase in unemployment not by restoring employment to the previous level but by cutting back even further. The fact of the matter is that there are no forces in a free-market economy that can guarantee that investment decisions (the key variable in the foregoing analysis) will be precisely (or even roughly) what is necessary to offset the decline in wage-goods

---

[67] See Keynes (1936, pp. 19–21 and books III and IV). A variation on Say's law is the "Pigou effect": A decrease in wages will cause prices to fall. Those with money will feel richer and thus will spend more. The reply to that would seem to be obvious: Perhaps they will – or perhaps not. A slumping economy might well induce financial caution.

demand that occurs when wages are reduced. Hence there is no reason to assume that an equilibrium, if reached at all, will be a full-employment equilibrium.

It should be noted that the preceding argument undercuts the conservative contention that labor unions (and minimum-wage laws, another frequently cited factor)[68] are responsible for unemployment. Quite the contrary. Insofar as labor unions, minimum-wage laws, and various welfare provisions prevent demand from falling as low as it might otherwise go during a slump, they apply a brake to the downward spiral. Far from being responsible for unemployment, they actually mitigate it.

It should be obvious to anyone who cares to look that the empirical record of actually existing capitalism gives no support whatsoever to the alleged full-employment tendency. Wallace Peterson reminds us of "the basic fact that, except during wartime, there has *always* been a chronic shortage of jobs in the United States."[69] Blinder reminds us that in Western Europe, unemployment rates rose more or less steadily from 1974 to 1985 – from 3 percent to more than 13 percent in the United Kingdom, from 2.8 percent to 10.5 percent in France, and from 1.6 percent to 8 percent in West Germany. ("Some young men in these countries have *never* held a job and may never be productive workers.")[70] Lest we think that the fault lies with labor unions, minimum-wage laws, and welfare provisions, Alexander Keyssar reminds us of the high unemployment rates during the preunion, prewelfare "good old days."[71] Not without reason did Marx give the unemployed (the "industrial reserve army") a central place in his model of capitalism.[72]

Most contemporary economists now acknowledge that capitalism has a full-employment problem. One speaks now of the "natural" rate of unemployment – defined to be that level of unemployment below which inflation would accelerate.[73] This, of course, gives the game away, because there is nothing at all natural about this quantity. Involuntary

---

[68] See Friedman (1962, p. 180): "The state can legislate a minimum wage rate. It can hardly require employers to hire at that minimum all who were formerly employed at wages below the minimum.... The effect of the minimum wage is therefore to make unemployment higher than it otherwise would be." Friedman and Friedman (1980, pp. 237–8) later repeated that claim, adding that "the minimum wage rate is one of the most, if not the most, anti-black law on the statute books," because it "requires employers to discriminate against persons with low skills."

[69] Peterson (1982, p. 86). As Peterson and many others have pointed out, the official statistics significantly underestimate the extent of involuntary unemployment, because they do not count "discouraged" workers who have stopped looking, or those working part-time who would prefer full-time work, or the millions more who claim to want to work but who do not fit the Bureau of Labor Statistics unemployment criteria (Peterson, 1982, pp. 84–7).

[70] Blinder (1989, p. 120).   [71] Keyssar (1986).   [72] Marx (1967, ch. XXV).

[73] See Samuelson (1980, pp. 771–2) for a succinct account.

unemployment may be natural to capitalism, but if so, that fact hardly counts in capitalism's favor.

There would seem to remain only the last-ditch argument fashionable in conservative "New Classical" circles: Unemployment is not involuntary, but is freely chosen by workers, who calculate that their time is better spent searching for more highly paid employment. As Robert Lucas would have it, "to explain why people allocate time to . . . unemployment, we need to know why they prefer it to all other activities."[74] If ordinary experience does not suffice to cut short a discussion of this "argument," one might consider two well-established facts: First, when unemployment rises, it is layoffs, not quits, that are rising. Second, unemployed workers normally accept their first job offer.[75] Neither of these fits well with the hypothesis that most unemployment is a free choice of leisure.[76]

There is one "empirical" argument in support of the claim that capitalism always provides jobs for those who want them that I would think too simpleminded to mention were it not for the fact that one of my students reported having been subjected to it by an economics professor, who brandished a copy of the *Chicago Tribune*'s help-wanted section as proof that there is no involuntary unemployment. It should be obvious that this "proof" means nothing in the absence of a correspondence between the number of jobs advertised and the number of unemployed – to say nothing of a correspondence between the required skills and the available skills.[77] One study counted 228 jobs advertised in a local paper in an area reporting 7,800 unemployed – and few of these jobs were found to be reasonable options for the most of the unemployed. (One that was reasonable, three dollars per hour for a motel night clerk, drew seventy applicants within twenty-four hours after the advertisement appeared.)[78]

We must conclude that there are no sound theoretical arguments, nor any empirical evidence, in support of the contention that Laissez Faire tends to full employment.[79] Unemployment is a fundamental efficiency

---

[74] Lucas (1987, p. 54).   [75] Blinder (1989, p. 118).

[76] Robert Solow (1980, p. 7), in his presidential address to the American Economics Association, assessed the claim that "people who give the vague impression of being unemployed are actually engaged in voluntary leisure" with appropriate incredulity: "It is astonishing that believers have made essentially no effort to verify this central hypothesis. I know of no convincing evidence in its favor, and I am not sure why it has any claim to be taken seriously."

[77] Try telling a young philosopher, fresh Ph.D. degree in hand, that the many listings under "Jobs for Philosophers" prove that there is no involuntary unemployment in the profession.

[78] Meyer (1978, pp. 88–95). Meyer's analysis of all the want ads that appeared one day in the local Middletown, New York, newspaper revealed that of the 228 ads, only 142 were for full-time jobs within commuting distance, and of those, 100 called for some special skill. The employers offering the remaining 42 jobs were swamped with applications.

[79] A novel argument has recently been put forth by MIT's Martin Weitzman (1985), purporting to show that the unemployment tendency, admitted to be endemic to traditional

defect of the conservative ideal. If unemployed workers face idle factories simply because of a lack of effective demand that would stimulate employers to hire them, then the system does not come close to Pareto optimality.

We should not take lightly the debilitating effects of chronic unemployment; they have been widely documented and indeed are plainly visible. The early research of the 1930s revealed the stages: shock, followed by an active, optimistic search for another job, followed by active distress and increasing pessimism, concluding with fatalistic resignation, the "broken attitude."[80] Nearly two decades ago, Harvey Brenner demonstrated a stable correlation, going back 127 years, between rates of unemployment and rates of mental-hospital admissions.[81] Recently, Emile Allan and Darrell Steffensmeier have shown a (scarcely surprising) connection between unemployment and juvenile and young-adult crime.[82] The costs of unemployment, whether measured in terms of the cold cash of lost production and lost taxes or in the hotter units of alienation, violence, and despair, are likely to be large under Laissez Faire.[83]

I have argued that Laissez Faire is likely to experience unemployment inefficiencies. There is no reason to suppose they will not be severe. We must now ask about Economic Democracy. Interestingly enough, that tendency of worker self-management that earlier raised inequality and efficiency concerns, namely, the reluctance of a firm to employ more workers when costs decline, has a more desirable counterpart relative to a decline in demand, for if a self-managed firm is hesitant to take on more workers when times are good, it is also reluctant to reduce its ranks when times are bad. The face-to-face democracy within such an enterprise militates against shifting the burden of a business slump onto a few, especially if the slump is likely to be temporary.[84] This burden

forms of capitalism, is not inherent in capitalism per se, but only in capitalist economies that pay wages. To solve the unemployment problem, Weitzman argues, we need to shift to an economy that pays workers a contracted share of the profits, rather than a contracted wage. Unfortunately, Weitzman argues from within the same neoclassical framework that so misleads conservative economists. Though he couches his argument in terms of imperfect rather than perfect competition, he, too, assumes that production will automatically expand if labor costs drop. That is to say, he ignores Keynes's basic insight. For additional critiques of Weitzman, see Nordhaus (1986) and Rothschild (1986-7).

[80] Eisenberg and Lazarsfeld (1938, p. 378).
[81] Brenner (1973).
[82] Allan and Steffensmeier (1989).
[83] Eastern European intellectuals take note: The unemployment accompanying a move toward Laissez Faire need not be temporary.
[84] This solidarity could be, and probably should be, backed by a law prohibiting the dismissal of a worker simply for reasons of financial exigency. Considerations of equity and efficiency converge here. Such worker rights not only increase the likelihood of full employment (which is required for Keynesian efficiency) but also, as noted earlier, are likely to enhance X-efficiency.

sharing, which is natural to Economic Democracy, is far from natural to capitalism. Capitalist firms generally negotiate a wage contract that guarantees a wage rate, but not employment. When demand declines, an employer has little choice but to lay off workers, because it is not open to him to abrogate the wage contract.[85]

Of course, if the decrease in demand (under Economic Democracy) proves to be more than temporary, the incomes of everyone will decline, and workers will want to seek employment in more profitable concerns. This is as it should be. Some will shift toward areas where demand is stronger, thus allowing the incomes of those remaining to rise again. Labor will reallocate itself smoothly, without the violent disruptions of involuntary unemployment.

Worker solidarity in the face of a business slump will prevent a sharp drop in employment, but it cannot guarantee full employment. There are always new workers entering the labor force, young people in particular, but also workers leaving firms that are in decline, or simply people looking for something better. More active government intervention is needed here – and is provided by our model. The key mechanisms are the ones associated with that feature of Economic Democracy little discussed thus far: social control of investment.

Recall the basic features: Investment funds will come from a use tax on the capital assets of society and will be returned to communities on a per capita basis. Each community will then apportion its share to its banks. Each bank's share of those funds, as well as that bank's income, will be determined by its prior record in making profitable grants and in creating employment. Most banks will have entrepreneurial divisions that will work at encouraging employment expansion in affiliated firms and at developing new self-managed enterprises. The experience in Mondragon suggests that such procedures and institutions can be effective. In Mondragon, deliberate efforts are made by each of the cooperatives, as well as the bank, to expand employment. As a result, "cooperatives have continued to increase employment under adverse economic conditions, whereas industrial employment creation on the provincial level has fallen strongly."[86]

If these mechanisms prove insufficient, *the government should become the*

---

[85] This is not an axiomatic feature of capitalism, but one that is likely to prevail under Laissez Faire. The employer has no incentive to apply "share the burden." Individual workers have little incentive, because in the absence of worker democracy they have little motivation to concern themselves with their more expendable "comrades."

[86] Thomas and Logan (1982, p. 49). It should be noted that the economy of the Basque region continued to degenerate during the worldwide recession of the early 1980s, to the point that new job creation in cooperatives virtually ceased. The cooperative complex, however, unlike the rest of the region, was able to avoid contraction. (Unemployment in Spain hit 18.4 percent in 1983, the highest rate in Europe.) See Bradley and Gelb (1987).

employer of last resort, guaranteeing public-service jobs to all who are able to work. Unemployment is too serious a problem to be tolerated. Full employment is a part of the socialist heritage that should not be relinquished. The effects of unemployment – financial, psychological, social – are so devastating, and the promise of full employment so central to the socialist project, that Economic Democracy should, without hesitation, guarantee every citizen a genuine "right to work."[87]

The conservative response to such a suggestion is to predict labor indiscipline. If workers do not have to face the sack, why work hard or effectively? This concern would seem to have empirical support. When the socialist economies of Eastern Europe and the Soviet Union were full-employment economies, labor inefficiency and worker indifference were widespread. ("They pretend to pay us, and we pretend to work.") But notice that Economic Democracy, unlike command socialism, offers a strong positive incentive for good work: Incomes are tied directly to enterprise profits. To be sure, there may be shirkers, but such workers run the risk of social displeasure – and the threat of being fired. A self-managed firm can dismiss members for cause, and probably would not hesitate to do so, knowing that the person in question will not be too badly hurt.[88]

Those who remain unpersuaded should remember that Japan's most dynamic sectors offer virtual lifetime employment and that recent developments in Eastern Europe do not suggest that unemployment is a great spur to efficiency. On balance, the evidence indicates that the positive effects of employment security on X-efficiency well outweigh the negative effects, when coupled with profit sharing and participation.

There remains one conservative objection that should be mentioned. It is argued that government intervention to secure full employment leads inevitably to inflation.[89] As we shall see in Chapter 6, this charge is not without substance when directed, as it usually is, against Keynesian liberalism. But it has little force against our model. There is no reason

---

[87] As an alternative to public employment (or perhaps as a supplement), communities might want to institute "rotating layoffs." During periods of significant unemployment, communities could agree to provide unemployment compensation to those laid off, to cushion the financial shock, while firms could agree to recall those laid off after a specified period, laying off others in their stead if necessary. The underlying rationale for "rotating layoffs" is twofold: The effects of unemployment on the individual (and hence on the community) are far less severe if the financial loss is not too great nor the time too long (indeed, not a few might welcome an unexpected vacation); second, worker solidarity in the firm is enhanced by burden sharing. (My thanks to Patsy Schweickart for this suggestion. During her employment as a plant engineer for General Motors in the early 1970s, she found workers often looking forward to temporary layoffs.)

[88] There might be an argument here (the strength of which would depend on empirical experience) for funding employment-of-last-resort jobs at significantly less than the rate at which the fired person was paid.

[89] Hayek (1960, pp. 280–1, 324–39); also see Hayek (1972) and Friedman (1962, p. 76).

whatsoever that government spending of funds collected by taxation for the purpose of financing new enterprises should be inflationary. The conservative critique of liberal full-employment policies is directed at deficit spending, but such spending is not the unemployment remedy we propose. (As we shall see, the inflationary pressures that might threaten Economic Democracy come from another source.)

The conclusion of this section is obvious: Laissez Faire cannot guarantee full employment; it can only hope that an equilibrium approaching full employment will occur. Being laissez faire, it opposes all government intervention to reduce unemployment. By contrast, our model incorporates structures and governmental policies that should make it possible for everyone who wants to work to do so, and in addition it gives those who do have work considerable job security. Even if these mechanisms work imperfectly, unemployment will not be the pervasive problem it is under Laissez Faire.

More trouble: the sales effort

Every product is a bait by means of which the individual tries to entice the essence of the other person, his money. Every real or potential need is a weakness which will draw the bird into the lime. – Karl Marx

The full-employment assumption is not the only problematic assumption underlying the Laissez Faire case for efficiency. Another basic – and controversial – assumption is that of "consumer sovereignty." The consumer is king in the neoclassical conception of laissez faire. The economy exists to respond to his desires. These desires are presumed to be his own, and to accord with his own best interests. (The king who is routinely manipulated is not really sovereign.) Because the market signals consumer preferences with great facility, and provides incentives for their summary satisfaction, one can conclude that the market is optimally efficient in promoting each consumer's well-being (at least within the constraints imposed by his income) if the satisfaction of preferences expressed by market purchases does in fact promote an individual's well-being. This is the consumer-sovereignty assumption: If a consumer reveals by his purchase a preference for *A* over *B*, then *A* in fact contributes more to his well-being.[90]

[90] "A fundamental value judgment that is made in almost all welfare analyses is the sovereignty of consumer choice – that the preferences revealed by a consumer's demand behavior correspond exactly to an ordinal indicator of his welfare, or even to a cardinal indicator if choice under uncertainty is being discussed and if the expected utility hypothesis is satisfied" (Hammond, 1989, p. 193). Hammond is right that this assumption underlies almost all welfare analysis, but he is wrong that this a value judgment. It is an assumption about empirical reality, or at least about some stylized version of empirical reality.

It is important to recognize that what is being assumed here is an empirical thesis, not a normative one. The assumption is that a consumer's well-being is maximized, subject to his income constraint, when he freely chooses his consumption. This should be distinguished from the normative judgment that an individual should be the ultimate judge of his own welfare. Also, a denial that consumer sovereignty obtains should not be confused with the normative judgment that manipulation is wrong (in Jon Elster's formulation, that "exploiting intrapsychic mechanisms that are unknown to the individual can never be justified").[91] These normative judgments are bound up with the issue at hand, as we shall see, but we need to keep them separate from the empirical claim.

Needless to say, consumer sovereignty will not strictly obtain in any realistic market system. Minimal criteria, such as physical health, or an individual's retrospective self-evaluation, suggest clear conterexamples. But an argument such as ours cannot insist on strict compliance, because no system that allows consumers any freedom of choice can guarantee that there will be neither self-destructive consumption nor ignorant or soon-regretted purchases. The relevant questions concern the relationships between the frequency of the failure of consumer sovereignty and the structural features of Laissez Faire and Economic Democracy.

If one steps from the mainstream of contemporary economics, one encounters a great many critics of the consumer-sovereignty assumption. John Kenneth Galbraith, in his presidential address to the American Economics Association, could not resist tweaking his colleagues. To insist on consumer sovereignty, he declared, is to turn away from "a remarkably obvious question: Why does the modern consumer increasingly tend toward insanity, increasingly insist on self-abuse?"[92]

Such criticisms are not suffered lightly by those at the center of the profession. The standard response invokes the specter of repression. MIT's Robert Solow fires back at the critics: "The attack on consumer sovereignty performs the same function as the doctrine of 'repressive tolerance.' If people do not want what I see so clearly they should want, it can only be because they don't know what they 'really' want."[93] Friedman writes in a similar vein: "Indeed, a major source of objection to a free economy is precisely that it does its task so well. It gives people what they want, instead of what a particular group thinks they ought to want. "[94]

But these charges of elitism and intolerance are off the mark, deriving from a failure to observe the distinction noted earlier. The consumer-sovereignty assumption is the *empirical claim* that freely made consumer purchases really do tend to maximize well-being; it is not the *normative claim* that people ought to decide for themselves what is good for them.

[91] Elster (1979, p. 83).   [92] Galbraith (1973b, p. 3).
[93] Solow (1970, p. 105).   [94] Friedman (1962, p. 15).

One can well oppose the idea that a paternalistic authority ought to decide for consumers what is good for them, and still deny that consumer sovereignty obtains in a particular economy. One might wish to see the system reformed so as to make it less likely that consumer choice would conflict with well-being (truth-in-advertising laws, perhaps). One might want the market replaced by some other democratic procedure. One might even want to maintain the system as it is because of other, overriding, ethical or economic concerns.[95] None of these normative views entails elitism or intolerance. To infer intolerance from a denial of consumer sovereignty is to confuse an empirical claim with a normative one.

This is all charge and countercharge. The conventional response to the attack on the consumer-sovereignty assumption may be wide of the mark, but that does not end the matter, certainly not for us. Because we are comparing ideal models, we must inquire more carefully into structural relationships.

One fact is quite clear: Just as capitalism provides incentives for innovation, efficient management, and close attention to consumer demand, it also encourages the stimulation of demand. Galbraith points to the familiar institutions and puts the matter bluntly:

> The control or management of demand is, in fact, a vast and rapidly growing industry in itself. It embraces a huge network of communications, a great array of merchandising and selling organizations, nearly the entire advertising industry, numerous ancillary research, training and other related services and much more. In everyday parlance this great machine, and the demanding and varied talents that it employs, are said to be engaged in selling goods. In less ambiguous language, it means that it is engaged in the management of those who buy goods.[96]

Demand stimulation is so commonplace in our lives that we may fail to appreciate just how peculiar the phenomenon really is – nonexistent in earlier modes of production, nonexistent in some contemporary ones. No one in a primitive or feudal economy (apart from a few traders) has any reason to entice people to increase their consumption. Neither master nor slave, lord nor serf, has the slightest interest in persuading people to eat more bread or drink more wine. Nor does the production manager in a command economy, because quotas are set by an independent agency. Indeed, it well might strike a visitor from another planet as exceedingly odd that in a world where so many have so little, so much effort goes into persuading those who have a lot to consume even more.

---

[95] A terminological clarification for the careful reader: Although it is true, as I have argued, that economic values are normative, and indeed may be considered "ethical," I shall use "ethical values" and "ethical concerns" as shorthand for "noneconomic ethical values" and "noneconomic ethical concerns."

[96] Galbraith (1967, p. 200).

In a market economy, however, demand stimulation is an integral part of the system. With financial reward tied to sales, there exists an inevitable tendency toward "salesmanship." Of course, the strength of this tendency varies considerably with particular circumstances. In the early stages of capitalist development, when emerging capitalist farmers and manufacturers engaged in successful competition with small landholders and craftsmen, there was not much need to a stimulate demand. The markets were there, to be captured by offering goods at lower prices. But as traditional markets became saturated and as capitalist production transformed the peasant and artisan classes into wage laborers, the pressure intensified to develop new markets, new products – and new sales techniques. More and more people, more and more resources, came to be devoted to the selling of goods.

To put this development into perspective, consider just a few numbers. In 1867, $50 million was spent on advertising in the United States. By the turn of the century, such spending had risen to $500 million. In 1967, the total was in excess of $17 billion. By 1988, worldwide expenditures on advertising alone reached $225 billion, more than $100 billion of it spent in the United States – the latter sum equal to total U.S. expenditures on gasoline, oil, and coal that year.[97]

If it is clear that the market encourages the development of sales techniques, it is also clear that there is nothing in the structure of Laissez Faire to inhibit this development. To the contrary, if a technique proves effective, competitive pressures will ensure its adoption. For a capitalist firm to forgo an effective technique would be to deny itself potential profits and to subject itself to the competitive risk of serious loss.

It is obvious that a large sales apparatus is likely to develop under Laissez Faire. But would that be detrimental to the economic well-being of society? The sales effort has its defenders. Jules Backman, for example, concludes his study with the assessment that "on balance, it seems clear that advertising makes a major contribution to our national economic well-being and to the competitive nature of our economy."[98] A more common (and more cautious) view is expressed by Solow:

No one who believes, as I do, that profit is an important business motive could possibly argue that advertising has no influence on the willingness of consumers

---

[97] Simon (1970, pp. 188–9); Clark (1989, p. 14). Simon estimates that total promotional expenditures, including advertising, but also "most of what salesmen do . . . window displays, publicity, and the display of goods so that customers can examine them, including trade fairs," are roughly three times the advertising expenditures alone (Simon, 1970, p. 26). This puts the promotional bill in 1967 at $51 billion. The same multiplier for 1988 would put total promotional expenses at $300 billion – a figure somewhat larger than what was spent on national defense that year.

[98] Backman (1967, p. 160). I cannot resist noting that Backman was aided in his work by a grant from the Association of National Advertisers.

to buy a given product at a given price. After all, how could I then account for the fact that profit-seeking corporations regularly spend billions of dollars on advertising? But I should think that a case could be made that much advertising seems only to cancel other advertising, and is therefore merely wasteful. I should think it obvious that this almost has to be true – for otherwise there would be nothing to stop the cigarette industry and the detergent industry from expanding their sales to their hearts' desire and the limit of the consumer's capacity to carry debt. . . . It is open to legitimate doubt that advertising has a detectable effect at all on the sum of consumer spending or, in other words, on the choice between spending and saving.[99]

Let us consider Solow's position for a moment, because it is both widely held and influential. Solow's conclusion comes to this: Advertising affects how people spend their money, but not how much they spend; most advertising is self-canceling and thus merely wasteful.

The first thing we observe is that the argument that advertising almost has to be self-canceling, "for otherwise there would be nothing to stop the cigarette industry and the detergent industry from expanding their sales to their hearts' desire," is egregiously fallacious. To say that advertising can increase total consumption is not to say that consumption can be increased beyond all bounds, any more than to say that fertilizer makes marigolds grow larger is to say that they can be grown larger than sunflowers.

There is a deeper problem with Solow's analysis. Whether the sales effort shifts the volume of consumption or merely shifts consumption patterns is not the relevant ethical question. Of course, if the sales apparatus has little effect (either quantitative or qualitative) on consumption, then it would certainly appear wasteful (i.e., detrimental to efficiency), because the people and resources so employed could be put to better use.[100]

If sales techniques do have an effect (and it is difficult to believe they do not – those billions of dollars, after all), then the crucial question is whether or not the effect is to make people better off. The question whether people consume more and save less as a result of the sales effort or merely consume more of brand X than of brand Y is not the central issue. What we need to know is the effect of such behavior on well-being.

As might be expected, given the difficulty of constructing controlled experiments, there is little empirical evidence to go on. Among the many problems, there is the fact that a consumer who has made a purchase that subsequently seems to have been ill-advised often is reluctant to express regret, because the decision reflects on his judgment and character.

[99] Solow (1968, p. 48).
[100] There has been surprisingly little research done on the effects of advertising. More surprising still, what research has been done has been hard pressed to find any correlation between advertising expenditures and results on sales. See Schudson (1984, pp. 17–18).

Despite the lack of empirical evidence, however, it seems to me that we can venture an answer if we properly pose the question. Let us ask simply if there are any good reasons for thinking that the sales effort is likely to bring people's consumption patterns into better alignment with what would maximize their well-being. Are there any "invisible-hand" forces at work that tend to produce this result?

We observe that an invisible-hand explanation is necessary. The direct, conscious intention of producers is not to maximize customer well-being, but to make what will sell and to sell what has been made. Adam Smith long ago observed that "it is not from the benevolence of the butcher, the brewer or the baker that we expect our dinner, but from their regard for their own interest. We address ourselves, not to their humanity but to their self-love, and never talk to them of their own necessities but of their advantage."[101]

Of course, if we assume that the only things that will sell are those that will maximize well-being, then an invisible-hand explanation presents itself immediately: People who are free to choose will buy only what will make them truly happy. But is such an assumption plausible? On the one hand we have salesmanship and sales resistance, which suggests that consumers often perceive their own interests to be distinct from the interests of those with products to sell. On the other hand, there is the fact that a sale cannot be consummated without the buyer's consent. No one, after all, is forced to buy.

Now if a person can be convinced only by a demonstration that the purchase of the product in question is in his rational self-interest, then the assumption that only those things that will profitably sell are the things that will maximize well-being is firmly grounded. In this case, the sales effort consists in conveying true and complete information concerning the advantages and disadvantages of the commodity in question, so that the consumer may make as rational a choice as possible.

It is obvious that our discussion has strayed into Fantasyland. Rational demonstration is not the only sales technique.[102] No one who has watched an hour or two of commercial television can have any doubts, nor anyone who has read any of the popular exposés of the more esoteric practices.[103]

---

[101] Adam Smith [1976, p. 27 (I.ii.2)].

[102] As one advertising executive explained, "if you sell purely on rational needs, the next manufacturer can not only duplicate those factors, but can make a feature of one upmanship. In the fifties and sixties detergents got clothes white. Then it was white and bright. Then it was white and bright and fresh. Then it was white, bright, fresh and soft" (Clark, 1989, p. 24).

[103] Among the best-sellers of some years ago were works by Packard (1958, 1960) and Key (1973, 1976). For a critique of Key's sensational charges of "sexploitation," see Clark (1989, pp. 119–24). For an entertaining, if chilling, presentation of material only slightly less dramatic, read the rest of Clark.

For additional evidence, one can turn to the former head of a major advertising agency:

Claude Hopkins, whose genius for writing copy made him one of the advertising immortals, tells the story of one of his great beer campaigns. In a tour through the brewery, he nodded politely at the wonders of the malt and hops, but came alive when he saw that the empty bottles were being sterilized with live steam. His client protested that every brewery did the same. Hopkins patiently explained that it was not *what* they did, but what they *advertised* they did that mattered. He wrote a classic campaign which proclaimed "OUR BOTTLES ARE WASHED WITH LIVE STEAM!" George Washington Hill, the great tobacco manufacturer, once ran a cigarette campaign with the now-famous claim: "IT'S TOASTED!" So, indeed, is every other cigarette, but no other manufacturer had been shrewd enough to see the enormous possibilities of such a simple story. Hopkins, again, scored a great advertising coup when he wrote: "GETS RID OF FILM ON YOUR TEETH!" So, indeed, does every toothpaste.[104]

Thus we see – and of course we knew it all along – that nonrational sales techniques are available and are commonly employed by those who can afford the price.[105] We know that advertisements do much more than convey information so as to aid rational choice. We know that

the ads say, typically, "buy me and you'll overcome the anxieties I have just reminded you about," or "buy me and you will enjoy life," or "buy me and be recognized as a successful person," or "buy me and everything will be easier for you," or "come spend a few dollars and share in this society of freedom, choice, novelty and abundance."[106]

Marx may have exaggerated his own period when he wrote that "no eunuch flatters his tyrant more shamefully or seeks by more infamous means to stimulate his jaded appetite, in order to gain some favor, than does the eunuch of industry, the entrepreneur, in order to acquire a few silver coins or to charm the gold from the purse of his dearly beloved neighbor."[107] An exaggeration today? "Brooke Shields was fifteen when she made the still arresting Calvin Klein jeans ad: Legs splayed wide apart, she asked, 'You want to know what comes between me and my Calvins? Nothing.'"[108]

---

[104] Reeves (1961), quoted by Baran and Sweezy (1966, p. 129).

[105] By "nonrational sales techniques" I mean those that deviate from the ideal of supplying the consumer with that information, and only that, relevant to his making a rational decision about a purchase. Needless to say, there is nothing irrational or nonrational, from the point of view of the producer, in employing these techniques.

[106] Schudson (1984, p. 6). Or, as put by a German theorist, "an innumerable series of images are forced upon the individual, like mirrors, seemingly empathetic and totally credible, which bring their secrets to the surface and display them there. In these images, people are continually shown the unfulfilled aspects of their existence. The illusion ingratiates itself, promising satisfaction: it reads desires in one's eyes, and brings them to the surface of the commodity" (Haug, 1986, p. 52).

[107] *Economic and Philosophical Manuscripts of 1844*, in Fromm (1966, p. 141).

[108] Clark (1989, p. 115).

We may presume that these techniques are effective. If they are not, then the most sophisticated enterprises of modern capitalism must be indicted for awesome stupidity. But if they are effective, and if the producers in a competitive capitalist economy have little direct, conscious interest in promoting consumer well-being, then the invisible-hand argument can be saved only by a most untenable assumption: that the only commodities that people can be persuaded to buy – by either rational or nonrational means – are those that do in fact maximize well-being. Without this assumption one cannot conclude that Laissez Faire is efficient in promoting consumer well-being.

It is worth noting that the foregoing argument does not presume that producers are smart and consumers are stupid. But producers are likely to be more rational in the pursuit of their goal (selling their products) than consumers are in pursuing theirs (maximizing well-being). A sales project is a consciously undertaken venture with clearly defined criteria for success. Because it often involves considerable expense – and promises significant gains – it is carefully evaluated, often with the help of expert (and expensive) personnel.[109] (In 1985, General Motors and Ford spent nearly $1.4 billion in their advertising battles, and Pepsi and Coke more than $680 million in theirs. One Diet Coke commercial, shot at Radio City Music Hall, is reputed to have cost $1.5 million.)[110]

The consumer's project exhibits sharply contrasting features. The goal is less precise and is rarely aimed at consciously. Purchases tend to be made piecemeal, not as part of a coordinated plan. Moreover, they do not ordinarily involve sufficient expense to warrant expert advice.[111] The consumer is not helpless; he must, after all, be persuaded to buy. But the sales effort pursues its goal with considerably more rationality than the consumer pursues his. To the extent that success correlates with rationality, the producer has a decided advantage. (We might also take note of the fact that the consumer is targeted quite young, well before the onset of reason. Action for Children's Television has pointed out that advertisers spend more than $600 million per year selling to children on television and that children see about 20,000 thirty-second commercials each year.)[112]

---

[109] For a nice account of how advertising campaigns are planned, see Schudson (1984, ch. 2).

[110] Clark (1989, p. 27).

[111] Staffan Linder (1970) cites two studies, one showing that 50 percent of consumer purchases can be classified as impulse purchases, the other showing that even in the area of durable goods, "only about a fourth of [the] buyers displayed most of the features of deliberate decision-making – planning, family discussions, information seeking, as well as choosing with respect to price, brand and other specific attributes of the commodity" (Linder, 1970, p. 68).

[112] Clark (1989, p. 188).

I have argued that nonrational sales persuasion will render Laissez Faire inefficient. But there is a major problem with this argument, at least as it relates to the larger thesis of this book. I have gone on at length about nonrational sales persuasion under Laissez Faire. But Economic Democracy will also be a market economy; it will also rely on profit maximization, and so it will also harbor a tendency toward nonrational sales persuasion. Does not the argument against Laissez Faire apply full force against Economic Democracy as well?

That Economic Democracy will have a structurally generated tendency toward nonrational sales techniques cannot be denied. However – and this is the important point – *this tendency will be significantly weaker under Economic Democracy than under Laissez Faire*. Not all market economies are the same, not even with respect to market-induced behavior. Let me offer three reasons in support of that assertion.

First, our model shares an advantage with modern liberalism. Because we are not committed to Laissez Faire, we are not averse to regulating or barring certain techniques judged (by means of a suitably democratic procedure) to be immoral or offensive, nor are we averse to prohibiting the marketing of products that would seriously threaten health or safety. Under Laissez Faire, the government, democratic or not, must not impinge on economic freedom. Unlike the situation under Laissez Faire, we need not rely wholly on caveat emptor.

A second reason is more directly related to a specific feature of our model. Consider an aspect of Laissez Faire that is problematic even apart from its relation to the sales effort: the inability of workers to opt easily for a labor–leisure trade-off. This difficulty (along with many others) is assumed away in the standard neoclassical model, but it cannot be dismissed in our more realistic version. Under Laissez Faire I am quite free to alter the qualitative pattern of my consumption or my consumption–saving ratio. There are no institutional barriers to my doing so. If my taste shifts from apples to oranges, I go to the market and buy oranges instead of apples. If I want to cut my consumption by a quarter in order to save more, I simple spend less and deposit the remainder in my savings account. But what if I should prefer to consume one-quarter less, and work only six hours per day instead of eight? Do I notify my employer and come in the next day at ten o'clock instead of eight? Do I find another job like the one I have, except with six-hour shifts instead of eight?

And yet, without the availability of a labor–leisure trade-off, the system is not Pareto-optimal. If I am willing to consume somewhat less in exchange for a bit more leisure, then I can be made better off, and no one else worse off, if I am granted this option. In the standard neoclassical model, an employer would immediately acquiesce to this, because, full employment assumed, employers must attend carefully to the desires of their workers. In our more realistic model, employers are not likely to be so responsive.[113]

In addition to causing direct Pareto nonoptimality, the absence of a labor–leisure trade-off bears significantly on sales-effort inefficiencies. If a person has money, and little to do with it but spend it on consumer goods, he is particularly susceptible to the blandishments of an aggressive sales apparatus. And for the vast majority (in existing capitalist societies and presumably under Laissez Faire) this is precisely the situation. One can save instead of spend, but this is simply the choice to consume later instead of now.

It should be noted that this is not so for the wealthy. For the wealthy, saving is not simply the choice to consume later. If one has a large quantity of discretionary funds, then saving and investing have tangible benefits quite distinct from future consumption, because one can increase one's power, prestige, and influence by purchasing productive assets. One can avoid labor altogether by "putting one's money to work." But for the large majority, the only attractive alternative to consumption is leisure, and that is not a real option under Laissez Faire. So one might as well spend, now or later, on things that (one often truly knows) will not enhance well-being.

Under Economic Democracy the labor–leisure option will be a more realistic possibility. To be sure, one cannot simply come in at ten instead of eight. But because workers will democratically control the conditions of their work, a majority vote is all that will be needed to reduce the working day, or to allow some members greater flexibility in return for lower incomes. The labor–leisure choice is more than an abstract possibility when a forum exists for the presentation of one's case, and a majority vote is sufficient to effect a change. With leisure a genuine alternative, one's sales resistance is likely to increase, making rational consumption more probable.

Nonrational persuasion should be less troublesome under Economic Democracy than under Laissez Faire for yet a third reason. As we have seen, the worker-managed firm has less interest in expansion. This peculiar feature of our model – that it does not have a growth impera-

---

[113] For a more detailed presentation of this argument, backed up by original research, see Schor (1991). How much leisure we could have chosen is quite striking: "We [in the United States] could now produce our 1948 standard of living (measured in terms of marketed goods and services) in less than half the time it took that year. We actually could have chosen the four-hour day. Or a working year of six months. Or, *every worker in the United States could now be taking every other year off from work – with pay*" (Schor, 1991, p. 2); emphasis in original. Schor demonstrates further that the hours of work, contrary to what theorists had been predicting, have been steadily increasing over the past twenty years.

tive – has already been discussed in connection with allocative inefficiency and unemployment, but we are still far from having fully elaborated its significance.

A self-managed firm is less inclined to expand because growth usually entails taking on more workers, with whom the extra profits must be shared. Under constant returns to scale or declining costs, there exists no monetary incentive for a worker-managed firm to expand, whereas a profitable capitalist firm under these conditions will expand indefinitely. Thus a capitalist firm has a much stronger incentive to increase sales than does a worker-managed firm, and hence a much stronger motivation to put money and effort into selling. A self-managed firm is less motivated to advertise. It probably will have fewer means as well, because self-managed firms are likely to be smaller than their capitalist counterparts, and so have smaller advertising budgets to begin with.

There is yet another reason, distinct from the issue of nonrational sales persuasion, for awarding Economic Democracy higher marks for consumer sovereignty than Laissez Faire. This reason derives from public control of investment. Although the consumer is allegedly king under Laissez Faire, the fact of the matter is that products are initiated by producers, not by consumers; new tastes and new "needs" develop not in response to what consumers think they might want but in response to what producers think consumers might want – more accurately, in response to what producers think consumers might be persuaded to want. Although this dynamic does not disappear under Economic Democracy, it is attenuated by the previously discussed factors, and it is supplemented by community input into investment planning. Under Economic Democracy, but not under Laissez Faire, it is possible to mandate that certain products be encouraged. (It might be decided, for example, that investment funds should be made available to enterprises willing to set up on-premise day-care centers, or that more funds should be made available for the development of nonpolluting technologies.) Under Economic Democracy, but not under Laissez Faire, it becomes possible to talk and act collectively concerning anticipated wants and needs.[114] This is an enhancement of consumer sovereignty, because consumer choices are more likely to promote well-being if the array of available goods and services better approximates what one wants.

Let me conclude this discussion by raising an issue of a different sort, one that will muddy the waters a bit. I have argued that without the patently absurd assumption that the only products people can be persuaded (by any means) to buy are those that will maximize well-being, the case for the efficiency of Laissez Faire (in promoting well-being)

---

[114] For a good discussion of this issue, see Fraser (1989).

collapses. I have argued further that Economic Democracy should be less vulnerable (though not wholly immune) to the sorts of nonrational sales techniques that are at the heart of this problem.

The first argument is in fact an easy argument to make. Who would deny that the enormous effort that a contemporary capitalist society expends in creating desires is wasteful? Yet, curiously, this glaring efficiency defect of contemporary capitalism elicits little public or private criticism. Politicians talk endlessly about unemployment and about government waste, but not about the waste of resources that go into selling. Few people will defend the obviously manipulative character of much of the modern sales effort, and yet few people, publicly or privately, seem very upset about it. Most people probably would affirm the normative judgment that it is wrong to exploit the "intrapsychic mechanisms that are unknown to the individual," and yet few of us wax indignant when techniques that do just that are directed at us so as to persuade us to buy. It is worth asking: Why not?

At least part of the answer, I submit, is that we often enjoy being so manipulated. We rather enjoy being cajoled; we enjoy the energy and eroticism and good feeling invoked by sophisticated commercials. It all seems quite harmless, particularly because no one believes the content anyway. The literary critic Northrop Frye offers an arresting analysis: "Advertising can be taken as a kind of ironic game. Like other forms of irony, it says what it does not wholly mean, but nobody is obliged to believe its statements literally. Hence it creates an illusion of detachment and mental superiority even when one is obeying its exhortations."[115]

Do we or don't we "obey its exhortations"? Few of us feel manipulated, certainly not in an offensive manner, and the empirical evidence is inconclusive. So what is the problem? If we enjoy the feeling of mental superiority, and perhaps also an enhancement of self-esteem at being the focus of the seller's attention, not to mention the aesthetic, erotic, and humorous aspects of a good ad – and get free television to boot – why should we complain?

These reflections bear on our critique of the sales effort in the following sense: We have been assuming that the sales effort should be evaluated in terms of its effects on consumption, to wit, whether or not it induces the correct (i.e., welfare-maximizing) pattern of consumption. But we have not taken into account the possibility that the activity itself may be welfare-enhancing. Might it not be the case that even though the sales effort distorts an individual's consumption patterns from what would truly maximize that person's welfare, this distortion is more than compensated for by the general pleasure that the sales effort itself provides?

[115] Frye (1967, p. 26).

I find this claim highly implausible, but I must confess that I do not see how it can be definitively refuted. Let us be clear, though, about its status. We observe that this claim is not about "consumer sovereignty" – the assumption that consumer purchases maximize well-being. The analysis we have given negates the thesis that consumer sovereignty is likely to obtain under Laissez Faire, and with it the "proof" that Laissez Faire is optimally efficient. The new claim we are considering concedes that the sales effort undermines consumer sovereignty, but proposes that the deviation from overall well-being caused by the sales effort is more than compensated for by the overall pleasure this effort affords. This claim, of course, is purely conjectural. I do not see how to refute it, but I do not see how one can prove it either.[116]

We can say this: Because consumers have no choice as to how many of society's resources are devoted to the sales effort, there is no invisible hand tending to produce the optimal amount. (A firm will try to run a cost-effective sales campaign, but its "effectiveness" will be measured in terms of sales, not in terms of the pleasure given to those who experience the campaign.) There is clearly an invisible hand encouraging the development of ever more sophisticated techniques, encouraging also the expenditure of ever increasing sums to persuade people to buy things they do not need or had not even dreamed of wanting prior to the persuasive effort.

We can also assert with assurance that this invisible hand will be less insistent under Economic Democracy. We may conclude that Economic Democracy will allocate fewer of its human and material resources to the sales effort.[117] A sales effort – including nonrational persuasion – will persist under Economic Democracy, but it should be significantly less than the epic efforts under contemporary capitalism, which may be expected as well under Laissez Faire.

These considerations suffice to establish that consumer behavior is likely to be more rational under Economic Democracy than under Laissez Faire. Purchases are more likely to enhance long-range well-being. But I have

---

[116] One could sidestep the issue altogether and attack the sales effort by appealing to the normative principle of nonmanipulation: Whether or not people enjoy having various psychic buttons pushed, it should not be done. The sales effort fails to accord human beings the respect we deserve as rational agents. This response suffices to condemn the nonrational sales techniques of Laissez Faire (at least for those who accept the normative principle), but it does so by removing the issue from the efficiency framework within which the analysis of this chapter has proceeded.

[117] A sales effort will be present, but this is by no means undesirable. Consumers need to know what is available and why it is useful. It is also good, from the customer's point of view, that producers must put some effort into selling – a feature sadly lacking in Soviet-style command economies. Polish economist Wlodzimierz Brus (1972, p. 7) described the relationship between producer and consumer in a command economy as the producer's "terrorization" of the consumer.

not demonstrated that this gain will exceed the pleasure that a massive sales effort gives consumers. Those enchanted by TV commercials and shopping malls may as yet be unpersuaded. (In a recent survey, some 93 percent of American teenage girls listed shopping as their favorite pastime.)[118] This pleasure, however, must be set against the other benefits that can be expected from Economic Democracy, benefits beyond those of fuller employment and greater consumer rationality. To examine these, we must move beyond the efficiency framework of this chapter.

[118] Brown *et al.* (1991, p. 163).

4. Capitalism or socialism?: growth

There are difficulties with Laissez Faire, as we have seen. It is vulnerable to unemployment and to the emergence of a massive apparatus for nonrational sales persuasion. But the argument is far from over, for it is open to an advocate of Laissez Faire to counter with the claim that these difficulties, real though they may be, pale in the face of capitalism's stunning accomplishment: its unparalleled record of innovative growth. Whatever its faults, the advocate might say, capitalism has been and remains a remarkable engine of progress. To discard it would be idiotic. This is the issue we must now join. Our fixed-technology assumption, which has kept this question at bay, must now be dropped.

A serious investigation of the connection between capitalism and growth is as much an ethical inquiry as was our investigation of efficiency, and so it will also involve an appeal to values. We need not expand our basic list, but some qualifications are in order. Human happiness remains our touchstone. We continue to regard material goods as good, but we do not want to assume without question that more is necessarily better. We continue to assume that individuals are generally the best judges of their own well-being, but we shall have to consider more carefully just how individual preferences are to be aggregated into social choices. We shall encounter *democracy* in this chapter, but not yet as a distinctive value. Like equality, democracy is a value about which classical liberals have reservations, although fewer today than in times past. Contemporary conservatives are generally willing to concede democracy instrumental, if not intrinsic, value. For the arguments in this chapter, that will suffice. Hayek's judgment that "however strong the general case for democracy, it is not an absolute value and must be judged by what it will achieve" need not be disputed.[1]

To plunge into the growth issue, we might begin by asking if it can be proved that the investments of capitalist entrepreneurs generate optimal growth. Cambridge economist Maurice Dobb finds such a suggestion incredible: "Only myopic concentration upon stationary equilibrium could breed the supposition that there is even a *prima facie* case for regarding long-term investments under free-market constraints as optimal."[2] To be

---

[1] Hayek (1960, p. 106).
[2] Dobb (1969, p. 149). Joan Robinson is of a similar opinion: "What theory has ever been advanced of how private self-interest directs *new* investments into lines that best provide for the needs and desires of society as a whole?" (Robinson, 1976, p. 9).

sure, one can construct a formal proof if one makes the appropriate assumptions, but these assumptions do not pretend to even rough correspondence with reality. E. S. Phelps provides a typical list: Not only must a perfectly competitive equilibrium be attained (no mean condition itself, as we have seen), but also we must assume that

1. There is perfect information about current and future prices (including interest rates and wage rates) over the lifetime of the population and also perfect information about current and future supplies of public goods.
2. Producers have perfect information about current and future technology over the lifetime of the population.
3. There are no externalities of production.
4. Consumers have perfect information about current and future tastes over their lifetimes, and their preferences will be unchanging over time.
5. There are no externalities of consumption other than public goods whose production we take as given.[3]

It is obvious from this that we need not concern ourselves with formal proofs. But it is also plain, upon reflection, that formal proofs are not the real issue. Dobb's remark seems hyperbolic, for there most certainly is a prima facie case for capitalism: the empirical record of its accomplishments. Long before the "end of history" was proclaimed, defenders of capitalism pressed this point:

Judged solely by [economic] standards, it would seem that history has already awarded the contemporary rivalry to private capitalist enterprise. In all the statistical rankings of nations according to their accumulated wealth or per capita income, those which have fostered capitalism occupy the top positions on the list.[4]

An empirical argument such as this must be approached cautiously. We must be careful about the famous logical fallacy *post hoc ergo propter hoc*. The reign of capital may be contemporary with technical innovation and the rise of material prosperity, but are these phenomena causally linked? Temporal coincidence suggests a connection, but it also suggests connections between capitalism and the African slave trade, global imperialism, and the most destructive wars known to humanity – connections that proponents of capitalism presumably would call accidental. We must ask about the *structural features* of capitalism (Laissez Faire in particular, because that is the ideal we are investigating) that are conducive to innovation and growth.

Innovation, risk, and reward: the entrepreneurial spirit

The structures of Laissez Faire that promote growth are surely no mystery. Advocates will immediately point out that both competitive pressure

[3] Phelps (1970, p. 498).   [4] Monsen (1963, p. v).

and the hope of great gain encourage individual initiative and the taking of socially beneficial risks. Capitalism thus gives free rein to that "entrepreneurial spirit" that, in seeking out and transforming into reality new ideas for products and technologies, relentlessly stimulates the economy to innovative growth.

This is an extremely important argument; so let us approach it with some care. First, let us note that the core values to which it appeals are not unproblematic. Setting aside for now the question of growth itself, what about "innovation"?

It might seem odd even to raise this question. Few of our contemporary normative judgments would seem more settled than the judgment that the restless, creative spirit associated with this concept is an essential good. But this contemporary judgment was not always widespread. It seemed quite obvious to Plato (and most other ancient and medieval thinkers) that change was as likely to be for the worse as for the better.[5] For the Greeks, "new" was scarcely synonymous with "better." Paul Wachtel points to Goethe's handling of the Faust legend as representative of the asendancy of the new, "modern" sensibility. In contrast with earlier versions of the legend,

the overall sense one has of Faust in Goethe is clearly not of a villain but of a struggling hero. Faust is the man who *dares*. His virtue is our modern virtue: restlessness. In his wager with the devil it is the very insatiability of his desires, his conviction that he will never be satisfied, that he counts on above all. This is the great virtue, which God Himself endorses in Goethe's tale. The great sin to which the devil tries to tempt him is to enjoy, to be content, to find pleasure. What he must maintain, at the risk of his soul, is ceaseless activity, unbridled striving after achievement and new experience. He agrees that he should perish if ever at any moment he should say, "Tarry awhile, you are so fair."[6]

Having raised a question about the value of the innovative spirit, let me pull back, for I do not want to claim that this spirit is no longer needed. The last thing I want to suggest is that our present state is one of perfection, and hence in no need of change. But we should be clear that the innovative spirit is but one value, one that might conflict with other values (the need for stability, for example) and must be assessed in terms of the more basic value of human happiness.

The specific form of this spirit that concerns us here is the *entrepreneurial spirit*, the spirit associated with the taking of economic risks and with economic innovation (i.e., changes in the processes or products of production that benefit consumers). These two elements of the entrepreneurial spirit are distinct, not just conceptually, but often in practice. One can take an economic risk that is not particularly innovative (e.g., opening

[5] See Plato's account of the decline and fall of the perfect state, *The Republic*, Books VIII and IX.

[6] Wachtel (1983, p. 93).

a new restaurant or buying some shares of IBM); one can be economically innovative without much risk (e.g., working in a company's research laboratory). It is in the hope of promoting the latter element that the former is encouraged.

It can scarcely be denied that Laissez Faire gives great encouragement to the risk-taking element. George Gilder, prominent theorist of the New Right, in his rhapsody on the entrepreneur, observes that

some 4,700 small manufacturers are spawned in this country each week, while some 4,500 others fail. More than two-thirds of all ventures collapse within five years, and the median small businessman earns less than a New York City garbage collector. Of the thousands of plausible inventions, only scores are tested by business, and only a handful of these [achieve] economic success.[7]

One might see in all this activity – so much of it doomed – a remarkable lack of prudence and wonder about how bad ordinary jobs must be to induce so many people to take such risks. At the same time, one can scarcely deny that such "creative destruction" has its positive side, providing a capitalist economy with a continuing supply of economic innovations.

One might wonder if the stimulus to innovate here is optimal, if the risk element might not be excessive. But the more important question, surely, in light of recent history, is whether or not socialism can engender anything like this sort of spirit. If it cannot, then the choice is indeed stark: between a dynamic, innovative economy, admittedly with lots of problems, and an economy that, whatever its other virtues, is essentially stagnant. Not a happy choice, not at a time when "there are more hungry people in the world today than ever before in human history, and their numbers are growing."[8]

Several arguments are commonly put forth in support of the charge that socialist societies will be insufficiently innovative. The most common is the claim that a bureaucratic state, responsible for everyone's cradle-to-grave needs, kills off human initiative. Needless to say, whatever force this argument might have against certain forms of socialism, it has little against Economic Democracy. Economic Democracy will be a market economy. People's incomes will depend on how well their enterprises fare in competition with other enterprises.

A second argument is more technical and is directed specifically at worker-managed enterprises. It derives from James Meade's observation that

while property owners can spread their risks by putting small bits of their property into a large number of concerns, a worker cannot easily put small bits of his

---

[7] Gilder (1981, p. 296). I must confess that it is unclear to me why Gilder celebrates these facts, so obviously full of pain.
[8] World Commission on Environment and Development (1987, p. 29).

effort into a large number of different jobs. This presumably is the main reason we find risk-bearing capital hiring labour rather than risk-bearing labour hiring capital. Moreover, since labour cannot spread its risks, we are likely to find co-operative structures only in lines of activity in which the risk is not too great.[9]

The argument here is that capitalists will take more risks than workers, because capitalists can diversify their risks, whereas workers cannot. If workers borrow to finance their own enterprise, they put all their eggs in one basket. The general conclusion to be drawn is that an economy of worker-managed firms will be more risk-averse than will a capitalist economy – presumably more risk-averse than is socially desirable.[10] But notice, this argument assumes that when workers borrow, they must pay back the loan – hence the great risk. That is so for cooperatives in a capitalist economy and in certain models of market socialism, but not under Economic Democracy. Recall that an enterprise seeking to innovate or expand will receive a grant from its bank, not a loan. It will take on an additional obligation, namely, the tax on that grant, but the grant itself will not be repaid.

In effect, risk will be socialized even further under Economic Democracy than under capitalism. When an investment fails under capitalism, society loses, in that the labor and materials that went into the buildings and equipment that were constructed or purchased are, at least to some degree, wasted; workers in the enterprise lose, in that they lose their jobs or take pay cuts; capitalists lose, in that their money is gone. Under Economic Democracy, a bad investment will entail the same losses to society and to the enterprise's workers – but there are no capitalists to suffer. The peculiar risk that the capitalists take (of their money) will have been spread to society at large, because the fund from which the grants will derive will have been tax-generated.

I do not think one should conclude that firms under Economic Democracy will be more inclined to take risks. Because the long-range gains from an investment cannot be projected with any sort of precision, one would not expect a systematic bias. So long as the tax rate on capital assets is significantly positive, firms must be careful. Worker-managed firms and capitalist firms should make essentially the same risk–gain evaluations when considering a possible innovation.[11]

If we shift our attention from demand to supply, we find no systematic bias here either. There is no a priori reason to suppose that banks under Economic Democracy will be more or less prone to take risks than are banks or investors under capitalism, because the incomes of the grant

---

[9] Meade (1972, p. 426).
[10] See Jensen and Meckling (1979, pp. 481–4) for another rendition of this argument.
[11] This assertion will be slightly qualified later in light of the observed tendency of worker-managed firms to treat labor as a fixed cost.

officers will be tied to their making successful grants. Nor is there any reason to suppose that the size of the investment fund will be smaller under Economic Democracy than under Laissez Faire, or, for that matter, any larger. If banks have insufficient funds to cover the investment opportunities available, the fund can be increased by raising the tax rate. If the fund is too large, the rate can be cut. Unlike the situation under Laissez Faire, society will be able to make a conscious decision as to the size of its investment fund.[12]

So far we have been unable to come up with a good reason for thinking that Economic Democracy will be less innovative than Laissez Faire. There is no reason to think that the supply of investment funds will be less under Economic Democracy, nor any reason to think that self-managed firms will be more averse to taking risks. But we have yet to address a key motivational factor: the lure of great reward. High risk will inhibit innovation, but the absence of high risk does not guarantee a positive response. Capitalism not only is structured so as to allow investors to keep risks down (via diversification, and also limited liability) but also provides a positive incentive that seems to be lacking in Economic Democracy: the possibility of making a killing, of seeing one's investment double, triple, skyrocket in value. This possibility will not exist under Economic Democracy.

This argument is not so easily answered. It is indeed the case that the possibility of great individual wealth will be much less under Economic Democracy than under Laissez Faire. It will be argued in the next chapter that this is one of Economic Democracy's strengths. But it must be admitted that the possibility of great wealth is a spur to entrepreneurial activity.

Let us begin by thinking about what it is that we want the entrepreneurial spirit to accomplish. Above all, we want better processes of production, and we want better products – better in terms of promoting material well-being, which we presume to correlate positively with human happiness. Now, I take it as obvious that much of what is stimulated by the possibility of great gain under capitalism has little to do with promoting better processes or products. There are the high-stakes financial games so popular in the eighties: hostile takeovers, leveraged buy-outs, junk bonds, real-estate speculation, and the like.[13] There are the myriad products designed specifically to facilitate the nonrational sales techniques discussed in Chapter 3. There are the thousands upon thousands of small

[12] The governments of contemporary capitalist countries often try to increase investments by using such devices as investment tax credits and accelerated depreciation, but these are contrary to the spirit of laissez faire.
[13] I am not saying that such activities have no connection to the real economy, but the justificatory apologetics here are so transparent that they cannot be taken seriously.

businesses – restaurants, convenience stores, small retail outlets – that bloom and fade every year like dandelions.

This last item merits an aside. I do not deny that these small businesses serve useful purposes, but they involve precious little innovation, and often considerable exploitation of employees, family members, and the owners themselves, not to mention the high rate of heartbreaking, purse-breaking failure. I would not argue that such small "petty capitalist" concerns should be prohibited under Economic Democracy. It would make more sense to set a size limit (say ten employees). If the company grew larger than that, the workers would have the right to run the firm democratically.[14] These petty capitalists would be allowed to seek funds from private individuals and also from the community banks, although in the latter case they would have to pay back the loans.

It seems to me that such small enterprises have a role to play in a healthy, functioning community. They might even shed some of their worst features in a society that is committed to full employment and is economically more stable (as Economic Democracy, it will soon be argued, will be). But one would not expect them to be a significant source of innovations, no more so under Economic Democracy than under capitalism.

To return to the main argument: Much of what is stimulated in a capitalist society by the promise of riches has little to do with genuine innovation. But some of it does. An important part of it does. What can Economic Democracy offer as a substitute? Let us consider.

Under Economic Democracy, innovations can be expected to come from existing or newly formed cooperative enterprises, and also from basic research. We can expect more basic research to be funded under Economic Democracy than under Laissez Faire. Kenneth Arrow, some thirty years ago, called attention to the insufficiency of market forces in this regard:

Thus basic research, the output of which is only used as an informational input into other inventive activities, is especially unlikely to be rewarded. In fact, it is likely to be of commercial value to the firm undertaking it only if other firms are prevented from using the information. But such restriction reduces the efficiency of inventive activity in general, and will therefore reduce its quantity also.[15]

---

[14] Two issues come up here that I shall leave undeveloped: Should the owner be compensated? Must the workers exercise this right? As to the first question, it seems reasonable that the owner should be paid a fair price by the state for his assets, which now become social property. As to the second, I am inclined to argue that the important principle is the right of workers to form a cooperative, as opposed to the principle that all enterprises over a certain size should be self-managed. If workers wish to continue their status as wage laborers, they can be allowed to do so. I do not think we need fear a "creeping capitalism" here.

[15] Arrow (1962, p. 618).

Under Economic Democracy, expenditures for basic research would doubtless be one of the significant appropriations made by the national legislature (capital expenditures coming from the investment fund, and salaries of researchers from general tax revenues). The results of this research would be freely available to all enterprises.[16]

Basic research may be necessary to economic innovation, but it is by no means sufficient.[17] It is at least as important to have enterprises structured so as to take advantage of innovative possibilities. David Mowery and Nathan Rosenburg, in their careful study of this issue, call attention to such factors as on-sight research capabilities (so that enterprises can keep abreast of developments and see how these might fit with their processes and projects), a flexible work force, innovative ideas coming from below, and much horizontal communication.[18]

Mowery and Rosenburg give particularly high marks to Japanese firms in this regard, but anyone familiar with Mondragon cannot but be struck by how well it scores. Mondragon firms tend to be small, a factor not at all at odds with innovativeness. In fact, it has long been recognized that technical innovations tend to originate in small companies.[19] Because they are small, each firm does not have in-house research facilities, but the Mondragon complex itself has one (Ikerlan) to serve their collective needs.[20] The Mondragon work force would seem to be as flexible as the work force of a Japanese firm. Workers not only move about within their enterprises but also transfer from one cooperative to another when necessary. There is also much emphasis on continuing education.[21] Because the institutions of Economic Democracy are modeled on Mondragon (i.e., cooperative enterprises linked via second-degree cooperative banks), one would expect a similar capacity to innovate.

In capitalist societies, many of the process and product innovations originate within existing enterprises, but entrepreneurial individuals also play a role – individuals who set up new businesses that employ new processes or make new products of the sorts that constitute genuine advances in material well-being. Under Economic Democracy there will

---

[16] Government funding for basic research is, of course, a common feature of contemporary capitalism. This is consonant with the modern liberal models of capitalism (which we shall investigate later), but not with Laissez Faire.

[17] In point of fact, basic research need not be a major component in every country's budget – an important consideration for developing countries. As Mowery and Rosenburg (1989, p. 218) have observed, "it is easy to exaggerate the extent to which national economic growth depends on a first-rate domestic scientific research capability. This should not be terribly surprising. The fruits of scientific research have always been portable."

[18] Mowery and Rosenburg (1989, pp. 219–36).

[19] See Du Boff (1990, pp. 61–4).

[20] See Whyte and Whyte (1988, pp. 63–7). Ikerlan was begun in 1972 at Arizmendi's urging; in 1982 the Basque government agreed to provide half of the financing.

[21] See Whyte and Whyte (1988, pp. 150–6, 200–5).

also be a role for entrepreneurs, but their function, and hence the characteristics associated with that function, may be somewhat different.

Rather than speculate about this abstractly, let us consider how the entrepreneurial role is filled in Mondragon. Roy Morrison considers this role, which he calls "cooperative entrepreneurship," the core of the Mondragon model.[22] The emphasis is not so much on the individual entrepreneur as on the entrepreneurial group.

Attached to the Caja Laboral Popular is the Empresarial Division, charged with monitoring and assisting existing cooperatives and with creating new enterprises. It is this latter function that concerns us here. Many new firms are established in Mondragon by a process of hiving off from existing firms; others start from scratch. The former process has no counterpart under capitalism. The owners of a capitalist firm have no interest whatsoever in breaking up their enterprise into separate, independent entities. Efficiency considerations often dictate the "divisionalization" of a firm into semiautonomous units, but the units remain in the firm – with profits flowing to the owners. But for a self-managed firm, it makes good economic sense to separate into smaller units, so long as economies of scale are not sacrificed. The democratic, participatory character is enhanced in smaller firms (with, presumably, a gain in X-efficiency and, perhaps, a gain in innovative capability), and there is no loss to the members of the parent firm, because per-capita income is not affected. Moreover, all Mondragon firms remain linked through the central bank; so the success of a hived firm does not detract from, but indeed enhances, the security of the parent firm.

It seems likely that many new firms under Economic Democracy would begin, as they do in Mondragon, as units within a larger firm, from which they would separate. The associated bank's entrepreneurial division could provide advice and perhaps adjustment finance, as does the Empresarial Division in Mondragon. Others would be formed de novo. In Mondragon, in the creation of new firms from scratch, three elements are particularly striking. First, the process of formation usually is initiated from without (though sometimes there is recruitment): A group of people interested in starting up a new enterprise approach the Empresarial Division. They may have a product in mind, or they may ask for assistance from the section of the Empresarial Division that maintains a "product bank" of feasibility studies. Second, the project is carefully advised and monitored from the earliest stages until it reaches a break-even point, often six or seven years later. If the initiators prove to be ineffective, or the product unfeasible, the project is terminated. Third, in planning, labor is treated not as variable capital but as fixed. That is to say, it is assumed

---

[22] See Morrison (1991, pp. 111–34).

that additional workers, once brought into the enterprise, will not be laid off or fired. Unlike a capitalist enterprise, the new worker-managed enterprise cannot plan on varying its labor force as demand fluctuates. Planning is thus more "conservative" than under capitalism. This conservatism and the expert assistance that is made available doubtless account for the remarkable success rate of new Mondragon cooperatives: only three failures ever.[23]

Why do small groups of people want to undertake the surely anxious task of setting up a new enterprise? So far as I know, no data have been gathered on the Mondragon "entrepreneurs." Morrison suggests that "the initiative for a new co-op may come from a group motivated by the challenge and excitement of beginning a new enterprise or by the need for jobs and community development in their region."[24] Are such motivations sufficient? Will they continue to be sufficient for Mondragon? Would they be sufficient for a general system of Economic Democracy? In the case of Mondragon, some concern has been expressed by co-op leaders about "an apparent slackening of the entrepreneurial drive among young Basques."[25] As for Economic Democracy, it is impossible to say.

But I hasten to add: Should a reliance on spontaneous entrepreneurial drive prove to be inadequate, various combinations of monetary incentives and nonmonetary enabling mechanisms could be instituted by concerned communities to supplement nonmonetary incentives. Business- and engineering-school programs to emphasize entrepreneurial skills could be instituted. (Psychologist David McClelland has long insisted that such skills, as well as motivations, can be enhanced by careful training.)[26] Substantial financial prizes could be given to individuals or groups who succeed in launching successful enterprises. One could even go so far as to allow firms to be run as capitalist enterprises, with all profits going to the initiators, until a certain size is reached or a certain time period has elapsed, at which point they would be nationalized (with compensation), and then turned over to the workers.[27] Here, as in many other instances, flexibility is important. Communities should have the leeway to experiment. Economic Democracy, it should be clear, has a structure that allows decentralized experimentation to be readily undertaken.

[23] Ibid., p. 174.   [24] Ibid., p. 117.
[25] Whyte and Whyte (1988, p. 81). In Mondragon, not only the Empresarial Division but also individual firms attempt to encourage potential entrepreneurs.
[26] See McClelland and Winter (1969) for a detailed account of one project. See McClelland (1984, ch. 17) for a survey of the literature.
[27] John Roemer (1991), in his model of market socialism, makes this proposal. Roemer's model, which differs significantly from Economic Democracy, will be analyzed in Chapter 8.

Can we conclude from the foregoing analysis that Economic Democracy will be as innovative as Laissez Faire? I hesitate to say yes. Both systems can be expected to be innovative, but I do not see how we can predict with any confidence which system will provide the greater stimulation for innovation. But that is not the important question anyway. To try at this point to determine which will be more innovative would be to rush past a vital issue. A defense of capitalism based on its ability to motivate economic growth presupposes that the innovative growth of the kind produced by capitalism is a good to be maximized. It presupposes that an alternative society should strive to equal or surpass such growth. But such presuppositions are far from self-evident. A deeper analysis is in order, to which we now turn.

What kind of growth?

Anyone who regularly reads the financial papers or business weeklies would conclude that the world is in reasonably good shape and that long-term economic trends are promising. . . . Yet on the environmental front, the situation could hardly be worse. Anyone who regularly reads scientific journals has to be concerned with the earth's changing physical condition. Every major indicator shows a deterioration in natural systems: forests are shrinking, deserts are expanding, croplands are losing topsoil, the stratospheric ozone layer continues to thin, greenhouse gases are accumulating. – *State of the World 1991*

To address the question of growth, let us distinguish the qualitative aspect from the quantitative. In this section we shall consider the kind of growth; in the next we shall look at the rate. Two kinds of growth are most often singled out by critics of capitalism as problematic: the paradoxical growth common in the Third World that seems to increase rather than diminish poverty, and the growth that seems to threaten our planet's ecological balance. These specific tendencies, we shall see, are concrete manifestations of more abstract difficulties with Laissez Faire. Let us first survey the abstract terrain before turning our attention (somewhat cursorily) to the concrete issues.

Objections to the specific products and technologies generated by Laissez Faire are not unfamiliar. Economists themselves have long pointed out that "externalities" or "neighborhood effects" render certain market transactions nonoptimal. When a transaction affects others than those directly involved, either positively or negatively, the market mechanism does not give an accurate account of costs and benefits. Environmental deterioration is the commonly cited example. The costs to a community of air pollution are not reflected in the free-market price of commodities produced by a highly polluting technology. If two technologies yield the same marketable output, but the cleaner technology is more costly, the producer has a powerful economic incentive to select the more polluting one. Because the market neither encourages the development of low-polluting technologies nor thwarts the development of high-polluting ones, technologies tend to evolve in a nonoptimal manner.

Production externalities force Laissez Faire growth away from optimality. So do consumption externalities. These present even deeper problems for classical liberalism (and for capitalism generally), problems less amenable to simple reform. A basic assumption of neoclassical economics is that an individual's consumption is a private matter affecting only herself. This, of course, is manifestly untrue in a large number of cases. The decision of my neighbor to buy beer in disposable bottles has consequences that affect me: an increase in litter, a decline in the natural resources available to my children, a rise (eventually) in the cost of municipal waste treatment. The private decisions of many individuals to buy automobiles instead of horses changed the physical and social structures of continents – for those who purchased them and for those who did not.

At issue here is something other than unforeseen consequences, a difficulty from which no social system can hope to be immune. (To foresee the effects of disposable bottles is scarcely beyond the power of the human mind.) In a free-market economy, the collective effects of new consumption patterns follow from major investment decisions, and investment decisions fall within the "private" sphere, outside the democratic process. In most cases, citizens are not even aware of these decisions until long after they have been made. (Disposable bottles, unbeckoned, appear. People buy them. Soon enough refillables vanish.)[28]

After the decisions have been made, and after their effects have been felt, political action is possible (if we assume for a moment that political action regarding a free-market response to consumer preference is not ruled out of court by classical liberalism), but by then the context has been altered significantly. When investment decisions have solidified into brick and steel and have given jobs to many people, the moral as well as physical environment has shifted. Bottle companies are not wrong to appeal to the human sacrifice involved in reconverting plants, in laying off workers, in rupturing old habits – moral considerations that would not have applied when the decisions were originally made.

Individual action – refusing to buy – is also possible under capitalism. This is the response much preferred by classical liberalism, but individual action has even less chance of success. As Sen's "isolation paradox" demonstrates, the very logic of individual decision making is

[28] I introduced the beer-bottle example earlier (Schweickart, 1980). At that time it was still possible to choose between returnable and disposable bottles for beer and soft drinks. Since then, the market has worked its magic. Few have this option today.

different from that of collective choice.[29] When confronted as an individual consumer with the option of buying a six-pack of beer in disposable bottles, I might well decide that the convenience is worth the disutility, the latter being the effect on the environment of six more bottles. Confronted with the analogous choice in a political context, however, I might decide – without any logical or moral inconsistency – that the convenience of disposable bottles is not worth the disutility, for now the option is an environment free of disposable bottles. It follows that a society of quite rational people, all of whom would prefer a litter-free environment to the convenience of disposable bottles, might well find themselves inundated anyway – if they allow the market to effect the decision. Such an outcome clearly is not optimal, not even in terms of the individual's own preferences.[30]

The problem here (called by some the "tyranny of small decisions")[31] is not confined to beer bottles:

Purchase of books at discount stores eventually removes the local bookshop. Yet book buyers can never exercise a choice as between cheaper books with no bookshop and dearer books with one. The choice they are offered is between books at cut price and books at full price; naturally, they take the former. The effective choice of continuance of a bookshop at the expense of dearer books is never posed. Everyone has the choice of living in the city as it is or in the suburb as it is, but not between living in the suburb and the city as they *will be* when the consequences of such choices have been worked through. The house in the suburbs appears desirable in itself (just like the lower price tag on the book). Whether its attractions outweigh the subsequent deterioration of suburban amenities and perhaps the effective destruction of the city, which this choice in company with other people's carries in its train, is never put to the test.[32]

As these cases make quite clear, a market determination of investment decisions is not always preferable to a political determination. Of course, one should not conclude that it never is. Even apart from the fact that it would be impossible in practice for votes to be taken on every investment choice, it is by no means evident that if some people want hula hoops or digital watches or anchovies on their pizzas, then the community should decide. Democratic decision making has drawbacks of its own, among them time consumption, a bureaucratic tendency, and the possibility of a "tyranny of the majority," which must be balanced against

[29] This paradox is the "prisoner's dilemma" extended to an n-party world. See Sen (1961, pp. 479–95).

[30] We see here the logical fallacy of blaming consumers for the deleterious effects of many contemporary developments. What we get is not necessarily what we want, nor what we would have chosen had the alternatives been differently posed. Macroscopic outcomes need not reveal the preferences of even quite rational consumers.

[31] By Fred Hirsch (1976), following Alfred Kahn (1966).

[32] Hirsch (1976, p. 40).

the "tyranny of small decisions."[33] What is plainly required for optimal growth is a suitable mix of consumer sovereignty and citizen sovereignty.

Externalities of production and consumption are not the only drawbacks to Laissez Faire growth. It is widely recognized by economists that if investment projects are not coordinated, then growth will not be balanced, in which case potential profitability will not reflect social desirability. As noted long ago by Scitovsky:

> Only if expansion in the ... industries were integrated and planned together would the profitability of investment in each of them be a reliable index of its social desirability.... Complete integration of all industries would be necessary to eliminate all divergence between private profit and public benefit.[34]

The reason for this is easy to illustrate. Suppose, at given market prices, new housing looks highly profitable. Investments will flow into this area, creating a sharp increase in demand for building materials, and consequently a rise in their prices. But this makes housing less profitable, and so some construction is halted, and investment funds are shifted toward building-materials enterprises instead. This process clearly involves a degree of waste that could have been avoided had coordinated investment decisions channeled funds simultaneously into housing construction and the building-materials industries.

The projected profitability in the foregoing example overstates the economic desirability of a particular type of investment. In other cases it understates it (e.g., when a new technique reduces the costs of intermediate goods). In either case, deviation from optimality occurs that is not due to random acts of nature or unpredictable changes in consumer preferences, but to a lack of coordination among decision-makers.

This defect can be and often is mitigated somewhat under capitalism by the collection and dissemination of information by government and private agencies and also by the integration of independent firms into single corporations. This latter movement, however, with its tendency toward monopoly, is scarcely an unmixed blessing. The former is hampered by the sharp separation, under capitalism, between the public sector and the private sector. If a decision is made to locate a plant in a particular

---

[33] Social decision making is beset with theoretical difficulties that have occupied much attention since the publication of Kenneth Arrow's celebrated "impossibility theorem." Arrow (1951) proved that if one wants a procedure for ranking alternatives that is "rational" (i.e., transitive, reflexive, and complete over an unrestricted domain), that is unaffected by "irrelevant alternatives," and that is reflective of individual preferences (at least to the extent that one state of affairs will be more highly ranked than another if everyone prefers it), then the only possibility is dictatorship. Neither majoritarian democracy nor any other voting mechanism will suffice. We shall not concern ourselves with Arrow's result, because that result, quite unlike the "tyranny of small decisions," has no practical bearing on the issue at hand – or on any other real-world matter, so far as I can tell.

[34] Scitovsky (1954, p. 149).

area, then investments should be made not only in the raw-materials industries serving the plant but also in housing for the workers, in power and sewage facilities, and so forth. The market mechanism sometimes produces these results. If an entrepreneur decides to locate a plant in a particular region, and if he pays his employees enough to generate a demand for new housing, then housing will eventually be constructed. And if the tax base is sufficiently increased, social services may be increased also. These developments might follow, but then again they might not. An alternative scenario is not unknown: People flock to the source of new jobs; housing, schools, and public services become overloaded; social conditions deteriorate; the plant moves elsewhere, abandoning the community.

The sharp separation of public investment and private investment has many other consequences. To cite one of Galbraith's frequently quoted observations from the late 1950s:

The family which takes its mauve and cerice, air-conditioned, power-steered, and power-braked automobile out for a tour passes through cities that are badly paved, made hideous by litter, blighted buildings, billboards and posts for wires that should long since have been put underground. They pass on into a countryside that has been rendered largely invisible by commercial art. . . . They picnic on exquisitely packaged food from a portable icebox by a polluted stream and go on to spend the night at a park which is a menace to public health and morals. Just before dozing off on an air mattress beneath a nylon tent, amid the stench of decaying refuse, they may reflect vaguely on the curious unevenness of their blessings.[35]

Laissez Faire thus founders on the shoals of externalities and unbalanced growth, the latter exacerbated by the public–private distinction regarding the sources of investment funding. These factors puncture the claim that the profitability of an investment measures its social utility. So, too, does a third factor. If balanced growth and an absence of externalities are necessary for private profitability to reflect social desirability, so, too, is an equitable distribution of wealth. Because projected profitability is based on a survey of dollar votes, a misallocation of income will misallocate not only the existing consumer goods but also the funds for those investment projects designed to increase consumer goods in the future.

I have not yet argued that the distribution of wealth under Laissez Faire is inequitable. (That is one of the tasks for the next chapter.) But setting aside the question of justice, it is not difficult to see how an inegalitarian distribution of wealth (justified or not), when coupled with Laissez Faire, can lead to the paradoxical phenomenon mentioned at the beginning of this section: growth that generates poverty. The scenario is

[35] Galbraith (1958, pp. 199–200).

familiar and important. Consider a poor country in which a small minority own most of the land. The farm workers grow crops that feed the population and provide the landowners a handsome profit. Suppose the landowners decide to invest, rather than simply consume, this profit (that is, to act as capitalists rather than as traditional landowners). It is pointless to increase the production of basic foodstuffs, because the population is too poor to pay for increased consumption. But there exist vast numbers of people in rich countries willing to pay for special crops – coffee, chocolate, bananas, nuts, sugar, vegetables out of season, fast-food beef – and so investments are made to convert to export crops. The supply of basic foods decreases, prices go up, and poor people eat less. Because the new agriculture usually is more capital-intensive than the old, there is also less employment. The country is now richer (the new crops generating more revenue than the old), but more people are poorer. The market (combined with private property and wage labor) has again worked its magic.

In theory, of course, this extra revenue could be used to make the poor better off than before, but that is hardly to be expected under Laissez Faire. The increase belongs to the rich. The state has no right to interfere. As Adam Smith has reminded us, we cannot count on benevolence in economic dealings.[36] So the more likely course is more of the same: more investment in export crops, more poverty, and more dependence on the vagaries of the world market. There is no invisible hand to call a halt.

Needless to say, the actual evolutions of Third World economies are vastly more complicated than this simple model suggests, but the model points to a tendency that is clearly perverse. This perversity is often amplified by other considerations. The shift to "agribusiness" can also have severe ecological and even gender consequences. As physicist-feminist-ecologist Vandana Shiva points out, in most of the Third World, traditional agriculture – and the complex knowledge associated with it – has been an important source of women's power. But now

the worldwide destruction of the feminine knowledge of agriculture, evolved over four to five thousand years, by a handful of white male scientists in less than two decades has not merely violated women as experts; since their expertise in agriculture has been related to modelling agriculture on nature's methods of renewability, its destruction has gone hand in hand with the ecological destruction of nature's processes and the economic destruction of the poorer people in rural areas.[37]

The structural tendency toward growth that intensifies poverty, present in many forms of Laissez Faire, would not exist under Economic

---

[36] "Nobody but a beggar chooses to depend chiefly on the benevolence of his fellow-citizens" [Smith, 1976, p. 27 (I.ii.2)].
[37] Shiva (1989, p. 105). Shiva's extended argument for this claim is profound and compelling.

Democracy. There are two basic reasons for this, one connected to the cooperative dynamic, the other to the investment mechanism. First, if certain cooperatives turned successfully to export production, the gains would tend to diffuse throughout society. Because nobody would be laid off, aggregate demand would go up with income. Workers in the export sectors would have more to spend, thus increasing the demand (presumably) for basic foods, which in turn would lead to higher prices and hence higher incomes for the basic-food producers. Basic-food production would then be more profitable than before, and so there would be less pressure to convert more land to export production. The invisible hand would have given a pull in the right direction.

If the profit that can be made by producing for export remains much larger than what can be made by producing for home consumption, many more cooperatives will want to convert. But to do so, they will need investment funds, which, recall, will be tax-generated, and hence subject to democratic control. Various public bodies will be in position to coordinate (and perhaps ration via higher tax rates) the investment grants given out for export conversion, if it is deemed undesirable to shift away from food self-sufficiency. The invisible hand will thus be supplemented by the visible hand of democratic control.

Let us consider now the other often-remarked defect of Laisssez Faire growth. This is not the place for a full-blown analysis of the various environmental crises now upon us (which are not unrelated to the poverty issue just discussed),[38] but it will be a useful exercise to compare Laissez Faire and Economic Democracy regarding their ability to cope with one serious environmental threat. Let us consider the massive overload that industrial societies are placing on the regenerative capacity of the planet's atmosphere. How do we deal with air pollution?

"Air pollution" encompasses more than the familiar smog; I mean the term to include also the three great, invisible specters – acid rain, upper-atmospheric ozone depletion, and the "greenhouse effect" – all occasioned by the buildup of various gases, primarily sulfur dioxide in the first case, chlorofluorocarbons in the second, and carbon dioxide in the third.[39] As with most ecological problems, the larger causes are complex and interconnected. Among other things, air pollution relates to energy policy, which relates to transportation policy (automobile exhaust is a major source of carbon dioxide and other harmful emissions), which

[38] See Tietenberg (1990), Shiva (1989), and World Commission on Environment and Development (1987).

[39] For a careful, accessible, distressing analysis of these interconnected phenomena by a scientist from the National Center for Atmospheric Research, see Firor (1990). "It may well be that the real tragedy of air pollution is not that it will kill us, but that it won't; we will adjust to the changes and forget the possibilities that disappeared with the earlier world" (Firor, 1990, p. 107).

relates to how our cities are structured. How might we get a grip on these interrelated concerns?

Let me begin with two observations. The first is that strict Laissez Faire cannot even pretend to deal with these problems. The second is more surprising: A modified Laissez Faire would seem to be able to do whatever Economic Democracy can do. I shall conclude by arguing that what seems to be is not so.

Strict Laissez Faire requires that government keep it hands off the economy: The government should protect the country from being preyed upon by other countries, and citizens from preying upon one another. The fundamental duty of government is to protect property (including each individual's property in his own person).[40]

Consider now the question of air pollution. What steps might we take to rein it in? Here is a partial listing, drawn from suggestions and recommendations in *State of the World 1991*:

1. Stop subsidizing industries and technologies that are polluting.
2. Ban or set strict limits on the discharge of certain substances into the atmosphere.
3. Enact an effluent tax, a per-unit charge on harmful emissions set high enough to discourage heavy polluters and to reward countermeasures.
4. Impose a carbon tax, an energy tax on all carbon-based fuels.
5. Undertake serious reforestation.
6. Shift away from an automobile-dominated transportation system by (a) upgrading interurban rail service and (b) restructuring cities to make them people-, bicycle-, and tram-friendly, auto-unfriendly.[41]

Of all these measures, strict Laissez Faire can countenance only the first. All the other measures involve government interference with the economy. Because the air belongs to no one, no one can claim a property-right violation by its defilement.[42] The strict laissez-fairist's hands are tied. Nothing can be done beyond ending subsidies, which, although by no means insignificant,[43] falls far short of what is needed.

The argument just given will not do as a serious critique of strict Laissez Faire, because no contemporary conservative takes so strict a

---

[40] The classic formulation of this notion is to be found in John Locke's *Second Treatise on Government*.

[41] Brown et al. (1991, ch. 2–4).

[42] Theorists of a libertarian bent (the contemporary position that comes closest to advocating strict Laissez Faire) often try to concoct a property-rights case against pollution using the argument that if your pollution causes me lung cancer, then you have indeed violated one of my fundamental rights. See Nozick (1974, pp. 79–80). The problem, of course, is that in practice it is impossible to say exactly whose pollution caused specific harm to my lungs, exactly whose pollution did how much damage to the ozone layer, etc.

[43] The role of governments and international agencies in promoting "development" schemes that wreak havoc on the atmosphere (above all, energy subsidies and policies that encourage deforestation) should not be underestimated. See Shiva (1989).

hands-off view. Not even Adam Smith maintained so stringent a position. Indeed, he held it a *duty* of government to erect and maintain those facilities that, "though they may be in the highest degree advantageous to a great society," will not be provided by the market.[44] Smith had in mind "good roads, bridges, navigable canals, harbours, etc.," but the principle – that government must provide what the market will not – applies as readily to negative externalities as to positive ones. This has long been recognized. One should not be surprised to find Milton and Rose Friedman acknowledging that "the preservation of the environment and the avoidance of undue pollution are real problems and they are problems concerning which the government has an important role to play. . . . When the costs and benefits or the people affected cannot be [readily] identified, there is a market failure."[45]

If what we are calling Laissez Faire is to represent the modern conservative ideal, we must not interpret Laissez Faire so strictly as to rule out those government measures that neoclassical economics itself countenances. We may presume a certain reluctance on the part of a conservative to endorse government intervention whenever and wherever there is market failure, but we should not tie his hands completely. Milton Friedman's position may be taken as representative of the (modified) Laissez Faire position:

> In any particular case of proposed intervention, we must make up a balance sheet, listing separately the advantages and disadvantages. Our principles tell us what items to put on one side and what items on the other, and they give us some basis for attaching importance to the different items. In particular, we shall always want to enter on the liability side of any proposed government intervention, its neighborhood effect in threatening freedom, and give this effect considerable weight.[46]

If we look back at our list of pollution remedies, it is clear that none of them are in essential conflict with Laissez Faire principles thus understood. Conservatives instinctively oppose the outright banning of products, appealing to consumer freedom,[47] but if the danger is as clear and present as, say, chlorofluorocarbons are to the ozone layer, they can assent to such measures. Effluent and energy taxes are not problematic at all to a neoclassical conservative, because these are merely attempts to bring market prices into line with real costs (including costs to the environment), nor are reforestation projects, because these can be thought of as public works, justified by positive externalities. The shift away from

---

[44] Smith [1976, p. 723 (V.i.c.1)].

[45] Friedman and Friedman (1980, p. 214).   [46] Friedman (1962, p. 32).

[47] Recall that the term "conservative" is used throughout this work to designate economic conservatism, not social conservatism. The former is libertarian in orientation. The latter, which is eager to ban many things (most having to do with sex, drugs, or rock and roll), is not.

automobiles, at least insofar as this is a consequence of taxes and public works that compensate for externalities, can also be supported.

But if this analysis is correct, are there any reasons for thinking that Economic Democracy might better deal with the air-pollution problem? Are there any structural features of Economic Democracy to which we might point? The vague (or acute) feeling that people who are anticapitalist are more likely to be proenvironment will not do, certainly not with the environmental record of Eastern Europe now plainly in view.[48]

A decisive affirmative answer to these questions becomes evident only if we look at the problem not from above (i.e., from the point of view of national legislation) but from below. Let us start with a factory. To the extent that emissions affect the workers directly on the job (as they often do), we can expect a self-managed firm to pollute less. Workers will control the technology; it will not be imposed on them from without.

To the extent that emissions affect the local community, they are likely to be less severe, for two reasons. First, workers (unlike capitalist owners) will necessarily live nearby, and so the decision-makers will bear more of the environmental costs directly. Second – this is very important – a self-managed firm will not be able to avoid local regulation by running away (or by threatening to do so). The great stick that a capitalist firm holds over the head of a local community will be absent. Hence absent will be the macrophenomenon of various regions of the country trying to compete for firms by offering a "better business climate" (i.e., fewer environmental restrictions).

Not only will local firms not run away, but fresh capital will not avoid the region. The tax-generated investment fund will be apportioned to regions per capita; regions will not compete for funds. It can be expected that those firms immediately affected by tougher emission standards or higher effluent taxes will protest, and not without reason, because their incomes will be adversely affected, but it can also be expected that investment grants to cover the costs of upgrading to a cleaner technology will be forthcoming from the community investment fund. To the extent that those communities where their competitors are located follow suit in establishing tougher emission standards or higher effluent taxes (again, more likely than under capitalism, because their firms cannot run away either), the relative disadvantage suffered by the firms first affected will dissipate.[49]

We can draw two conclusions thus far: Self-managed firms will be less likely to pollute in the first place than are their capitalist counterparts,

[48] For one horrific account, see Brown et al. (1991, ch. 6).
[49] It should be recalled also that a competitive disadvantage will be less likely to lead to bankruptcy for a firm under Economic Democracy than under capitalism, because the competing firms will be less expansionary.

and if they do, such legislative remedies as measures 1–4, listed earlier, are more easily implemented locally.

With respect to measures 5 and 6, the single most important difference between Laissez Faire and Economic Democracy is that the latter will not have the sharp distinction between public and private in regard to investment funds.

Under Laissez Faire (and capitalism generally), public and private investments are strictly segregated. Funds for the former are tax-generated, and apportioned politically. Funds for the latter are enticed from individuals and are apportioned privately. At no point is a democratic body, at any level, in a position to decide as follows: This is what we have to invest; this much we want to go to public capital expenditures, and this much to private capital formation.

Not only are the two investment flows segregated, but under Laissez Faire, private investment leads public investment. That is to say, private investment funds are generally easier to obtain in the first place; moreover, if they are not obtained, public investment also suffers.

Private investment is cajoled from the wealthy by promising not only that they will get their investment back but also that they will get back more than they laid out. Public investment, by contrast, can be obtained only by persuading the lower and middle classes (for the most part) to give up for the "common good" a portion of what they consider to be their hard-earned income – quite often to repair the damage done by private investment. Not surprisingly, the former funds are more easily generated than the latter. Not surprisingly, the public sector is more often strapped for funds (apart from those segments serving powerful capitalist interests, e.g., military contractors and the highway lobby).

Moreover, as we shall see more clearly in a later section of this chapter, the health of a Laissez Faire economy depends on private investors investing. If they do not, we get a recession, which not only places major strains on public safety-net programs but also causes tax revenues to fall.

Consider now the impact of these differences in investment mechanisms on air-pollution-abatement measures 5 and 6. Consider reforestation. Reforestation is a capital investment; so under Economic Democracy, funds for this will come from the investment fund. The local (or state or national) legislature can set aside a portion of this fund for that purpose. Of course, this will diminish the amount available for new cooperative investment, and so the pros and cons must be weighed.

Three points should be noted here. First, the choice is differently posed than under capitalism. To free up funds for reforestation does not require that we cut other government programs or raise taxes. We have a third option: shifting investment funds from the cooperative sector.

Second, a contraction in funds for new cooperative investment does not spell recession, because it is automatically offset by an increase in public investment. Third, if such environmental investment puts too great a strain on the investment fund, it is open to a community to supplement this fund with other tax revenue – perhaps from the effluent or energy tax.

None of these considerations, or even all taken together, can guarantee that more money will be allocated for reforestation under Economic Democracy than under Laissez Faire. Decisions will be democratically reached; so we cannot predict their outcomes with certainty. But it is clear, I think, that the choice will be more rationally posed under Economic Democracy. It is not presupposed that the private-sector (or cooperative-sector) investment will come first.

Consider one final element of the pollution-abatement package: inter-city rail transport and intracity electric mass transit (a key element of city restructuring). It is easy to see here the damage done by the separation under capitalism between public investment and private investment, although in this case the problem is not one of too little public funding, but of sectoral imbalance. Under Economic Democracy, capital funding for roads, railway tracks, and electric-tram grids will are be on a par. All will come from the same source. Because roads are provided as a public good, so, too, should railway lines and tram grids.[50] Because all capital allocations will be from the same fund, the community will have control over developmental priorities. It may, if it so chooses, shift away from "autocracy"[51] by allocating relatively more capital funds to the rail and mass-transit sectors, coupling these allocations with funding for the construction of bicycle paths, bicycle parking, and pedestrian amenities. It may also encourage the integration of housing construction with enterprise placement, so that people can live nearer their places of work. Such comprehensive, locally initiated planning[52] obviously will be more feasible when the community has the kind of control over the investment fund that it will have under Economic Democracy, but not under Laissez Faire.[53]

---

[50] Whether the railroads and urban mass-transit systems should be run as public enterprises or should be self-managed, profit-making cooperatives can be determined by the relevant legislatures.

[51] Kenneth Schneider's term (Schneider, 1971).

[52] For many more ideas on restructuring cities to make them ecologically sound, see Gordon (1990).

[53] By way of stark contrast, see David St. Clair's balanced, well-researched, deeply disturbing account (St. Clair, 1986) of the destruction of the thriving mass-transit systems in the United States by General Motors and its various accomplices and front organizations. In an Economic Democracy, an outside company will not be allowed to come in, buy out a transit system, wreck it (by converting to far less efficient buses), and then sell off the remains. See also Kwitney (1981).

Perhaps the most surprising result of the foregoing analysis is that the main advantage of Economic Democracy over Laissez Faire with respect to air pollution and many other environmental issues is not so much its greater legitimacy in overriding market criteria, nor even its greater degree of planning (both of which are often thought to be the major virtues of socialism), but rather the increased control over these matters afforded to local communities.

As we have seen, there are few environmental measures that a democratic citizenry would be inclined to undertake that would be ruled out, in principle, by (modified) Laissez Faire. But precisely because capital is so mobile under Laissez Faire, few of these measures could be implemented locally, at least not without far more extensive compromises with local business interests than would be necessary under Economic Democracy. Hence, environmentalists must turn to the national government, which must draft national legislation. But (as conservatives are the first to point out) such legislation, precisely because of its scope, cannot be finely tuned to local conditions, and so it often generates much local opposition.

There is a great irony here: The socialism of Economic Democracy will give far more control to local communities than can the capitalism of Laissez Faire. I take this to be an extremely important point, for it is increasingly recognized by ecologists that the large-scale projects that can be undertaken only by national governments directly, or with significant national-government subsidies (nuclear power plants, coal gasification, giant hydroelectric facilities, large-scale irrigation projects, interstate highway systems), are often the projects most damaging to the environment. To be sure, national governments and international agencies must play active roles in grappling with the serious, perhaps catastrophic, problems we now face, but it is extremely important that we allow space for local initiatives to flourish. Economic Democracy will provide such space – much more than Laissez Faire does.

How fast to grow?

Marx says that revolutions are the locomotives of world history. But the situation may be quite different. Perhaps revolutions are not the train ride, but the human race grabbing for the emergency brake. – Walter Benjamin

Let us turn from the qualitative dimensions of growth to the quantitative. It will be impossible to keep these aspects rigidly separate, but for now let us assume that the kinds of investments made under Laissez Faire are not problematic. Let us assume that the goods and services produced have no serious externality effects and are produced in balanced proportions unskewed by an inequitable distribution of income.

Even with these assumptions it does not follow that maximal growth is desirable. In fact, it is not clear what "maximal growth" means, because production involves resource and labor costs. At the very least, "maximal" is subject to the proviso that the future remain open, that resources not be so used that future generations will have no future. It must also be qualified – to the point that the term "maximal" is inappropriate – by reference to labor time. If people work sixteen-hour days, they will produce more than if they work eight. The optimal rate of growth must involve a balance of consumption now versus consumption later, and also consumption now versus leisure now.

An important value issue arises here. We have been assuming that material goods are indeed good. Does it follow that more are necessarily better? Every major religious tradition says no:

He who knows he has enough is rich. (Tao Te Ching)

Whoever in this world overcomes his selfish cravings, his sorrows fall away from him, like drops of water from the lotus flower. (Dhammapada)

Excess and deficiency are equally at fault. (Confucius)

Poverty is my pride. (Muhammad)

Give me neither poverty nor riches. (Proverbs 30 : 8)

It is easier for a camel to go through the eye of a needle than for a rich man to enter into the kingdom of God. (Matthew 19 : 23–4)[54]

These quotations differ in emphasis, some advocating moderation, some extolling poverty, but all condemn excess. All suggest that the drive for ever greater consumption is folly. But is this "wisdom," or is it resignation – consolation offered by the haves to the have-nots? Is it not true that, in fact, richer people are happier than poorer people?

Interestingly enough we have some data on this question. The empirical answer seems to be yes, and no. A study some years ago drawing on thirty surveys conducted in nineteen countries concluded that

in all societies, more money for the individual typically means more individual happiness. However, raising the incomes of all does not increase the happiness of all. The happiness–income relation provides a classic example of the logical fallacy of composition – what is true for the individual is not true for society as a whole.[55]

Of course, the evidence does not show that every rich person is happy and every poor person unhappy, but in every country surveyed the percentage of people in a given income category identifying themselves

---

[54] Quotations compiled by the Worldwatch Institute, reprinted in Brown et al. (1991, p. 166).
[55] Easterlin (1973, p. 4).

as happy correlated positively with the ranking of that income category. Within a given country, those who have more are happier than those who have less. However, raising everyone's income does not increase overall happiness, nor does a country's GNP ranking correlate with its self-reported level of happiness.[56]

Needless to say, one should be cautious about drawing policy conclusions from what people (of very different classes and cultures) write on their happiness questionnaires. But the evidence strongly suggests that economic growth per se does not increase happiness. Michael Worley, of the National Opinion Research Center at the University of Chicago, notes that the percentage of Americans who today report that they are "very happy" is no higher than it was in 1957, despite a doubling of per-capita personal consumption since then.[57]

This is not difficult to understand. My own experience has not been unlike that of Jonathan Freeman (both of us having been students in the days before student life meant student debt):

As a student I lived on what now seems like no money at all, but I lived in a style which seemed perfectly fine. My apartment then seemed (and in retrospect still seems) like a lovely apartment, though it was not luxurious. I ate out as often as I thought I wanted to. I do not remember denying myself anything because of money, though I suppose I did. When I got a job, my income more than doubled. My rent also just about doubled. I ate out as often as before, but the restaurants were a little more expensive. I do not remember denying myself anything because of money, though I suppose I did. As my income has grown since then . . . I have spent more on everything, and I consider buying more expensive items. None of this has had any appreciable effect on my life or on my feelings of happiness and satisfaction.[58]

How do we explain what appears to be a systemic irrationality? Economic growth does not increase happiness, and yet capitalist countries strive mightily to grow.[59] And they seem never to learn. They strive to grow. They grow. They are no happier. So they strive for more growth.

Let us begin with a popular answer that I think is wrong: Each individual, thinking that more will make him happier, strives for more, and hence the economy grows. But because all are striving, (almost) all remain in the same relative positions, and so the happiness level remains

---

[56] Durning (1991, pp. 156–7) cites a major study conducted in 1974 that found Nigerians, Filipinos, Yugoslavs, Israelis, Japanese, and West Germans to be at about the same level of overall happiness – near the world norm – whereas both Cubans and Americans were much happier.

[57] Durning (1991, p. 156).

[58] Freeman (1978, p. 140). Freeman's life has been atypically free of financial anxieties (as has my own), but the general point seems broadly applicable: Once basic needs are satisfied, rising income often has little effect on personal happiness.

[59] Not only capitalist countries. Socialist countries, too, have made growth a high priority, but that is a separate issue that need not concern us here.

the same – as does its inverse, the level of discontent – and so each strives for more, and the cycle repeats.

There are two basic problems with this account. First, the direction of causality is assumed to run from intent to effect. But are we so sure that the desire for more on the part of the general population causes growth – or does growth perhaps create the desire? Notice that if one's relative position is the important variable in happiness, then in a growing economy one must consume more simply to avoid losing ground. One must consume more "to keep up with the Joneses" only if the Joneses are consuming more.

Second, there has been a lack of attention to intervening structures. A person may want more, and strive for more, but how does that translate into economic growth? People do not always get what they want, nor that for which they strive. We do not seem to get increased happiness. How is it that we get growth?

To arrive at a better explanation of our growth paradox, we need to ask how the rate of growth is in fact determined under Laissez Faire. We see at once that growth is not the outcome of a conscious, collective social choice. It is not the case that all of us (or even a majority) decide on a certain rate of growth, and then act to bring it about. To be sure, no society can determine in advance how fast it will actually grow, even if a consensus could be reached as to what rate would be desirable, because growth depends significantly on primary uncertainty, especially on technological innovation. A society can, however, make decisions that will affect the growth rate in important ways. It can decide, for example, what percentages of its human and natural resources should be devoted to research and development, to the establishment of new production facilities embodying the latest technology, and the like.

Under Economic Democracy, the decision most relevant to the growth rate will be the decision concerning the tax rate for capital assets, for this tax will be the source of new investment funds. It is this decision that will determine the portion of the national product to be devoted to capital expenditures for education, research and development, factory retooling, and introduction of new technologies. This is a decision to be made consciously and publicly by the national legislature.

Under Laissez Faire, the analogous decision is not made by an elected body, nor is it the outcome of individual preferences as revealed by their market purchases. Under capitalism, the societywide decision as to how much will be invested is made consciously by no one. This societal decision is the unplanned outcome of the individual decisions of firms and entrepreneurs who have (or can borrow) funds to invest. In no sense is the decision democratic. The undemocratic character of this decision is well illustrated in Keynes's description of pre–World War I capitalism:

This remarkable system depended for its growth on a double bluff or deception. On the one hand the laboring classes accepted from ignorance or powerlessness, or were compelled, persuaded or cajoled by custom, convention, authority and the well-established order of Society into accepting a situation in which they could call their own very little of the cake that they and Nature and the capitalists were cooperating to produce. And on the other hand the capitalist classes were allowed to call the best part of the cake theirs and were theoretically free to consume it, on the tacit underlying condition that they consumed very little of it in practice. The duty of "saving" became nine-tenths of virtue and the growth of the cake the object of true religion.[60]

If this account acknowledges the undemocratic character of capitalist growth, it also suggests a defense, made more explicit in Keynes's next paragraph:

The cake was really very small in proportion to the appetites of consumption, and no one, if it were shared all round, would be much better off by the cutting of it. Society was not working for the small pleasures of today but for the future security and improvement of the race, – in fact for "progress."[61]

What we have here, of course, is a utilitarian defense of a nondemocratic procedure, much like the standard defense of Stalin's forced industrialization: The people, if allowed to choose, would not choose wisely.

We may look with suspicion at such a defense, but it cannot be dismissed out of hand. We are not assuming at this point that democracy is necessarily good. So far, we have granted democracy only instrumental value, allowing, with Hayek, that "it must be judged by what it will achieve."

But can one seriously believe that a rate of growth that is the unplanned outcome of decisions taken by a small class of people answerable only to themselves (and stockholders) will more likely accord with what the majority of the populace need or want than a rate of growth that follows from a democratic decision procedure such as that proposed for Economic Democracy? Can one seriously believe that a rate of growth "privately" determined produces more overall happiness?

Perhaps. Classical liberals are fond of stressing the depths of human ignorance and our inability to subject everything to human reason.[62] So they might well deny that people can make an intelligent decision about the rate of investment. They might well maintain that such a decision would be shortsighted, resulting in a growth rate in no way comparable to the rate achieved under capitalism. I take this to be the import of Hayek's remark that "I have yet to learn of an instance when the deliberate vote of the majority (as distinguished from the decision of some governing elite) has decided on such sacrifices in the interests of a better future as is made by a free-market society."[63]

---

[60] Keynes (1971, pp. 19–20).   [61] Ibid., p. 20.
[62] See Hayek (1960, pp. 22–38).   [63] Ibid., p. 52.

To evaluate this charge, we must consider more closely what will be involved in reaching a decision about the overall rate of investment under Economic Democracy. Is it likely to be systematically distorted in ways that would jeopardize "the interests of a better future"?

The initial rate, of course, is rather arbitrary. A society will have the historical investment rates of capitalist and socialist societies to go by, but the precise figure to be set for the tax rate on capital assets (which will determine the size of the investment fund) will be a free choice. Subsequently, the national legislature will have to decide whether or not the selected rate is satisfying expectations. If not, the rate may be raised or lowered.

Let us consider this decision. Looking back over the preceding year, the legislature can see whether or not that portion of the investment fund made available to cooperatives for new investment was sufficient. If there are funds left over, it can do one of two things: It can lower the tax rate (which will simultaneously make the grants more attractive and diminish their supply), or it can allocate a larger portion of the investment fund to public capital goods. If, rather than having funds left over, the funds were insufficient (relative to cooperative demand), the legislature can do the opposite: It can raise the tax rate (increasing the supply, but making grants more expensive), or it can allocate a smaller portion to public capital funding.

The first point to note here is that neither raising nor lowering the capital-assets tax will have serious adverse effects on individual incomes, so there would not seem to be a systematic bias either way. Lowering the capital tax will raise all the incomes in the cooperative sector, but at the cost of making investment funds harder to get.[64] Raising the capital tax will cut into current income, but this will increase the supply of investment funds going to communities. In either case the income effect will be small, because the benefits and burdens will be shared by all the cooperatives. By way of example, if we assume that the cooperative sector constitutes three-quarters of the economy, and that 15 percent of the GNP goes to new cooperative investment, then decreasing the investment fund by 10 percent will raise all incomes in the cooperative sector, on average, by 2 percent; increasing the investment fund by 10 percent will lower incomes in the cooperative sector by 2 percent.

The second important point to note is that the supply of investment funds under Economic Democracy will be more tightly linked to demand

---

[64] Income will be increased, because costs of production will be reduced. Lest it be thought that most workers would be inclined to go for the bird in hand (i.e., to prefer a sure increase in income, as opposed to a possible investment grant for their firm), we should remind ourselves that this is a decision taken by a national legislature charged with looking out for the well-being of the entire economy. One can imagine individual voters lobbying for a tax cut, but there will be opposite pressure from both communities and cooperatives worried about investment funds coming up short.

than is the case under Laissez Faire. There is no danger of too much saving, as there is under capitalism. In a typical capitalist economy, massive quantities of funds, generated by their property holdings, accumulate each year in the hands of the wealthy, far more than could ever be "consumed." Retained corporate profits swell the pool of savings. All these must be invested. But where? If there are promising projects in the productive sectors of the economy, they will receive funding, but there are other options as well. Funds can be lent to governments (to be repaid with interest, of course), or they can be employed speculatively in real estate, in the stock market, and elsewhere. And if these outlets prove insufficient? Investors can hold on to their funds (exercising their "liquidity preference"), in which case (as we shall see more clearly in the next section) we get a recession.

What does not happen under capitalism is what will happen readily under Economic Democracy: The excess funds will be returned to the direct producers (by way of a cut in the assets tax). Under Economic Democracy, but not under Laissez Faire (or any other form of capitalism), the supply of investment funds is a (strongly) *dependent variable*, not a (relatively) *independent variable*. The national legislature will assess the likely demand for investment funds and then decide how much to "save" (i.e., what the assets tax will be).

The foregoing analysis brings into view a striking feature of Economic Democracy: The microeconomic tendency observed earlier – that a self-managed firm lacks the expansionary tendency of a capitalist firm – has a macroeconomic counterpart. *Economic Democracy is not biased in the direction of a high rate of growth.* Laissez Faire (and capitalism generally) contrasts sharply on this point. As Keynes observed, "the growth of the cake [is] an object of true religion." As Marx observed, "Accumulate, accumulate! That is Moses and the prophets!"[65] More recently, Nobel physics laureate Dennis Gabor has observed that "growth has become synonymous with hope, and man cannot live without hope."[66]

Capitalism is structured for growth. On the supply side, concentrated property holdings generate large pools of income too extensive to consume. Investment becomes a necessity for the individual capitalist, although scarcely a painful necessity, for a successful investment can enhance not only the investor's wealth but also his power and prestige. On the demand side, firms are eager to expand. "Grow or die" is a business byword. Large size enhances a firm's ability to act aggressively

---

[65] Marx (1967, p. 595).
[66] Quoted by Wachtel (1983, p. 50). Gabor adds that "under the day-to-day pressure of business, even highly intelligent people refuse to think of the long term, and if they think about it at all, they unconsciously repeat St. Augustine's prayer, 'Lord make me good, but not yet.' Let exponential growth continue in my time."

against competitors and to resist their threatening moves. (Notice that we have here an answer to the paradox of why capitalism keeps growing, even though growth does not increase the general happiness: Those whose decisions determine the rate of growth have neither the motive nor the means to allow considerations of the general happiness to bear significantly on their decisions.)

So we see that the conservative critic is right that the rate of growth under Economic Democracy may differ substantially from what would be achieved under Laissez Faire, but wrong about the reason. It is conscious choice, not shortsightedness or ignorance, that likely will cause the difference. Notice that if an Economic Democracy decides that it wants to grow, it has the means at its disposal. It can increase the size of its investment fund by raising the capital-assets tax; it can allocate more funds to research and development and to capital funding for education; it can offer encouragement grants to firms willing to upgrade their technology, and perhaps additional incentives to entrepreneurial individuals and collectives. But Economic Democracy is not structurally biased in the direction of increased growth. It can cut back on investment without dire consequences, or it can use its investments to reduce the hours of work or to improve working conditions. If consumers really want more goods of a particular type, their demand likely will be met, but the system does not push relentlessly in the direction of ever greater consumption. Economic Democracy, unlike Laissez Faire, should function perfectly well without such growth.[67]

So our critic is right about the fact, but not about its significance. It is true that growth rates under Laissez Faire and Economic Democracy are likely to be different, but it hardly follows that this conclusion favors Laissez Faire. The rate of investment under Laissez Faire is in no way subject to popular approval. One gets what the invisible hand decrees, but the market reflects no societal preference whatsoever here.[68]

Our critic, who is committed to democracy only as an instrumental value, has one final retort: Growth, rapid growth, is good, whether people want it or not. This would seem to be Hayek's view. The "free" society, he says, is the maximally progressive one. It is irrelevant whether we would be happier if we stopped growing today or had stopped a

---

[67] This point will be elaborated more fully in the next section.

[68] The market, which can legitimately be regarded as a quasi-democratic mechanism for registering societal preferences for various sorts of consumer goods, has no such legitimacy as an indicator of societal preference for a rate of investment. It is not implausible to say that a person who buys apples is expressing a judgment as to how many apples he would like in the future; hence, the aggregate of consumer purchases is a reasonable approximation of what people would like to have produced. But it makes no sense to say that a person who saves a hundred dollars is expressing a judgment as to how much investment he would like society to undertake.

hundred years ago; the point is not to stop: "What matters is the success-ful striving for what at each moment seems attainable. It is not the fruits of past success but the living in and for the future in which human intelligence proves itself. Progress is movement for movement's sake."[69] Hayek admits that it "is not certain whether most people want all, or even most of the results of progress. For most of them it is an involun-tary affair which, while bringing them much they strive for, also forces on them many things they do not want at all."[70] So be it.

This argument leads us back to the question raised at the beginning of this section, then set aside, concerning the desirability of economic growth. As we have seen, Laissez Faire encourages rapid growth.[71] Such growth is largely independent of the perceived needs, desires, or wishes of the general populace, arising as it does from competitive pressures and the desire of investors to make money with their money. Economic Demo-cracy, by contrast, will not be so automatically growth-oriented. Indi-vidual firms will not tend to expand unless there is an exogenously generated increase in demand. The amount of funding to be made avail-able for new investment will be the conscious decision of the national legislature.

So the case for Laissez Faire rests on a two-part premise: that growth really is of overriding importance to society, and that a democratic elec-torate is unlikely to understand this. Let us confine our attention to the first part of the premise. The issue, of course, is not growth versus no growth, but whether or not the rapid growth in personal consumption generated by Laissez Faire (when it is functioning as it is supposed to function) is optimal growth, whether people want it or not. Let us think this through just a bit more.

First, we should note that the value Hayek places on "successful striv-ing" is not a value linked logically to growth in personal consumption. Surely one can strive and develop in the absence of material advance. (Moral excellence was once thought to be a worthy goal.) One might even argue – and many have – that beyond a certain point, material advance can be a hindrance to the pursuit of other, perhaps more desir-able goals. One need not be an ascetic to see that certain kinds of striving require unhurried leisure and that material wealth can sometimes con-flict with leisure. The "paradox of domestic consumption," for example, is a well-documented phenomenon: Housework time, both for women

---

[69] Hayek (1960, p. 41). The reader will recognize here the Faustian sensibility (Goethe's *Faust*) remarked on at the beginning of this chapter. God forbid that we should "tarry awhile" and enjoy.

[70] Hayek (1960, p. 51).

[71] I do not mean to suggest that the structures of Laissez Faire guarantee rapid growth. As we shall see in the next section, many things can go wrong. But when Laissez Faire is functioning as it is supposed to function, it is a high-growth system.

who worked outside the home and for those who did not, increased substantially between 1930 and 1960.[72]

But without growth, won't we all die of boredom? This question always comes up. Frankly, it has always astonished me that serious thinkers should worry about the boredom of a nongrowing economy. The tradition goes back to Adam Smith: "The progressive state is in reality the cheerful and hearty state to all the different orders of society. The stationary state is dull."[73] Even so thoughtful a critic of growth as Kenneth Boulding can write that

> perhaps the most fundamental and intractable problem of the stationary state is, as Adam Smith saw so clearly, that of dullness. The second law of thermodynamics, the principle of increasing entropy, is a special instance of a much more general principle which might be described as the "second law of practically everything." This is the principle of the exhaustion of potential, that once a potential had been realized it is "used up" and cannot be realized again....
>
> One could postulate a second law of cultural dynamics, that creative acts are essentially non-repeatable, that once they have been done they cannot be done again.... The progressive state, however, puts a high value on creativity which is the main reason why it is cheerful and hearty. In the stationary state creativity may become pathological.[74]

I do not understand such arguments. To me, they reflect a failure in logic, to say nothing of imagination. A stationary economy is one in which the average material standard of living does not decline. I grant that if that standard is quite low, as it was in Adam Smith's day, then a stationary state is no happy prospect, but if stabilization occurs at a much higher level, why should it be dull? Why should it be duller or less creative to maintain a relatively constant level of material consumption – and thus to have the leisure to develop the skills, to read the books, to visit the places, to cultivate the friends that one has always wanted to – than to increase consumption? A human being, after all, is lucky to reside on this earth for more than three-quarters of a century, and that residence is all new to each of us at birth. Are more gadgets really necessary to keep boredom at bay? Might not gadgets be part of the problem?[75]

---

[72] See Gershuny (1984, p. 48). Gershuny argues that this trend has reversed itself since 1960, although it remains true that middle-class men and women have less leisure time now than they did in 1935. Working-class men and women appear to have more leisure time now, although for men (but not for women) the gain is wholly taken up by television viewing (Gershuny, 1984, p. 54).

[73] Smith [1976, p. 99 (I.viii.43)].   [74] Boulding (1973, p. 97).

[75] See Scitovsky (1976) for the more plausible argument that contemporary affluence generates boredom. Consider also Keynes's reflection on the future: "I see us free, therefore, to return to some of the most sure and certain principles of religion and traditional virtue – that avarice is a vice, that the exaction of usury is a misdemeanor, and the love of money is detestable, that those walk most truly in the paths of virtue and sane wisdom who take at least thought for the morrow. We shall once more value ends above means and prefer the good to the useful" (Keynes, 1963, pp. 371–2).

Advocates of growth are likely to respond to these musings by noting that increasing leisure also requires growth. Robert Solow, who usually can be counted on for a clever defense of orthodoxy, defines "the progrowth-man [as] someone who is prepared to sacrifice something useful and desirable right now so that people should be better off in the future."[76] But this definition distorts the central issue. The no-growth or slower-growth proponents also call for current sacrifice (specifically, a slowdown in material consumption) for the sake of the future. The distortion is particularly acute relative to the question of systems choice. Laissez Faire is structured to promote the growth of private consumption, not the "growth" of leisure or the "growth" of better working conditions. Economic Democracy will be far more conducive to these latter kinds of "growth."

If rapid growth is unnecessary, is it perhaps also harmful? If so, the case for Laissez Faire deteriorates further. By now, the most common argument against material growth is known to everyone: Our planet can no longer bear the increased air, water, soil, and other pollutions that accompany rapid economic growth. Industrial production has increased fififtyfold since 1950.[77] The current trends simply cannot continue. Boulding has remarked that only a madman or an economist would believe that exponential growth can go on forever in a finite world.[78]

The fact of the matter is that progrowth advocates in advanced industrial countries often score effectively against many of the antigrowth arguments and proposals – some of which, it should be said, are sharply at variance with democratic and egalitarian values[79] – but they have little to offer in the way of arguments in favor of growth, apart from a concern for boredom and some fatuous pronouncements about the fate of poor, underdeveloped countries if the industrialized countries do not grow. Solow, to his credit, notices that "if economic growth with equality is a good thing, it doesn't follow that economic growth with a lot of pious talk about equality is a good thing."[80]

If we add to the ecological-limit considerations the evidence cited earlier that increased growth does not increase happiness once the basic needs have been satisfied, then the case for Economic Democracy, as opposed

---

[76] Solow (1973, p. 41).

[77] World Commission on Environment and Development (1987, p. 4).

[78] Reported in Olsen and Landsberg (1973, p. 97).

[79] For an elegant and amusing depiction of the "right-wing" environmentalist scenario, see Stretton (1976, pp. 15–39). For a good many scores against antigrowth arguments, see Beckerman (1974).

[80] Solow (1973, p. 41). I have omitted the argument that is ubiquitous during political campaigns: that growth is necessary to create jobs. I take this to be an admission that capitalism does indeed have the structural problem with respect to employment that was analyzed in Chapter 3.

to Laissez Faire, would seem to be overwhelming. In advanced industrial societies, the pressing need is to alter production and consumption patterns so as to reduce the burden these activities place on the environment. We certainly need new technologies, and lots of human initiative and creativity, but we need an economic structure that will encourage (or at least not discourage) the channeling of such human strivings toward goals other than increased personal consumption. Economic Democracy, in allowing more scope for substituting leisure or a higher-quality work environment for increased income, and in allowing more scope for local initiatives in restructuring our communities, will better fit the bill than does Laissez Faire.

There is one more issue that must be addressed here, so as to avoid a major misunderstanding. It is surely true that current trends in environmental deterioration cannot continue, not without catastrophic consequences. But we must be careful with this argument. The greatest beneficiaries, by far, of the post–World War II growth explosion have been the wealthiest one-fifth of humanity, the 1 billion people whose

appetite for wood is a driving force behind the destruction of the tropical rain forests, and the resulting extinction of countless species. Over the past century, their economies have pumped out two-thirds of the greenhouse gases that threaten the earth's climate, and each year their energy use releases perhaps three-fourths of the sulphur and nitrous oxides that cause acid rain. Their industries generate more of the world's hazardous chemical wastes, and their air conditioners, aerosol sprays, and factories release almost 90 percent of the chlorofluorocarbons that destroy the earth's protective ozone layer.[81]

Current trends cannot continue. It does not follow that the remaining four-fifths of humanity must give up all hope of a decent life. The empirical evidence does not support that brutal conclusion. A recent study by José Goldemberg and associates has concluded that the entire world population could live modestly but comfortably at a level comparable to that in much of Western Europe, and do so without placing undue stress on energy and environmental resources.[82] But clearly this cannot take place if the "less advanced" 80 percent of the world's population attempt to emulate the development patterns of the "more advanced." Nor could it take place without drastic alterations in the consumption patterns of these more advanced industrial countries – alterations difficult to imagine so long as these countries are so structured as to make growth "an object of true religion," "Moses and the prophets," "synonymous with hope."

---

[81] Durning (1991, p. 156).
[82] Goldemberg et al. (1987); cited and discussed by Durning (1991, p. 157).

In the less developed countries the case for economic growth is far stronger than it is in the industrialized countries. Members of the World Commission on Environment and Development are not wrong to see "growth to be absolutely essential to relieve the great poverty that is deepening in much of the developing world."[83] The commission is also correct that "poverty is a major cause and effect of global environmental problems [and that] it is therefore futile to attempt to deal with environmental problems without a broader perspective that encompasses the factors underlying world poverty and international inequality."[84]

These considerations, however, do not imply that Laissez Faire remains the option of choice for the Third World. As we saw in the preceding section, the kind of growth generated by Laissez Faire can very well increase, rather than decrease, a poor country's poverty. Moreover, if one looks to the Third World "successes" commonly cited in defense of capitalist development, one sees something quite different from Laissez Faire. As Amartya Sen points out:

> The difficulty in reading great significance into the performance of South Korea as a success story for the "invisible hand" is the fact that the hands that reared South Korean growth were very visible indeed. . . . The South Korean government had control over two-thirds of the investment resources in the country in the period of its rapid acceleration of growth. . . .
> In fact it is remarkable that if we look at the sizeable developing countries, the fast growing and otherwise high-performing countries have all had governments that have been directly and actively involved in the planning of economic and social performance. . . . Their respective successes are directly linked to deliberation and design, rather than being just the results of uncoordinated profit seeking or atomistic pursuit of self-interest.[85]

These considerations tell against Laissez Faire, but they do not demonstrate that Economic Democracy is preferable to other forms of capitalism in meeting the legitimate needs of the Third World. That argument must wait until Chapter 7. But if the choice is between Economic Democracy and Laissez Faire, the choice seems clear. I have argued that Economic Democracy will be structured so that it can allow for a high rate of growth if high growth is desired. Moreover, Economic Democracy will allow for a degree of conscious planning that currently is ruled out of bounds by Laissez Faire, a degree of conscious planning that seems absolutely essential to equitable, ecologically sustainable development.

---

[83] World Commission on Environment and Development (1987, p. 1). This commission is an independent United Nations body chaired by the former prime minister of Norway, Gro Harlem Brundtland. The majority of its members are from the Third World. Its 1987 report is unstinting in its insistence that the world's majority must have a say in formulating environmental policies.

[84] World Commission on Environment and Development (1987, p. 3).

[85] Sen (1984, pp. 102–3).

Instability

The profit motive, in conjunction with competition among capitalists, is responsible for an instability in the accumulation and utilization of capital which leads to increasingly severe depressions. Unlimited competition leads to a huge waste of labor, and to the crippling of the social consciousness of individuals.

                                                                    – Albert Einstein

In arguing that the case for rapid economic growth is far from compelling, I have omitted one class of progrowth arguments that are frequently advanced: the destabilizing effects of an economic slowdown. I have not omitted these arguments because they are trivial, much less because they are invalid. In fact, many of them are sound. As we shall see, steady, sustained growth (whether or not it is desirable or even possible) is *necessary* for stability. Capitalist stability, that is. This conclusion does not bode well for Laissez Faire, because steady, sustained growth (as we shall also see) is far from inevitable.

Instability arguments are commonly and rightfully associated with Marx: The "laws of motion" of capitalist development drive the system to self-destruction. Although Marx offered no comprehensive crisis theory, still less a fully developed breakdown theory, he did provide numerous suggestions, partial arguments, and insights that are important to an understanding of capitalist instability.[86]

Non-Marxist economic theory, for its part, virtually ignored the crisis question until the Great Depression and Keynes forced a reconsideration.[87] Keynes addressed the problem of short-run instability. Soon after, the Keynesian Roy Harrod raised the question of capitalism's long-range stability. Harrod's arguments spawned a debate that raged fiercely for several decades, pitting neo-Marxists and post-Keynesians against the neoclassicists. Mathematical models and accompanying theorems proliferated, but in the end little was settled. After a while, the antagonists simply stopped talking to one another.[88]

Models are, in fact, quite helpful in analyzing stability issues. Using models, drastic simplifications can be made so as to bring out the essential elements. It will not be necessary for us to analyze the complex models associated with the aforementioned debate, but it will prove useful

---

[86] See Sweezy (1942, pp. 133–234). This remains one of the best discussions of the Marxian view of economic crises.

[87] I am overstating somewhat. Not all pre-Keynesian economists were untroubled by the view that the system would automatically and appropriately adjust to equilibrium disruptions (though their criticisms had little effect on mainstream opinion). See Hansen (1953, ch. 1) for documentation.

[88] Harrod (1939). This essay and a good sampling of the subsequent debate have been edited by Sen (1970). For an update on the neoclassical view, see Solow (1988). Note his bitter evaluation of the Cambridge controversy: "a waste of time, a playing-out of ideological games in the language of analytical economics" (Solow, 1988, p. 309).

to look at a couple of simple models that highlight the variables most relevant to our concerns.

Our aim is to identify some of the necessary conditions for capitalist stability. Let us understand an *unstable economy* to be one whose development over time likely will place severe strains, periodically or indefinitely, on the social fabric. One such condition for stability is a steady or rising average rate of profit. Since Keynes, it has become a commonplace that a healthy capitalism requires investor confidence. If confidence declines, so does investment. A decline in investment lowers aggregate demand, which leads to layoffs, which reduce demand further, which provokes further layoffs, and so on – the all-too-familiar downward recessionary spiral. The "animal spirits" (Keynes's characterization) of investors are contingent on the expected rate of profit. If an investor can expect a high return on his investment, he is happy. But if the economy experiences a period of declining profits, investor confidence will erode, to be followed by recession, rising unemployment, and social instability.

Declining profits are destabilizing in another way, more often stressed by Marxian thinkers: A decline in profits tends to intensify class antagonisms. When profits decline, individual capitalists (or their managerial representatives) seek to fend off the decline by increasing the pace of work, lowering wages, and/or extending the length of the working day (e.g., by means of mandatory overtime).

When we say that a steady or rising rate of profit is a "necessary condition" for capitalist stability, we are, of course, speaking of very high probability, not logical necessity. It could happen that the profit rate would decline so gradually that it would upset neither investor confidence nor class relations. It could happen that the decline would be gradual and uniform, reducing profits to the point that all excess would be consumed by the capitalist class, and none at all (beyond depreciation reserves) invested. The resulting economy would be a no-growth stationary state – an outcome envisaged by many classical economists. As John Stuart Mill remarked, "it must always have been seen, more or less abstractly, by political economists, that the increase in wealth is not boundless; that at the end of what they term the progressive state lies the stationary state."[89] Mill, unlike most of his predecessors and successors, did not view this prospect with alarm:

I am inclined to believe that it would be, on the whole, a very considerable improvement on our present condition. I must confess I am not charmed with the ideal of life held out by those who think that the normal state of human beings is the struggle to get on; that the trampling, crushing, elbowing, and treading on each other's heels, which form the existing tempo of social life, are the most desirable lot of human kind.[90]

[89] Mill (1965, p. 752).   [90] Ibid., p. 754.

Such an evolution could happen under Laissez Faire, but the likelihood is minimal. Profit rates cannot be expected to be uniform, and so a general decline in the average rate of profit likely would correspond to a period of widespread business difficulties, bankruptcies, and economic disruption, a period of recessionary nonoptimality in which idle workers would face idle factories, while labor would be intensified for those still working.

It is unlikely that any existing capitalist economy could evolve gradually to a stationary state via a slow decline in the rate of profit, but even if one did so, it would not be free from instability. To see why not, let us sketch a simple model. Let us suppose that society is composed of two classes: capitalists, who own the means of production, and workers, all of whom are employed by the capitalists. For convenience, we may think of the capitalist class as embodied in a single capitalist. Let x_i represent the total output of the ith production period. We can think of the production period as a year, and its output as some uniform consumer good, say wheat. Let w_i be the wage bill (in bushels of wheat) for the ith production period, advanced to the workers at the beginning of the period. Let r be the (constant) rate of profit.

A stationary state may be described follows: A capitalist begins with x_0 bushels of wheat. (Where he got them need not concern us; perhaps he saved, perhaps he stole – no matter.) He advances this wheat to his workers; thus, $x_0 = w_1$. They return to him $x_1 = (1 + r)x_0$ bushels of wheat at the end of the first production period. The capitalist consumes the surplus rx_0 bushels. He again advances x_0 to the workers, and the cycle repeats. It can continue indefinitely, each x_i equal to x_1, each w_i equal to x_0.

Can it continue indefinitely? The case would seem to be economically stable, because the profit rate is steady, and no technical difficulties are evident. But politically there is a problem, for here we have a society that looks suspiciously feudal. One class of people live without laboring; those in the other class labor indefinitely without any improvement in their condition. (At best there is no improvement; if the population is increasing, there is impoverishment.) It must be doubted that such a society could long persist in the absence of either a rigid, hierarchical tradition or an authoritarian government. Free and effective communication, to say nothing of democracy, would certainly be troublesome. Such a society might persist if indoctrination and propaganda were sufficient to keep people content, but open class struggle would seem more likely.

If capitalism is not stable without growth, let us build growth into our model. Let us drop the assumption that the capitalist consumes the surplus, and replace it with the assumption that he invests it. For simplicity we shall assume that he abstains completely, and invests all of the surplus.

(Nothing important hangs on so drastic an assumption; if anything, we are strengthening the case for capitalism.)

We find ourselves here with a puzzle. What, exactly, does "investment" mean in the context of our model? Our capitalist at the end of the first year has $x_1 = (1 + r)x_0$ bushels of wheat, x_0 of which he must set aside for his workers' wages. But what can he do with the surplus rx_0 so as to increase production to $x_2 = (1 + r)x_1$ at the end of the second year?

One solution is to do what he did before, but on a wider scale. Let us call this *extensive growth*. He must hire more laborers. Because we have assumed full employment, growth in this manner (i.e., without technical progress) requires a growing population. If all workers are equally productive, and if there are no diminishing returns to scale, stability (i.e., maintaining a profit rate r) requires that $n_i = (1 + r)n_{i-1}$, where n_i represents the number of workers available for period i. [If we allow for diminishing returns, then n_i must be greater than $(1 + r)n_{i-1}$.] Now, if population growth satisfies this condition, the system appears to be stable. It is economically stable because the profit rate is maintained, and it is politically stable because the capitalist is not consuming the surplus, but rather investing it. Individual workers are not improving their condition over time, but at least there is no impoverishment. In any event, they can hardly blame their condition on the (nonconsuming) capitalist, who is here a paragon of social virtue.

The problem with this case, of course, is its reliance on a geometrically expanding population. In reality, the capitalist cannot continue indefinitely "to do what he did before, but on a wider scale." He can for a while. This model is not inappropriate for certain periods of capitalist development. The population of Europe more than doubled, and that of North America sextupled, between 1750 and 1950. World population increased 6.4 percent per decade during that period, in contrast to about 6 percent per century between A.D. 0 and 1750.[91] But as anyone who has ever thought about it knows (and if one has taken an elementary calculus course, one can draw the terrifying graphs), exponential population growth cannot go on forever. If capitalism requires a geometrically expanding population for its stability, then capitalism is not stable.[92]

But there is a way out: The capitalist need not continue "to do what he did before." Capitalists can act out their historical role by inventing, innovating, revolutionizing the means of production. Let us model this sort of growth. Let us reverse the population assumption of our second model and assume that the work force is constant. This is a simplifying

---

[91] Kuznets (1965, pp. 8–9).

[92] This is not strictly true, because the geometric ratio could be so small as to be insignificant in the foreseeable future. However, in order for population growth to sustain the profit rates normally expected in existing capitalist societies, it would have to far exceed demographic stability.

assumption, but not an unrealistic one in light of recent population trends in industrial nations. Let us assume that all growth comes from techno-logical innovation. Let us call this *intensive growth*. To maintain the profit rate, investments must cause output to grow steadily: $x_i = (1 + r)x_{i-1}$ for all i. Because by hypothesis, our capitalist consumes nothing, and the work force is fixed, this growth rate translates into a steady increase in per capita consumption, also at the rate of r per year: $w_i = x_i/n$, where n is constant and x_i is steadily increasing. This is clearly the "golden age" of capitalist development. The profit rate is steady, keeping the capitalist happy; wages increase exponentially over time, to the delight of the work force; and the population remains constant, to the relief of everyone. Here, certainly, is a case of capitalist stability.

Such a state is logically possible. Such a state is also necessary, for the three models we have considered are the only (pure) possibilities, and the first two are decidedly unstable.[93] But if steady growth via techno-logical change is both possible and necessary, is it also likely? How likely? What variables must interact, and how, for his happy state to persist as the unplanned outcome of a free market? (What role the government might play in securing this state will be discussed in Chapter 6.)

The key variable here, obviously, is productivity: output per worker. If productivity does not rise at the rate r, then profits cannot be main-tained. If x_i bushels of wheat are invested in period i, then $(1 + r)x_i$ must be returned to the capitalist.[94] Perhaps this steady increase in productiv-ity can go on indefinitely. Perhaps technological innovation will always overcome the problems of diminishing returns and resource scarcity.

This premise is closely related to the limits-to-growth controversy dis-cussed in the preceding section. There I emphasized the environmental constraints on limitless growth. Resource constraints also are often in-voked in that context, but I chose not to do so. Although the issue is by no means settled, the best evidence to date suggests that resource ex-haustion, per se, will not be the barrier it was once thought to be.[95]

However, resource considerations do enter our argument here. To avoid

---

[93] Neoclassical economists often distinguish between growth due to technological change and growth that comes simply from using more capital (movement from one production function to another versus movement along a given production function). This distinc-tion is not relevant to our purposes. Both kinds of growth (if they really can be distin-guished) we call "technological," because both involve actions by capitalists to increase the productivity of labor.

[94] Our one-commodity world avoids – at the cost of realism – the indexing problem. (If 1,000 bushels of wheat are produced in period 1, and 500 head of cattle in period 2, how much has the economy grown? Or has it declined?) This complication, however, does not affect our basic point: The growth that is essential to capitalist stability (measured by some suitable index) requires productivity gains (measured by the same index).

[95] For a recent assessment by a distinguished interdisciplinary team, see Gordon et al. (1988). Their most serious reservations about the available resources concern water and energy, but in the latter case, anyway, the problem has to do with the environmental constraints, not any physical insufficiency.

instability, not only must resources be physically available, but technical innovation must offset their rising scarcity costs (including those one should expect to see imposed politically to contain the associated environmental degradation). Perhaps this will happen. But if not, then recessionary instability and an intensification of the class struggle, both triggered by declining profits, are highly likely.[96]

Productivity increase is the sine qua non of stable capitalism. It is the most fundamental of the necessary conditions, but it is not the only one. The simplicity of our model conceals several others. In actuality, the increase in productivity is only one moment of a three-part movement, each of which must succeed in order for capitalist expectations to be satisfied and stability to obtain. The capitalist, possessing a surplus rx_i at the end of year i, must find an outlet for that surplus. It will be returned to the workers only if they represent an investment outlet that promises sufficient profit to attract the funds. The funds must be invested. This is the first moment. Second, the anticipated productivity increase must materialize. Third, the new products must be sold.

The second moment we have already analyzed. The limiting factor here is technological innovation: Will it be forthcoming, and fast enough to overcome diminishing returns and environmental constraints? The first moment was alluded to when we discussed "investor confidence" at the outset of this section. Investment, we know, is essentially the channeling of workers and resources from where they are less productive to where they are expected to be more so. If individual capitalists do not see opportunities for productive investment sufficient to warrant risking their capital, they have other options: consume the surplus, or invest in nonproductive speculative assets, or send their capital abroad in search of more promising opportunities, or exercise their "liquidity preference" by holding their surplus in wait. If there is excessive capitalist consumption or speculation, then the productivity increase necessary for long-range stability is unlikely. If either of the latter two practices suddenly becomes widespread, aggregate domestic demand drops, and recessionary instability ensues forthwith.

Whether or not opportunities for productive investment are really diminishing is a controversial issue. The American Keynesian Alvin Hansen advanced this "stagnation thesis" in the late 1930s. Marxist economists Paul Baran and Paul Sweezy revived it in the mid-1960s and

---

[96] Robert Heilbroner (1974, p. 123) agrees: "Why societal peace persists in the face of an outlandishly skewed distribution of income is a perennial puzzle, especially in a democratic society.... To the extent that environmental and other difficulties require a slowdown in the pace of economic growth, the struggle for place is apt to become more marked [and we are likely to see] a reappearance of the 'vanished' problem: Disraeli's War Between Two Nations – the Rich and the Poor."

made it the focus of their influential critique.[97] Mainstream opinion, not surprisingly, remains skeptical. For our part, we need not take sides in this debate, because nobody denies that diminishing outlets for investment could pose a problem for capitalist growth. What is important to note for our argument is that the stagnation problem involves two factors. The first is technological: whether or not and to what degree productivity increases are technically possible. The second is psychosocial: whether or not a certain class of people will exercise their "freedom" (to invest) appropriately. As we shall see shortly, the psychosocial factor is quite different under Economic Democracy.

The third moment essential to a Golden Age of capitalist stability is the selling of the goods produced at the anticipated prices. This condition is not captured at all by our model, for we have the capitalist advancing the product directly to his workers. Our scenario is useful in illustrating certain relations, but it obscures the fact that, in reality, workers must buy the product of the capitalist, and do so with the money wages paid to them.[98]

This third moment reveals two additional sources of potential instability: First, workers must have sufficient money to buy the capitalist's product. Second, they must want to spend it. The first is the problem of aggregate demand; the second is that of "consumer confidence" and the sales effort.

In Chapter 3 we examined the case against a large-scale, sophisticated sales effort. I argued that it is improbable in the extreme that the needs and desires generated by nonrational techniques will genuinely contribute to individual well-being. Here we see the reverse phenomenon: the potential for economic disruption (and hence a lowering of well-being) posed by the lack of an aggressive sales effort. Capitalism requires growth, which in turn requires investor confidence, which in turn requires consumer confidence. If consumers do not continue to buy in ever increasing amounts, then products will remain unsold, the capitalists' animal spirits will wane, layoffs will follow, and so on. We have here another of those peculiar "contradictions" of capitalism: The economy exists to satisfy consumers, but if they become too satisfied, a crisis will ensue.

The problem of aggregate demand has already been discussed in connection with the unemployment problem. So far as Laissez Faire is concerned, there is nothing more to add. Laissez Faire in no way ensures that aggregate demand will always be sufficient for full employment.

[97] Hansen (1938); Baran and Sweezy (1966).

[98] Heilbroner (1989, p. 100) recalls the story, perhaps apocryphal, of Henry Ford II and union organizer Walter Reuther walking through a newly automated engine factory: "Walter," says Ford to Reuther, "how are you going to organize these machines?" To which Reuther replies, "Henry, how are you going to sell them cars?"

Conditions for capitalist stability: three best cases (nondeclining rate of profit)

	Population	Worker consumption	Problem
No growth	Stable	Constant	Political
Extensive growth	Increasing	Constant	Population
Intensive growth	Stable	Rising	None: Golden Age

The three moments of Golden Age growth:
1. Capitalists must invest
2. Productivity must increase
3. Products must be sold
   a. Consumers must have sufficient money
   b. Consumers must be willing to buy

Corresponding difficulties:
1. Insufficient investor confidence
2. Insufficient technological innovation
3. Insufficient sales
   a. Insufficient effective demand
   b. Insufficient consumer confidence

More must be said concerning government intervention to maintain demand, but that topic belongs to our discussion of Keynesian liberalism, and so it need not concern us here. (Contemporary classical liberals often abandon their commitment to Laissez Faire at this juncture. The government must do something to ensure adequate demand. The solution most favored in conservative circles is *monetarism*: The government should regulate the money supply.[99] This "solution" will be discussed in Chapter 6.)

We are now in position to compare the stability of Laissez Faire with that of Economic Democracy. The accompanying table summarizes our analysis to this point. The most significant difference between Laissez Faire and Economic Democracy is that the latter does not have a growth imperative. Laissez Faire (indeed, capitalism generally) needs to grow; Economic Democracy does not. A stationary state under Economic Democracy would not generate the peculiar political problem inherent in capitalism, for there would be no affluent ownership class in need of justification. This is not to say that distributional disputes will vanish under Economic Democracy. So long as there are inequalities and

---

[99] Cf. Friedman (1962, ch. 3). The latest wave of conservative economics, the New Classical economics, tends to disagree. Not even monetarism will work, it is argued, because agents will rationally anticipate governmental behavior, and adjust accordingly. See Barro (1977). In a sense, the new classicals embrace a purer form of Laissez Faire than Friedman's.

material scarcity (which there will be under Economic Democracy), there is the potential for political conflict. But what will give Economic Democracy its decisive edge will be the absence of a class, plainly unproductive in a stationary economy, whose historical and contemporary justification is rooted in growth.[100]

Economic Democracy will be able to function quite well as a stationary state; hence it will require neither an expanding population nor technological innovation at a pace sufficient to guarantee increased production. It will also be able to make the transition from a growth state to a stationary state without undue disruption. If consumers begin to purchase less, the effect will be to increase leisure time among producers, leisure that will be shared by those firms first affected, and then gradually spreading to other sections.[101] The violent spasms of layoffs triggering further layoffs to which Laissez Faire is so vulnerable will be absent. Nor will Economic Democracy face the threat of an "investment strike," because no class will have a "liquidity" option. There will be no class whose animal spirits must be sustained if stability is to be ensured. Under Economic Democracy, investment funds will be generated by taxation and made available to those who want them. If too few projects are proposed, then national or state or local governments can encourage more initiatives, and/or the national legislature can cut the capital tax. If society does not want to grow, it does not have to. A high level of investment is not required for stability.[102]

There remains one important issue to consider. Our analysis thus far has centered on *recessionary instability*. But what about the other large problem that is often associated with instability, namely, *inflation*? Perhaps Economic Democracy simply trades one problem for another?

There would seem to be reason for concern on this score. I have frequently noted that under Economic Democracy there will be less cutthroat competition than under capitalism, because firms will have little

---

[100] To quote Heilbroner again: "[Capitalism's] largely uncritical worship of the idea of economic growth is as central to its nature as the similar veneration of the idea of divine kingship or blue blood or doctrinal orthodoxy has been for other regimes" (Heilbroner, 1989, p. 102).

[101] The idea here is this: Because a worker-managed firm is reluctant to lay off its members, the demand decline will translate into shorter hours for all. Their incomes will decline, of course, so they will contract their spending also, thus decreasing the demand for other products, etc. Of course, if the contraction is very sharp in certain industries, some workers will seek work elsewhere. Given the mechanisms discussed in Chapter 3, they should be able to find it.

[102] A positive rate of investment will always be necessary so long as problems of resource depletion and diminishing returns persist. But the slower the growth of the economy, the less severe these problems. The greater the investment for the purpose of growth, the greater must be the research to counter diminishing returns – another paradoxical state of affairs that does not favor capitalism.

or no incentive to drive competitors out of business or to capture large shares of their markets. It has been seen that various desirable consequences should follow from this feature, but here is one that seems not so good: In the absence of tight competition, what is to prevent a firm from raising its prices at will? Clearly, the workers in the firm would benefit. Even if sales fell off somewhat, they might be better off than before. (A firm takes in the same revenue selling n widgets at $2X$ as it does selling $2n$ widgets at X, but it pays out only half as much for the raw materials, and its workers need work only half as many hours.) A firm would refrain from such price hikes if it appeared likely to lose its customers to a competitor firm, but in Economic Democracy the competitor firm might not be much interested in expanding production. It could simply increase its prices as well. In this way, both firms would benefit, and a price rise having nothing to do with higher costs would spread throughout the industry.

The standard, theoretically sanctioned answer to this problem is free entry of new firms: If the widget industry becomes suddenly lucrative, enterprises making other things will want to shift to widget production, or workers will want to leave existing firms and set up widget factories. The supply of widgets will go up, and prices will have to come down. But is this an adequate answer? In practice, new firms cannot be set up quickly. Large amounts of start-up capital would have to be committed to what could turn out to be a bad investment if the existing firms simply cut back their prices to what they were before.

To analyze this problem properly, we need to think through two distinct questions. Will Economic Democracy exhibit a stronger tendency toward inflation than Laissez Faire? Will the consequences of inflation be the same for both systems? Let us consider the first question. If we stick to our characterization of Laissez Faire as a capitalist economy that is (1) free of government interference and (2) free of monopoly, the answer must be yes. A firm under Laissez Faire will be more reluctant to raise its prices than will a comparable firm under Economic Democracy, because the former will have greater reason to fear that a competitor will try to capture its market.

At this point it is necessary to reflect on our characterization of Laissez Faire, for the two defining conditions are not, in fact, compatible.[103] It is clear theoretically and empirically that a capitalist economy tends toward unequal concentrations of market power. Big firms tend to swallow

---

[103] The reader will recall that we made the assumption that there are no monopolies under Laissez Faire, so as to better understand the claim that a competitive capitalist economy is efficient. Because even without monopolies the efficiency claim turned out to be false (because of unemployment and the sales effort), it was not necessary to question the legitimacy of the no-monopoly assumption.

up little firms or drive them out of business. It is highly unrealistic to assume that a capitalist economy with minimal government interference will be tightly price-competitive. As Adam Smith observed, "people of the same trade seldom meet together, even for merriment and diversion, but the conversation ends in a conspiracy against the public, or in some contrivance to raise prices."[104]

Clearly, the more central of the two defining characteristics of Laissez Faire is minimal government intervention.[105] So we can assume that there will be many firms under Laissez Faire that will be able to raise prices beyond what would be the case under conditions of vigorous price competition, just as there will be many such firms under Economic Democracy. It is not obvious which system will exhibit the more pronounced tendency. Although it is true that competition in general will not be as intense under Economic Democracy as under Laissez Faire (because firms will be less inclined to want to drive their competitors out of business), it is also true that firms under Economic Democracy likely will be smaller and hence may have to be more careful about losing customers. In both systems, a price increase is a gamble. A firm is always tempted to raise prices simply to increase its income, but it knows that sales may drop off as a result and that customers lost may be difficult to regain.

Let us grant that there does exist a tendency toward inflation in both Laissez Faire and Economic Democracy.[106] What are the consequences? Let us ask the root question: What is wrong with inflation? Surprisingly, economists do not have an easy answer. As MIT economist Paul Krugman concedes, "it is one of the dirty little secrets of economic analysis that even though inflation is universally regarded as a terrible scourge, most efforts to measure its costs come up with embarrassingly small numbers."[107]

Clearly, if prices are rising at a uniform rate and incomes are rising by the same rate, there is no real effect on anyone's well-being. Everyone's actual consumption and relative consumption remain unchanged. Even when the rates are uneven, no great harm need occur – some relative inequity, some loss of Pareto optimality as prices deviate nonuniformly from costs, but nothing too serious. The most significant disutility

[104] Smith [1976, p. 145 (I.x.c.27)].

[105] Conservative theorists are generally reluctant to have the government do too much to block the tendency toward monopoly, for they feel (not without reason) that such attempts often backfire. See Friedman (1962, pp. 119ff.).

[106] The connection between monopoly power and inflation is not so straightforward as it might appear. If resources remain fully employed (and the money supply remains constant), higher prices in one sector will be offset by lower prices in another, so that there will be no overall inflatic n. But because, in reality, quantity adjustments are at least as likely as price adjustments (i.e., a firm will contract production rather than lower prices), an inflationary tendency seems likely in an economy that is not highly competitive.

[107] Krugman (1990b, p. 52).

identified by economists is that the inflationary "static" in the price system makes long-range planning more difficult, but even this problem would seem manageable. Indeed, virtually all capitalist economies, when healthy, experience price inflation, sometimes quite acute.[108] So long as incomes keep up, there would seem to be little reason to worry about instability.

Economists often suggest that the widespread societal opposition to inflation is due to a certain irrationality on the part of workers.[109] Workers see their own rising incomes as being due to their own merit, but they view rising prices as independent of, rather than caused by, their rising wages. So they feel put upon, their hard-won gains eaten away by inflation.

There is probably some truth to this account, at least enough to dispose people to accept the media-mediated portrayal of inflation as a terrible evil.[110] But the real opposition to inflation, I submit, comes from another quarter. So long as we confine our attention to wages and consumption, it is difficult to see why inflation should be a "terrible scourge," as opposed to an annoyance or a frustration. But if we think of borrowing and lending, a quite different picture comes into focus. In general, inflation hurts those who lend money more than those who borrow. When I borrow $X, I must pay back $X (setting aside interest), but during a period of inflation the $X that I pay back will purchase less (i.e., are worth less) than the $X I received. During periods of inflation, lenders tend to lose, and borrowers tend to gain.

It is by no means a remarkable fact that people with money to lend tend to be wealthier than people who want to borrow. There are, of course, many exceptions, but as a general rule it can scarcely be doubted. So, contrary to what "inflation-fighters" constantly suggest (making reference to widows on fixed incomes), inflation (certainly "wage-push" inflation) tends to shift the distribution of income downward, from capital to labor. When inflation is accelerating, it can even push the real interest rate into negative territory – a horrifying prospect to those for whom interest income is fundamental (i.e., for the upper class).[111] Should

---

[108] It was noted in Chapter 2 that the Japanese economy grew, in real terms, fifty-five-fold between 1946 and 1976. During that period of astonishing real growth, consumer prices increased nearly twenty-five-fold. See Leisner (1985, p. 116).

[109] See Blinder (1987, pp. 51–4).

[110] The rhetoric that inflation calls forth is quite amazing. Here is President Ford in 1974: "Our inflation, our public enemy number one, will, unless whipped destroy our homes, our liberties, our property, and finally our national pride, as surely as any well-armed enemy" (Blinder, 1987, p. 46).

[111] One important way in which inflation bites the capitalist class is via taxation. One pays taxes on wages and interest income, both calculated in nominal, not real, terms. Suppose a person receives $30,000 interest on a $300,000 bond when the rate of inflation is 10

we be surprised to find a rising clamor to " Whip Inflation Now" (to recall the Gerald Ford slogan), even if that means throwing the country into massive recession (as was done in the 1980s, Krugman reminds us, deliberately and with bipartisan support)?[112] Of course, the political justification always advanced is to protect those hordes of poor people on fixed incomes – never, God knows, to protect the moneylenders. But this is a disingenuous justification, given the fact that the pain that attends a recessionary "solution" dwarfs the pain that inflation would inflict on those supposedly being protected.[113]

I do not mean to suggest that inflation can never hurt innocent people or can never be destabilizing. When the effects of inflation fall disproportionately on classes that have significant potential for disruption, serious instability can indeed ensue. In capitalist societies, unionized workers and large industrial capitalists are fairly well insulated from the adverse effects of inflation. Unions can bargain forcefully for wage increases, and their bosses can pass the costs of those increases on to consumers. Small businessmen, unorganized workers, and finance capitalists are more vulnerable. Now, if finance capitalists begin to lose heart, this loss of "investor confidence" can trigger a recession. If inflation becomes extreme, worse may be in store. Rampant inflation often has been a prelude to a fascist usurpation of power (one thinks of Italy before Mussolini, Weimar Germany, Allende's Chile), the key supporters of which usually are small businessmen, unorganized workers, and finance capitalists. Under advanced capitalism, of course, inflation is rarely allowed to get so far out of hand, because the government has the power, and usually the will, to step on the monetary brake and induce a recession.

So we see that inflation under capitalism does pose a stability problem. If it is left untreated, investor confidence may be shaken. In a worst-case scenario, one gets fascism. If the government intervenes, it will be to engineer a recession – less severe, it hopes, than the one that would result if investor confidence were too badly shaken – but a recession nonetheless.

Will inflation under Economic Democracy have the same consequences? We note that the three classes mentioned earlier as being particularly

percent. His real wealth has not changed, because the $30,000 merely offsets the decline in real value of the bond. Yet he must pay (if he is in the 33 percent tax bracket) $10,000 to the government. He is not happy.

[112] Krugman (1990b, p. 58).

[113] If the real concern were poor people on fixed incomes, an obvious solution would be to index welfare payments to the cost of living and to give tax relief to those in the low-income brackets who depend on modest interest and dividend payments. That such measures are never proposed by "inflation fighters" ought to raise doubts about their real motivations.

vulnerable to inflation will not exist under Economic Democracy. There will be no finance capitalists or small businessmen, and all workers will belong to democratic collectives.[114] Should we conclude that inflation under Economic Democracy would be harmless? This question does not admit of a simple answer. Suppose the technology, work force, and consumption preferences of an Economic Democracy remained fixed, but all enterprises raised their prices by the same percentage. Would consumption stay the same? Not necessarily. Not unless the money supply was also increased by the same percentage.[115] If not, then lack of purchasing power would necessitate that fewer goods be sold, and so the economy would contract. We would have the analogue of capitalist "stagflation": both higher prices and an economic slowdown.

Would this be a bad thing? It would not be as bad as under capitalism, because a contracting economy in an Economic Democracy would mean cutting back on the hours of work for everyone in the affected firms. In effect, people would trade consumption for leisure. Still, such socialist "stagflation" can hardly be viewed as optimal. It is one thing for workers, either individually or collectively, to choose to work less, so as to exchange consumption for leisure. It is quite another for this to be the unintended consequence of the separate decisions of individual enterprises to raise their prices.

I think we must concede that stagflation is a potential problem for Economic Democracy. It is not, however, a stability problem, because an inflation-induced contraction is not likely to feed upon itself. If firms are having a hard time selling their goods, they will not continue to raise prices. Nor is stagflation a problem before which the government is powerless. There are three basic tools that it can employ: monetary policy, tax policy, and price controls.

This is not the place for a full-blown analysis of monetary, tax, and price policies under Economic Democracy (much of which would of necessity be speculative), but some basic elements may be ventured. Perhaps the most important general point, relative to the issue at hand, is that the government of an Economic Democracy will have considerably more control over its money supply than does the government of a capitalist economy, because there will be no private banks or other financial institutions of the sort that play such major roles in a capitalist economy. In a capitalist economy, the government's central bank creates money essentially by printing it, and then using it to pay for government

---

[114] I am thinking of the model in its pure form. In reality there likely will be some small businesses run by private individuals who hire wage labor, but this sector will be small, and not central enough to the economy to be capable of destabilizing it.

[115] A technical point: I am assuming here and in the ensuing discussion that the velocity of money is constant.

purchases.[116] But banks and other such institutions also "create" money, in effect by extending credit.[117] A central bank has various instruments that it can employ in an attempt to monitor and control the total amount of credit being extended, but in a capitalist economy the financial institutions often find ways, via new debt instruments, to circumvent the regulators. Because there is big money to be made from the interest payments, they have a powerful incentive to do so. In an Economic Democracy, the central bank also will be able to print money, and it must also monitor the credit that producers are extending to their customers, but in the absence of interest there will not be the other institutions to worry about.

To return to the case of stagflation: Prices are rising, and production is declining. In dollar terms the GNP is stationary, but in real terms production is declining, because the higher prices are absorbing the money that otherwise would have been spent on more goods. Theoretically, the solution is simple: The central bank should allow the money supply to keep pace with the rise in the inflation index. This could be done simply by cutting taxes and printing money to cover the shortfall. This would increase the effective demand by the requisite amount. Theoretically, that solves the problem. Prices will have gone up, but incomes will have risen too, and so people will be able to buy what they did before. Nothing has really changed.

There are a couple of problems with this solution. We have assumed that all prices would go up uniformly. Unfortunately, there is no reason to suppose that such would be the case. Each firm will set its own prices. Those with more market power (i.e., less to fear from price competition) presumably will raise theirs more than will firms with less market power. This will introduce both inequity and allocative inefficiency into the economy.

It seems highly unlikely that the inefficiencies would be serious enough to require special measures. After all, real-world capitalist economies, even those deemed most efficient, are rife with inequalities in market power. Observers from Adam Smith onward have noted that capitalist firms do not like to price-compete. They go to great lengths to avoid it. Large corporations are especially adept at this.[118] Real-world capitalist prices deviate markedly from those that would be set under conditions of perfect (or even vigorous) competition – to little ill effect, economically. If serious problems are generated by the lack of vigorous price

---

[116] This will be discussed more carefully in Chapter 6.

[117] Bank loans and credit cards are only the most obvious forms. Whatever the form, if a person has a line of credit, he can make purchases as if he had cash; so this credit constitutes a part of the money supply.

[118] See Galbraith (1967, ch. 16–17) for a detailed description.

competition under Economic Democracy, they are more likely to be equity problems than efficiency problems. If these problems become severe, the government will have several options: It can impose a graduated income tax (targeted to wealthier individuals) or a graduated profits tax (targeted to wealthier firms) or selective price controls (targeted to firms with excessive market power). None of these is a perfect solution, but some version of one or the other should be workable. All are routinely used in advanced capitalist societies.

There is another problem with the monetarist solution to stagflation that might seem far more serious. If the central bank were to increase the money supply so as to avoid stagflation, it would seem to be undercutting the discipline of the price system. If firms know that the government will step in to head off the contraction that their price rises will cause, then all restraints will be off. In solving the stagnation part of stagflation, we would generate a pure inflation with runaway potential.

It seems to me that this concern is overblown, for four reasons. First, all restraints are not off. Individual firms that raise their prices will have to worry that their consumers will stop buying or will go elsewhere. The tax cut that comes may come too late. Second, it is clear from the record of capitalist countries that significant inflation often accompanies real growth. It is not true that inflation invariably runs away. It is certainly not true that the "static" of inflation makes planning impossible. Third, consider once more who is hurt by inflation. I argued earlier that lenders tend to be hurt, and borrowers helped. But who will be the lenders in Economic Democracy? There will be no lenders. The money for investment will come from the assets tax, not from private savers. The only "victims" of inflation under Economic Democracy will be those on fixed incomes or those with personal savings, but both of these groups could be protected by indexing. Finally, and perhaps most importantly, the government will have ultimate control over the money supply – more control, as we have seen, than does the government under capitalism. If inflation should threaten to get out of hand, the government need not stand helplessly by. It can step on the monetary brake.

We have seen in this chapter that relaxing the assumption that technology is fixed, and allowing for the possibility of innovation and growth, can do little to enhance the case for Laissez Faire. In fact, they make it worse. The kind of growth stimulated by the free market is likely to be unbalanced, plagued by externalities, and skewed by an inequitable distribution of income. Its rate is also likely to deviate from optimality. Laissez Faire is structured to grow, and it will grow (whether or not growth is desirable or desired) until it runs up against one or more of the various barriers we have discussed. These barriers, however, do not brake the growth process in a smooth and natural fashion; instead, they tend to trigger recessionary unemployment and class conflict.

This is not to say that a smoothly functioning, optimal, Golden Age Laissez Faire is impossible. But the Golden Age is not likely. There are no structural forces to keep the economy on the golden path. Reason and experience point to instability. Unless there are extremely important noneconomic considerations in favor of Laissez Faire, its desirability as a societal model would seem to be outstripped by the promise of Economic Democracy.

5. Capitalism or socialism?: liberty, equality, democracy, autonomy

Arguments purporting to demonstrate the economic nonviability of socialism have been advanced with more or less vigor, depending on the vicissitudes of economic conditions. During the Great Depression it was the economic viability of capitalism, more than that of socialism, that was called into question. During the post–World War II period that brought Marxian revolutionary victories in the Third World (essentially 1949 to 1979, the period framed by the Chinese and Nicaraguan revolutions), the success of Soviet industrialization and the success of countries like China and Cuba in eliminating chronic hunger and in taking control of their natural resources (thus providing a compelling model for national liberation) caused Western policymakers much concern.[1] But whatever the economic health of a particular socialist society, the noneconomic argument has always been put forth: Such systems are not free! They are not democratic! The individual becomes a mindless cog in a great totalitarian machine!

These charges, variously modulated, have been constant features of antisocialist thought, long antedating the empirical support provided by the example of the Soviet Union under Stalin.[2] The charges, of course, reek of hypocrisy, in view of the Western embrace of tyrants and thugs (too many to list) so long as they are *our* sons of bitches."[3] But these charges have often been true – not all of them all the time, but too many and too often.

We need not attempt here to sort out the details, because historical specifics are not directly relevant to the argument at hand. What is relevant, however, and what must be addressed, is the frequently repeated

[1] To cite but one example: Department of Defense documents from 1959 report that the State Department feared that "a fundamental source of danger we face in the Far East derives from Communist China's rate of economic growth," with the Joint Chiefs of Staff adding that "the dramatic improvements realized by Communist China over the past ten years impress the nations of the region greatly and offer a serious challenge to the Free World." See Chomsky (1973, pp. 31ff.) for documentation and discussion.

[2] *The Communist Manifesto* (1848) notes that the abolition of capitalism "is called by the bourgeoisie abolition of individuality and freedom!" (Marx and Engels, 1948, p. 24).

[3] FDR's remark has been often (and bitterly) quoted, e. g., by Ernesto Cardenal (1980, p. 14) in his great poem "Zero Hour":

As the sonofabitch Roosevelt said to Sumner Welles:
"Somoza is sonofabitch but he's ours."

claim that socialism, by its very nature, is incompatible with certain noneconomic, ethical values. It is one thing to point to specific abuses in specific countries; it is another to assert that these abuses flow from the very structure of socialism. This latter charge must be confronted.

To do so, and to develop further the positive case for Economic Democracy, we must look more closely at values. The overall anticapitalist argument of this book has thus far proceeded by appealing to values acceptable even to most conservatives. The underlying ethical commitments have been quite modest: Human happiness is good; material well-being is good; scarce resources ought not be wasted; it is generally better to labor less than more, but involuntary unemployment is bad; individuals are the best judges of their own welfare; if a course of action or structural change will make some people better off and no one worse off, then it should be undertaken. In all cases, the judgments are prima facie only, capable of being overridden when they conflict with other values.

There may be a break in this conservative-liberal-Left harmony (at the level of values) in this chapter. Some of the arguments here will appeal to values that differ (or are at least weighted differently) from those of many conservatives. Specifically, we shall be dealing with liberty, equality, and democracy. Conservative assessments of these values do not always coincide with liberal-Left assessments.[4]

One means for clarifying the differences between conservative (classical liberal) and liberal-Left value judgments is to situate liberty, equality, and democracy with respect to autonomy, a value often regarded (since Kant) as fundamental to human dignity.[5] Etymologically, "autonomy" means self-rule, and it was first applied by the ancient Greeks to a *polis* that was not under the dominion of another city-state or foreign power. With Rousseau, the concept of self-rule became "freedom," defined (famously) as "obedience to a law one prescribes to oneself,"[6] and was used to defend democracy as the only form of government that does not conflict with an individual's natural liberty. With Kant, the term "autonomy" was resurrected, given a Rousseauvian twist, but transposed from the political realm to the realm of private morality. Kant defined autonomy as the act of binding oneself to the moral law, which is one's own law because it is the law one would legislate for all rational beings.[7] For Kant,

---

[4] The term "liberal-Left" will refer to values or judgments common to both the modern-liberal and democratic-socialist traditions. (It should not be confused with "Left-liberal," a term commonly used to refer to one end of the liberal political spectrum.) I use the term "liberal-Left" to underscore my conviction that there are no significant differences, relevant to the arguments of this book, between modern-liberal and democratic-socialist value commitments. The differences, as we shall see in Chapter 6, lie elsewhere.

[5] For a sampling of current philosophical views on personal autonomy, see Christman (1989). See also Dworkin (1988).

[6] Rousseau (1968, p. 65).   [7] Kant (1959, p. 51).

it is the capacity for autonomy that gives each human being worth and dignity.

If the concept of autonomy is construed narrowly, a conservative will have no trouble endorsing it. The notion of autonomy as personal self-government has strong affinity with the classical-liberal conception of liberty: "independence of the arbitrary will of another."[8] The Friedmans approvingly quote John Stuart Mill's dictum: "Over himself, over his own body and mind, the individual is sovereign."[9]

A narrow interpretation along Kantian lines also points to a notion of equality acceptable to classical liberalism. Human beings, in virtue of their capacity for autonomy, are worthy of equal moral respect and hence are entitled to equality before the law. "Not birth, nationality, color, religion, sex, nor any other irrelevant characteristic should determine the opportunities that are open to a person – only his abilities."[10]

The Rousseauvian link between autonomy and democracy is more problematic for conservatives. If Rousseau had really solved the problem of reconciling individual liberty with state authority – if the laws passed by a democratic assembly were always indeed one's own – then classical liberals would not demure. But because the "tyranny of the majority" is not a pseudoproblem, classical liberals are deeply suspicious of the propensity of democracy to encroach on liberty.

In a sense, the classical liberal construes autonomy narrowly as the right to govern oneself according to one's own lights, subject only to the restriction that one's actions not impinge on other parties' equal rights to self-determination. That is to say, autonomy is identified with (negative) liberty, and liberty is given absolute weight vis-à-vis the values of equality and democracy. Liberty may be curtailed only for the sake of greater liberty.[11] Democracy is valued insofar as it serves to protect liberty, but neither equality nor democracy has independent weight. For Nozick, "the entitlement conception of justice makes no presumption in favor of equality."[12] For Hayek, "democracy . . . is probably the best means of achieving certain ends, but it is not an end in itself."[13]

The liberal-Left perspective construes autonomy more broadly. If personal self-government is important, it seems reasonable to be concerned not only with the right to live by one's own lights but also with the means

---

[8] Hayek (1960, p. 12).
[9] Friedman and Friedman (1980, p. 2). The quotation is from Mill's *On Liberty*. Notice that the classical-liberal formulation of liberty divorces freedom from the Kantian notion that autonomy is obedience to universal moral laws. With Kant, two distinct ideas are held in tension: that the individual is bound only by his own laws, and that these laws are universal.
[10] Friedman and Friedman (1980, p. 132).
[11] See Hayek (1960, p. 6) and Nozick (1974, p. ix).
[12] Nozick (1974, p. 223).   [13] Hayek (1960, p. 106).

to do so. If all have equal rights to self-government, then all should have equal opportunities for self-government – "opportunity" here implying access to the necessary means.[14] What exactly is meant by "necessary means" has been a subject of intense philosophical debate in recent years, but the details need not concern us.[15] Almost all of a liberal-Left persuasion share what Kai Nielsen describes as a conviction "so close to Bedrock here that it is difficult to know what to say" regarding "the sense of unfairness which goes with the acceptance, where something non-catastrophic could be done about it, of the existence of very different life prospects of equally talented, equally energetic children from very different social backgrounds."[16] Almost all are convinced, as conservatives are not, that (substantial) material inequalities require justification. In Rawls's famous formulation, "All social primary goods – liberty and opportunity, income and wealth, and the bases of self-respect – are to be distributed equally unless an unequal distribution of any or all of these goods is to the advantage of the least favored."[17]

The liberal-Left conception of autonomy is broader than the conservative conception along another decisive dimension. The liberal-Left concern is not only with individual self-government but also with collective self-government. Neither modern liberals nor democratic socialists, no more than conservatives, think that Rousseau solved the conflict between personal liberty and state authority, but most modern liberals and democratic socialists, much more than conservatives, are attracted by his participatory ideal, his democratic elaboration of the medieval maxim that "what touches all should be decided by all." This ideal might be formulated as a "principle of participatory autonomy": An individual has a right to participate in making those rules to which she must submit and those decisions whose consequences she must bear.[18]

The liberal-Left commitment to democracy follows readily from the commitment to participatory autonomy, but it should be noted that participatory autonomy is not equivalent to democracy. Eighteenth- and

[14] For a careful, if controversial, attempt to demonstrate that all persons have equal moral rights to freedom and well-being, see Gewirth (1978).

[15] Among the contenders: opportunities for welfare (Arneson), primary goods (Rawls), resources (Dworkin), capabilities (Sen), and access to advantage (Cohen). See Cohen (1989) for an explication of the differences.

[16] Nielsen (1985, pp. 7–8).

[17] Rawls (1971, p. 303). Not everyone of a liberal or Left persuasion accepts Rawls's specific formulation, but almost all accept something comparably egalitarian.

[18] Rawls's version of this principle is designated the "principle of (equal) participation": "All citizens are to have an equal right to take part in, and to determine the outcome of, the constitutional process that establishes the laws with which they are to comply" (Rawls, 1971, p. 221). Rawls, we observe, formulates his principle so as to apply only to the realm of traditional politics, but his reasoning would seem to allow for a more general formulation. See Gould (1988, p. 84) and Walzer (1980, p. 254) for formulations similar to the one I have proposed.

nineteenth-century political thinkers frequently appealed to the principle of participatory autonomy to justify democracy (often in the face of classical-liberal opposition),[19] but in the twentieth century democratic theory took a different turn. Taking their cue from Joseph Schumpeter, many theorists have concluded that Rousseauvian democratic theory, with its emphasis on participatory "rule by the people," is unrealistic and impractical. Democracy, they argue, should be regarded as a quasi market where politicians compete to offer their leadership services to an electorate. The essence of democracy is held to be not the active deciding of issues by an electorate but an institutional arrangement for selecting political leaders by means of a competitive struggle for the people's votes.[20] The value of democracy, it is said, does not lie in its enhancement of participatory autonomy. To the contrary, too much such autonomy, too much participation by the citizenry, can be destabilizing. As Harvard's Samuel Huntington put it in his report to the Trilateral Commission, "the effective operation of a democratic political system usually requires some measure of apathy and noninvolvement."[21] Democracy is held to be valuable because it checks the governors. Just as the market constrains producers to seek out and satisfy consumer preferences, competitive democracy similarly constrains politicians. This constraint, not participation, is the essence of democracy.

This is not the place to debate the merits of a participatory conception of democracy versus a competitive conception, but it is useful to inquire which conception is more congenial to classical liberalism. To put the question more bluntly: Does a conservative value participatory autonomy? The answer, I think, is no. At least not much. The concept is explicitly attacked by Nozick:

Others have no right to a say in those decisions which importantly affect them that someone else . . . has a right to make. . . . After we exclude from consideration the decisions which others have a right to make, and the actions which

[19] Polanyi (1970, p. 266) notes that "inside and outside England, from Macaulay to Mises, from Spencer to Sumner, there was not a militant liberal who did not express his conviction that popular democracy was a danger to capitalism."

[20] See Schumpeter (1962, p. 269).

[21] Crozier, Huntington, and Watanuki (1975, p. 114). The Trilateral Commission, brainchild of David Rockefeller, was founded in 1973 to bring together the right sort of people from the United States, Western Europe, and Japan to discuss "common problems." The 1970s witnessed considerable panic in ruling-class circles concerning the democratic "excesses" of the 1960s and the decline of traditional authority. Crozier et al. (1975, p. 2) wrote that "in recent years, acute observers on all three continents have seen a bleak future for democratic government." Huntington, in his contribution to that volume, pointed out that at the end of the 1950s, three-quarters of the American people thought that their government was run primarily for the benefit of the people. By 1972 that figure had declined to 38 percent, with a full 53 percent thinking that it was "run by a few big interests looking out for themselves" (Crozier et al., 1975, p. 78).

would aggress against me, steal from me and so on and hence violate *my* (Lockean) rights, it is not clear that there are *any* decisions remaining about which even to raise the question of whether I have a right to a say in those that importantly affect me.[22]

He adds, by way of example, that "if one starts a private town, on land whose acquisition did not and does not violate the Lockean proviso, persons who chose to move there or later to remain there would have no *right* to a say in how the town was run, unless it was granted them by the decision procedures for the town which the owner had established."[23]

In addition to the values associated with a broad conception of autonomy, the arguments of this chapter will also appeal to some of the values enumerated at the beginning of this section that grounded our earlier arguments. Of particular importance is human happiness. The preceding analysis has stressed material well-being as the form of happiness to be optimized in a well-ordered society; here we shall also refer to psychological happiness.

Two components will be particularly important. We shall assume that, in general, people are happier when the work they do calls for an exercise of skill. We shall assume that what Rawls calls the "Aristotelian principle" is true: "Other things equal, human beings enjoy the exercise of their realized capacities (their innate or trained abilities), and this enjoyment increases the more the capacity is realized, or the greater its complexity."[24] There is, in fact, some solid empirical evidence that "the effect of substantive complexity of work on intellectual flexibility is real and remarkably strong"[25] and that work that involves the use of initiative, thought, and independent judgment has important positive effects on personality. One study found that such work

leads to self-directed orientations to self and society: men who are self-directed in their work are consistently more likely to become nonauthoritarian, to develop personally more responsible standards of morality, to become self-confident and not self-deprecatory, to become less fatalistic, less anxious and less conformist in their ideas.[26]

A second component of psychological well-being to which we shall appeal is that of achieving the right balance in one's life between labor

---

[22] Nozick (1974), p. 270.

[23] Ibid. It is striking how markedly Nozick's (conservative) intuitions conflict here with those of the liberal-Left. It seems perfectly clear to Michael Waltzer, in his quite similar story of a "bold, adventurous, energetic and very smart" young man who founds a town, that founding or reforming a town or state "generates no right of ownership and none of the subsidiary rights that ownership brings with it." See Walzer (1980, pp. 279–84).

[24] Rawls (1971, p. 426).   [25] Kohn and Schooler (1978, p. 24).

[26] Kohn and Schooler (1982, p. 1272). For a similar study of women workers, see Miller et al. (1979). I shall assume that the various good effects that have been mentioned correlate positively with happiness.

and leisure. As E. F. Schumacher has observed, these elements are complementary and cannot be separated without "destroying the joy of work and the bliss of leisure."[27] We shall assume that psychological well-being requires useful work, but not excessive work.

The values to which the subsequent arguments will appeal have not been defended here, nor will they be defended later in any systematic fashion. The aim here, as in similar prior discussions, has been to state and clarify the moral values underlying the arguments against capitalism that will follow. It should be clear that these values are widely, if not universally, shared in our society. Most, though perhaps not all, are acceptable even to conservatives. To the extent that they are not, a conservative may not be persuaded by the arguments that follow. To the extent that they are, he should be.

Liberty

Under socialism you would not be allowed to be poor. – George Bernard Shaw

Liberty, for a classical liberal, is defined as the absence of coercion, and "coercion occurs when one man's actions are made to serve another man's will, not for his own but for the other's purpose."[28] Liberty is associated with an assured "private sphere" wherein one is free from interference. It is sharply distinguished, in classical liberalism, from one's ability to accomplish desired ends or from having a range of opportunities. This is a controversial delimitation, but the controversy will not detain us here. What we want to investigate is a concrete issue: the claim that one has more liberty, in the classical-liberal sense, under Laissez Faire than under Economic Democracy.

The first thing we observe is that a great many of the traditional liberty-based arguments against socialism have no force against our particular model. For Hayek, "the common features of all collectivist systems may be described, in a phrase ever dear to socialists of all schools, as the deliberate organization of the labors of society for a definite social goal."[29] For Friedman, "in a socialist society, there is only the all-powerful state."[30] But neither of these characterizations applies to our model. The significant enlargement of governmental control will involve only new investment, and even that will be highly decentralized. The labor of society will not be directed toward a "definite social goal" by an "all-powerful state." Firms will be controlled by their workers, not by the government. Economic Democracy, no less than Laissez Faire, draws a line between

---

[27] Schumacher (1973, p. 52).   [28] Hayek (1960, p. 133).
[29] Hayek (1944, p. 56).   [30] Friedman (1962, p. 18).

political power and economic power and allows one to check and counterbalance the other.

"But," a conservative is bound to reply, "Economic Democracy would represent an extension of governmental power, a power that is already enormous and constantly growing. A 'mere' 10–15 percent more GNP coming under governmental control (the estimate in Chapter 2) could raise the government's total share of the economy to 50 percent or more, a frightful and frightening figure." As Hayek has argued, "once the communal sector, in which the state controls all the means, exceeds a certain proportion of the whole, the effects of its actions dominate the whole system. Although the state controls directly the use of only a large part of the available resources, the effects of its decisions on the remaining part of the economic system become so great that indirectly it controls almost everything."[31]

To respond to this charge is not so easy. We can begin by noting that it is by no means a foregone conclusion that the government will absorb a larger share of the GNP under Economic Democracy than it does under contemporary capitalism. It need not run to 50 percent. Many government programs in contemporary capitalist societies are necessitated by the underlying contradictions of capitalism itself. For example:

1. Unemployment and underemployment are more fundamental to capitalism than to Economic Democracy.[32] Hence, larger, more expensive (and more divisive) welfare programs are required.

2. The enormous outlays for national "defense" have been driven, at least in part, by (a) an anticommunism rooted in ruling-class fear that anticapitalist sentiment would prove "contagious," (b) the need for a steady source of effective demand to mitigate the inherent instability of Laissez Faire, and (c) the need to maintain control over a large enough portion of the world's resources to sustain capitalist growth. None of these considerations applies with comparable force to Economic Democracy.

3. The large drain on the federal budget occasioned by the national debt (interest payments, mostly to the wealthy, here and abroad) is a present expense reflecting the past unwillingness of the government to acknowledge to its citizens (by taxing them appropriately) the full costs of the weaponry and warfare deemed necessary to uphold the existing order.[33]

In short, a smaller, not larger, government might well be appropriate

[31] Hayek (1944, p. 61).

[32] This was demonstrated in Chapter 2 with respect to Laissez Faire. Chapter 6 will extend the argument to modern-liberal forms of capitalism.

[33] To take but one year: If defense expenditures had been cut in half in 1989, the U.S. government would not have had to borrow $150 billion to balance its budget, and subsequent generations would have been spared the eternal interest payments.

to Economic Democracy, even though a democratic socialist society likely would choose to provide its citizens with free health care and free education (as in all actually existing socialist countries, and in some, though obviously not all, advanced capitalist societies).

This response should call into question the immediate identification of socialism with big government, but it does not go to the heart of the matter. I have already argued that control of new investment is of strategic importance. Although quantitatively not large, new investment does determine the rate and quality of growth and the overall health of the economy. Hayek has a point. Control here does give, in an important sense, control over the whole economy.

Indeed, such control is precisely what is intended: political control of investment so as to head off the anarchy of the market, to subject the growth of the economy to human direction, and to eliminate the boom–bust cycles of capitalism. Efficiency and material well-being served as the normative bases for these claims in the arguments of the preceding chapters, but an appeal could also have been made to autonomy. Private investment decisions affect the lives of everyone in quite decisive ways; everyone should have some input into those decisions.

Although we must grant that the government (by design) will play a larger economic role under Economic Democracy than under Laissez Faire, we need not concede that this role will conflict with liberty. The question is, is a person's free space significantly limited (or are individuals more subject to the arbitrary wills of other individuals) when democratically elected bodies decide the rate at which enterprises will be taxed, or decide to offer encouragement grants to enterprises or individuals willing to undertake projects deemed worthy of promotion? I would not argue that liberty (in the classical-liberal sense) will be enhanced by these measures, but it would hardly seem to be curtailed.

For most people, it is not political control of investment that comes to mind when "socialism" is juxtaposed with "liberty." What is troubling to all people of good will is the repression of dissent in actually existing socialist societies. Procapitalist theorists commonly explain this fact as an inevitable consequence of structure. Friedman, for example, argues that dissent under socialism will never be as free as under capitalism, because the two systems differ in crucial respects:

1. In a socialist society, all jobs are under direct control of the government, and so an advocate of capitalism risks being denied all forms of employment.
2. In a capitalist society, publishers need not agree with an advocated cause. If a book or magazine will sell, it will be published; not so under socialism.
3. In a socialist society, an advocate of capitalism, even if he had the funds, "would have to persuade a government factory making paper to sell to him,

a government printing press to print his pamphlets, a government post office to distribute them among the people, a government agency to rent him a hall, and so on."
4. To gain support for a cause, one needs funds. Under socialism, the only wealthy people will be government officials, whereas under capitalism there are many independently wealthy people from whom "to get funds to launch any idea, however strange."[34]

We see immediately that Friedman's first three points do not tell against Economic Democracy. Control over new investment may give national, regional, and local governments some strategic control over the economy, but it by no means gives them control over employment or printing presses. The economy will be a decentralized, market economy. The profit motive will operate within a worker-managed publishing house as it does within a capitalist one.

If points 1–3 do not apply, what about point 4, the contention that the existence of an independently wealthy upper class enhances liberty? Friedman's argument here smacks of intellectual fraud. It is simply false to say, as he does, that "radical movements in capitalist societies . . . have typically been supported by a few wealthy individuals" – at least if the referents are radical Left movements.[35] The radical Right, of course, is another matter.[36] The suppression of socialist ideas and Left political movements by the power that concentrated wealth can command has been massive. Friedrich Engels did indeed help Marx through some hard times, and Left movements occasionally attract wealthy individuals, but this must be set beside Blackshirt, Brownshirt, White Hand, and the myriad other forms of right-wing, wealth-backed terror. The "role of inequality of wealth in preserving political freedom . . . is seldom noted," says Friedman.[37] For good reason.

So much for Friedman's argument, but let us pursue the matter just a bit further. Concern for the status of free speech and other civil liberties under socialism is by no means misplaced. No socialist society yet established has had a record on civil liberties as good as the best of Western capitalism. There has been much repression. Why that has been so is a question of enormous importance. Although the historical issues are too complex to treat properly here, a couple of perhaps obvious observations are in order.

[34] Friedman (1962, pp. 16–18).
[35] Ibid., p. 17. This passage, in context, suggests that wealthy patrons provide the primary support; it is not the trivially true observation that some wealthy persons have supported radical causes.
[36] On wealthy benefactors bankrolling fascists and Nazis, see Sarti (1971) and Turner (1969). On the role of Houston's wealthy builders, bankers, and oilmen in fanning local McCarthyism in the 1950s, see Carleton (1985).
[37] Friedman (1962, p. 17).

To understand contemporary socialist societies, we must take specific historical factors into account, notably (1) the fierce resistance to socialism on the part of prior regimes and the rest of the capitalist world, (2) the absence of liberal and democratic traditions in those countries where revolutions were successful, and (3) the severity of underdevelopment in those countries. The Industrial Revolution in the West, it should not be forgotten, was also a brutal affair. One should not forget the genocidal impact that the opening up of the New World to nascent capitalism had on the native inhabitants. One should not forget the African slave trade. One should not forget the enclosure movements, child labor, and all the rest. These events do not exculpate socialist barbarism, but an honest comparison of the historical records of capitalism and socialism should keep them in mind.

To return to the main question: If investment funds collected by taxation and distributed via a network of community-mediated banks will not pose a threat to liberty, and if a free press is to be expected under Economic Democracy, can we conclude that Economic Democracy will be as free as Laissez Faire? We observe that Economic Democracy will accord its citizens the full range of civil liberties associated with Western democracies: freedom of speech, the press, assembly, and the like. As to economic liberties, under Economic Democracy people will be free to seek work where they will, to change work as they will, not to work at all if they can find someone to support them. Economic Democracy implies no restriction of private ownership of nonproductive property: the food, clothing, shelter, or the thousands of other personal possessions people might want to purchase. One's home will remain one's castle.[38] One can even own a productive facility, so long as one works it alone or with one's family. The line, remember, is drawn at wage labor and at the making of money in virtue of ownership rather than work.[39]

To be sure, Economic Democracy (like modern liberalism) will permit the national, regional, and local governments to enact laws regulating the manufacture of specific items and the rental of land and dwellings, but it is not evident that such laws will significantly restrict an individual's free space, much less subject her to the arbitrary will of another. It is worth pointing out that one of the greatest champions of individual liberty, and an ardent supporter of the free market to boot, did not think that the justification of Laissez Faire was liberty. For John Stuart Mill, "Restraints

---

[38] Socialists have been insufficiently appreciative of the case for private housing as a component of well-being and of the fact that private housing in no way conflicts with the basic principles of socialism. An important and articulate exception is Stretton (1976).

[39] As indicated earlier, a limited amount of wage labor might be permitted. But to keep the principles clear, I shall assume an absolute prohibition.

[on trade] are wrong solely because they do not produce the result which it is desired to produce by them. . . . The principle of individual liberty is not involved in the doctrine of free trade."[40]

Nozick, for one, would object: Liberty is indeed curtailed under socialism. "The socialist society will have to forbid capitalist acts between consenting adults."[41] This much-quoted conclusion is derived from the following scenario:

> Notice also that small factories would spring up in a socialist society, unless forbidden. I melt some of my personal possessions and build a machine out of the material. I offer you and others a philosophy lecture once a week in exchange for yet other things, and so on. . . . Some persons might even want to leave their jobs in socialist industry and work full time in this private sector. [This is] how private property even in means of production would occur in a socialist society.[42]

Despite the implausibility of the scenario, the substance of Nozick's argument is to the point: Certain capitalist acts might be forbidden under Economic Democracy. Our model is not so severely benevolent as the socialism envisaged by Shaw in the epigraph to this section. One will be allowed to be poor if one wishes – but one might not be allowed to work at a productive facility constructed with private funds unless the owner agrees to relinquish his ownership claim and run it cooperatively. One might not be allowed to pay interest to private individuals to entice them to invest in one's enterprise. The basis for these prohibitions, if enforced, would not be paternalism, nor would it be the fear that Economic Democracy would evolve into a capitalist society in the absence of such restrictions. (I find that eventuality about as likely as the peaceful resurrection of the antebellum South should the prohibition of slavery be repealed.)[43] The basis would be the concern that "capitalist acts" could generate inequalities sufficient to be destabilizing, even if the vast majority were clear in their preference for worker self-management, and the economy as a whole remained far from capitalist. A few individuals with a lot of money can generate much mischief.

I am not altogether certain that this empirical judgment upon which the legal prohibitions of "wage slavery" and "usury" are based is correct, but I do find it plausible. It might be the case, however, that allowing wage labor and interest payments to private individuals in a society where cooperative employment and public financing were readily available would not have any dire consequences, in which case these minor restrictions on liberty need not be imposed. I take this to be a judgment call, to be made democratically by the citizenry.

---

[40] Mill (1978, p. 94).   [41] Nozick (1974, p. 163).   [42] Ibid., pp. 162–3.
[43] For a debate on this issue, see Arnold (1987a,b,c) and Schweickart (1987a,b).

The argument of this section has thus far been defensive, claiming that Economic Democracy would not curtail liberty much, if at all. In fact, there are reasons for thinking that Economic Democracy might be freer than Laissez Faire.

First, we notice that Friedman's concern that workers under socialism will be afraid to express their opinions turns against him when the comparative term is Economic Democracy. Dissent under Economic Democracy should be easier than under Laissez Faire, because employment will be more secure. As we have seen, workers in a self-managed firm are likely to be given substantial job protection by law, for reasons of both equity and efficiency. A capitalist employer, certainly under Laissez Faire, can fire an employee for political reasons.[44] A worker-managed firm will have more difficulty.

Second, if we stay on the shop floor, and if we recall Hayek's definition of coercion ("when one man's actions are made to serve another man's will, not for his own but for the other's purpose"), it would be difficult not to conclude that workers under Economic Democracy will be freer, in the classical-liberal sense, than under Laissez Faire. Under the latter, a worker must surely serve the owner's will (as transmitted by management), not for his own purpose, but for the owner's purpose. Granted, a worker can always quit (as he can also under Economic Democracy), but under Economic Democracy the "other" whose purpose he must serve will be the collective of which he will be a voting member. Under Economic Democracy he will have the option of "voice" as well as "exit."[45] Under Economic Democracy he will also share directly in the profit. Theses two facts render it less likely that his purpose will be sharply at variance with the purpose of the "other."

There is a third reason, of a very different nature, for thinking that Economic Democracy might promote liberty more effectively than would Laissez Faire. Those who assert the connection between capitalism and liberty rarely ask about the relationship between liberty at home and support for repressive regimes abroad. Yet, as Noam Chomsky and Edward Herman duly note, "the common view that internal freedom makes for humane and moral international behavior is supported neither by historical evidence nor by reason."[46] Long ago, Machiavelli ventured to assert

---

[44] "I should explain here, for those who may not know, that every nonunion employee in the U.S. is an 'employee at will.' He can be fired for *any* reason, good or bad, for his tie, for the color of his eyes, or for no reason at all. It is amazing to me how many people, even bright, college-educated people, have no idea that this is the case" – labor lawyer Thomas Geoghegan (1991, pp. 273–4). Geoghegan overstates the case here, but not by much. Certain specific reasons may not be used, e.g., race, sex, or age, and public-sector employees sometimes have seniority-based job protection.

[45] See Hirschman (1970) for an elaboration of this famous distinction.

[46] Chomsky and Herman (1979a, p. 1).

that "of harsh servitude, the harshest is to be in servitude to a republic [because] the aim of a republic is to enervate and weaken its subject lands in order to increase its own prosperity."[47]

Perhaps Machiavelli puts the case too strongly, but a dispassionate look at the empirical evidence surely must make one wonder. Capitalist regimes, even when internally liberal and democratic, have time and again given precedence to Chomsky's "Fifth Freedom" (to exploit the human and material resources of other countries) over Roosevelt's more celebrated "Four Freedoms" (of speech, of worship, from want, and from fear).[48]

It is open to the procapitalist to argue that these unfortunate incidents are historical accidents, unrelated to structure, but a strong opposing case can be made. Capitalist institutions – above all, private ownership of the means of production, coupled with wage labor – are particularly well adapted to making money abroad. Wages are paid in accordance with local conditions of supply and demand; profits accrue to the owners, wherever they may reside. So unless there are specific barriers to their doing so, successful capitalist enterprises will seek beyond their national boundaries for productive resources and low wages.

The barriers to their doing so are invariably political – above all, the governments or insurrectionary movements in target countries that want to keep control of, or take back, their own resources. Capitalist enterprises thus have a powerful economic motive to remove such governments or defeat such movements. Because they lack direct means, they are powerfully motivated to extend financial support to those elements of the target country that can be persuaded to open up the country to foreign capital, or to keep it open, as well as to those political parties in the home country willing to use military force, when in power, to that end.[49] And if civil liberties in the target country suffer? No problem: Ideological justifications are ready at hand (white man's burden in the old days, anticommunism today). These need not be terribly cogent, because the electorate in the (democratic) home country is little affected by repression abroad. Indeed, many among the electorate benefit from the less expensive goods that these policies yield.

Consider, by way of contrast, an economy organized along the lines of

---

[47] Machiavelli (1966, p. 117).

[48] Chomsky (1985, p. 47) puts the Fifth Freedom more bluntly as "the freedom to rob and exploit." For unsparing details and careful documentation, consult the whole of Chomsky (1985), together with Chomsky and Herman (1979a).

[49] For a couple of particularly appalling case studies, see Schlesinger and Kinzer (1983) on the role of the United Fruit Company in the U.S.-engineered overthrow of the democratically elected Arbenz government in Guatemala in 1954, and see Hersh (1983, ch. 21, 22) on the roles of ITT, Chase Manhattan, Anaconda, and other U.S. corporations in toppling the democratically elected Allende government in Chile in 1973.

Economic Democracy. An enterprise can certainly trade with foreign countries, but it will have little incentive to invest abroad. It can request a grant from the community bank to purchase property abroad, but the request is not likely to be granted, given that job creation in the local community will be a prime criterion in determining awards. It can use some of its own depreciation funds to invest abroad, but if the purchased property is to be worked by workers there, those workers must be given full democratic rights in the organization, an arrangement that likely would prove unwieldy and would, in addition, negate the benefit (that accrues to capitalist firms) of low wages abroad.[50]

In sum, a worker-managed firm will have little motive to expand abroad, and hence little motive to press a home government to keep foreign economies "open" (with whatever suppression of liberty there that might entail).[51] Notice that this argument appeals to structures, not to human nature. I am not claiming that the citizens of an Economic Democracy are likely to be better informed than the citizens under capitalism regarding the consequences of government foreign policy, nor less selfish in pursuing their own interests. I am pointing out that, in contrast to capitalism, the citizens of an Economic Democracy will not have the same means at their disposal, given the structure of their economic institutions, to profit from the repression of others.

One final observation: Those who assert the connection between capitalism and liberty in order to deny that socialism is compatible with liberty invariably identify capitalism with the market. But the fundamental socialist objection to capitalism is to the other two defining characteristics of capitalism: private ownership of the means of production and wage labor. There are problems, to be sure, with the market, but a valid case can be made that there is a connection between the market and liberty. Private property (in the means of production) is another matter. Yale political scientist Charles Lindblom has noted that "the traditional liberal argument is incomplete unless it defends private property as itself consistent with freedom, a point on which it is silent. It is simply blind to the implications for freedom of Proudhon's 'Property is theft!' as well as to the implications of less extreme interpretations of how property is established and instituted."[52] I can do no better than quote his argument:

In liberal thought a world of exchange is conflict-free. Everyone does what he wishes. When all social coordination is through voluntary exchange, no one

---

[50] Whether or not an enterprise should be permitted to invest its depreciation funds in stocks, bonds, or other property abroad is a matter to be left to the community, because these funds, properly speaking, will belong to society, not to the firm.

[51] Reinforcing this tendency to "stay at home" is the structural tendency, already frequently noted, for worker-managed firms to be less expansionary, in general, than comparable capitalist firms.

[52] Lindblom (1977, p. 46).

imposes his will on anyone else. But how, we ask, can such a happy state be possible? It's possible only because the conflicts over who gets what have already been settled through a distribution of property rights in the society. Was that distribution conflict-free? Obviously not. Was it noncoercively achieved? Obviously not. The distribution of wealth in contemporary England, for example, is a consequence of centuries of conflict, including Viking raids, the Norman Conquest, the early authority of the Crown and nobility, two waves of dispossession of agricultural laborers from the land, and the law of inheritance.[53]

Property may not always be theft, and wage labor may not always be slavery, but the relationship of private ownership of the means of production and wage labor to liberty is so problematic that restricting private ownership so as to eliminate both wage labor and interest should enhance, not detract from, society's overall system of liberty, and indeed the world's.

Equality

Having wealth is unjustified, but the Rockefellers justify it by doing good. I had to cut through all this and understand that there *is* no rational justification for my family having the amount of money that it has, and that the only honest thing to say in defense of it is that we like having the money and the present social system allows us to keep it. – Steven Rockefeller

The value to which the arguments of this section appeal is more controversial than liberty. It is the basic value about which classical and modern liberals have such conflicting intuitions. On the one hand, modern liberals, virtually without exception, regard material equality as good – not absolutely, but certainly prima facie. That is, all assume that inequalities of wealth and power require justification. Conservatives, on the other hand, are often skeptical that equality has even that much worth. Recall Nozick: "The entitlement conception of justice in holdings makes no presumption in favor of equality.... It cannot be merely *assumed* that equality must be built into a theory of justice."[54]

We are at an impasse of sorts. I want to list equality among the values to which our arguments can appeal, and yet I do not want the conservative reader to stop short. Let us postpone the confrontation for a bit. Let us be clearer about the facts before bringing values to bear. Let us first establish two nonnormative theses: that Laissez Faire tends to produce massive material inequalities, and that Economic Democracy will be much more egalitarian.

The theoretical basis for the first thesis is clear and straightforward. Poor people are to be expected under Laissez Faire because there is no

[53] Ibid. [54] Nozick (1974, p. 233).

tendency toward full employment under Laissez Faire, nor toward a minimum wage that would pull a worker from poverty.[55] Individuals having great wealth are to be expected under Laissez Faire because wealth breeds wealth under Laissez Faire. Not only do successful companies expand rapidly, driving out or absorbing their less successful competitors, but if one has money, one can "put that money to work."

Our first thesis is supported powerfully by the empirical evidence. The United States is a relevant case. Although far from Laissez Faire, the United States has long ranked near the bottom of the advanced capitalist countries in public expenditures on social welfare and in effective redistributive policies.[56] Moreover, for more than a decade now the United States has been governed by administrations committed in theory and in practice to giving freer rein to the market (by cutting taxes for the rich and reducing welfare programs for the poor).

These movements in the direction of Laissez Faire have resulted in a surge in inequality. Recent Census Bureau figures show that the share of the national income going to the wealthiest one-fifth of the population (and the share going to the richest 5 percent) is higher than at any point since 1947; the share going to the poorest one-fifth is the lowest since 1954.[57] *Business Week* has reported that in 1980 the average chief executive officer (CEO) of a major corporation made forty-two times more than the average rank-and-file worker; by 1990 he was making eighty-five times more.[58] This widening gap is not merely relative. MIT economist Paul Krugman observes:

In the 1980s increasing inequality in income distribution, rather than growth in productivity, was the main source of rising living standards for the top 10 percent of Americans. And the 1980s were the first decade since the 1930s in which large numbers of Americans actually suffered a serious decline in living standards.[59]

Just how unequal is this inequality? All who have examined the figures have concluded that the inequality is pronounced, but it is difficult to grasp, from the numbers alone, just how pronounced. Unless one has a rare feel for figures, it is difficult to comprehend its dimensions. Some heuristic assistance is needed.

Perhaps the best device is one introduced some years ago by Dutch neoclassical economist Jan Pen to describe income distribution in England.[60]

---

[55] $4.25/hour, 40 hours/week, 50 weeks/year = $8,500.
[56] See Magaziner and Reich (1982, p. 12ff.) for many tables of comparative statistics.
[57] Figures reported in the *Boston Globe*, September 27, 1990, p. 24.
[58] Byrne (1991, p. 95). Thurow (1992, p. 138) puts the ratio of top CEO income to average worker income at 119 : 1.
[59] Krugman (1990a, p. 5).   [60] Pen (1971, pp. 48–53).

Let me adapt his approach to the present-day United States. We begin by telling a story. As will shortly be evident, we can give our story the same title as his: "A Parade of Dwarfs (and a Few Giants)."

Imagine each of the 93 million households in the United States represented by a member whose height is proportional to the household's income. Imagine a parade, which will last exactly one hour, starting with the shortest (poorest) people and ending with the tallest (richest) people. Suppose you are six feet tall (which we shall take to be average height, to keep the numbers simple) and you are standing on the same level as the marchers. Your six-foot height represents an annual income of just under $50,000 (in 1989).[61]

The one-hour parade begins with very short people, the marchers slowly increasing in size. After eight minutes, the person passing is about a foot and a half tall. That person (most likely female, most likely white)[62] has not yet reached the height of your knee, but she has reached the poverty line ($12,675 in 1989). Behind her are heads of households in which live some 31.5 million persons (12.8 percent of the population).

The parade continues, the heights of the marchers increasing, but very slowly. Your attention flags. Half an hour passes. You look again, perhaps expecting to see someone your own height, but to your surprise the parade is still a parade of dwarfs. The person passing at the thirty-minute mark is a mere three feet eight inches. (Median household income in 1989 was $28,900.) You will have to wait until nearly three-quarters of the parade has passed before someone of average height comes by. Only then will income have reached $ 50,000.[63]

After forty-five minutes, the parade begins to bring taller people more rapidly into view, although at first the change is not startling. At fifty-five minutes, the marchers coming by are nine feet tall ($75,000, the household income of a pair of tenured associate professors in the

---

[61] Per capita personal income in 1989 was $17,500; average household size was 2.7 persons. The figures on which my story is based, unless otherwise indicated, are from *Information Please: Almanac, Atlas and Yearbook, 1991,* and from the Census Bureau study reported in the *Boston Globe,* September 27, 1991.

[62] Of all poor families, 51.7 percent are managed by women with no husband present; two-thirds of the poor are white. Data from U.S. Bureau of the Census (*Boston Globe,* 1991, pp. 2, 4).

[63] Pen (1971, p. 51) calculates that in England the person of average height will pass at the forty-eight-minute mark; my calculation for the United States is somewhat less. Crucial note for those not familiar with the terminology: Statisticians distinguish between "median" (the value of the variable located at the midpoint of the sample) and "mean" or "average" (the sum of the variables, divided by the sample size). For example, the sequence 1, 2, 3, 4, 5, 6, 14 has a median of 4 and an average of 5. When the dependent variable (income, in our story) is concentrated at the upper end, the average will be higher than the median. The degree of concentration will determine the size of the gap.

humanities, say). Two and a half minutes later, the size of the marchers has increased another three feet; they are now twice the average height, twelve feet, representing $100,000.

Suddenly the figures begin to shoot upward. A minute later, with only ninety seconds remaining, the president of the United States passes by, twenty-four feet tall.[64] Then, in the final seconds, the figures explode. The million-dollar incomes pass – 120 feet, five times taller than the president. Then come those top CEOs reported by *Business Week* to be in the $5–20-million range.[65] The chairman of International Telephone and Telegraph (ITT), for example, at $11 million, strides by at 1,320 feet tall, several stories above the Sears Tower (which, as all Chicagoans know, is the world's tallest building).

But even these giants are small in comparison with the colossi that flash by in the parade's final microseconds. *Fortune* researchers uncovered sixty U.S. billionaires in 1990.[66] If we allow them a modest 5 percent return on their wealth, that is an annual income of $50 million – and a parade height of more than a mile. The last person in the parade would, until recently, have been Sam Walton (owner of Wal-Mart), whose estimated family fortune was $21.1 billion. He would have towered above us, and everything else on earth, twenty-four miles up, more than four times the height of Mt. Everest.[67]

Such is the distribution of income in the United States. And as everyone knows who looks into such matters, the distribution of wealth (i.e., net assets, as opposed to annual income) is even more unequal. I shall not attempt a story to describe that. It would be of the same general form, but with the dwarfs much, much smaller, and the giants much, much larger.

For the statistically minded, here is a snapshot. If we divide the *national income* into thirds (as in the parade we have just described), we find that

one-third goes to the bottom 60 percent of the population,
one-third goes to the next 30 percent of the population, and
one-third goes to the upper 10 percent of the population.[68]

---

[64] This is assuming that the president's only income is his $200,000 salary (1989). He stands nearly twice as tall as a member of Congress.

[65] Byrne (1991). The *Business Week* survey of the top two executives in 365 top corporations turned up 400 persons making more than $1 million, and 30 making more than $5 million.

[66] Reese (1991).

[67] Sam Walton died in 1992, at the age of seventy-four. As of this writing, it is unclear who will succeed to the title "Richest American." As to the source of Walton's fortune: "Last year, with sales of $32.6 billion, Wal-Mart outsold, not just the mom and pop stores it's been putting out of business in small towns across America, but also retailing giant Sears" (Reese, 1991, p. 59).

[68] Thurow (1987, p. 30).

If we divide the *national wealth* into thirds, we find that
   one-third goes to the bottom 90 percent of the population,
   one-third goes to the next 9 percent of the, and
   one-third goes to the upper 1 percent of the population.[69]
It might also be noted that the bottom 55 percent of the population have
zero or even negative financial assets, home equity and durable goods
being the only wealth of those with positive worth.[70]

Without making any value judgments, let us reflect for a moment on
our parade, on the facts depicted there. The first thing we notice is that
in this "affluent" society, a large majority of families are far removed
from the popular image of the "typical" American family: nice new house
full of nice new appliances, with a couple of nice new cars in the drive-
way, and a vacation to the Caribbean in the offing. No one can live that
way on $30,000 per year. And remember that $30,000 in income is the
upper limit for those in the bottom 50 percent of the population.

If there are lots of poor people in the United States, and hundreds of
millions more who are far from affluent, there are also lots of rich people.
As a percentage of the population, the rich group is not large, but in
absolute terms it is. The upper 1.6 percent (all those who passed by
during the last minute of our one-hour parade) comprises some 3.3 million
individuals having assets in excess of $500,000. Of these, about 1 million
are millionaires, 25,000 have more than $10 million, and sixty or so are
billionaires. Each of these 3.3 million people has, on average,
   $400,000 in corporate stock,
   $400,000 in real estate,
   $120,000 in bonds, and
   $125,000 cash on hand.[71]
The first nonnormative thesis of this section has been established. But
what about the second? It seems beyond reasonable doubt that Laissez
Faire will generate massive inequalities. One might wonder, however, if
Economic Democracy would be much different. After all, both Laissez
Faire and Economic Democracy will be market economies. In both, en-
terprises will have to compete for talented managers and skilled work-
ers. In both, luck will play a significant role, because unexpected shifts

[69] Carroll (1991, p. 13). His figures are from a 1986 Federal Reserve Board report. The
reader should be aware that accurate estimates of wealth at the top are notoriously
difficult to compile, because there are no laws requiring disclosure. Different agencies of
the federal government often come up with different estimates. The Internal Revenue
Service (IRS), for example, thinks that the upper 1.6 percent of the population own only
28.5 percent of the national wealth (*Chicago Tribune*, August 23, 1990).
[70] Thurow (1987, p. 32).
[71] These figures are from the IRS study reported in the *Chicago Tribune*, August 23, 1990.
One should, of course, be careful in interpreting the *averages* listed earlier, because wealth
is enormously skewed even (especially) in this top bracket. The assets listed are average,
but not typical. Most of the 3.3 million have much less (though none are uncomfortable).

in consumer demand or the advent of new technologies will profit some firms and cause hardship for others. Should one not suppose that the structure of inequality will be essentially the same in each system?

The answer is perhaps obvious by now. At the low end: There will be less poverty under Economic Democracy than under Laissez Faire because there will be less unemployment. The employment claim was demonstrated in Chapter 3. At the upper end: There will be few (if any) "super-rich" under Economic Democracy, because (1) earned incomes will be more egalitarian, and (2) there will be no unearned income.

Consider point 1. The basis for this claim is that income differentials within an enterprise will be decided democratically. The equalizing tendency of democracy is not insignificant. It is reflected even in a society such as the United States, where large fortunes do not contradict the prevailing ideology, and large salaries are regarded as essential to good management. Even in this society the salaries of top public officials are far from sufficient to allow for a large accumulation of wealth. According to one calculation, the salaries and bonuses paid to the fifty-six officers and directors of one corporation (General Motors) exceeded the combined remunerations received by the president of the United States, the vice-president, the 100 senators and 435 representatives, the nine Supreme Court justices, the ten cabinet members, and the governors of all fifty states.[72]

To this line of reasoning it is sometimes objected that market forces will necessarily override democratic egalitarianism.[73] In a market economy, one is paid according to one's marginal contribution (it is said). If a chief executive is paid $X under Laissez Faire, it is because he contributes that much. Because he would contribute that much under Economic Democracy as well, competitive forces would set his salary there at $X. If he were paid any less, another enterprise would hire him away.

This objection takes neoclassical theory much too seriously. It rests on the presupposition that salaries are indeed set in accordance with marginal contribution, which itself rests on another presupposition: that marginal contributions can be readily assessed. But common sense indicates otherwise (as does the empirical evidence). Consider Mr. Rand Araskog, the aforementioned CEO of ITT, who in 1990 was paid a salary of $7 million and earned an additional $4 million in bonuses, perks, and restricted stock.[74] Is it conceivable that an ITT accountant calculated that, all else equal, ITT's $20.4 billion in revenues that year would have been

---

[72] See Heilbroner and Thurow (1984, p. 478). In our society, politicians become rich not by saving a large fraction of their salaries but by dabbling (legally or otherwise) in the "free market."

[73] See Arnold (1987a) for a version of this objection.

[74] Details on ITT and Araskog are from a *Boston Globe* article, May 8, 1991.

only $20.389 billion in Mr. Araskog's absence – hence determining his marginal contribution to be $11 million?

In reality, of course, no such calculations are ever attempted. Corporate committees (composed of highly paid executives) propose salary structures to a board of directors (composed of wealthy individuals), who know quite well that however high these salaries are in absolute terms, they are so small a percentage of overall costs that stockholders will not feel the squeeze.[75]

A key difference, then, between Laissez Faire and Economic Democracy is that in the former the incomes of top management must be justified (in practice) to a small number of individuals, usually quite wealthy, who not only have little to lose in granting huge salaries but also are predisposed to see the top managers as being very much like themselves, and hence entitled to comparable incomes. By contrast, the incomes of top management in a worker-managed enterprise will have to be justified to a workforce whose members experience more immediately the relationships between management's incomes and their own, and they, too, will be predisposed to see their top managers as being rather like themselves.

Of course, one might worry that this egalitarianism will conflict with efficiency, but as we saw in Chapter 3, that worry is groundless. One might add that the examples afforded by Japan (whose executives are far less highly compensated than their U.S. counterparts), to say nothing of Mondragon (with its only rarely exceeded 4.5 : 1 ratio between highest and lowest salaries), indicate that Keynes's suggestion (taken up by Economic Democracy) is not unrealistic:

Thus we might aim at a practice . . . which allows the intelligence and determination and executive skills of the financier, the entrepreneur *et hoc genus omne* (who are certainly so fond of their craft that their labour could be obtained much cheaper than at present) to be harnessed to the service of the community on reasonable terms of reward.[76]

If the egalitarian tendency of workplace democracy can be expected to flatten the curve of earned incomes, even more significant is the absence of "unearned income." Remember, there will be no capitalists in Economic Democracy, nor will there be any interest payments to private individuals. This is extremely significant. The acquisition of income-

---

[75] Stockholders occasionally challenge the level of executive salaries, but rarely to effect. In Mr. Araskog's case, the California Public Employees Retirement System, which holds 1 percent of ITT's stock, did object, but was silenced with the assurance that Araskog's pay was a "fair reflection of long-term performance."

[76] Keynes (1936, p. 376). Notice that the high–low ratio at ITT is about 1,000 : 1. The *Business Week* study reported that for large corporations, the ratio between top executives to average rank-and-file workers (at 85 : 1) is about five times greater than that in Japan (Byrne, 1991, p. 73).

generating property (making money with money) is the major path to large-scale accumulation under capitalism. The popular consciousness may associate spectacular incomes with athletic prowess or musical talent or a medial degree, but the really big money flows through different channels.[77] With the only inequalities in income being due to different degrees of effort or talent, massive accumulation is virtually impossible. Without property income or the magic of compound interest, anyone desirous of becoming a billionaire during a fifty-year working lifetime would have to save $20 million each year, every year. To accumulate even $1 million, one would have to sock away $20,000 per year. Why anyone under Economic Democracy would want to save that much money is hardly clear, for in contrast to the situation under capitalism, there will be little to do with money but spend it on personal consumption. One will not be able to purchase the power and prestige of owning productive wealth, nor can one simply sit back and watch one's money grow.[78]

It is time to confront the normative issue. We have established that Laissez Faire will generate massive material inequality, far greater than that under Economic Democracy. So what? What is wrong with inequality?

Harry Frankfurt has recently argued that "economic equality is not, as such, of particular moral importance. What *is* important from the point of view of morality is not that everyone should have *the same* but that each should have *enough*."[79] Frankfurt has a point. When people object to inequality, to what are they objecting? Many (perhaps most) are looking at the first part of our parade, at the tens of millions of poor, and of those who find the parade's dramatic finale unsettling, many no doubt feel that there must be a causal connection between the mountainous personages at the end and the dwarfed figures at the beginning. But if there were found to be no connection, would we still object?[80] If there were no poor, would we still object? Are there any ethical grounds for objecting? Or is the appeal here simply to envy?

In a very real sense our overall argument is independent of this issue, and so it could be sidestepped. As we have seen, Laissez Faire will produce more unemployment than Economic Democracy, and *eo ipso* more

[77] Peruse the list published by Reese (1991). *Fortune* researchers uncovered 202 billionaires worldwide, and not a healer or entertainer or professional athlete on the list.

[78] *Fortune* writer Patricia Sellers (1991, p. 52) rhapsodizes that you could "put a billion dollars in a humble NOW account yielding only 5 percent, and you could skim off $137,000 in interest every glorious day!"

[79] Frankfurt (1987, p. 21).

[80] The classical Marxian connection, however appropriate in some contexts, cannot be invoked here. There are too few full-time workers among those below the poverty line to produce the surplus value from which the incomes of the super-rich derive.

poverty. One can agree with Frankfurt and still condemn Laissez Faire, although, strictly speaking, the normative ground would not be inequality, but material insufficiency.

But to sidestep in such a manner would not be wholly satisfactory. Not only would it be disappointing, coming on the heels of our startling parade, but a conservative might reply (as in fact almost all conservatives do) that welfare measures to help the truly needy would not be unacceptable.[81] Granted, such government intervention would break with the canons of strict Laissez Faire, but it would be a small enough price to pay (a conservative might say) to save us from the egalitarianism of Economic Democracy.

The reader will recall that it is not part of the project of this book to defend the values upon which its arguments rest. But given this conservative reply, not to mention the perceived centrality of equality to the conservative–liberal-Left divide, a brief canvass of the issue seems not out of place. We cannot actually settle the value controversy here, but perhaps we can clarify it a bit.

It should be clear from the foregoing that we need not concern ourselves with arguments for or against absolute equality ("equality of outcome," conservatives like to say).[82] The two terms of the comparison are economic systems involving inequality, albeit of quite different degrees. The arguments we need to consider are those that bear on relative equality, specifically, on the choice between Economic Democracy and (a modified) Laissez Faire that will take care of its poor. We want to see if there are good arguments concerning equality that will help us choose between two quite specific societies, each of which (we shall assume) will provide its poorer members with material sufficiency, but only one of which will feature massive inequalities at the upper end comparable to those of contemporary capitalism.[83]

It is important to distinguish arguments from strongly held "moral intuitions" or (what some would see as the same thing) strongly held "preferences." Individuals in our society are quite divided on the question of equality. Even if there were no poverty, an egalitarian would be inclined to the following view: "It's just not right that some should have so much more than others. It's just not fair, 'the existence of very different life prospects of equally talented, equally energetic children from

---

[81] Friedman (1962, pp. 190ff.) is typical in this regard. His specific proposal is the negative income tax.

[82] Friedman and Friedman (1980, p. 134); Flew (1989, p. 178).

[83] We are assuming here, for the sake of argument, that Laissez Faire can be suitably modified so as to eliminate such dire poverty at the bottom as one finds in the United States. I do not think this is a plausible assumption (for reasons that will be given in the next chapter), but it is a necessary assumption if we are to get clear about the normative critique of inequality per se, disconnected from insufficiency.

very different social backgrounds.' If the inequalities are needed so as to ensure that the society as a whole is better off, that's one thing, but if they are not needed, why should they be tolerated?"

To which the inegalitarian might reply: "I happen to like living in a society where great wealth is possible. So long as no one is hurt, what's wrong with that? I like thinking that one day I might reach that pinnacle. The possibility adds excitement to my life. If I don't make it, well, in the meantime I've been mightily entertained by the 'lifestyles of the rich and famous,' and properly edified by the rise and fall of the Boeskys and Helmsleys and Trumps and all the greedy others whose reach exceeded their grasp. I don't see the problem."

Personally, I feel the force of the conservative reply. So long as no one is hurt, what is wrong with inequality? But notice that this reply allows for rational contestation: Is it true that no one will be hurt by the inequalities of (modified) Laissez Faire? What are the arguments?

Let us begin at the other end, with arguments in favor of the inequalities of Laissez Faire. The two most common (and, to my mind, most significant) have already been considered and disarmed. It is commonly argued that capitalist inequality is necessary for efficiency and/or necessary for innovative growth. Chapters 3 and 4 should have persuaded the reader that those claims are false.

Hayek offers another argument, of a somewhat different nature:

The contention that in any phase of progress the rich, by experimenting with new styles of living not yet accessible to the poor, perform a necessary service without which the advance of the poor would be very much slower will appear to some as a piece of far-fetched and cynical apologetics. Yet a little reflection will show this is fully valid and that a socialist society would in this respect have to imitate a free society. It would be necessary for a planned economy (unless it could simply imitate the example of other more advanced societies) to designate individuals whose duty it would be to try out the latest advances long before they were made available to the rest. . . . A planned economy would have to provide for a whole class or even a hierarchy of classes, which would then differ from that in a free society merely in the fact that the inequalities would be the result of design and the selection of particular individuals or groups would be done by authority rather than by the impersonal process of the market and accidents of birth and opportunity.[84]

We need not spend much time on this, because the choice is not the one proposed by Hayek (either capitalism or a planned society that specifies a hierarchy of classes). Economic Democracy will be a socialist economy without central planning and without an exceedingly wealthy upper class. One can expect significant material inequality under Economic Democracy,

---

[84] Hayek (1960, p. 41).

and hence a significant market for "new styles of living."[85] One should not expect palatial estates, servants, private jets, and the various other amenities of the super-rich, which, by their very nature, can never "trickle down."[86]

If there are no good arguments in favor of the kind of material inequality to be expected under Laissez Faire, are there any good arguments against it, arguments against inequality per se, that is, inequality in the absence of poverty?[87]

Perhaps the most common argument has its roots in ancient Greece. Although they differed radically on their proposed solutions, both Plato and Aristotle worried a great deal about political instability occasioned by the disparities between rich and poor.[88] Sharp inequalities can induce social disorder: violence, crime, and, in extreme cases, revolution and/or tyranny.

This, I think, is a powerful argument against unmodified Laissez Faire, but does it tell against our modified version that has assumed away poverty? Perhaps yes. Both Plato and Aristotle were concerned with the deleterious effects on character that can be occasioned by wealth, as well as by poverty. Concerning the former, Aristotle observed that "the evil begins at home; for when they are boys, by reason of the luxury in which they are brought up, they never learn, even at school, the habit of obedience. [Hence, when grown, they] cannot obey, and can only rule despotically."[89]

---

[85] One can only speculate as to how much actual inequality there might be under Economic Democracy, because so much will depend on cultural and economic variables that cannot be specified in advance. We can say with confidence that there will be no giants towering above the earth, because it will be impossible to accumulate that much from saving alone. We can speculate that within a firm, the ratio of highest-paid to lowest, democratically determined, will be of an order of magnitude comparable to that in Mondragon (4.5 : 1, maybe 6 : 1 in exceptional cases), because that seems sufficient for efficiency. We can expect market fluctuations, technical innovations, and the like to produce windfall profits on occasion, so that some firms will be much better off than others – at least until redirected new investment exerts its equalizing influence. If we allow that no household should fall below the poverty line (raised, say, to $15,000), then a 6 : 1 ratio would put the upper incomes at $90,000, with windfall conditions pushing some individuals occasionally much higher, though probably not for extended periods. Very few people, if any, would likely fall outside the 10 : 1 ratio, with an income in excess of $150,000.

[86] See Harrod (1958) on the distinction between "democratic" wealth and "oligarchic" wealth; also see Hirsch (1976) on the social limits to growth.

[87] Frankfurt is correct that inequality and poverty are not logically connected. Suppose the United States were an Economic Democracy, without extremes of wealth or poverty. If each of us threw $1 in to a kitty, and then drew 250 lots, we would have 250 millionaires, but no one poor.

[88] See Plato, *The Republic*, especially Books III and VIII, and Aristotle, *Politics*, especially Books IV and V.

[89] Aristotle, *Politics*, 1295b.

Our specific worries are not quite those of Aristotle, but the question remains: Does excessive wealth corrupt? We cannot say "always and everywhere," because decent, law-abiding members of the upper class are not uncommon. But the flood of financial scandals that accompanied and have followed the "What a time it was!" Reagan eighties ought surely to give one pause. When great wealth is possible and can be enjoyed with full social approval (both conditions obtaining under Laissez Faire), the temptation to cut legal corners (and worse) is powerful. And the spectacle of corruption at the top, often unpunished (given the political and legal resources that money makes available), can provoke a corrosive cynicism throughout society.

This argument should give one pause, but is it substantial enough to affect the choice at hand? Are we to expect less cynicism and degradation under Economic Democracy than under Laissez Faire? I find this to be a difficult question. I think the answer is yes, but I do not have a convincing proof. The difficulty lies in establishing a direct link between inequality and moral corruption, given the host of culturally differentiated intervening variables. I would like to say that there is a correlation between inequality and crime, but the distribution of wealth in low-crime England is even more unequal than that in high-crime America.[90] The Soviet Union under Brezhnev was considerably more egalitarian than the United States, and yet corruption there was rampant.[91] These facts do not disprove the thesis that, all else equal, the more egalitarian society will be less crime-ridden and corrupt, but clearly the ceteris paribus clause makes proof difficult.

A second argument against (extreme) inequality is offered by Rawls. He worries not about the effects of wealth on those at the top but about the tendency of great inequality to generate envious, hostile feelings in those at the bottom. It is not common to regard envy as the basis for an ethical objection, but Rawls bites the bullet here. Given "human beings as they are," great disparities in income and wealth are bound to induce envy, and may even wound a person's self-respect. Under such circumstances, a person cannot "reasonably be asked to overcome his rancorous feelings." Such envy is "excusable." A society that permits excessive inequality is not.[92]

---

[90] The annual murder rate in the United States tends to be about twenty times that in Great Britain, and the robbery rate about ten times higher. See Archer and Gartner (1984, unpaginated appendix) for yearly comparisons. See Samuelson (1980, pp. 83–4) on comparative wealth.

[91] Peter Wiles (1974, p. 48) calculated that the income ratio of the top 10 percent to the bottom 10 percent was twice as high in the United States as in the Soviet Union in 1968.

[92] Rawls (1971, p. 534). Rawls grants that some inequality is justifiable for reasons of incentive (making everyone, or at least the least advantaged, better off); his argument is directed against inequality that goes beyond that.

It should come as no surprise that conservatives contest this line of reasoning. Nozick argues that reducing inequality might make matters worse. This is because self-esteem is based on differentiating characteristics (he says) and because

some simple and natural assumptions might even lead to a principle of the conservation of envy. And one might worry, *if* the number of dimensions is not unlimited and if great strides are made to eliminate differences, that as the number of differentiating dimensions shrinks, envy will become more severe. For with a small number of differentiating dimensions, many people will find they don't do well on *any* of them.[93]

I confess that I find it difficult to take this argument seriously. What Nozick is suggesting is that if inequalities of income were reduced, then one who was ugly, ignorant, and untalented would truly be miserable (and hence more envious), because he could not even compensate by becoming rich.[94] But even if this rather bizarre proposition were true, Nozick's general conclusion would not follow, for if there were a "principle of conservation of envy," then reducing inequalities could not make envy any worse, because ex hypothesi its quantity is unchangeable.

I do not think we need take Nozick's objection seriously, but it does not follow that Rawls's argument is sound. His argument works as a justification for restricting inequality at the top only if those rancorous feelings that concern him derive from comparing oneself with those at the top. But is it not the case that envy is based, in most instances, on a comparison of oneself with someone similarly situated, not on a comparison with someone far removed? (I suspect that among my colleagues, for example, the department member who gets an impressive raise in salary is resented far more intensely than is Sam Walton or Mr. Araskog.)[95] If so, then an appeal to envy, however "excusable," does not lend much support for Economic Democracy over Laissez Faire.

There is a third argument against massive economic inequality (to my mind, the most important and most cogent argument against the degree of inequality that will appear under Laissez Faire), but we shall set it

[93] Nozick (1974, p. 245).

[94] Perhaps this argument should be understood as Nozick's answer to the young Marx, who mused about the power of money to affect fundamental ontology: "I *am* ugly, but I can buy the *most beautiful* woman for myself. Consequently, I am not *ugly*, for the effect of *ugliness*, its power to repel, is annulled by money. . . . I am a detestable, dishonorable, unscrupulous and stupid man, but money is honored and so also is its possessor. Money is the highest good, and so its possessor is good" (*Economic and Philosophical Manuscripts of 1844*, in Fromm, 1966, pp. 165–6).

[95] British philosopher Alan Ryan (1984, p. 179) makes the same point thus: "Three men digging in the same hole to locate gas, water and electricity mains will be acutely aware of differentials in their pay; about the wealth of Lord Cowdray they neither know nor care. . . . So long as they are not too hard up, they do not begrudge other people what they happen to get. Being Lord Cowdray is like winning the pools – good luck rather than legally licensed robbery." For empirical confirmation, see Runciman (1966, part 3).

aside for now. The thesis is simply stated: Such inequality undermines democracy. But because this argument appeals to the value and its supporting institutions that are the topics of our next section, it is more properly treated there.

It is appropriate here to take stock of our investigation. We have established that massive inequalities are to be expected under Laissez Faire and that Economic Democracy will be much more egalitarian. There appear to be no good arguments in favor of the sorts of inequalities to be expected under Laissez Faire. The arguments against these inequalities (as distinct from arguments against poverty) point to the destructive effects that great wealth can have on character (effects on those who have and on those who have less), and to the undermining of democracy. The character arguments appear to be inconclusive. Consideration of the latter charge is being deferred.

For those who share the intuitions of an egalitarian, the case for Economic Democracy should be greatly enhanced by the analysis in this section. However, if one does not share those intuitions, and if, further, one is (1) unperturbed by the magnitude of the inequality to be expected under Laissez Faire, (2) unconvinced that Laissez Faire breeds poverty that cannot be alleviated by slightly modifying the system, and (3) unpersuaded that great wealth at the top will have a corrupting effect on character, then one will not be moved by the arguments just presented. Perhaps an appeal to democracy, rather than to equality, will have more effect.

Democracy

It is easy to perceive that the wealthy members of the community entertain a hearty distaste to the democratic institutions of their country. The populace is at once the object of their scorn and their fears. – Alexis de Tocqueville

Democracy is less highly valued than liberty by classical liberals. The "classical" classical liberals brooded that the masses might use their power to impinge upon property, the bulwark (in their eyes) of liberty.[96] Many found Plato's account of democracy compelling: that the natural evolution of democracy is toward a redistribution of wealth, which provokes civil war, which in turn leads to tyranny.[97] Modern history has revealed a somewhat different course of events. It could be argued that Weimar Germany and post–World War I Italy fit rather well that ancient paradigm of class struggle, but these instances have been exceptional to

---

[96] Even so liberal a classical liberal as John Stuart Mill feared this and sought to safeguard property from what he saw as the inevitable implementation of universal suffrage. See Mill (1958, pp. 94ff.).

[97] Plato, *The Republic*, Book VIII.

Western capitalism, not the rule. Universal suffrage has come to pass in the West, and yet property rights have remained intact, and property holdings have remained concentrated. The democratic threat to property now appears rather remote.

This is not to say that in times of stress conservatives can be counted on to support the democratic agenda. In 1975, Leonard Silk and David Vogel interviewed a large number of high-level corporate executives, a fair cross section, they claim, of the country's business leadership. They were startled to find that "many leading businessmen have begun to wonder if democracy and capitalism are compatible. . . . Many see a trend toward a more 'authoritarian' or 'controlled' system as inevitable if the corporation is to survive." Consider one executive's anxious query: "Can we still afford one man, one vote? We are trembling on the brink."[98]

But the "democratic distemper"[99] of the sixties and early seventies has subsided. Order having been restored, conservatives today are more favorably disposed toward democracy. They are not committed to participatory autonomy, but they are again expressing the conviction that democracy is the best check to liberty-usurping tyranny. After all, democracy was the rallying cry that toppled the house of communism.

The argument is often made that only a capitalist society is compatible with democracy. A famous and forceful articulation of that thesis was published nearly fifty years ago by Hayek:

> It is now often said that democracy will not tolerate "capitalism." If "capitalism" means here a competitive system based on free disposal over private property, it is far more important to realize that only within this system is democracy possible. When it becomes dominated by a collectivist creed, democracy will inevitably destroy itself.[100]

The argument for this claim is abstract, but important:

> It is the price of democracy that the possibilities of consensus are restricted to the fields where true agreement exists and that in some fields things must be left to chance. . . . Democratic government has worked successfully where, and so long as, the functions of government were, by a widely accepted creed, restricted to fields where agreement among the majority could be achieved by free discussion; and it is the great merit of the liberal creed that it reduced the range of subjects on which agreement was necessary to one which was likely to exist in a society of free men.[101]

---

[98] Silk and Vogel (1976, pp. 189ff.). It is another executive's view that "one man, one vote will result in the eventual failure of democracy as we know it." Another puts the matter frankly: "We are not a democracy in business. We are on top, we are used to having our own way. We are, therefore, not used to dealing with the democratic process."

[99] The phrase is Harvard's Samuel Huntington's, from his contribution to the Trilateral Commission's famous anti-democratic volume (Crozier et al., 1975, p. 102).

[100] Hayek (1944, pp. 69–70).

[101] Hayek (1944, p. 69). Notice, that Hayek uses "liberal" here to mean "classical liberal," i.e., "conservative".

Friedman makes essentially the same argument:

The use of political channels, while inevitable, tends to strain the social cohesion essential for a stable society. The strain is least if agreement for joint action need be reached only on a limited range of issues on which people in any event have common views. Every extension of the range of issues for which explicit agreement is sought strains further the delicate threads that hold society together. If it goes so far as to touch an issue on which men feel deeply yet differently, it may well disrupt the society. Fundamental differences in basic values can seldom if ever be resolved at the ballot box; ultimately they can only be decided, though not resolved, by conflict. The religious and civil wars of history are bloody testament to this judgment.[102]

This argument cannot be dismissed simply by pointing out that Economic Democracy will not be centrally planned. The market structure of Economic Democracy will deflect some of the argument's force, but the fact remains that under Economic Democracy more issues will be subject to a conscious, democratic, decision procedure than under capitalism (especially Laissez Faire). But the Hayek-Friedman argument is abstract. To evaluate it, we must be more concrete. What are the specific issues that Laissez Faire, but not Economic Democracy, will remove from the field of free discussion? How much strain would their inclusion place on the social fabric?

First, there is the matter of workplace organization. Under Laissez Faire, the capitalists (and/or management) will have de jure control; under Economic Democracy, the workers will. Will democracy at work involve greater conflict? We can hardly say that workplace democracy will be conflict-free. Some workers may wish to use a technology that is boring but productive; others may have reverse priorities. More significantly (to judge from the historical experience of worker self-management), those with managerial authority in a firm may feel hampered by democratic constraints and may, with varying degrees of success, strive to minimize them.[103] But these disputes will be confined within an enterprise; there is neither theoretical argument nor empirical evidence to suggest that such local disputes will erupt into civil disorder, much less bloody civil war. Set this prognosis against the historical record of violent capital–labor confrontations: worker insurrections, strike waves, the Ludlow Massacre, Harlan County, and on and on.[104] Surely the truism is true: One of the great merits of the democratic process is that it allows problems to surface, to be debated, and to be resolved before they reach a flash point.

---

[102] Friedman (1962, p. 24).
[103] See Comisso (1979) for a study of this issue in the Yugoslav context.
[104] For a well-told tale of the U.S. experience, see Brecher (1972). We should note that the most violent episodes have occurred during capitalism's relatively laissez-faire phase.

A second basic issue that will be subject to democratic control under Economic Democracy, but not under Laissez Faire, is the overall direction of economic change. The investment mechanism of Economic Democracy will be explicitly designed to give the national, regional, and community legislatures more conscious control over the investment decisions that will impact their constituencies. Here, again, there is bound to be conflict.

To see how this might be played out, let us consider a specific issue. A socialist society, no less than a capitalist one, must make difficult choices about energy. The question of nuclear power must be addressed. Because nuclear power requires massive, concentrated capital investment, the decision under Economic Democracy to embark (or continue) along the nuclear road would have to be decided by the national legislature. Hearings would have to be held; debate would ensue; the national legislature would vote. Under Laissez Faire, by contrast, the decision will rest with the utility companies. The business of generating power is the business of business, not the business of government.

We need not speculate as to the outcomes of these respective procedures, for that is not the relevant question here.[105] What we must ask is, Which system will resolve the issue more peacefully?

What seems obvious is that the answer is not obvious, and this lack of clarity tells against the Hayek-Friedman argument. A democratic decision would be preceded by debate, perhaps sharp debate. And there is no guarantee that the discontented minority, if the pronuclear forces prevailed, would rest content, refraining from civil disobedience. But – and this is the crucial point – there is no guarantee that the same thing would not happen if the decision were privately made. It is surely wrong to think that decisions that have such evident and significant consequences for people's daily lives could (or should) be kept off the political agenda, at least in a political democracy.

Conservatives, in fact, are not thinking about workplace disputes or nuclear power when they make their abstract argument. They are thinking mainly of something else. The fundamental issue that conservatives want kept from the ballot box, the issue that abstraction tends to obscure, is the one that has always evoked their deepest fear: redistribution of

---

[105] The answer toward which speculation would incline is perhaps surprising. It seems to me that Laissez Faire would be less likely to opt for the nuclear road than would Economic Democracy, for if the industry were made to bear the full costs of the project, including waste-disposal costs, insurance premiums against accidents, and the like, no self-respecting capitalist would take the risk. I doubt that Economic Democracy would opt for nuclear power either, but it would be better placed to socialize the costs and risks. (The systems most likely to go nuclear are centralized, nondemocratic systems and those modern capitalist systems that allow a large and bureaucratic government to work in economic partnership with big business.)

wealth or income. Above all, distribution of income must be handled by the market.[106]

But notice that the distribution of income under Economic Democracy will be handled by the market, at least the distribution of the national income among firms. The firms that are more efficient, better organized, and/or luckier will make more than their less successful counterparts. Even within a firm, market forces will impinge, for although incomes will be decided democratically, firms must compete for talented personnel. To be sure, progressive taxation is not ruled out under Economic Democracy if unseemly inequalities develop (as it is under Laissez Faire), but that is not going to result in "bloody conflict." All modern capitalist societies (over strenuous conservative objection) have instituted precisely such taxation schemes, with no such dire consequences.[107]

Because the argument that democracy will work only under capitalism has failed to survive examination, let us reverse the question. Will democracy work at all under capitalism? Is there not substance to the charge, made by Marxists (among others), that "bourgeois democracy" is a sham?[108]

To make sense out of these questions, we need to introduce a new term. Following Robert Dahl and Charles Lindblom, let us call a system whose political leaders are selected via regular popular elections from among competing candidates a *polyarchy*.[109] Most contemporary advanced capitalist societies are now polyarchies. None of the recently deceased communist societies fit this description.

Following Dahl and Lindblom, we shall keep "democracy" close to its etymological meaning and define it as a system in which (1) the electorate comprises all sane adult members of the society, and (2) the electorate is "sovereign." To be sovereign, an electorate must satisfy two conditions: (2a) Its members must be reasonably well informed about the issues to be decided by the political process and reasonably active in contributing to their resolution. (2b) There must exist no stable minority

---

[106] See Friedman (1962, ch. X), Hayek (1960, ch. 6), and Nozick (1974, ch. 7).

[107] The effectiveness of such schemes under capitalism is another matter, which will be addressed in the next chapter. Here we are concerned with the claim that allowing such items on the agenda will undermine democracy.

[108] In what follows, I shall not be endorsing the claim that bourgeois democracy differs in kind from the "proletarian democracy" of a one-party state and that only the latter is true democracy. That claim has been convincingly refuted in theory by Frank Cunningham (1987) and in practice by recent historical events. What I shall be arguing is that Economic Democracy is much more likely than Laissez Faire to fit our common understanding of democracy.

[109] See Dahl and Lindblom (1953). Dahl (1989, p. 220) characterizes polyarchy as a political order in which "citizenship is extended to a relatively high proportion of adults, and the rights of citizenship include the opportunity to oppose and vote out the highest officials of government."

class that is "privileged" (i.e., in possession of political power at least equal to that of elected officials and unmatched by that of any other stable grouping.)[110] In short, democracy is a system in which a universal electorate is well informed and active and is unobstructed by a privileged minority class.

Our question is this: Is the classical-liberal ideal compatible with democracy (so defined)? The historical record demonstrates that capitalism, even in its relatively laissez-faire forms, can coexist with polyarchy. This is no small thing. As Dahl observes:

Although the institutions of polyarchy do not guarantee the ease and vigor of citizen participation that could exist in principle in a small city-state, nor ensure that governments are closely controlled by the citizens, or that policies invariably correspond with the desires of a majority of citizens, they make it unlikely in the extreme that a government will long pursue policies that deeply offend a majority of citizens.[111]

But polyarchy is not democracy. Laissez-faire societies have never satisfied condition 1. Universal suffrage did not come to the United Kingdom until 1929, France until 1945, or Switzerland until 1971. In the United States, women did not get the vote until 1920; large numbers of African-Americans were excluded until the Voting Rights Act of 1965. By those dates, all of these countries were far from Laissez Faire.

But, above all, the empirical record raises doubts not just about Laissez Faire but about capitalism generally concerning condition 2b: privilege. Lindblom argues that business occupies a privileged position in all contemporary polyarchies.[112] In a similar vein, William Domhoff defends the thesis that "there is a social upper class in the United States that is a ruling class. . . . It is socially cohesive, has its basis in the large corporations and banks, plays a major role in shaping the social and political climate, and dominates the federal government through a variety of organizations and methods."[113]

According to both Lindblom and Domhoff, businessmen contribute vastly greater sums of money to political campaigns than do other groups.[114] Moreover, they are better organized to represent their special interests, they have special ease of access to government officials, and they are disproportionately represented at all upper levels of government. In addition, given their control of the mass media, they are in

---

[110] See Lindblom (1977, p. 172).   [111] Dahl (1989, p. 223).

[112] Lindblom (1977, pp. 170–88).   [113] Domhoff (1983, p. 1).

[114] Of the $500 million spent during the 1972 U.S. presidential election campaign, unions contributed roughly $13 million. In 1956, a year for which direct union–business comparisons are possible, the contributions of 742 businessmen matched the contributions of unions representing 17 million workers (Lindblom, 1977, p. 195). So much for the equality of "big business" and "big labor" – and that was several decades ago, well before labor's precipitous decline.

position to exert direct influence on the opinions and perceptions of the general population.[115]

The case made by Lindblom and Domhoff (set out by each in fascinating detail) seems to me irrefutable. But we must remember that such empirical arguments do not automatically overturn the classical-liberal position. Friedman, Hayek, Nozick, and others concede, indeed insist, that much is wrong with contemporary capitalism – for it has become infected (they would say) with modern liberalism. So we must interrogate the structures of Laissez Faire. We must ask if the empirical reality points to an inherent incompatibility between democracy and capitalism, rather than an accidental aberration perhaps brought on by too many concessions to the liberal Left.

I contend that there is indeed an inherent incompatibility. If it is granted (as it must be) that wealth will be highly concentrated under Laissez Faire, there would seem to be only one plausible case that a classical liberal might make as to why Laissez Faire would not give rise to a politically privileged upper class (such as we find in all existing capitalist countries). It might be put like this: Laissez Faire will keep economic matters off the political agenda; hence the capitalist class[116] will have no reason to undermine democracy. If the government keeps its hands off the economy, there will be no reason to suppose that the interests of capitalists will be threatened by a democratic process.

The central fact that undermines this argument was established in Chapter 4: Laissez Faire is inherently unstable. Thus it is inevitable that a democratic government will attempt to prevent or mitigate instability. If the electorate is sovereign, it will refuse to allow unemployed people to face idle factories indefinitely. It will demand that the government do something about "the economy." As history well demonstrates, laissez-faire ideology cannot contain such discontent.

---

[115] For confirmation of this latter claim, see Chomsky and Herman (1988), who point out that not only does the business class own most of the mass media (television, radio, newspapers, publishing houses), the bulk of which depends for its existence on advertising revenue (from private business), but also it provides a substantial share of "experts" for news programs (either from its own ranks or from privately funded "think tanks") and generates massive and intimidating "flak" when it feels it is being unfairly treated.

[116] Terminology here is somewhat controversial. Lindblom and Domhoff avoid the term "capitalist." Lindblom identifies the privileged class as the "business class," but this term seems problematic, because the tens of millions of small businessmen that this category includes have little more access to the levers of power than do ordinary workers. Domhoff identifies the ruling class as the "social upper class," consisting of the wealthiest 0.5 percent of the population. This strikes me as better, though the cutoff point is somewhat arbitrary. I prefer to give the class its functionalist title. We might define "capitalists" operationally as those who own sufficient income-generating property that they can, if they so desire, live comfortably without working. In the United States, this would be roughly the 1 percent of the population who own one-third of the wealth.

But if the government can be expected to play a significant role in a capitalist economy, then it becomes imperative that businessmen protect their interests. Thus they have a strong motive to press for political power. They also have the means, for two reasons: First, and most obvious, they have wealth. Second, they occupy so strategic a position in the economy that an elected government must acquiesce to most of their demands. Let us reflect briefly on these two points.

Consider the first reason: In a polyarchy, wealth can be employed in a variety of ways to enhance the probability that the outcome of a nominally democratic process will reflect the interests of the wealthy. These are well known, but they bear enumerating. There are the mechanisms to ensure that their collective interests are well formulated.

1. Private foundations and institutes can be set up to study ways to protect and advance their interests, and to formulate "model legislation."[117]
2. Privately funded "roundtables" can be set up to bring together high government officials, sympathetic academics, and corporate leaders so as to build support for their positions.[118]

There are mechanisms to ensure that the general public will acquiesce:

3. The owners of major media (all of which will be in private hands under Laissez Faire) can mobilize against political campaigns that run counter to the general interests of their class. Indeed, they can fairly well block even respectful consideration of the arguments.
4. Institutional advertising can be undertaken that will directly advance the interests of the wealthy, or (what is usually more effective) give the "appropriate" slant to issues of popular concern: "People start pollution; people can stop it" (i.e., don't blame the corporations or capitalism).

There are mechanisms to get the appropriate acts passed by the legislature:

---

[117] In the United States there are twenty-six general-purpose foundations with endowments of $100 million or more, and dozens of corporate foundations (Domhoff, 1983, p. 92). The impact of wealth on policy, when channeled through such institutions, can be enormous. As Domhoff points out, "the major funding for most of the new ultra-right organizations of the 1970s and 1980s came from one extremely conservative member of the Mellon family of Pittsburgh, Richard Mellon Scaife, who was giving $10 million a year through four foundations and trusts in addition to an unknown amount of money from the income of a personal fortune estimated to be worth $150 million" (Domhoff, 1983, p. 94). (As I write this, I look at a fund-raising letter that just came, indicating that *In These Times*, the only independent socialist weekly newspaper in the United States of national scope, may be forced out of business because of an outstanding debt of $100,000 – a paltry sum, a mere 1% of what one right-winger gives away each year in support of his causes.)

[118] See Domhoff (1983, pp. 85ff.) for descriptions of the Council on Foreign Relations, the Conference Board, the Committee for Economic Development, the National Association of Manufacturers, the Chamber of Commerce, and more.

5. Politicians and other government officials can be bribed.
6. Large contributions can be given to election campaigns.
7. Highly paid professional lobbyists can be employed to put pressure on elected officials.

Taken together, these mechanisms constitute a powerful bulwark against any tendency by democracy to encroach on property rights. As a measure of their effectiveness, one might cite Domhoff's analysis of twentieth-century labor legislation in the United States. The National Labor Relations Act of 1935, which legitimized the rights of workers to unionize and to engage in collective bargaining, had been bitterly opposed by nearly all elements of the business community.

> This defeat suffered by the corporate community demonstrates that it does not have total control within the policy-planning process on all issues. On the other hand, it was the first serious defeat it had suffered on a labor issue up until that point in American history, and subsequent major legislative victories on collective bargaining in 1947 (the Taft-Hartley Act) and 1977 (the Labor Law Reform Act) showed it was to be the only defeat it would suffer on the issue of labor relations in the first 80 years of the century.[119]

Thus, U.S. business suffered one major defeat this century, and that one was effectively reversed.[120]

There is a second reason for thinking that the owners of the means of production under Laissez Faire will be privileged, quite apart from the influence their wealth will buy. Look at society from the point of view of a political figure. A politician, no less than a businessman, values economic stability. Politicians must pay attention to those groups that threaten that stability. It is clear that labor unions and rebellious ethnic minorities can disrupt things, but these groups must be organized to be effective, and force can be brought to bear against them if they go too far. In sharp contrast, capitalists need not be organized to employ what is perhaps their most fundamental weapon: the "investment strike."[121] And the threat of force is impotent against them.

As we saw in Chapter 4, investor confidence is the key to capitalist stability. If a government initiates policies that capitalists perceive to be opposed to their interests, they may, with neither organization nor even spitefulness, become reluctant to invest in the offending country (or region or community), not if "the climate for business is bad." The out-

---

[119] Domhoff (1983, p. 146). See also Useem (1984) for a detailed account of how corporate interests in Great Britain and the United States mobilized in the late 1970s to redirect the political agendas of their respective countries.

[120] See Geoghegan (1990, pp. 51–4) for a succinct account of the impact of Taft-Hartley. For more details, see Goldfield (1987, ch. 9).

[121] "Most fundamental" in the sense that it is tied to their functional role, not to their inordinate wealth. The capitalist class would remain privileged even if Laissez Faire were relatively egalitarian.

come of such isolated acts is an economic downturn, and hence political instability. So a government under Laissez Faire (or any other form of capitalism) has no choice but to regard the interests of business as privileged. In a very real sense, what is good for business really is good for the country. If business suffers, so will everyone else.

The arguments set out should have persuaded the reader that Laissez Faire and democracy are indeed incompatible. But two troubling issues remain, each related to the question, Would it be all that different under Economic Democracy? The first is the suspicion that democracy as we have defined it is wishful thinking. The second is the suspicion that moving closer to this "democratic ideal" would not make much real difference in anyone's life.

Consider the first issue: Is it really possible to have an active, informed, sovereign electorate that comprises the entire adult population? Would Economic Democracy (its name aside) be any less incompatible with (true) democracy than Laissez Faire? These are difficult questions. I cannot prove that the democratic ideal is wholly realizable. I rather doubt that any political ideal is wholly realizable. But I think there are good reasons to believe that Economic Democracy will come closer to the democratic ideal than will Laissez Faire.

Above all, there is the issue of privilege. Under Economic Democracy there will be considerably less inequality than under Laissez Faire, and there will not exist a class of private individuals capable of an investment strike. Capitalists will not be able to dominate the government, for there will be no capitalists. But might there not arise a "new class"? The chief contender here would seem to be the government bureaucracy. This indeed is a possibility. One can imagine the civil service as a stable class possessing political power at least equal to that of elected officials and unmatched by that of any other minority group. A conservative might argue that given the choice between business as privileged and the civil service as privileged, society will be better off with the former.

There is a fundamental problem with this argument. If the analysis offered thus far is correct, the realistic choice is not between business privilege and civil-service privilege. The contradictions of Laissez Faire will necessitate government intervention; the more the economy develops, the greater the contradictions, and the greater the contradictions, the greater the intervention. The historical development of modern capitalism (which everywhere features a large civil service) confirms this theoretical assessment. So the real choice is between a government bureaucracy without a privileged capitalist class and a government bureaucracy with a privileged capitalist class. No contemporary economy can do without a government bureaucracy of some sort.

Must this bureaucracy necessarily be "privileged," in the sense we have accorded the term? I am prepared to grant possibility, but I see nothing like necessity, not in a society where major political officials will be elected. It is difficult to imagine structural features guaranteeing bureaucratic privilege that would be comparable to those we have just examined, which guarantee privilege to the capitalist class. Nonelected government employees under Economic Democracy will possess nothing like the wealth possessed by capitalists. Neither will they be capable of an investment strike.

If this analysis is correct, then to choose capitalism over Economic Democracy would be to choose a system that would have at least one and perhaps two privileged classes (if the bureaucracy under capitalism is privileged). To choose the reverse would not guarantee democracy, but a fundamental obstacle would be removed.[122]

There is another important consideration that supports the choice of Economic Democracy. The absence of a privileged class is a requirement for democracy, but so is our earlier condition 2a: an active and informed electorate. The extension of democratic procedures to the workplace, important in its own right, bears on this issue. It is an old argument, but one worth repeating: One addresses the ills of democracy with more democracy.[123] People develop democratic interests, attitudes, and skills by practicing democracy.[124] Under worker self-management, crucial decisions that will have immediate impact (organization of work and distribution of income, to name only two) must be made democratically by the individuals affected. However imperfectly the democratic structures function, they provide a greatly expanded opportunity for participation. It seems not unreasonable to expect democratic sensibilities, cultivated at the workplace, to carry over into the wider political arena.[125]

---

[122] Another candidate for "privileged class" is the "technostructure." John Kenneth Galbraith (1967, ch. 6) has argued forcefully that managerial-technical elites dominate contemporary capitalist societies, and would as readily dominate socialist ones. This is a serious charge, to which I would answer that (1) it is by no means clear that the charge is true with respect to capitalism, (2) if it is true with respect to capitalism, it need not be true with respect to Economic Democracy, and (3) in any event there is no reason to think it would be worse under Economic Democracy. For a more detailed response to Galbraith on this point, see Schweickart (1980, pp. 203–5).

[123] Cunningham (1987, p. 65) calls this strategy (which he endorses) "the democratic fix." For the opposing view, here is Harvard's Samuel Huntington: "Applying that cure at the present time could well be adding fuel to the flames. Some of the problems of governance in the United States today stem from an excess of democracy" (Crozier et al., 1975, p. 113).

[124] For a nice portrait of the "democratic personality" and a rebuttal to the charge that such character traits can never become widespread, see Gould (1988, pp. 283–99).

[125] Greenberg (1986) offers impressive empirical confirmation of this expectation. His study of the plywood cooperatives of the Pacific Northwest demonstrates that "with the exception of voting, about which no differences were found, worker-shareholders were significantly more active in all phases of political life than workers in conventional

There are two issues relevant to the general question, Would it be all that different under Economic Democracy? I have responded to the suspicion of wishful thinking by trying to demonstrate that Economic Democracy, if not wholly satisfying the democratic ideal, will at least come closer than will Laissez Faire. The second issue is essentially the "So what?" question. Even if it does come closer, what difference will that really make?

Of course, this question is beside the point to a true democrat, because democracy, for such a person, is a value in its own right. But I suspect that "true democrats" are rather rare in a capitalist society. William Buckley is doubtless expressing the opinion of many when he claims that the right to spend one's money as one wants is more important than the totality of democratic rights.[126]

In a sense, this question questions the *value* of democracy, and so it need not be addressed here. But let us not dismiss it too quickly, for it need not be interpreted as a rejection of democracy *tout court*. Let us interpret it as this more modest question: Why is not polyarchy enough? Granted (it might be said), polyarchy does not fully realize the democratic ideal, but many of the reasons one might give in support of the value of democracy apply also to polyarchy. What is to be gained from moving somewhat closer to the democratic ideal than we are at present?

In light of the analysis in this section, this is seen to be a question about the congruence of capitalist and democratic interests. We have seen that under Laissez Faire the capitalist class will be better positioned to advance and protect its interests than will any other group in society. Although this class may constitute only a tiny minority of the population, its real interests are almost never thwarted. However (it may be said), if these real interests are congruent with the real interests of the majority, then we really have no problem, do we? Polyarchy may not be government by the people, but it is government for the people (or at least not government against the people). Should not that be enough?

firms" (p. 131). It should be noted that Greenberg's findings do not support many of the claims that advocates of workplace democracy are wont to make. Greenberg did not find significantly less alienation among the cooperative workers, or significantly greater feelings of cooperation, equality, generosity, or solidarity with other workers. The negative findings of that study are discussed in later sections of this book.

[126] Buckley does not put the matter quite so bluntly. He offers a wordier proposition of vastly more complicated syntax: "Give me the right to spend my dollars as I see fit – to devote them, as I see fit, to travel, to food, to learning, to taking pleasure, to polemicizing, and, if I must make a choice, I will surrender to you my political franchise in trade, confident that by the transaction, assuming the terms of the contract are that no political decision affecting my sovereignty over my dollar can be made, I shall have augmented my dominance over my own affairs." Quoted by Wachtel (1983, p. 267).

Let me conclude the general discussion of Economic Democracy, Laissez Faire, and democracy that has occupied us throughout this section with a quite concrete answer to that question, an answer not found in philosophical discussions of democracy, but to my mind hugely important. Let me set aside those areas where the economic interests of the capitalist class conflict, prima facie, with the interests of large numbers of other citizens (e.g., control of the workplace, unemployment, consumer protection, redistribution of wealth). I want to focus instead on a noneconomic issue, "noneconomic" in the sense that it does not impinge so directly on the immediate material well-being of the citizenry that large numbers can be mobilized by a political campaign that connects the issue to their immediate economic interests.

Let us consider *foreign policy*. It is a truism of political science that the government of a polyarchy has a far freer hand in its conduct of foreign policy than in its conduct of domestic policy. The economic effects of domestic policy are felt rather directly, and so the government is constrained to move cautiously. Abrupt changes can be made only in exceptional circumstances. In sharp contrast, sudden initiatives and reversals of long-standing policy can be effected almost overnight in the area of foreign policy: enemies become friends; friends become enemies; countries are invaded without prior consultation; insurgency and counterinsurgency operations are secretly funded, and so forth.

Let us think about what is surely one of the remarkable aspects of our century: the degree to which anticommunism has served to motivate Western foreign policy. Let us consider the relationship of anticommunism to capitalism and democracy. Let me offer three basic theses:

1. The foreign policy of a capitalist country will be anticommunist, and it will tend to value anticommunism over democracy when these values conflict.
2. A foreign policy that values anticommunism over democracy will be far more destructive of life, liberty, democracy, and national autonomy than will a foreign policy that gives priority to democracy.
3. The foreign policy of Economic Democracy will not value anticommunism over democracy.

This is not the place for a complete defense of these claims. Such a defense would require some qualification of the theses, and more justification than I can give here for a methodology that invokes historical evidence in support of structural claims. But let me advance the following considerations, which, to my mind, would constitute the core of the full-scale defense:

Thesis 1: We know that the government of a capitalist country is little constrained by its polyarchical structure in its conduct of foreign policy and that the capitalist class is disproportionately represented (to put it mildly) on agenda-forming agencies outside and within government, including those that deal with foreign policy. So it is fair to say that in general, foreign policy represents what the capitalist class take to be their general interests.

It is often claimed that the "anticommunism" of Western foreign policy has been a screen behind which more blatantly economic interests have hidden, and this may well be true. At the same time, we should not doubt that anticommunism deeply permeates the upper classes in all capitalist countries, and for good reason. To a greater extent than any other ideology (and in opposition to many), communism, as an ideology, calls capitalism into question. To a greater extent than any other ideology, communism challenges the right of the rich to the privileges they enjoy.[127] All wealthy people know that such rhetoric is dangerous; all know that the massive inequalities of capitalism seem to be unfair and could be "demagogically" exploited. It thus becomes a matter of highest priority that this threat be kept at bay. It is quite reasonable for the capitalist class to treat "communism" as a virus, to be resisted, quarantined, sabotaged, stamped out wherever possible, for it is indeed dangerous to the interests of capital – as an idea, and even more so as a successful social experiment.[128]

Because the foreign-policy interests of a capitalist country reflect the interests of the capitalist class, and because the capitalist class has a far clearer and more immediate interest in opposing communism than in fostering democracy, thesis 1 follows.

Thesis 2: I presume that most wealthy people *believe* that capitalism, despite its inequalities, is better for the country as a whole than any form of socialism could be and that property income (the basis of their wealth) is justified. (There are not many who would say what Stephen Rockefeller said in the quotation that opened the preceding section.) But if the central thesis of this book is correct, they are wrong in that belief: Property income is not justifiable, for there does exist the possibility of a viable, more desirable alternative.

Might such a socialism have come into being in this century? We shall never know what might have been. It is not inconceivable that the currents of local and workplace democracy evident in the soviets that sprang into existence in Russia in 1905 and 1917 might have joined with the market mechanisms of Lenin's "New Economic Policy" to produce something like Economic Democracy – had the Russians been allowed to experiment in peace. But peace was not to be. The capitalist world has

---

[127] I am using the term "communism" here, rather than "Marxism," because communism, as an ideology hostile to and hated by the capitalist class, antedates Marxism, and also because it is the "communism" of Marxism (i.e., its attack on private ownership of the means of production) that most offends that class.

[128] Michael Hogan (1987, p. 45) cites a 1947 State Department memorandum defending the Marshall Plan initiative as a means of heading off "experiments in socialist enterprise and government controls" that might otherwise take root in Europe.

always been hostile to all forms of economic experimentation seeking to abrogate the "rights" of capital, and the Russian Revolution was no exception. As we know, European and U.S. troops were dispatched to aid the White Armies in the Russian Civil War, and although those interventions were unsuccessful, it can scarcely be doubted that capitalist hostility had a profoundly distorting effect on "actually existing socialism." Even a cursory investigation of Soviet history reveals how masterfully Stalin exploited the (hardly irrational) siege mentality of the Bolshevik leadership in order to consolidate his control and to justify his horrific policies of forced collectivization and manic industrialization.[129]

I do not claim that the horrors of anticommunism have exceeded the horrors of Stalinism, or that anticommunism was largely responsible for these and other atrocities committed in the name of Marx. (About these matters I remain agnostic.) But I think we can say with assurance that the policies motivated by anticommunism have accomplished little of value and have produced staggering carnage. As a thought experiment, try to imagine what this century might have been like had democracy rather than anticommunism guided Western foreign policy. It seems reasonable to assume that the United States (to confine ourselves here to the most important player)

1. Would not have sent troops to the Soviet Union in 1918 to oppose the revolution
2. Would not have looked so kindly on Mussolini's seizure of power in Italy nor supported so readily a policy of "economic appeasement" of Hitler [130]
3. Would not have supported the coming to power in the 1930s of the patriarchal dictatorships in Central America and the Caribbean (Hernandez Martinez in El Salvador, Somoza in Nicaragua, Ubico in Guatemala, Carias in Honduras, Trujillo in the Dominican Republic, Batista in Cuba)
4. Might have aided Republican Spain in its fight against Franco's antidemocratic revolt (which was supported materially and with personnel by both Hitler and Mussolini)
5. Would not have supported the corrupt rule of Chiang Kai-shek in China
6. Would not have supported the efforts of the French to regain control over Indochina after World War II

[129] See Deutcher (1967, pp. 288ff.). Whatever the real reasons behind the European response to Nazi rearmament (in blatant disregard of the terms of the Versailles Treaty), there is no doubt that Stalin and many other Russians perceived "appeasement" as a deliberate attempt on the part of capitalist interests to encourage the development of a powerful anticommunist force that likely would strike east.

[130] In his recent study of fascist Italy, historian David Schmitz (1988) notes that "based upon the earlier experience with Mussolini in the 1920s. . . . American policy toward Europe during the 1930s was built in part upon the analytical foundation that Fascism provided political stability in nations threatened with revolution, constituted an anti-Bolshevik bulwark, and promised favorable economic polices" (p. 6). Business leaders in the United States, he points out (p. 70), were wildly enthusiastic about Il Duce.

7. Might not have insisted on partitioning Korea after World War II or supported the installation of a brutal right-wing dictatorship in the South, and hence might have avoided the Korean War [131]
8. Would not have engineered the overthrow of the Iranian government and the installation of the shah in 1953
9. Would not have orchestrated the destruction of democracy in Guatemala in 1954 and encouraged the spread of military rule (with death-squad supplements) there and in El Salvador and Honduras
10. Would have recognized the right of the Vietnamese, Laotian, and Cambodian peoples to choose their own future, and hence would have avoided the Vietnam War
11. Would not have opposed the black-liberation struggles in southern Africa for many, many years
12. Would not have looked the other way (to put the best face on the matter) when the Indonesian military seized power in 1965 and massacred some 1 million "Communists"
13. Would not have aided and abetted the establishment of military rule of monumental savagery throughout most of South America in the 1960s and 1970s
14. Would not have embraced the Marcos dictatorship in the Philippines from its onset in 1972 until its penultimate moment in 1986
15. Would not have bankrolled murderous insurgency movements against the popular governments that came to power in the 1970s by overthrowing a hated dictator or a colonial power (Nicaragua, Angola, Mozambique)
16. Would not have worked ceaselessly, to the day of this writing, to destroy Cuba, the one society in Latin America that has eliminated starvation and homelessness

This is by no means an exhaustive list.[132] The United States has backed many more antidemocratic terror regimes than are listed here, and the United States has not stood alone in its anticommunist crusade. Most of the major European countries have backed most of these policies. Comparisons of this kind seem almost obscene, but still it should be said: The wars, coups, killings, terror, and torture that have been justified in the name of anticommunism have produced a body count that is surely close to (and may exceed) that of Stalinism.[133]

---

[131] Halliday and Cummings (1988) show how the United States, during its pre–Korean War occupation of Korea, undermined the Resistance government, and brought in the fiercely anti-Communist Syngman Rhee, who, supported by what a 1948 Central Intelligence Agency (CIA) report called "that numerically small class which virtually monopolizes the native wealth and education of the country" (p. 23), then imposed a reign of terror on the Left.

[132] There are many studies that detail the listed events and more. An excellent starting point, with extensive documentation, is Chomsky and Herman (1979a).

[133] Chomsky (1987, p. 24) offers some estimates: 4 million dead in Indochina, 500,000–1 million dead in Indonesia, 200,000 dead in Central America (since 1978), 200,000 dead in East Timor (since 1975). That is only a sampling.

Thesis 3: The common rejoinder to the argument I have been construct-ing is a cynical shrug: "Sure, the United States has been hypocritical in its foreign policy and has set aside its espoused values when they have conflicted with its real interests. All countries do that. Economic Demo-cracy, whatever high-flown virtues it claims for itself, would do exactly the same." This rejoinder has emotive power, particularly in the current climate dominated by "cynical reason,"[134] but against it I should like to pose two sets of facts.

Those who would affirm that the people of any polyarchy will initiate and unswervingly support a nondemocratic foreign policy must ac-knowledge that (1) not a single one of the foregoing sixteen instances of anticommunist activity can plausibly be viewed as the government's response to intense political pressure from an outraged electorate, (2) in most of these cases the American people were quite ignorant of what was really going on, and (3) in many of these cases there was conscious concern on the part of the policy-making elite to keep from the American people the true nature of their policy, for fear that it would not be accept-able.[135] I do not deny that once a policy has been decided upon, an administration usually can generate at least passive support for it, but that hardly counts as evidence for the claim that a government genuinely responsive to majority wishes would pursue the same policy.

The facts in the second set are structural. The basic institutions of Economic Democracy are not well designed for the exploitation of other countries; the basic institutions of capitalism are. This issue was broached in the preceding section, but let us take it a bit further. Notice that both a capitalist country and one structured along the lines of Economic De-mocracy will have two basic economic interests in other countries: They can serve (1) as markets for the goods produced in the home country and (2) as sources for goods or raw materials that cannot be (so cheaply) obtained at home. Both of these ends are served by trade, and both might be jeopardized if there should emerge in one of these foreign trading partners a regime that was excessively protectionistic or had monopolis-tic control over a vital resource. If such a regime came to power, it is not implausible to suppose that the citizens of the home country, either a capitalist country or an Economic Democracy, would demand interven-tion.

But here is a curious fact: If we look at the history of U.S. intervention

---

[134] See Sloterdijk (1987), who coined the term.

[135] For a meticulous examination of one of the most famous instances, see Chomsky's analysis of the "Pentagon Papers" (Chomsky, 1973, pp. 3–173). It is difficult to study government and elite think-tank documents not meant for general consumption without being struck by the palpable concern of so many policymakers about be "lack of sophis-tication" on the part of the American public about the "national-security" need for antidemocratic policies.

since the Russian Revolution, we find not a single target country that in fact possessed monopoly control over a vital resource,[136] and we find virtually no regime that refused to trade with us. In fact, the pattern has been the opposite: The United States has imposed economic sanctions on its "enemies." We, not they, have refused to trade.

Here is another curious fact: In no case have our interventions been justified to the American people primarily on economic terms, though such justifications have occasionally been floated. Eisenhower made reference to the "tin and tungsten" of Indochina, and, more recently, Saddam Hussein was said to threaten "our way of life." But such justifications have invariably fallen flat and have been replaced by noneconomic appeals: freedom, democracy, opposition to tyranny, and, above all, anticommunism. In light of these facts, one must surely wonder: If the American people cannot be moved to support foreign intervention by appeals to their economic interests, is it likely that the citizens of a more democratic society would be so moved?

Let us look more closely at structures. A nation's basic economic interests in a foreign country can be satisfied by trade, but certain institutions within a nation may have interests that go beyond trade. In particular, a capitalist enterprise will have an interest in (1) investment outlets for its profits and (2) cheap labor. The search for such "opportunities" are not structurally confined to the home country. So it will be in the interest of capitalists to press for a foreign policy that will oppose any attempt by a foreign country to restrict the capitalists' investment opportunities there or their access to that cheap labor, or (God forbid) to nationalize their existing investments in that country. But such restrictions were precisely what virtually all the governments or movements targeted for violent U.S. opposition had promised their followers. Should we be surprised that a government dominated by the interests of capital would be inclined to intervene?

Think now of Economic Democracy. A worker-managed enterprise will have not the slightest interest in cheap labor abroad, for labor power is not a commodity. (Any worker who joins an enterprise becomes a voting member.) Nor will it look for "investment opportunities" beyond the confines of its community. Recall that funds for investment will come from tax revenues. To secure an investment grant, an enterprise will have to demonstrate to the local bank that the funds will be profitably invested in the enterprise, either to enhance productivity or to increase local employment. The possibility of investing abroad will scarcely be an

---

[136] The recent war with Iraq might be counted as an exception to this claim. We need not pursue this issue, because if oil really was the motive (which many would dispute), the case remains exceptional.

option.[137] So there will not be any pressure on the government emanating from the "private sector" to meddle with a foreign "revolutionary" government or movement that is attempting to take control of its own economic destiny.

The conclusion of this extended sketch for an argument readily follows: The foreign policy of an Economic Democracy promises to be far more respectful of the aspirations of other countries for freedom, democracy, and self-determination than the foreign policy of a capitalist country. The bottom line: *It will indeed make a difference that Economic Democracy comes nearer the democratic ideal than does capitalism.*

A corollary that is also a prediction: I have argued that capitalist countries tend to be anticommunist. My analysis has made no reference to the military threat from the former Soviet Union, nor to any other characteristics of communist societies other than their anticapitalist ideology and their resistance to corporate penetration. If this analysis is correct, then anticommunism, despite the virtual disappearance of communism, will not disappear. It is possible (though to my mind unlikely) that some other term or terms will be substituted, but my analysis predicts that any government or movement anywhere in the world, regardless of how democratic it is, that challenges in a fundamental way the right to property income, or the right of corporations to invest in foreign countries as they see fit, will be opposed by the United States and most other capitalist countries.[138] It predicts further that the justification for this opposition will not be based on an appeal to the economic self-interest of capitalism's citizenry, but rather on an appeal to some higher principle.

I do not say that "anticommunism," so labeled, will always fill this role, but I suspect that it will be invoked far more often than one currently might be inclined to think. It is difficult for me to imagine that a concept that has served the ruling class so well, with its overtones of atheism, state terror, deprivation of liberty, and the like, will be lightly abandoned.

Meaningful work

To work at the bidding and for the profit of another is not a satisfactory state.
                                                              – John Stuart Mill

We come now to the objection to competitive capitalism most closely associated with the young Karl Marx. Capitalism, I shall argue, alienates

---

[137] It was noted in the preceding section that a firm might be allowed to invest some of its depreciation funds in foreign stocks and bonds, but that, if permitted, could not be expected to have an appreciable effect on foreign policy.

[138] Opposition movements or governments in Eastern Europe and the countries formerly in the Soviet Union will certainly not be excepted.

workers from their work. To put the charge in terms of our articulated values, the capitalist organization of work runs sharply counter to the autonomy and psychological well-being of employees. Specifically, I shall argue that Laissez Faire does not provide (1) an optimal degree of workplace participation, or (2) an optimal balance of labor and leisure, or (3) an optimal level of skill development at work.[139] I shall argue that Economic Democracy will better approximate what working people would choose were they truly free to make the relevant trade-offs.

The neoclassical theory that undergirds classical liberalism suggests that such nonoptimality is rare so long as competition reigns. Basic neoclassical economics inclines one to think that the levels of participation, work duration, and skill are what they are because workers have, in an important sense, chosen them to be so.

Marx takes a contrary view: Alienated labor is held to be absolutely central to capitalism. This is true for the young Marx and for the mature Marx as well. What distinguishes capitalism from simple commodity production is neither private property nor the market; it is the commodity character of labor power. Therein, Marx insists, lies the secret of capitalist production. He writes in *Capital*, following his analysis of market exchange:

The sphere we are deserting [the market] within whose boundaries the sale and purchase of labor-power goes on, is in fact a very Eden of the innate rights of man. There alone rule Freedom, Equality, Property and Bentham. Freedom, because both buyer and seller of a commodity, say of labor-power, are constrained only by their own free will. . . . Equality, because each enters into relation with the other as simple owners of commodities, and they exchange equivalent for equivalent. Property, because each disposes only of what is his own. And Bentham, because each looks only to himself. . . .

Each looks only to himself and no one troubles himself about the rest, and just because they do so, do they all, in accordance with the preestablished harmony of things, or under the auspices of an all-shrewd providence, work together for their mutual advantage, for the common weal and in the interest of all.

On leaving this sphere of simple circulation or of exchange of commodities, which furnishes the "Free Trade Vulgaris" with his views and ideas . . . we think we can perceive a change in the physiognomy of our dramatis personae. He, who before was the money owner, now strides in front as the capitalist; the possessor of labor-power following as his laborer. The one with an air of self-importance, smiling, intent on business; the other, timid and holding back, like one who is bringing his own hide to the market and has nothing to expect but – a hiding.[140]

There are many questions we might ask. Is it true that working people under capitalism receive a "hiding"? Perhaps they did in Marx's day, but do they now? Do they think they do? The empirical evidence is

---

[139] This conception of "alienation" is not identical with that of Marx, but it is sufficiently similar to warrant our appropriating his term. For a careful account of Marx's concept, see Ollman (1971).

[140] Marx (1967, p. 176).

ambiguous. Sociologist William Form observes that "from the earliest research to the present, most workers everywhere have reported job satisfaction."[141] Yet author Studs Terkel, who traveled the country some years ago interviewing workers, concludes that although

there are, of course, the happy few who find savor in their daily jobs, for the many, there is a hardly concealed discontent. The blue-collar blues is no more bitterly sung than the white-collar moan. "I'm a machine," says the spot welder. "I'm caged," says the bank teller, and echoes the hotel clerk. "I'm a mule," says the steel-worker. "A monkey could do what I do," says the receptionist. "I'm less than a farm implement," says the migrant worker. "I'm an object," says the high-fashion model. Blue and white collar call upon the identical phrase: "I'm a robot."[142]

The empirical evidence regarding the extent and depth of job dissatisfaction is difficult to assess. As Form points out, survey questions can be manipulated to vary the proportion of employees reporting dissatisfaction. Moreover, workers may report job satisfaction because they are happy to have a job rather than be unemployed, or because admitting dissatisfaction would suggest personal failure, or because their preferences have adapted to their prospects – or because they are truly satisfied.

Upon reflection, we see that this empirical difficulty is not really a problem for our argument. In defining "alienation" in terms of the nonoptimality of participation, labor–leisure, and skill development, we have loosened the connection between alienation and felt dissatisfaction. We are assuming that it is good to participate in decisions whose consequences one must bear and to develop one's skills, even if one does not experience the lack of such opportunities as a deprivation. We are allowing that certain structures might push one to work harder and longer than it is good for one to work.

It follows from these value assumptions that one can be alienated and not consciously feel dissatisfied about one's work. If one is an unskilled workaholic who is content to let superiors make all decisions, our value assumptions lead us to judge this situation prima facie nonoptimal. It does not follow that one should be forced to participate if one prefers not to, or forced to develop one's skills, or forced to slow down. It does follow from our value assumptions that if one system provides people with more opportunities than does another to participate or to develop their skills or to better balance their work and leisure, then that system is preferable.

The connection between alienation and felt dissatisfaction has been attenuated, but is has not been severed completely. Recall that the normative framework within which we have been working requires that a

[141] Form (1985, p. 11).   [142] Terkel (1975, p. xiv).

person's self-evaluation always be given prima facie weight. So if there were few or no reports of employee dissatisfaction under capitalism, then the argument of this section would not need to be taken too seriously. But of course there is dissatisfaction. The empirical debate is not about whether or not there is worker dissatisfaction, but about the degree of that dissatisfaction. No one denies that worker dissatisfaction exists.[143] At the same time, we must allow that this dissatisfaction does not automatically indict capitalism. Perhaps this dissatisfaction is due to human nature, or to an acceptable trade-off between work satisfaction and some other good. We need to investigate the structural linkages.

Are there any grounds for believing that capitalism will not be alienating, that it will in fact approximate optimal levels of participation, work duration and intensity, and skill development? This is where neoclassical economics enters the picture: The capitalist does not decide arbitrarily on the organization of work, it is said, but rather according to factors that allow for decisive worker influence. If work is less fulfilling than it might be, workers have chosen it to be so. Nozick's version of this argument proceeds as follows: We assume that productivity, under a reorganization scheme designed to make work more meaningful, may rise, remain the same, or fall. Therefore,

if the productivity of the workers in a factory *rises* when the work tasks are segmented so as to be more meaningful, then the individual owners pursuing profits will so reorganize the productive process. If the productivity of the workers *remains the same* under such meaningful division of labor, then in the process of competing for laborers firms will alter their internal work organization.

So the only interesting case to consider is that in which dividing a firm's work tasks into meaningful segments, rotation of labor, and so forth is *less efficient (as judged by market criteria)* than the less meaningful division of labor. This lessened efficiency can be borne in three ways (or in combinations of them). First, the workers in the factories themselves might desire meaningful work. It has all the virtues its theorists ascribe to it, the workers realize this, and they are willing to give up something (some wages) in order to work at meaningfully segmented jobs. They work for lower wages, but they view their total work package (lower wages plus the satisfaction of meaningful work) as more desirable than the less meaningful work at higher wages. They make a tradeoff of some increase in the meaningfulness of their work, increased self-esteem and so forth.[144]

---

[143] For two classic studies, see Sheppard and Herrick (1972) and U.S. Department of Health, Education, and Welfare (1973). To get a feel for what it is like to work in a manufacturing plant, see the account by Göran Palm (1977) of his year at LM Erikson (the largest private employer in Sweden), or the three-year study by Nichols and Beynon (1977) of a British chemical company, or the inside look provided by Balzer (1976) at a Massachusetts Western Electric plant. For an intriguing comparison of capitalist and state-socialist factory life, see Burawoy (1985, ch. 4), who sets his own experience against that described by Hungarian poet and sociologist Miklós Harasti (1977).

[144] Nozick (1974, p. 248); emphases in original.

We need not consider Nozick's other ways of bearing the lessened efficiency (consumer groups voluntarily subsidizing the less efficient firms, or the government prohibiting nonmeaningful work), because both are beyond the pale of standard neoclassicism, and neither is relevant to any realistic version of capitalism. His important claim concerns the first way: If a reorganization that makes work more satisfying is at least as productive as the original organization, then a capitalist pursuing his own interest will so reorganize. If it is less productive, he will still reorganize, provided that the workers accept a wage reduction sufficient to maintain his original profit margin. Hence, if work could be made more meaningful, but is not, it is because workers have been unwilling to bear the cost of making it so. This argument, if correct, has an important implication: The structure of work under Economic Democracy, and consequently worker alienation, will not be significantly different than under capitalism.

One might object that Nozick's argument presumes that a capitalist is entitled to his current rate of profit, but this objection will not take us far. Because the assets tax under Economic Democracy will be comparable to capitalist profit, we cannot assume that under Economic Democracy workers in a given firm will have a significantly larger pie to share. To do justice to Nozick and neoclassicism, we need to dig deeper. Although they will turn out to be interconnected, we need to examine separately the various components that figure in our definition of alienation.

First, there is the issue of participation. As we have already seen, there is a vast quantity of empirical evidence demonstrating that participatory workplaces tend to be places of higher morale and greater productivity than authoritarian workplaces.[145] Nozick doubtless would reply that such findings have in fact induced many capitalist firms to experiment with more participatory environments and that we may expect this trend to continue until optimality is reached, for precisely the reasons he has given. To counter Nozick on this point, we must be able to point to factors that will inhibit an expansion of participation even if productivity would be enhanced thereby.

Let me suggest several. First, if we allow that power has a positive valence in its own right, apart from its instrumental value in enhancing income, then it follows that a Laissez Faire workplace will be more authoritarian than it would be if efficiency criteria alone dictated structure. If managers or owners enjoy the exercise of power, then they will sacrifice some income to that end.

---

[145] Some of this evidence was canvassed in Chapter 3. More than two decades ago, Paul Blumberg surveyed twenty-five years of research. His conclusion still stands. "There is hardly a study in the entire literature which fails to demonstrate that satisfaction in work is enhanced or that other generally acknowledged beneficial consequences accrue from a genuine increase in workers' decision-making power" (Blumberg, 1969, p. 123).

For middle managers the incentive to resist participatory schemes is even greater, because such changes often show many middle managers to be redundant. The resistance of middle management to participatory experiments, often bordering on sabotage, is well known and widely documented.[146]

If the appeal of power and the recalcitrance of middle management were the only inhibiting factors, a case might be made that competitive market forces would ultimately prevail: Owners, increasingly distant from actual management and hence from the intrinsic satisfactions of authority, would compel their agents to focus on bottom-line profit margins. If participatory arrangements were more productive, sooner or later they would be adopted. The root problem with this argument is the tacit assumption that increasing (technical) productivity is the only means for increasing profits, an assumption that neoclassical theorists often take for granted, and one that Marxists, with their emphasis on shop-floor class struggle, correctly contest. Marx himself highlighted the key points.[147] There are two means for increasing profits that resemble enhancing productivity, but that in fact are quite distinct. To increase productivity, one must get more output from the same inputs, one of which is labor. To increase (capitalist) profit, one must get more output from the same costs, one of which is the wage bill. But the link between a wage contract and the quantity and quality of the labor forthcoming is not a technical matter. It is possible to get more or less labor for a given sum of money. So there exists a strong incentive for capitalists to intensify the pace of labor. There exists also a strong incentive to reorganize the work process so as to minimize the need for skilled laborers, because skilled laborers are more costly than unskilled.

Both of these methods will be examined in more detail later, because they relate to the two other components of alienation we want to consider. For now, we need only note that both of these means of increasing (capitalist) profit would be threatened by a fully democratic workplace. Workers will not vote to increase the pace of their work simply to enhance the profits of the capitalist, nor will they vote to reduce their skill levels and take a pay cut. So the capitalist has good reason to resist full participation even if it promises to be more productive, because full participation would curtail these other means of enhancing profits.

---

[146] Adina Schwartz (1982, p. 646) cites a *Business Week* article on the "indifference and outright hostility" of managers at General Foods to a democratization plan, as well as a Polaroid director's explanation that a participatory scheme had to be terminated because "it was too successful. What were we going to do with the supervisors – the managers? We didn't need them anymore." See also Shoshana Zuboff's study of the implementation of new computer technology and the managerial resistance to the participatory possibilities that opened up (Zuboff, 1988, especially ch. 7).

[147] See Marx (1967, Part IV).

Let us look more closely at work intensity. This is but one of a complex of issues that Carmen Sirianni has called "the politics of time."[148] These issues, which include the pace of work, but also the length of the workday, vacations, flexible scheduling, job sharing, part-time work, work "sabbaticals," and more, belong in the category that I have identified as one of the three basic components of capitalist alienation: a nonoptimal balance between labor and leisure. It is this complex of issues we want to consider.[149]

There are good reasons for thinking that workers under capitalism are goaded to work harder than they would if they could freely choose their mix of leisure, income, and work intensity. Every instance of speedup may be regarded as an effort on the part of management to get more work from an employee than she thought she had contracted to do. Management can count on the fact that jobs usually are in short supply, and so employees can be induced, by an appropriate combination of technical speedup, tight monitoring, and threat, to do more than was bargained for. Of course, workers often resist, sometimes engaging in counterstrategies, but it is precisely this adversarial relationship that denies us any warrant for claiming that the resultant pace of work is optimal.

But speedup is only one facet of the problem. The macrodistribution of labor–leisure is also far from optimal under capitalism. Under Laissez Faire we can expect large numbers of people to have lots of leisure – we call them "unemployed." We can also expect overwork. Marx has pointed out the paradoxical fact that these two phenomena correlate positively under capitalism. The higher the unemployment rate, the easier it is for employers to demand more labor from their workers.[150] The situation is so common that we often fail to appreciate just how "unnatural" it is.

If we break free of the "naturalistic fallacy,"[151] a lot of questions come to mind regarding the way jobs are defined and apportioned. Why do we not guarantee everyone an opportunity to work? Why not let two people share a job? Why not make "flexitime" widely available? Why are part-time jobs paid proportionally so much less than full-time jobs, and usually devoid of benefits? Why not let all working people take sabbaticals

---

[148] Sirianni (1988, p. 7).

[149] I am using the concept "labor–leisure trade-off" to apply to a broader range of issues than the term usually denotes, partly for convenience, but also because it seems analytically appropriate. The pace of work, for example, is about how "leisurely" the work should be; flexitime allows one a less harried existence; etc.

[150] "The over-work of the employed part of the working-class swells the ranks of the reserve, whilst conversely the greater pressure that the latter by its competition exerts on the former, forces these to submit to over-work and to subjugation under the dictates of capital" (Marx, 1967, p. 636).

[151] Meaning here "that whatever is, is the way it is because of the nature of things," not what the term means in analytical ethics, namely, the (supposed) sin of deriving "ought" from "is."

on a regular basis? I presume that most people (certainly most working people) would agree that it would be desirable to have the opportunities suggested by these questions made widely available, provided, of course, that the costs were not excessive.

I submit that such opportunities whose costs (to the workers involved and to society at large) are not excessive will be far more likely to be realized under Economic Democracy than under Laissez Faire, for under Laissez Faire, but not under Economic Democracy, those with ultimate authority over the conditions of work have little to gain and much to lose from such reforms.

Capitalists have little to gain and much to lose from full employment. Their bargaining position vis-à-vis that of their workers is strengthened by high unemployment.[152] What do the owners of a firm have to gain from offering their employees sabbaticals, or flexible scheduling, or job sharing, or more opportunities for part-time work with proportional pay and benefits? The costs and risks are clear and direct, whereas the gain is at best indirect: a happier work force that may work harder and be more productive.

It is in the hope of just such a result that some firms do experiment with such reforms, but notice that the deciding factor is "the bottom line." But why should that be the deciding factor? Why should not a happier work force be a desirable end in itself? Under capitalism it is not, as was made clear by a highly placed executive in a large insurance company, who commented on the naiveté of "tender-minded academics":

[Clerical personnel] are easily trained for their jobs, [so] if they stayed on their jobs they would become wage problems – we'd have to keep raising them or end up fighting with them; they would form unions and who knows what the hell else. It's better to hire girls who are too well educated to stay happy with the jobs that we assign them to do.[153]

In a democratic workplace the situation will be different. The firm may lose some money on an organizational experiment, but the workers may well decide that it is worth it. Notice that they must bear the financial costs, but they also will experience the gains. Under capitalism, the costs and gains fall systematically on different persons – with those bearing the financial risk having the decisive power. In a democratic workplace, everyone would have their options increased by the reforms suggested earlier, and everyone would bear some of the costs if productivity were impaired. That is not to say that everyone will evaluate the costs and benefits the same way. There may well be serious disagreement and some bad decisions. Nevertheless, we are more likely to see an optimal

---

[152] This issue will be discussed in more detail in the next chapter.
[153] Sheppard and Herrick (1972, p. 176).

outcome when the process is not systematically distorted in the apportioning of costs and benefits.[154]

Let us consider the third basic component of capitalist alienation: the underdevelopment of work skills. Let us begin with a phenomenon quite familiar under capitalism: a shop-floor reorganization that increases capitalist profits by substituting lesser-skilled labor for workers of greater skill. (This reorganization may or may not involve capital investment; if it does, the savings in wages must more than offset the capital costs.) Let us assume for now that this reorganization will increase technical productivity – that is, that more output will be obtained from the same quantity of (lower-skilled, cheaper) actual labor.

Obviously, skilled workers will not choose to be replaced by unskilled workers. They might be permitted to stay on in this instance, provided they agree to change their work category and accept lower pay. But observe, their "choice of total work packages" is not the one proposed by Nozick. It is not between "more meaning with less pay" and "less meaning with more pay." It is between less meaningful, lower-paid work and no work at all. Even if a worker has other options (for skilled work elsewhere), she cannot be said to have, in any sense, chosen the reorganization.

Autonomy is not the only value at stake in such matters, of course. It might be argued that participatory autonomy is justifiably overridden in such cases by the enhanced well-being of the community at large: Production has been increased, and a valuable skill has been released for employment elsewhere in the economy. There is merit to this argument if the skill is needed elsewhere. If not, a crucial cost is incurred that is ignored by the market: The skilled laborer, to be employed at all, must sacrifice her skill, and with it perhaps some income, job satisfaction, and self-respect. This is a matter of great theoretical importance. The neoclassical argument for the optimality of competitive capitalism rests on the presumption that a competitive market compels those who make decisions to bear the social costs of their decisions. But here is a decision class of profound importance to individual well-being (decisions concerning skill requirements for productive processes) for which the social costs are not borne by the decision-makers. The capitalist decides, and a rise in profit confirms the choice. But the market does not register

---

[154] It should be noted that the reforms suggested here would have important bearings on "gendered time." The traditional capitalist workplace and traditional capitalist career models are deeply patriarchal. One is expected to give "full time" to one's job. Thus, powerful ideological support is given to a man's sense that housework and child care should be done by his spouse. (That this sense often persists even when she is also working "full time" outside the home can scarcely be doubted – male logic falters a bit here.) More flexible work arrangements should help to undercut this sense. See Sirianni (1988, pp. 22–7).

the cost to the skilled worker who is no longer allowed to exercise her skill.

Those concerned about consumer well-being may not be convinced. Granted, they might say, capitalism circumscribes a worker's autonomy; it may even at times interfere with her psychological well-being. But the reorganizations and innovations that have taken place, even when against the wishes of the workers involved, have contributed vastly to raising our living standards – for workers as well as for capitalists. Surely this more than counterbalances.

There is no way to prove that it does. The market, we have seen, does not correctly record all costs. It might well be the case that we would be a healthier, happier society if we had fewer goods and more meaningful work. As a matter of fact, this almost has to be true, given the evidence that work satisfaction is a major component of a person's overall happiness, whereas increased consumption is not.[155]

Here is an objection from another quarter: If the market incorrectly records the cost of skill loss, why should we expect Economic Democracy, which will be, after all, a market economy, to do any better? If competitive pressures favor the introduction of low-skill mass production under capitalism, why will they not do the same under Economic Democracy?

There are two independent answers to this objection. The first appeals to the fact that workers under Economic Democracy will face a different choice of "total work packages" than do workers under capitalism. Consider an example. Suppose it is technically more efficient, but less skill-enhancing, to set up an assembly line to produce automobiles than to produce them via production teams. If workers decide to adopt the former scheme, they will then face another choice. They may choose to produce the same number of cars as before, while working less, or they may choose to produce more cars, cutting prices some what so as to sell the extras. They have, in effect, a choice among three total work packages, each highlighting a different variable: skill, leisure, and consumption. They may choose production teams, emphasizing skill, or they may choose the assembly line and less work, or they may choose the assembly line and more income. But notice, if workers in plant A opt for production teams, while workers in plant B choose the assembly line, the workers in plant A will be unaffected if those in plant B choose the second option. Only if the workers in plant B opt for more income will those in plant A

---

[155] Freeman (1978, pp. 157–8) cites a study showing that 70 percent of those happy with their jobs were happy in general, but only 14 percent of those unhappy with their jobs were happy in general. He reports the major result of his own study to be that beyond a certain minimum, the amount of money one has matters little in terms of happiness (p. 136).

feel the effects, in which case they will be forced to lower prices to compete, and hence sacrifice some income. But even in that case, unless the productivity differential is truly substantial, they need not switch to assembly-line production themselves, for unlike the situation under capitalism, plant B will not rapidly expand by taking on more workers, and so the competition will be less intense. The income loss to plant A may well be bearable, well worth the skill enhancement.

The answer just given to the charge that things will be the same under Economic Democracy grants that skill reduction enhances technical efficiency. The second answer will question that assumption. It has already been suggested that capitalists might have an independent interest in reducing the skill levels of their workers: Skilled workers cost more. Let us probe more deeply. Why are unskilled workers cheaper? The reflex answer appeals to supply and demand: There are more of them. But why is that? Is it a fact of human nature that only a small part of the work force is capable of skilled labor, or is it part of the nature of capitalism to keep the level of skill devlopment low?

It has long been recognized by capitalists that the skilled worker is more difficult to control than the unskilled. The more complex the work and the more knowledge required, the more difficult it is to determine just what can be expected from a worker, just what constitutes a "fair day's work."

A correlation between skill and intransigence has often been remarked. Marx quotes from Andrew Ure's 1835 treatise *The Philosophy of Manufactur* (sic): "By the infirmity of human nature, it happens that the more skillful the workman, the more self-willed and intractable he is apt to become, and of course the less fit a component of mechanical system in which . . . he may do great damage to the whole."[156]

In this century, a whole philosophy, science, and technology of work has developed to deal with this problem. This development has such direct bearing on our concern that it merits a moment of our attention. The seminal figure is Frederick Winslow Taylor, the "father of scientific management." As conceived by Taylor, scientific management attempts to resolve "the greatest evil from which both workmen and employers are suffering," namely, "systematic soldiering." Systematic soldiering is the "loafing" that goes on not because of the "natural laziness of men" but as a result of "a careful study on the part of workmen of what they think will promote their best interests." As Taylor sees it:

The greater part of systematic soldiering . . . is done by the men with a deliberate object of keeping their employers ignorant of how fast work can be done.
So universal is soldiering for this purpose that hardly a competent workman

---

[156] Marx (1967, p. 367).

can be found in a large establishment, whether he works by the day or on piece work, contract work or under any of the ordinary systems of compensating labor, who does not devote a considerable part of his time to studying just how slowly he can work and still convince his employer that he is going at a good pace.[157]

Taylor's solution is justly famous: Management must take control of the workplace to a degree previously unknown. The labor process must be preplanned and precalculated to such a degree that the process no longer exists as a unified whole in the mind of the workman, but only in the minds of special management staff. As Taylor emphasizes, "all possible brain work should be removed from the shop and centered in the planning and laying-out department."[158] To this end, research and experimentation are necessary, because "the managers must assume the burden of gathering together all of the traditional knowledge which in the past has been possessed by the workmen, and then of classifying, tabulating and reducing this knowledge to rules, laws and formulae."[159]

Taylor's is but one of a series of "philosophies of work" that have emerged in the twentieth century, but at least in its general formulation it may well be what sociologist and management consultant Peter Drucker calls "the most powerful as well as the most lasting contribution America has made to Western thought since the Federalist Papers."[160] To be sure, many of the specific features of Taylorism have been superseded. Detailed daily instruction cards are no longer handed out, and even time-and-motion studies, pioneered by Taylor, have receded in importance. But two elements have persisted: a preoccupation with the problem of control, derived from an explicit or implicit recognition that the interests of workers are at variance with those of management, and an attempt to resolve the problem by reducing to a minimum the necessity for independent judgment on the part of the worker.[161] A top executive, recently interviewed by Shoshana Zuboff regarding the introduction of computer technology into paper production, puts the matter candidly: "The classic managerial role has been that of handler, manipulator, dealer, and withholder of information. . . . This means you never become overly depen-

---

[157] Taylor's three principal works, *Shop Management* (1903), *Principles of Scientific Management* (1911), and the public document, *Hearings Before the Special Committee of the House of Representatives to Investigate Taylor and Other Systems of Shop Management* (1912), are contained in a single volume (Taylor, 1947) and are separately paginated therein. The quotations are from *Shop Management* (pp. 32–3). My argument here owes much to Braverman (1974).

[158] Taylor, *Shop Management*, p. 98.

[159] Taylor, *Principles of Scientific Management*, p. 36.

[160] Drucker (1954, p. 280).

[161] See Edwards (1979) for   further elaboration of this thesis. Edwards downplays the specific influence of Taylor and sees "bureaucratic" control as superseding "technical" control in the more sophisticated corporations today. But the general result (the routinization and monotonization of work) remains the same.

dent on those hourly folks, who can become disloyal and walk out. There is a whole element here of control that we don't talk about." A worker in the plant sees it much the same way: "It seems management is afraid to let us learn too much about how this system operates. The more we know, the more we could sabotage it."[162]

If control is so clearly important to management, now as in Taylor's time, if "deskilling" is an important element of that control, and if (as we have assumed) the "Aristotelian principle" is true,[163] then this conclusion must follow: The structure of capitalism, which sets up a real opposition between owners and wage laborers, and which grants the former effective control over the workplace, tilts organizational and technical change in the direction of alienation, much more so than will Economic Democracy, because the fundamental conflict of interest that underlies the preoccupation with control under capitalism will not exist under Economic Democracy.

I should emphasize here that I am not claiming that skill levels under capitalism are lower now than they used to be. It cannot be denied that technological changes have often been introduced so as to better control the work force, quite apart from efficiency considerations.[164] But control is not the only motive. Increasing technical efficiency is also important, and such changes sometimes enhance skill levels. Paul Adler has argued that, on balance, skill levels have improved under modern capitalism.[165] I neither need nor wish to deny that claim. The relevant comparison for us is not early capitalism versus modern capitalism, but Laissez Faire versus Economic Democracy. What must be conceded is that under Laissez Faire (and under capitalism in general) there exists a powerful tendency to use technology as a means of controlling the work force by reducing, as far as possible (within the constraints imposed by the need for adequately efficient production), the skill levels of the work force. So strong and systematic a tendency will not exist when an enterprise is controlled democratically.

The overall argument of this section would seem to be complete. I have offered a variety of reasons for concluding that Economic Democracy will be less alienating than Laissez Faire: that the workplace will be more

---

[162] Zuboff (1988, pp. 250–1).

[163] "That all else equal, human beings enjoy the exercise of their realized capacities (their innate and trained abilities), and this enjoyment increases the more the capacity is realized, or the greater its complexity" (Rawls, 1971, p. 426).

[164] For some empirical studies that reach this conclusion, see Nobel (1984), Shaiken (1985), and Zuboff (1988).

[165] Adler (1986). He and some other theorists of work are now arguing that the latest technologies open up unprecedented opportunities for a more democratic workplace. See Piore and Sabel (1984), Hirshhorn (1984) and Zuboff (1988).

participatory, more flexible in its labor–leisure trade-off, and more encouraging of skill development. Well and good. Lovely in theory. But
how do I explain the discrepancy between what theory predicts and
what happens in practice? There remains that troubling assessment by
Edward Greenberg.

Will democratically run workplaces in fact choose their technology
and work organization so as to sacrifice some income for more meaningful work? Greenberg concludes from his firsthand research on the U.S.
plywood cooperatives of the Pacific Northwest and from his review of
the secondary literature that

> it remains inescapably the case that self-management in the U.S. plywood coop-
> eratives, at Mondragon, and in Yugoslavia has fewer beneficial effects on the
> diminution of alienation than is conventionally assumed by advocates of the
> democratic reform of the workplace. . . .
> It would not be unreasonable to conclude, at least tentatively, that workplace
> democracy, in most places and at most times, will likely enhance worker control
> over the product and the formal decision-making process and will make workers
> more satisfied with their work situation. Workplace democracy, in and of itself,
> however, seems unable to significantly alter those aspects of alienation having to
> do with the tyranny of the technical production process, the persistence of hier-
> archy and specialization, the lack of community and solidarity, and stunted mental
> health.[166]

Let me offer a three-part response. First, as Greenberg acknowledges,
workers can be expected to be more satisfied with their work in a democratic workplace than under capitalism, even if the technology remains
unchanged. Some elements of alienation, if not all, will be reduced. Second, the cooperative experiments most relevant to assessing the viability
and desirability of Economic Democracy are of relatively recent origin. It
was to have been expected that they would take over the prevailing
forms of technology and work organization. It was to have been expected
that the good prudential sense necessary to make a business work would
militate against trying to change too much too soon. But once certain
technologies have been adopted – and embodied in machine purchases
and plant design – they cannot be so readily changed.

Third, the empirical evidence is not uniformly grim. In Mondragon
there has developed a movement to change the organization of work,
and it has had some effect. A careful, cautious experiment in one section
of one cooperative in 1973 to replace a conveyor belt with a work table
(to allow for a more social environment, some task rotation, and more
self-determination of the work pace) has spread throughout the plant,
and now to some of the other cooperatives. In 1983 a new factory was
constructed that incorporated from the beginning the new philosophy of

---

[166] Greenberg (1986, p. 114).

work, with operators working in small groups, no assembly lines, no foremen. According to the general manager of the complex to which the factory belongs, "now the program in Vergara is well established. And the workers like it, as we have found from our surveys. Also, whenever a worker is transferred to another plant, he always wants to return to Vergara."[167]

Greenberg is importantly right to caution against seeing workplace democracy as an end to alienation. The work in the plywood cooperatives he studied (which have been in existence since the end of World War II) is indistinguishable from that in conventional mills, "universally noisy, dirty, dangerous, monotonous, and relentless."[168] He is also correct to emphasize that the larger social and political context of which workplace democracy is a part is of decisive importance.[169] But none of this undermines the basic claim defended in this section, which is not that workplace alienation will vanish under Economic Democracy, but that it promises to be less than under Laissez Faire. Indeed, Greenberg's findings, for all the cold water they throw on extravagant hopes, support this basic contention.

There remains one final counterargument to consider. I have argued that so long as organizational initiative remains with the representatives of capital, worker participation will be restricted, and worker choice will have little impact on the organization of work. The tendency toward alienated labor, although amenable to being checked somewhat by enrichment and participation schemes that enhance productivity, will persist. "But even if all that were true," an opponent might interject, "your case is inconclusive, because capitalists, in a free society, need not retain the initiative. If workers are genuinely dissatisfied, there are alternatives available to them. If they really want something better (and are willing to pay for the loss of efficiency), then they can take the initiative. Socialist acts, after all, are not forbidden under capitalism." Again, consider Nozick:

Of course, as an alternative, persons may form their own democratically-run cooperative firms. It is open to any wealthy radical or group of workers to buy an existing factory or establish a new one, and to institute their favorite micro-industrial scheme; for example, worker-controlled, democratically-run firms. . . . The important point is that there is a means of realizing the worker-control

---

[167] This quotation and the rest of the account are from Whyte and Whyte (1988).

[168] Greenberg (1986, p. 81). It is, in fact, more dangerous – an indication of significant self-exploitation (pp. 84–5).

[169] The extent to which such issues as flexitime, skill development, the gendered division of labor, etc., become part of the general public discourse will certainly have an effect on the extent to which democratic workplaces take them up. The important point is, there are not the structural obstacles to reform implementation in a worker-managed firm that there are in a capitalist firm.

scheme that can be brought about by the voluntary actions of people in a free society.[170]

This argument should not be dismissed on the grounds that few workers can afford to buy their factories and that the "radical rich" compose a small set indeed. Nozick's argument admits of a subtler interpretation. If workers really want worker self-management, he may be suggesting, then cooperatives will spring up, funded initially by radical philanthropists or wealthy workers. They will be few at first, as is the case with all innovative organizations, but if they are technologically and operationally viable, they will gradually attract workers away from the capitalists until the point is reached where everyone is satisfied. As a matter of fact, cooperatives have not undermined capitalism, and so they must be either nonviable economically or unattractive to workers or both. Worker self-management either does not work or is not wanted.

It is tempting to respond to Nozick by appealing to contingent historical facts to explain the failure of cooperative ventures that have appeared (not infrequently) on the capitalist stage. But such a response would focus on the wrong issue. The key issue is not the failure of specific ventures; the key question is why the movement as a whole has not steadily expanded.

But we know the answer to that question, or at least one important answer. The reason is structural. We know from our earlier analysis that a worker-managed firm lacks an expansionary dynamic. When a capitalist enterprise is successful, the owner can increase her profits by reproducing her organization on a larger scale. She lacks neither the means nor the motivation to expand. Not so with a worker-managed firm. Even if the workers have the means, they lack the incentive, because enterprise growth would bring in new workers with whom the increased proceeds would have to be shared. Cooperatives, even when prosperous, do not spontaneously grow. But if this is so, then each new cooperative venture (in a capitalist society) requires a new wealthy radical or a new group of affluent radical workers willing to experiment. Because such people doubtless are in short supply, it follows that the absence of a large and growing cooperative movement proves nothing about the viability of worker self-management, nor about the preferences of workers.

The absence of an expansionary dynamic may be the most basic reason for the failure of cooperative production to grow steadily at the expense of capitalist enterprises, but there are others. Cooperatives tend to be more egalitarian in their income structure; indeed, this egalitarianism is one of the features accounting for their X-efficiency. But this means that

[170] Nozick (1974, pp. 250, 252).

a cooperative firm operating in a capitalist environment is in constant danger of having its most skilled managers and workers hired away. Moreover, cooperatives in a capitalist environment are likely to have more difficulty in raising capital. Quite apart from ideological hostility (which may be significant), external investors will be reluctant to put their money into concerns over which they will have little or no control – which tends to be the case with a cooperative.[171] Because cooperatives in a capitalist environment face special difficulties, and because they lack the inherent expansionary dynamic of a capitalist firm, it is hardly surprising that they are far from dominant.

Note the conclusion that follows: Even if worker-managed firms are preferred by the vast majority,[172] and even if they are more productive, a market initially dominated by capitalist firms may not select for them. The commonsense neoclassical dictum that only those things that best accord with people's desires will survive the struggle of free competition has never been the whole truth with respect to anything; with respect to workplace organization it is barely a half-truth.[173]

I have argued that economic Democracy, as a system, will be less alienating than Laissez Faire. To summarize the reasons: Workers will have more participatory autonomy under Economic Democracy, because the degree of workplace democracy will not be restricted by the capitalists' need to keep open all options for profit. The labor–leisure trade-off should be more in accordance with the general interest under Economic Democracy, because workers will have a greater interest in promoting more

---

[171] For more details on these issues, see Putterman (1982), Levine and Tyson (1990, pp. 214–22), and Egan (1990).

[172] That this might in fact be the case is not wholly conjectural. Bowles, Gordon, and Weisskopf (1990, p. 321) report that two-thirds of the respondents in a 1975 poll said they would prefer to work in an employee-controlled company.

[173] I do not claim that cooperatives will always lose out in competition with capitalist firms. There is evidence to suggest that recent trends do not conform to the long-observed tendency for cooperatives in capitalist environment to succumb to capitalist competition, either through outright failure or by reconstituting themselves along capitalist lines. For formal models meant to explain this phenomenon, see Ben-Nur (1984) and Miyazaki (1984). The numbers of producer cooperatives have increased dramatically in most Western countries in recent years. From fewer than 20 in 1975, the number in the United Kingdom grew to 1,600 by 1986; in France the increase has been from 500 to 1,500; in Italy, some 7,000 new cooperatives came into existence between 1970 and 1982. See Estrin and Jones (1988). It is too early to tell if these trends will persist, but two explanatory factors might be cited. First, support structures have been developing to overcome some of the inherent difficulties facing isolated cooperatives and to encourage the development of new cooperatives. Second, it is possible that the newest "postindustrial" technologies will be found to be so well adapted to the cooperative form of work organization that cooperatives will prove significantly better at exploiting the productivity gains than their capitalist competitors. For more on this "postindustrial technology," see Block (1990).

flexible, less frantic, more meaningful working arrangements, as well as shorter hours and longer vacations, than do capitalists, who bear the costs and risks of such changes (under Laissez Faire) but do not receive the full benefits. Workers are likely to be more skilled under Economic Democracy, because neither competitive pressures nor the need for control will push so hard toward deskilling.

To be sure, conflict may be expected concerning all these issues, but a democratic resolution of a conflict that follows from free and open debate, that expresses the will of the majority of those involved, and that leaves open the possibility of revision and experimentation seems the best possible hope for an optimal outcome.

From the arguments of this and the preceding two chapters we may now draw a strong conclusion: All things considered, Economic Democracy is preferable to Laissez Faire.

6. Modern liberalism

I have completed the case against Laissez Faire, the heart and soul of classical liberalism. But there are other forms of capitalism. I contend that capitalism per se is no longer defensible. The preceding three chapters have shown that the conservative model is deeply flawed. This chapter extends the critique to the models that structure the reform agendas of modern liberalism.

Recall my brief against Laissez Faire. I argued that its claims to greater efficiency, better growth, and more liberty than will be found under socialism cannot be sustained, not when the socialism in question is Economic Democracy. I have countered its claims with a nine-count indictment, which can be put starkly as follows:

1. Laissez Faire will not approach full employment.
2. Laissez Faire undermines consumer sovereignty.
3. Laissez Faire encourages the wrong kinds of growth.
4. Laissez Faire promotes the wrong rate of growth.
5. Laissez Faire is economically unstable.
6. Laissez Faire constricts liberty.
7. Laissez Faire generates excessive inequality.
8. Laissez Faire is incompatible with democracy.
9. Laissez Faire alienates working people.

I contend that the same basic indictment will stand against other forms of capitalism. Modern-liberal models will be less culpable on many of these counts than Laissez Faire, but they still will suffer in comparison with Economic Democracy, as I shall try to show in this chapter. It will also be necessary to take up an issue hitherto neglected. Because one of the forms of modern liberalism to be taken up here concerns itself centrally with the issue of *international trade*, we shall have to consider how Economic Democracy will fare in relation to this issue as well.

Let us first consider what it is exactly that is now under scrutiny. Modern liberalism can be best understood as a reaction to the excesses of Laissez Faire. Modern liberals, like socialists, find Laissez Faire to be morally and economically unacceptable, but modern liberals, unlike socialists, judge the basic structures of capitalism to be sound. Modern liberals think the "contradictions" of the system can be alleviated without abrogating any of the three basic institutions: private property, wage labor, and the market. They concede, of course, that modifications are in order, but they do not regard any of these institutions as fundamentally flawed.

How might the contradictions be ameliorated? By dropping the laissez-faire provision and allowing the government to intervene. How should the government intervene? This question brings us to the division within modern liberalism discussed in Chapter 2. Modern liberalism wants a reformed Laissez Faire, but reform proposals will depend heavily on how capitalism is conceptualized. For a Keynesian liberal, capitalism is essentially as the neoclassical model describes it to be, except that it does not tend automatically to full employment. If full employment is ensured (via appropriate governmental measures), then the neoclassical model can be invoked to explain both the strengths and weaknesses of Laissez Faire and to suggest appropriate remedies for the latter. For a post-Keynesian, the neoclassical model is seen to be part of the problem, not part of the solution. Not only does it suggest the wrong kinds of reforms, but also it is part of a protective ideology that masks the real workings of the system.

In my judgment, there is much to be said for the post-Keynesian critique of the neoclassical paradigm, but that is an issue tangential to our central topic. What we must ascertain is the extent to which the reforms of Laissez Faire proposed by Keynesian and post-Keynesian liberals deflect the charges of our multicount indictment. Different conceptualizations of capitalism will suggest different reforms, but these reforms must be examined concretely. It is my contention that whatever set is proposed, reformed capitalism, when compared with Economic Democracy, comes up short.

This is a strong claim, a bit stronger than what I shall attempt to justify here. Instead of surveying the entire field of Keynesian and post-Keynesian liberalism and analyzing the myriad reforms implemented or advocated by those we would call modern liberals, my strategy will be to focus on a major figure in each tradition who has sketched and defended a reasonably comprehensive societal ideal, and then to examine those models closely. In seeing how these models fail, I think it will be clear that no other model that retains the basic institutions of capitalism is likely to succeed.

Such representative figures are not so easy to find. Historically, modern liberals have been preoccupied with specific, piecemeal reforms. Not too many have consciously articulated a comprehensive vision. A notable exception is the Harvard philosopher John Rawls. To be sure, Rawls's great work *A Theory of Justice* is not principally a treatise on liberal capitalism. Its primary aim is to develop and defend an original "theory of justice," the point of which (says Rawls) is to describe and clarify our ordinary, considered judgments regarding justice, much as a theory of grammar describes and clarifies a native speaker's ordinary language usage.[1] But these "considered moral judgments" are the judgments of a modern liberal.[2] Moreover, Rawls employs his theory to evaluate socio-economic formations. In doing so, he constructs a reasonably detailed model of a "property-owning democracy," and he argues that such a system would be just.[3]

It is this model of capitalism that we shall examine, for it well represents the Keynesian-liberal ideal. Unlike most political philosophers of his generation, Rawls does not, with the usual declaration of specialty noncompetence, shy away from economic issues, and when he does confront them, he does so from the perspective of the neoclassical (Keynesian-modified) paradigm.

That Rawls should adopt the neoclassical-Keynesian perspective without apparent hesitation is not surprising, given that he was writing and rewriting his treatise during the middle and late 1960s. From the end of World War II until the early 1970s – above all, during the prosperity of the 1960s widely regarded as having been ushered in by the Kennedy-Johnson (Keynesian-liberal) tax cuts[4] – the "new economics" of the mainstream seemed impregnably solid and irreproachably scientific. Dissent on the Right was regarded with amusement. The radical and post-Keynesian critics who had begun to chip away at the stately, flourishing, Keynesian-liberal paradigm were paid little notice. Rawls was not the only one impressed.[5]

Little did anyone realize, in 1971, that Laissez Faire (as an ideal, if not in reality) was soon to come roaring back. One could scarcely have guessed that "liberal," not "conservative," was soon to become the label from which politicians would flee. In the face of the conservative resurgence that began in the mid-1970s and continued through the 1980s, some

---

[1] See Rawls (1971, pp. 46–53). Rawls is not as committed to the status quo as the grammar analogy suggests. He allows that a correct theory of justice, unlike a correct theory of grammar, might move us to reconsider and modify our "ordinary usage."

[2] See Barry (1973) for an extended defense of this claim.

[3] See Rawls (1971, pp. 274–84). Rawls does not argue that only capitalist structures are just. His "ideological neutrality" is characteristic of modern liberalism, which, unlike classical liberalism, usually is content to argue that certain forms of capitalism can be just, without pressing the further claim that socialism cannot be. Rawls (1975) tilts even further to the left: "The principles of justice do not exclude certain forms of socialism and would in fact require them if the stability of a well-ordered society could be achieved in no other way" (p. 546). I shall argue in the next section that the latter clause is true.

[4] It was not at all respectable in those days to suggest that the prosperity was war-related.

[5] In those (economically) untroubled days, Milton Friedman would declare that "we are all Keynesians now," and Richard Nixon would say that "I am now a Keynesian." Quoted by Paul Samuelson (1973) in the ninth edition of his famous textbook *Economics*, and repeated through the eleventh edition (1980); in the twelfth edition (1985), those quotations were dropped. Times had changed.

liberal economists retained their Keynesian faith, many moved to the right, and some (particularly those who had already broken with their neoclassical heritage) began to formulate an alternative vision, distinct from both Reagan-Thatcher conservatism and standard (New Deal) liberalism.

A representative of this new thinking is Lester Thurow, "probably the most famous economist in America who has not been the host of a PBS television series."[6] A 1964 graduate of Harvard with a Ph.D. in economics, Thurow served as a staff economist for the president's Council of Economic Advisors; then, in 1968, he joined the faculty at MIT, where he has remained ever since. In 1983 he published *Dangerous Currents*, an attack on conventional economic theory (Keynesian as well as neoclassical). His 1985 book, *The Zero-Sum Solution*, offered a comprehensive reform agenda, building on his 1980 best-seller, *The Zero-Sum Society*. In 1992 he offered another, slightly amended version, *Head to Head: The Coming Economic Battle Among Japan, Europe, and America*. Thurow is currently serving as dean of MIT's Sloan School of Management, a post from which he passionately and relentlessly argues his vision – a vision, quite distinct from either classical or Keynesian liberalism, that we shall call post-Keynesian new liberalism, or simply new liberalism.[7]

Before taking up reforms and criticisms, let us do what we have done at the outset in each of the preceding three chapters: think for a moment about values. As we know, all criticisms of capitalism and socialism ultimately rest on value commitments. I have stated the commitments underlying the critique of Laissez Faire. Some are nonproblematical even to conservatives: human happiness, material well-being, efficiency, leisure, liberty. Others – notably, equality, democracy, and participatory autonomy – are more controversial, and so a conservative might balk at

[6] Mann (1990, p. 46). The comparison is with Milton Friedman and John Kenneth Galbraith, each of whom presided over a television series in the early 1980s ("Free to Choose" and "The Age of Uncertainty," respectively). Galbraith, recall, represents what I have called "early post-Keynesianism," as contrasted with Thurow's "late post-Keynesianism." A critique of Galbraith that follows the format employed here for Rawls and Thurow has been published (Schweickart, 1980).

[7] This vision is sometimes referred to as "neo-liberalism," but current usage assigns "neo-liberalism" contradictory meanings. The term sometimes designates the intellectual current touting free trade, privatization, and deep cuts in social services as the solution to the world's woes. This conservative "neo-liberalism" is quite different from (indeed on many points diametrically opposed to) the post-Keynesian "neo-liberalism" of Thurow. In this work, I shall use "New Liberalism" to designate the vision represented by Thurow. When capitalized, it will designate a model with specific structures, which will be described in a later section.

An important institutional base for (Thurovian) new liberalism is the Economic Policy Institute (EPI), a research center set up in the mid-1980s by Thurow, Jeff Faux, Robert Reich, Robert Kuttner, Barry Bluestone, and Ray Marshall to fill the void created as the Keynesian-liberal Brookings Institution moved to the right. See Faux (1992). Various EPI associates, Robert Reich being the most prominent, are now part of the Clinton administration.

the arguments I have marshaled against Laissez Faire that appeal to these values.

Few Keynesian liberals can pull up this way. The values I have articulated are almost as basic to their liberalism as they are to Economic Democracy. A hallmark of Keynesian liberalism is its commitment to reducing inequality. Few people of any political persuasion have expressed a deeper commitment to equality than John Rawls. Not only must society structure its institutions so as to allow fair (not merely formal) equality of opportunity to all; they must be shaped, he insists, so that all inequalities work to the advantage of the least advantaged. Inequalities are permitted, but only to the degree that they serve as incentives for the exercise of talent, and only if these incentives result in sufficiently greater efficiency and innovation that the benefits will reach the least well-off members of society.[8]

Keynesian liberalism has also been committed, historically and in principle, to democracy – to extending the formal franchise to excluded groups and to transforming formal rights into real opportunities. Rawls is explicit in this regard:

The authority to determine basic social policies resides in a representative body selected for limited terms by and ultimately accountable to the electorate. . . . All sane adults, with certain generally recognized exceptions, have the right to take part in political affairs, and the precept one elector one vote is honored as far as possible. . . . Moreover, they should have a fair chance to add alternative proposals to the agenda for political discussion. The liberties protected by the principle of participation lose much of their value whenever those who have greater private means are permitted to use their advantages to control the course of debate.[9]

As to participatory autonomy, the right of people to participate in the decisions that will affect them, the general picture is less clear. Historically, Keynesian liberalism has been somewhat ambivalent about this, with certain currents paternalistic and technocratic. Not Rawls, however. For him, active political participation is a right and a value. It "is an activity enjoyable in itself that leads to a larger conception of society and to the development of [one's] intellectual and moral faculties [which in turn] lays the basis for a sense of duty and obligation upon which the stability of just institutions depends."[10]

---

[8] Rawls (1971, pp. 73–8). I may have overstated slightly Rawls's egalitarianism here. Rawls (1977, p. 160) writes that "presumably there are various reasons for [inequalities that satisfy the difference principle], among which the need for incentives is but one." Rawls does not say what these other reasons might be, but whatever they are, the fact remains that the difference principle implies an extremely strong commitment to equality.

[9] Rawls (1971, pp. 222, 225).

[10] Ibid., p. 234. Rawls, it should be noted, does not call this principle "autonomy." His use of that term is more Kantian: "acting autonomously is acting from principles that we would consent to as free and equal rational beings" (p. 516).

It seems fair to say that the normative commitments of Keynesian liberalism differ little, if at all, from those to which I have appealed in making the case that Economic Democracy will be superior to Laissez Faire. Can we say the same about new liberalism? Is new liberalism as committed to the values of equality, democracy, and participatory autonomy as is Keynesian liberalism? The case here is a bit murky.

It is instructive to compare Thurow with Rawls. The economist is less explicit about his ethical commitments than the philosopher. Does Thurow give equality prima facie value? He finds "significant and disturbing" the shift in income and wealth that has taken place in the United States since the late 1970s: "the rich are getting richer, the poor are increasing in number and the middle class has trouble holding its own."[11] He notes that

> while Americans prefer not to think about inequalities, they are also uncomfortable that they exist. The discomfort starts with our religious heritage. Not many of us would want to explain to Saint Peter why we allowed children to go hungry and did nothing about it. . . . At a more self-interested level it is simply nicer to live in neighborhoods and cities without poverty and hunger. At the most self-interested level, there are few examples of democratic societies that have managed to survive while tolerating extreme disparities of income and wealth.[12]

It is characteristic of Thurow here and elsewhere to ground the normative dimension of his analysis as much as possible on appeals to self-interest. This may be no more than the disciplinary reflex of an economist, but I suspect it is more than that. Given the ferocity of the conservative attack on modern liberalism, it is not surprising that new liberalism has tended to adopt as tough-minded a stance as possible in defense of its reform proposals. To counter the charge that its proposals rely on the "soft" values of (Keynesian) liberalism, new liberalism puts its emphasis on values less vulnerable to conservative critique (i.e., stability, efficiency, and growth).

Whether this emphasis is strategic only or represents a rightward drift in value commitments I hesitate to judge. Thurow is clearly distressed by the inequalities of contemporary society. At the same time, he insists that what is at stake is not *equality*, but *equity* – and even that he grounds in efficiency. Equity, he says, is not equality, but "fairness." And "fairness," he says, "is a social phenomenon. What any population is willing to regard as fair depends upon history, institutions and values." What counts for Thurow (at least as he presents his case) is not equality, or even fairness per se, but the *perception of fairness* – for without the perception

[11] Thurow (1987, p. 30).   [12] Thurow (1985, pp. 111–12).

of fairness, voluntary cooperation breaks down, and the economy becomes inefficient.[13]

One senses similar tensions and ambiguities in his treatments of participatory autonomy and of democracy. Thurow and other late post-Keynesians, much taken by the lessons of Japan and Western Europe, repeatedly emphasize the importance of a more participatory workplace. (This stands in sharp contrast to the early post-Keynesians, who paid no attention at all to workplace democracy.) But worker participation (which for Thurow is never full workplace democracy) is always justified in terms of productivity enhancement.[14]

Thurow is a democrat (indeed, a Democrat, and a leading economic advisor to Democratic presidential aspirants), but he bristles at the suggestion that one should distrust experts and elected politicians, this being "at best a recipe for quietism and at worst a kind of tyranny of the cretinous." In his view, it is essential to the functioning of a democracy that there be an enlightened elite. What is crucial, he says, is that the elite constitute a genuine "establishment," not an "oligarchy."

Both are groups of well-connected rich people who marry each other and run the country. The difference between an establishment and an oligarchy is that an establishment says, "I'm interested in the long-run success of my country, and I am personally confident that if my country succeeds, I will succeed." An oligarchy is intrinsically insecure and has got to have secret Swiss bank accounts.[15]

Is this language heartfelt or only strategic? Especially now, as dean of a prestigious business school, Thurow speaks often to business leaders. Because he sincerely believes that the reforms he advocates will make business more efficient, and because he correctly perceives that such reforms will be difficult to implement in the face of business opposition, can he be expected to alienate his audience by saying that the business class is privileged, and hence incompatible with democracy? Could he be expected to say it even if he believed it? (Would he have been named dean of the Sloan School if he had ever hinted at such a belief?)

I take it as plausible, if not altogether certain, that (many) new liberals share the value commitments common to Keynesian liberalism and democratic socialism, but are simply more hesitant to proclaim them openly. So it is plausible, if not altogether certain, that arguments

---

[13] Ibid., pp. 120ff. "A society or firm that depends solely on the enforcement of rules and regulations is an inefficient society or firm. All societies need voluntary cooperation to be efficient" (p. 122).

[14] "Soft productivity is an untapped productivity vein of gold. America must tap this vein to create a winning economic team – but this means doing the things that are necessary to generate motivation, cooperation, teamwork" (Thurow, 1985, p. 125).

[15] This and the Thurow quotations in the preceding paragraph are reported by Mann (1990, p. 62). See also Thurow (1992, p. 266).

invoking these values will have force for a new liberal, even when directed against new liberalism itself. If not, then the new liberal will not be persuaded by all of what follows.

Keynesian-liberal "Fair Capitalism"

In *A Theory of Justice*, John Rawls sketches an ideal property-owning system that he thinks would be just. Let us call it "Fair Capitalism."[16] The model is elegantly rendered, its basic institutions defined so as to make their functions and interactions transparent. The political structure of this system is democratic; liberty of conscience and freedom of thought are taken for granted, as are other familiar civil liberties. The economic structure is capitalist, but this structure is overseen by a formidable government. Four government branches are assigned primary responsibility, each with a distinct set of functions. The *Allocative Branch* is charged with keeping the economy competitive and with using taxes and subsidies to compensate for cases in which competitive prices do not accurately reflect social benefits and costs. That is, it attempts to correct deviations from Pareto optimality caused by monopolies and externalities. The *Stabilization Branch* concerns itself with the macroequilibrium of the economy. It sees to it that strong effective demand brings about reasonably full employment "in the sense that those who want work can find it."[17] Together these two branches are meant to ensure a stable, efficient market economy.

More directly concerned with justice are the Transfer Branch and Distributive Branch. The *Transfer Branch* sees to it that no individual or household falls below the social minimum. It guarantees a certain level of well-being to all. The *Distributive Branch* occupies itself with the opposite end of the wealth spectrum. By a judicious mix of inheritance, gift, and expenditure taxes, it seeks to prevent a concentration of wealth that might jeopardize political liberty and fair equality of opportunity.

This model, we observe, is modern-liberal in its general presumption that the government has a major role to play in counteracting the harsher effects of the free market. It is Keynesian, as opposed to post-Keynesian, in taking the competitive market as its ideal of efficiency and in having the government deal with unemployment by maintaining strong effective demand.

We see what the government is supposed to do, but are the institutions adequate to the intentions? How likely is it that this Keynesian-

---

[16] Rawls does not call his model "capitalist," preferring instead the term "property owning democracy." But because the model features private property, wage labor, and the market, it is indeed a model of capitalism.

[17] Rawls (1971, p. 276).

liberal economy will be able to escape the various counts of the indictment brought against Laissez Faire? How likely in comparison with
Economic Democracy? To answer these questions, let us test Rawls's
proposal against our nine counts, taking the charges one at a time. To
facilitate the exposition, let us rearrange them slightly, and begin with
the noneconomic charges. The economic charge of instability will be
treated last, but it will be given the most extensive attention, because this
is the problem for which the policy prescriptions of Keynesianism deviate
most markedly from those of Laissez Faire.

In making the case for Economic Democracy over Laissez Faire, I
appealed to *liberty*. It is true that certain individuals are freer under Laissez
Faire than are their structural counterparts under Economic Democracy.
Owners and investors are constrained under Laissez Faire only by their
own perceptions of potential gain, whereas managers in Economic Democracy ultimately are answerable to the managed, and those who make
investment decisions must answer to democratic constituencies. But if
certain individuals are freer under Laissez Faire, far greater numbers are
less free (i.e., more subject to the arbitrary will of another), namely, most
working people and most community members, whose livelihoods and
well-being depend on policy and investment decisions over which they
have no control.

Fair Capitalism interferes only modestly with managerial prerogatives[18]
and scarcely at all with investment decisions, and so the foregoing argument tells against Fair Capitalism as well as against Laissez Faire. So,
too, does the argument that Fair Capitalism will be inclined to support
repressive regimes abroad. Capitalists under Fair Capitalism still will
look abroad for investment opportunities and cheap labor, and so they
can be expected to press their government to support regimes that will
keep those foreign economies "open" and their labor forces docile. As is
obvious to anyone who looks, the historical record of Keynesian liberalism in the United States (roughly, Franklin Roosevelt through Richard
Nixon) strongly supports this contention.

Equality, along with liberty, is a central concept of Rawls's theory of
justice. How egalitarian, then, is Fair Capitalism? Here a socialist can
only gasp in amazement. Rawls proclaims a profound commitment to
equality. His theoretical strictures on inequality are as severe as those of
the most ardent socialist. Yet he defends a system that admits, indeed
requires, property income, the basic source of contemporary inequality.
Interest, rent, stock dividends – the whole gamut of "income from ownership" – all persist under Fair Capitalism.

[18] Although Rawls does not discuss such things as regulations for occupational safety and
health, we shall assume that these and other standard components of Keynesian liberalism are included in Fair Capitalism.

To be sure, the government's Distributive Branch acts to dampen inequalities of income and wealth, but are its instruments adequate to their assigned tasks? Can they ensure that these inequalities will work to the benefit of the least advantaged? Notice that inheritance, gift, and expenditure taxes – the tools of the Distributive Branch – do not discriminate as to the source of income. Income differentials that serve as incentives for the performance of onerous work or the development of needed skills are not distinguished from those that derive from no productive contribution whatsoever. In fact, they cannot be so distinguished. Fair Capitalism relies on private savings to generate its investment fund, and when an economy relies on private savings for investment, property income must be permitted.[19] But as our analysis of Economic Democracy has demonstrated, private savings stimulated by the lure of interest are not necessary to a decentralized market economy – so it is difficult to understand how a theory of justice with so strong a commitment to equality as Rawls's can remain neutral with respect to property income. In fact, it is impossible to understand. Rawls's own theory, however neutral he wants it to be as between capitalism and socialism, plainly favors Economic Democracy over Fair Capitalism on this point.

I have argued that Laissez Faire is incompatible with genuine *democracy*. My first argument – that a concentration of wealth, inevitable under Laissez Faire, brings in its train disproportionate political influence – is acknowledged by Rawls. Institutions that ensure fair equality of opportunity, he says, "are put in jeopardy when inequalities of wealth exceed a certain limit, and political liberty likewise tends to lose its value, and representative government to become such in appearance only."[20] The Distributive Branch is specifically charged with preventing inequalities from exceeding this limit.

It must be seriously doubted that the Distributive Branch can keep wealth so bounded, given the inequalities made inevitable by property income, but even if it should succeed in maintaining a fairly wide dispersal of property, my second argument, which appeals to investor confidence, still holds. A capitalist economy, Fair Capitalism included, requires investor confidence for stability. Thus elected officials must give special weight to the interests of investors (be they few or relatively many), whether or not these interests are in accord with the majority interests of

[19] I do not mean to imply that tax schemes compatible with Keynesian liberalism could not distinguish at all among sources of income. Income taxes (which are not favored by Rawls, but are permitted under special circumstances) routinely do just that. However, tax rates for property income (1) cannot be too high and (2) cannot differ too much from other income-tax rates. If restriction 1 is violated, investment will be curtailed; if restrictions 2 is violated, much inefficient and/or illegal behavior will ensue.

[20] Rawls (1971, p. 278).

society. Thus investors constitute a privileged class, a class that oddly fits – or rather does not fit – our concept of genuine popular rule.

It might be thought that the interests of investors – let us call them capitalists, for that is what the significant investors will be, even under Fair Capitalism – are never at variance with the general interests of society. But this, I have repeatedly argued, is not so. The issue of *workplace alienation* is of particular importance. Here the arguments are identical with those directed against Laissez Faire, because Fair Capitalism offers little in the way of workplace reform. One can anticipate some experimentation with profit sharing and participation (also possible under Laissez Faire), but there is no reason to suppose that these modifications will result in an optimal level, not so long as the initiating power rests with those whose preeminent interest is the bottom line.

Notice that the value commitments to which we appealed in defining optimality preclude even genuine enhancement of productivity from serving as the ultimate criterion. Even if productivity were to suffer somewhat as a result of greater participation, the enhancement of work satisfaction might well be overriding. As Rawls himself notes:

It is a mistake to believe that a just society must wait upon a high material standard of life. *What men want is meaningful work in free association with others*, these associations regulating their relations to one another within a framework of just basic institutions. To achieve this state of things great wealth is not necessary.[21]

This is a prescription for Economic Democracy, not Fair Capitalism.

Turning now to the economic charges leveled against Laissez Faire, we observe that the one with which Keynesian liberalism most fully identifies is the charge that Laissez Faire will not approach *full employment*. The name Keynes is associated with nothing so much as unemployment – a revolutionary diagnosis and a putative cure. A remarkably simple cure at that, if contrary to common sense: When times are bad, spend, go into debt, do not save! If consumers are reluctant to oblige, then the government should step into the breach and unbalance its budget by spending more than it receives in taxes.[22]

The Keynesian remedy is simple to state, but is it effective? Can it cure

---

[21] Ibid., p. 290; emphasis added.
[22] Though "Keynesianism" now refers to the government's monetary and fiscal policies (which we shall examine later), Keynes himself did not hesitate to exhort the public. In a 1931 radio broadcast he urged the following: "Oh patriotic housewives, sally out tomorrow early into the streets and go to the wonderful sales which are everywhere advertised. You will do yourselves good – for never were things so cheap, cheap beyond your dreams. Lay in stocks of household linen, of sheets and blankets to satisfy your needs. And have the added joy that you are increasing employment, adding to the wealth of the country because you are setting on good useful activities, bringing a chance and a hope to Lancashire, Yorkshire and Belfast." Quoted by Elizabeth Johnson (1973, pp. 15–16).

unemployment without inducing other destabilizing consequences? Let us hold this question for a moment. We shall treat stability separately. Let us consider a different point. Suppose the Keynesian policies are able to ensure full employment. Will they be implemented? In 1943, Michael Kalecki, the independent co-creator of the "Keynesian" general theory, issued a famous dissent to the prevailing optimism. Kalecki, unlike the Keynesian liberals, saw class conflict as a decisive factor:

Indeed, under a regime of permanent full employment, "the sack" would cease to play its role as a disciplinary measure. The social position of the boss would be undermined and the self-assurance and class-consciousness of the working class would grow. Strikes for wage increases and improvements in conditions of work would be higher under a regime of full employment than they are on average under laissez-faire; and even the rise in wages resulting from the stronger bargaining power of the workers is less likely to reduce profits than to increase prices, and thus affects only the *rentier* interests. But "discipline in the factories" and "political stability" are more appreciated by business leaders than profits. Their class interest tells them that lasting full employment is unsound from their point of view and that unemployment is an integral part of the "normal" capitalist system.[23]

Business analysts often voice similar concerns, though without Kalecki's system-critical edge:

Unemployment remains too low for the workforce to have flexibility. Anytime the jobless total is less than two million even common labor is scarce. Many employers tend to hoard skills. And certainly, the labor unions are in the driver's seat in wage negotiations. More workers can be had, to be sure. But at considerable cost. And they probably wouldn't be the skills most desired. There's no assurance against inflation like a pool of genuine unemployment. That's a blunt, hard-headed statement, but a fact.[24]

It is also a blunt, hardheaded fact that under Economic Democracy there will exist no class of people with a specific interest in maintaining unemployment. Unemployment cannot generate downward pressure on wages, for there will be no wage laborers. It will enhance neither factory discipline nor the power of management vis-à-vis labor unions. Because the material needs of the unemployed must be financed from the taxes of those employed, the latter will have no interest whatsoever in preserving what Marx has called the "Industrial Reserve Army."[25]

This is not to say that Economic Democracy will experience no difficulty in providing work for everyone who wants to work, but the difficulty will not be structurally related to class interest as it is under capitalism, even Fair Capitalism, and hence will be more amenable to resolution. We should not forget the historical record. Capitalism, whether

[23] Kalecki (1972, pp. 424–5).
[24] *Business Week*, May 17, 1952. Quoted by Baran (1968, p. 102).   [25] Marx (1967, p. 628).

informed by the classical-liberal ideal or the Keynesian-liberal ideal, has always had problems with unemployment in peacetime.

The *sales effort* is another area where the interests of capital and those of the rest of society conflict. Neoclassical theorists, whether or not also Keynesian, have paid almost no attention to the sales apparatus. Rawls follows suit. None of the government agencies of Fair Capitalism is mandated to keep nonrational sales techniques in check. A close reader of Rawls may find this surprising, for Rawls is quite aware that "an economic regime is not only an institutional scheme for satisfying existing desires and aspirations but a way of fashioning desires and aspirations in the future."[26] Moreover, his analysis of "the good life" specifically identifies goodness with rationality. He presumes "that the members of a democratic society have, at least in an intuitive way, a rational plan of life in light of which they schedule their most important endeavors and allocate their various resources."[27] Given this emphasis on rationality, Rawls must surely look askance at an apparatus that propagandizes relentlessly, with the most sophisticated psychological techniques that money can buy, on behalf of consumption.

Both Economic Democracy and Fair Capitalism will be market economies, so both will be vulnerable to abuses of a nonrational sales effort. Neither will be as vulnerable as Laissez Faire, because both will allow government intervention to curb excesses. It does not follow that they will be equally vulnerable. The most important arguments of Chapter 3 on this topic apply to Fair Capitalism as well as to Laissez Faire. Individual enterprises under Fair Capitalism will be as growth-oriented as those of Laissez Faire, so they will be more inclined to invest massively in the sales effort than will enterprises under Economic Democracy. Moreover, Fair Capitalism will be as dependent on growth for stability as will Laissez Faire, so the government will be less likely to intervene to curb abuses than under Economic Democracy.[28]

My critique of the *kind of growth* promoted by Laissez Faire elaborated three themes: Inequalities distort development; growth is unbalanced; and growth is plagued by externalities, many of which are environmentally destructive. Rawls is not insensitive to these problems. Some income redistribution will be effected by the Transfer Branch and Distributive Branch of his model government. The Allocative Branch will attempt to correct "the more obvious departures from efficiency caused by the failure of prices to measure accurately social benefits and costs."[29]

---

[26] Rawls (1977, p. 160).   [27] Rawls (1988, p. 254). See also Rawls (1971, ch. 7).

[28] That firms under Fair Capitalism will be as growth-oriented as those under Laissez Faire is obvious. That growth remains as essential for Fair Capitalism requires a new argument, which will be supplied later.

[29] Rawls (1971, p. 276).

But the reply to that seems obvious: "Too little and too late." Under Fair Capitalism, inequalities are not likely to be sufficiently reduced. That was argued earlier. Because investment remains in private hands, decisions will not be coordinated – certainly not if the market is to remain competitive. With respect to externalities, the fundamental weakness of Fair Capitalism in comparison with Economic Democracy is that labor will be subservient to capital, not vice versa. Under Fair Capitalism, as under Laissez Faire, workers either must entice capital to come to them or must go to where the capital is. So capitalist enterprises can pit worker against worker, region against region, "externalities" be damned. Under Economic Democracy, capital will be apportioned to regions on a per-capita basis, which will give communities far more control over their (human/natural) environment than they will have under Fair Capitalism.

This last contention is especially important. Under both Fair Capitalism and Laissez Faire it is admitted that the market cannot be relied upon to resolve environmental difficulties. But as was pointed out in Chapter 4, so long as investment initiatives remain in the hands of private owners, government remedies must be national (or even international) in scope, for if they are local, companies can flee the restrictions. But this means (1) that an environmental problem will have to become exceedingly severe before a requisite consensus can obtain, (2) that the regulations likely will be weakened by industry and regional compromise, and (3) that the regulations will not be appropriately attuned to local conditions. Economic Democracy, though not a miracle cure for environmental difficulties, will be far better situated to manage them than will either Laissez Faire or Fair Capitalism.

If Fair Capitalism is ill-prepared to manage the quality of its growth, it is even less well prepared to control its *rate of growth*. Keynesian policies aim at establishing that equilibrium of saving and investment that will ensure full employment. When saving is in excess of investment, or vice versa, steps are taken to reduce one or increase the other. But the question is never raised whether or not the investment level sufficient to induce employers to hire all who want to work (the Keynesian condition) is in any way related to the socially desirable (or socially desired) rate of growth.

Rawls does not see this. If he did, it would be disconcerting, for Rawls treats the question of societal saving as one of considerable moral urgency. He discusses at length the problem of "justice between generations," and worries that a democratic electorate might "perpetrate grave offenses against other generations" by choosing to save too little.[30] What

[30] Ibid., pp. 284–98.

Rawls fails to notice is that Fair Capitalism provides no mechanism whatsoever for a conscious, conscientious determination of the saving or investment rate. The market decides each of these rates; then the government intervenes if there is an imbalance, so as to secure full employment.[31] There is no room in this process for an independent consideration of the needs of future generations. There is no place under Fair Capitalism – as there is under Economic Democracy – for a conscious, collective decision as to how much we should save.

It is worth remarking that Rawls's specific worry concerning the fate of future generations is likely misplaced. He worries about insufficient savings, but the tendency of capitalism, especially Keynesian capitalism, is toward a high rate of savings.[32] The tendency is for savings to outstrip investment, and this (as Keynes showed) will cause the economy to contract unless the government intervenes. Capitalism – especially Keynesian capitalism – is structured to save, to invest, and to grow. But it is precisely this growth, when driven by market forces unmediated by democratic procedures, that poses the threat to future generations, not any lack of aggregate savings.

If growth poses a problem for Fair Capitalism, so does its absence. In the last section of Chapter 4 it was shown that without growth, Laissez Faire is *unstable*. Recall the basic argument: If profits are merely consumed by the capitalist class, the resulting stationary state will be politically unstable, because the functionless character of property ownership will be apparent to all. So, for the capitalist class to appear (and to be) functional, a sizable portion of their profits must be reinvested. But even in this case, political instability may be expected if growth is not forthcoming. If the economy does not grow, then profits will decline, businesses will fail, investor confidence will be shaken. A cutback in investment will lead to layoffs, reduced demand, a recession. If the recession is long-lasting, then class (and other) antagonisms will become more virulent. Without a "recovery" (i.e., a resumption of growth), political instability will be the order of the day.

So Fair Capitalism must grow. But will it grow? We have seen that sustained growth requires three moments: Investments must be made, the anticipated productivity increases must materialize, and the products must be sold. We have seen that this latter moment depends on con-

---

[31] At least that is what it tries to do. How successful it is likely to be will be taken up later.

[32] It is commonplace these days to blame the economic woes of the United States on insufficient savings, but Lipsey and Kravis (1987) argue carefully (and, to me, convincingly) that this "insufficiency" is based on misperception. When properly measured, the United States is seen to save as much of its GNP as do our industrialized competitors. See also Lipsey and Tice (1989). In any event, increasing the national rate of savings need not correlate at all with the well-being of future generations.

sumer confidence and effective demand. With this schema in mind, we are well positioned to review the traditional Keynesian remedies and judge the likelihood of their effectiveness.

Keynesian policies fall into two categories: monetary policies and fiscal policies, that is, manipulation of the money supply on the one hand, and manipulation of taxation and government spending on the other. By now, even most conservatives are "Keynesian" in their conviction that the government must do something to avoid serious recessions,[33] but their strong preference is for the first category only (i.e., for "monetarism"): Government intervention should be confined to initiatives by the central bank to increase or decrease the money supply.[34] Friedman, for example, urges a legislative rule instructing the monetary authority to "see to it that the total stock of money [including currency outside commercial banks plus all deposits of commercial banks] rises month by month, indeed as far as possible, day by day, at a constant rate of X percent, where X is some number between 3 and 5."[35] If the market-driven rate of increase is too high, the central bank should intervene to cut it back; if the market-driven rate is too low, the central bank should make more money available.

The great merit of monetarism, in conservative eyes, is the minimalist character of the intervention. No taxation or government spending is involved. Money is made available, without government restrictions, to individuals willing and able to borrow. The market remains supreme in allocating investment and in distributing income.

The logic of monetarism is easy to grasp. So long as the money supply is steadily increasing, investors can finance expansion, and consumers can buy the goods produced. But is this sufficient to avoid recessionary instability? It will not ensure full employment, nor do monetarists claim that it will. According to Friedman, there is a "natural" rate of unemployment consistent with stable prices; to try to reduce unemployment

---

[33] It became fashionable in the mid-1970s for conservatives to disavow the Keynesian label. This may be attributed, at least in part, to the rise of the "New Classical Economics," which not only attacked the theoretical foundations of the Keynesian paradigm but also claimed (appealing to its "rational-expectations theory") that neither monetary nor fiscal policy could have much effect on aggregate output. By now, most of the claims of this iconoclastic movement have been discredited – though a stigma akin to that attached to the term "liberal" remains attached to the term "Keynesian." For a good (if partisan) review of the debate, see Blinder (1989).

[34] The central bank has a number of tools at its disposal for doing this. The most commonly used is the buying and selling of government securities. Buying government bonds with newly created money expands the supply; selling them takes money out of circulation, and hence contracts the supply. Because of fractional reserve requirements, there is a multiplier effect. These reserve requirements are also set by the central bank and may be adjusted if it is deemed necessary.

[35] Friedman (1962, p. 54). See also Lucas (1981, pp. 249–61).

below that rate is to invite runaway inflation.[36] But unemployment aside, will such a monetary policy ensure growth?

Joan Robinson puts her finger on the problem: "There is an unearthly, mystical element in Friedman's thought. The mere existence of a stock of money somehow promotes its expenditure."[37] Merely making money available does not guarantee that investors will invest, that productivity will increase, or that consumers will buy. Friedman and fellow monetarists point to the historical record, but that is unsatisfactory, because the correlation between business booms and expansions of the money supply does not demonstrate causality. As Robinson points out, a sharp rise in business activity is likely to be preceded by an increase in the money supply, because a rise in borrowing for working capital will show up sooner in the statistics than will an increase in the value of the output. This does not mean that an increase in the money supply caused production to increase.[38]

Moreover, the recent historical record has not been kind to monetarism. Monetarist policies, consciously adopted by the Federal Reserve in 1979, were successful in stopping inflation, but they ushered in the worst recession since the Great Depression. They were then abandoned in favor of (unacknowledged, if traditional) Keynesian fiscalism: massive government spending on "Star Wars" and other such war toys without compensating tax increases.

Keynesian liberals agree with the foregoing conclusion: Monetarism is not enough.[39] Fiscal policy, they say, is also needed. At one level, the logic of fiscal policy is as transparent as that of monetarism, though at a deeper level it is not. Consider the first level. Suppose there is an excess of savings, relative to investment. This, as we have seen, will cause the economy to contract, because effective demand will fall off if savings are not offset by investment. But (so goes the logic of fiscal policy) if insufficient investment is being made by the private sector, then the government can invest directly – in armaments, public works, space shuttles, whatever – and finance these programs by doing the borrowing itself. There is no need to wait for the private entrepreneurs to do their duty.

Here's the rub that requires a deeper analysis. When an economy is in recession, it does not look like it has excess savings. When an economy

---

[36] Friedman (1968). Although most economists have accepted this, Blinder (1989, p. 120) suggests that given the empirical evidence, "it may well be that Keynesians caved in too readily to the natural rate hypothesis."

[37] Robinson (1971, p. 87).

[38] Ibid., p. 86. It will be recalled from our discussion of inflation in Chapter 4 that the central bank does not have complete control over the money supply. The money supply fluctuates on its own in response to business and financial activity; the central bank reacts to these autonomous movements with countervailing movements of its own. Hence the difficulty of identifying causal connections.

[39] See Hahn (1984), especially his article "Why I Am Not a Monetarist."

contracts, both consumption and savings contract. The excess savings that may have precipitated the recession quickly disappear. Here the Keynesians make their subtlest argument: When an economy is in recession, *investments can create savings*. One does not have to have savings before one invests. One can invest first, and then cover the investment from the resulting savings. This is quite counterintuitive. Granted, individual entrepreneurs routinely invest before they save, and then repay the loans from their profits, but they have to borrow from someone who earlier had saved. Don't they?

The Keynesian answer is no: It is not true that there must first be savings before there can be investment. Once again a certain fetishism clouds our understanding. Suppose I would like to "invest" in some new machinery for my factory. I can go to the bank and take out a loan (presumably of someone else's savings), and then place my order. Or I can place my order directly. If the machine manufacturer is running slack, he may be willing and able to sell to me on credit. His workers, already on hand, will make the machine; I shall install it and use it, and then pay him for the machine from my subsequent savings.[40] In this case, notice, first came the investment, then came the savings. That this is not only possible but also important is one of Keynes's most basic insights.

The policy implication that flows from this insight is startling: The government should spend what it does not have. A country in recession need not wait for spontaneous saving to occur (the traditional Laissez Faire approach). The government can create something from nothing. It can spend more than it collects in taxes. If there are private savings lying fallow, the government can borrow them. If there are no such savings, *it can borrow from itself* (by simply printing more money). The point is to stimulate investment by stimulating overall spending, either directly by making government purchases or indirectly by putting money into the hands of people more likely to spend than to save (e.g., by cutting taxes for the low and middle classes). If spending goes up, investor confidence will go up, more private investments will be made, and growth will be restored. Why wait for an invisible hand (which may or may not ever come) when high-profile, visible intervention can set the ball rolling?

Such is the logic of Keynesian fiscalism. Will such policies work? Their intent, we see, is to increase investment by increasing aggregate demand, but there are some obvious difficulties. If the government cuts taxes, that might simply increase consumer saving, or reduce consumer debt, not increase consumer spending. If the government borrows from the private sector to finance its deficit, that borrowing might crowd out private

[40] And if the workers had already been laid off? They might be willing to extend their labor on credit. Clearly, the barriers to their doing so are social and psychological, not material. The Keynesian policies are designed to breach these barriers.

borrowing. If the government borrows from itself (by printing more money), that might simply lead to higher prices. Clearly, there is no logical necessity for fiscal policies to work.

If we think back to our basic schema, the fundamental problem becomes clear. An appropriate mix of monetary and fiscal policies can keep aggregate demand at a high enough level to keep investment in line with savings, but these policies plainly do not impinge on the key moment of the growth process: *productivity increase.* Or, rather, they impinge in conflicting ways. On the one hand, an increase in aggregate demand will enhance investor confidence; investments tend to increase productivity, as does direct government subsidy of research and development. On the other hand, a growing money supply can fuel purely speculative ventures that will have no effect at all on productivity; government expenditures can generate deadweight bureaucracies and/or divert resources and talented personnel into areas that contribute little or nothing to productivity (most military expenditures, to cite the obvious example). But when government stimulation fails to increase productivity, the result is not growth, but inflation – and the instability that if brings in its train. The simple fact is that neither monetary nor fiscal policies can guarantee growth, the growth that is so essential to capitalist stability.[41]

Compare Economic Democracy. The most important point: It does not need to grow. A stationary-state economy will not expose the capitalist class as functionless, for there will be no capitalist class. If a growing economy begins to slow its rate of growth, there will be no need to worry that the resulting lack of investor confidence will throw the economy into recession. Because new technologies can be employed to increase leisure, as well as output, there is no a priori reason to suppose that there will be a slowdown in the demand for investment funds. And if there is, the excess funds (being tax-generated) can be rebated to the citizenry, thus giving the economy a stimulatory boost. The basic cause of capitalist instability, present in Fair Capitalism as well as Laissez Faire, will be absent: the economy's dependence on the "animal spirits" of the capitalist class.[42]

We have completed our survey of the nine-count indictment originally directed at Laissez Faire. I have argued in this section that on most counts

[41] The "supply-siders" of the early Reagan years, however misguided in their own policy prescriptions, were not wrong in their critique: Keynesianism concentrates on stimulating the demand for goods, but increased demand without increased supply means inflation. At bottom, Keynesianism rests on the faith that market forces will suffice to increase the supply of goods, so long as the demand is there. In light of recent history, this faith seems misplaced.

[42] The reader will recall that the question of inflationary instability in an Economic Democracy was discussed in Chapter 4. It was concluded that inflation, although not unlikely, should not be a stability problem.

Keynesian liberalism is less guilty than is Laissez Faire, but in no case does it fare as well as Economic Democracy. It was noted in the preceding section that the value commitments prompting the Keynesian-liberal reforms are even more consonant with the values underlying the case for Economic Democracy than are the value commitments of classical liberalism. It follows that although the problems with Fair Capitalism may be less severe than those of Laissez Faire, Keynesian liberals have fewer ethical reasons than have classical liberals for preferring their model to Economic Democracy. Indeed, they have none.[43]

Post-Keynesian "New Liberalism"

Apart from trade and investment relations with the Third World, we have paid scant attention thus far to the international dimension in any of our models. Laissez Faire, Fair Capitalism, and Economic Democracy have all been presumed to be more or less self-contained economies. That lacuna will have to be addressed in this section, because new liberalism is about nothing so much as *international* competitiveness. Thurow emphasizes over and over that the increase in international trade and the rapidity of flow of international currency and capital have changed the nature of the economic game. New Liberalism is specifically designed to play in that game. What about Economic Democracy? Can it, too, play in that game? Can it play as well as an economy structured according to the precepts of new liberalism? If not, then what? Is socialism in one country a viable option? Before turning to these questions, we need a clearer picture of the new-liberal model and a sense of how it stands vis-à-vis our nine-count indictment of capitalism. Let us deal with these issues first.

Lester Thurow is typically modern liberal in his focus on reforming an existing system, as opposed to laying out an ideal model. He is concerned above all with redesigning the U.S. economy so as to meet the challenge posed by Europe and Japan. Still, it is possible to extract from his writings a model that is consistent with his reform agenda, indeed, a model that I think captures the essence of his vision.[44] Let us call this model "New Liberalism."[45]

---

[43] I am referring here to reasons relative to the intrinsic desirability of the respective models. A Keynesian liberal might agree, but counter that Fair Capitalism has a better chance of being implemented than does Economic Democracy. This "transition problem" will be discussed in Chapter 7.

[44] Thurow's various reform proposals have undergone modifications and shifts of emphasis over the years: *The Zero-Sum Society* (1980) emphasized equity and guaranteed employment. *The Zero-Sum Solution* (1985) stressed worker participation. *Head to Head* (1992) gives more attention to business groups. The model that follows combines elements from all of these works. It represents what I take to be his best case.

[45] Following the convention adopted with Laissez Faire, I shall use the capitalized term to designate a specific model instantiating the general orientation.

The model is plainly post-Keynesian. Perhaps the most characteristic and revealing feature of post-Keynesianism is its treatment of what is traditionally called "monopoly." For the neoclassical economist, monopolies and oligopolies are bad. A monopoly will use its power to keep goods in short supply so as to drive up their prices. Therefore, it is *inefficient* (the ultimate pejorative for the strict neoclassical). Society finds itself with less of what it really wants and more of what it wants less strongly: Pareto nonoptimality. A monopoly will also tend to be lazy and slack, lacking in innovative drive.

Post-Keynesians find this analysis preposterous. The conclusions follow from the neoclassical assumptions, they say, but these conclusions do not match reality. Large, oligopolistic firms rarely keep goods in short supply, and they are not necessarily lazy. The most productive, efficient, and innovative firms often are those with considerable market power. Antitrust legislation aimed at blocking enterprise collusion and forcing firms to be more price-competitive, say the post-Keynesians, has been informed by a false conception of the way the world works, a conception that takes the corner grocer as the model for a productive, efficient, innovative enterprise. IBM or Mitsubishi or Siemens would better serve, if reality, rather than outdated theory, were the guide.

Post-Keynesian New Liberalism derives from the conviction that the two most successful advanced capitalist economies today, Japan and Germany, share certain structural features that are very different from those of either classical or Keynesian capitalism, and it is argued that these differences reflect a kind of paradigm shift. For Laissez Faire, competition is the central category: The competitive market coordinates all economic activity. Keynesian capitalism gives government a larger role to play, but competition remains the economy's driving force. New liberalism reconceptualizes the economy in terms of two fundamental categories: competition and cooperation. From the microeconomic level to the macroeconomic level, both of these elements must be recognized, and given their due. Within a firm, among firms, between firms and the government, and at the international level the proper balance must be struck between competition and cooperation. According to new liberalism, neither classical nor Keynesian liberalism appreciates sufficiently the cooperative dimension of economic activity, and so the institutions that instantiate these perspectives give too much weight to competition, and too little to cooperation.

The basic features of the specific model we are calling New Liberalism reflect the concern to balance these two categories. To see this, let us examine the model, level by level, beginning with the firm.

Within the firm, New Liberalism wants more worker participation, more teamwork. It wishes to create within the firm "an environment where the labor force takes a direct interest in raising productivity."[46] It also calls for job security and a seniority wage – provisions that look inefficient from the neoclassical point of view, but which, Thurow argues, will promote worker identification with the company, a willingness to share skills, and a spirit of flexibility that will pay efficiency dividends in the long run.[47] It also wants profit sharing, or, better still, a bonus system, based on the value added, that will account for as much as a third of a worker's annual income.[48] The principal aim of all these features is to replace competition within the firm with cooperation, so as to make the firm itself more competitive.

Thurow, in accordance with post-Keynesian dictates, wants the existing antitrust laws repealed. He wants them replaced by a legal framework that will encourage (rather than make illegal) the formation of "business groups that are the equivalent of those that now exist in West Germany and Japan – and that used to exist in the United States prior to the Great Depression."[49] In order to be able to compete effectively in the international arena, corporations today need more, not less, market power. They must be allowed to integrate themselves horizontally and vertically by means of merchant banks or holding companies. In this way, management can free itself from the *tyranny of the stockholder* – the ever present threat of a hostile takeover that compels managers to focus on the short-term quarterly profit statement and prevents them from undertaking the risky ventures and long-range planning so essential to the overall health of the economy.

Firms within a business group will cooperate with one another, but they will compete with the firms in other groups and with their international rivals. At the center of the business group (which will be modeled on the Japanese *keiretsu*) will be a financial institution that will hold enough of each member firm's stock to give it controlling interest. The financial

---

[46] Thurow (1985, p. 148).

[47] See Thurow (1983, pp. 196–215) and Thurow (1985, pp. 170–80). On the issue of job security, Thurow points out that one does not assume that every worker is, or can be made to be, conscientious and hard-working: "Every manager I talked to [in Japan] said that he had workers who were not performing adequately. They were described in very unflattering terms, and according to company officials immense social pressure was brought to bear upon them to get them to start working. But they were not fired, even if 'they had not worked in years'" (Thurow, 1985, p. 173). But this defect is more than counterbalanced by the cited gains. In particular, security of employment (coupled with a seniority wage) allows Japanese workers to embrace, rather than resist, new technology, because innovations will neither cost them their jobs nor force them to take wage reductions.

[48] Thurow (1985) argues that "value added" (i.e., the difference between gross revenues and the costs of nonlabor inputs) is a more straightforward measure of workers' collective contribution, and hence is more likely to motivate. "Labor is rightly suspicious," he notes, "of the creative accounting that lies behind those profit figures" (p. 161).

[49] Thurow (1992, p. 288).

institution will have representatives on the board of directors of each member firm. It will play an active role in the hiring and firing of member-firm management. It will oversee the strategies and investments that will make each firm, and the group as a whole, successful.[50]

The relationship between government and business will also be characterized by greater cooperation, in that government will be less adversarial, less distant, more intimately involved in the details of economic development. Government will not police the private sector to make sure that firms compete rather than collude. Nor will it confine its economic interventions to arm's-length monetary and fiscal policies aimed at securing full employment. Thurow argues that antitrust laws are misconceived (as we have already noted) and that Keynesian macromanagement no longer works.

More precisely, only half of Keynesian macromanagement works. Governments do indeed have the power to create a recession, and thus cool off inflation. Cutting back on the money supply can do that, although the social costs are very high. What Keynesian policies are currently unable to do is reverse the process and pull an economy out of recession. The problem is, according to Thurow, that national economies are now too integrated into the world economy. Keynesian policies are based on the premise that when a government runs a deficit, the demand so stimulated will stimulate domestic investment. But with foreign goods now so easily available, the excess demand readily translates into increased imports instead.[51]

The new-liberal answer to the defects of classical and Keynesian liberalism is to propose a more active and integrative economic role for government. To ensure full employment, the government cannot rely on Keynesian macromanagement. It must itself provide jobs for those who cannot find employment in the private economy – real jobs, with decent wages, that produce goods or services needed by society.[52] Keynesian

[50] Ibid., pp. 280–90. I am inferring an ideal from Thurow's reform proposals. Thurow wants to encourage the formation in the United States of business groups. He is sympathetic to the form I have described, but he would not insist that all business groups have precisely this form or that all enterprises belong to business groups. I am giving the model a uniform character simply to highlight the basic structure.

[51] The Keynesian remedy was tried by the Mitterand government in France in the early 1980s and failed. Thurow grants that the massive defense-spending deficit of the Reagan years did work, but such policies, he predicts, will never work again. "America's strong macroeconomic stimulus in 1982 was the last such solo effort the world will see" (Thurow, 1992, p. 239).

[52] Thurow (1980, pp. 204–6). It must be said that this element of Thurow's reform agenda has dropped out of his later writings. Thurow (1985) shifts to a Weitzman "share economy" model. (See our brief, critical discussion of Weitzman in Chapter 3.) Thurow (1992) does not offer any specific reforms aimed at securing full employment. I include his early proposal in the model presented here in order to make New Liberalism as strong as possible vis-à-vis Economic Democracy.

policies cannot be relied on, either, to ensure that societal savings will be sufficient for investment needs. If savings are in short supply (as Thurow thinks they are in the U.S. economy), the government should restrict consumer credit and should institute a consumption tax.[53]

In addition, the government of a new-liberal economy should maintain monetary and fiscal policies that are the precise opposite of those of the Reagan years. Instead of tight monetary controls and loose fiscal controls (i.e., high interest rates, massive deficit spending), the government should loosen the former and tighten the latter. Sufficient money should be made available to keep interest rates low. The budget should be balanced.

With a balanced budget keeping public consumption in line, and with restrictions on personal consumption, investment funds will be plentiful. With interest rates low, they will also be cheap. These savings must next be invested – and in ways that will enhance productivity. Once again, New Liberalism interferes with the free market. "Too often, Adam Smith's 'invisible hand' becomes the hand of a pickpocket. Free unfettered markets have the habit of discovering very profitable but nonproductive activities."[54]

The government should tax and regulate nonproductive investments. But these negative measures are not enough. New Liberalism wants an "industrial policy": "We do not need central economic planning in the sense of an agency that tries to make all economic decisions, but we do need the national equivalent of a corporate investment committee to redirect investment flows from our 'sunset' industries to our 'sunrise' industries."[55] The government – in close consultation with the industries involved – must engage in strategic economic planning. It must make judgments as to which technologies are the most promising, and then aid in their funding.[56] It must be willing to protect these industries in their early phases (but only in their early phases). It must also be willing to make hard decisions about restricting credit in those industries that can no longer be competitive in the international market. To the traditional argument that such planning cannot work, Thurow replies that it can and does. Japan and Germany do it, and their economies outperform those that do not.

[53] See Thurow (1992, pp. 262–73). As was noted in the preceding section, Lipsey and Kravis (1987) and Lipsey and Tice (1989) dispute this contention.

[54] Thurow (1992, p. 285).

[55] Thurow (1980, p. 95). Industrial policy is a hallmark of all forms of post-Keynesian new liberalism. It has been a recurring theme in all of Thurow's major works. See Thurow (1985, ch. 9) and Thurow (1992, pp. 290–7).

[56] To ensure that private industry is sufficiently involved, Thurow proposes that the government put up not more than half the capital for a selected project. If no firm or consortium of firms is willing to risk the other 50 percent, then the project should be abandoned.

A decade ago it was possible to argue that instead of experimenting with strategic-growth policies to stimulate investments (physical and human), business groups, and national strategic planning, America could solve its problems by moving to a more vigorous form of traditional Anglo-Saxon capitalism. Both Mrs. Thatcher in Great Britain and Mr. Reagan in the United States were elected on such platforms. . . . Both experiments are now more than a decade old. Neither succeeded.[57]

The institutional reforms just described constitute the core of the new-liberal agenda, at least insofar as it relates to the domestic economy. (Its perspective on international trade will be considered later.) We are in position now to compare this model with Economic Democracy.

The reader has doubtless been struck by the degree to which the reforms that distinguish New Liberalism from Laissez Faire and Fair Capitalism resemble the structural features of Economic Democracy.[58] Individual firms under New Liberalism will be committed to worker participation and employment security. Firms will be clustered in *keiretsu*-like groups. The government will play an active role in generating and allocating investment funds.

There are, of course, major differences: Worker participation is not full workplace democracy; the new-liberal firms and groups will be much larger than the locally based Mondragon-type groups of Economic Democracy; the new-liberal investment fund still will come from private savings and still will be allocated primarily by the market.

How significant are these differences? Is New Liberalism a close enough approximation to Economic Democracy that our nine-count indictment must be dropped? Might New Liberalism be less vulnerable than Economic Democracy on some of these issues? Let us check and see. I shall be relatively perfunctory on most counts, because the reader should now be familiar with the basic moves. As in the preceding section, I shall rearrange the counts to facilitate exposition.

Unemployment. New Liberalism will provide "jobs to everyone who is willing and able to work regardless of age, race, sex, or education."[59] Can this be done? Can capitalism do without an "industrial reserve army" of the unemployed? Can capitalism do without the "discipline of the sack"? New Liberalism points to Japan, where, at least for that half of the work

---

[57] Thurow (1992, p. 297).
[58] Although the models have been developed independently, the resemblance is not accidental. Both Economic Democracy and new liberalism are responses to a deep dissatisfaction with U.S. capitalism; both are deeply skeptical of the neoclassical worldview; both insist on looking at empirical reality for clues to what works and what does not. The root difference between the two perspectives, of course, is the conviction of the former, disputed by the latter, that capitalism per se is the problem.
[59] Thurow (1980, p. 204).

force in the advanced sector of the economy, guaranteed employment seems to work. But it must be kept in mind that the curious dual structure of the Japanese economy – thousands upon thousands of small companies subcontracting to the large and powerful firms – shifts the burden of economic hard times downward. Workers in the core are secure. Those on the periphery are not.[60] If all workers have secure employment, and if all have participatory rights, will workers remain content with less than full democracy? Will they remain "responsible" in their wage demands? One should hesitate, I would think, before answering too quickly in the affirmative.

Sales effort. One can expect a massive sales effort under New Liberalism, both at home and internationally. New Liberal theory pays no attention to this problem. In practice, nonrational sales persuasion seems to play as large a role in Germany and Japan as in the United States.[61] Neither country is inhibited in using the most sophisticated sales techniques available to market its products abroad. Any American television viewer can attest to that.

Liberty. With employment security and participatory rights, workers will be freer under New Liberalism than under other forms of capitalism. But the international problem remains. It can scarcely be denied that firms under New Liberalism will strive for unimpeded access to Third World labor, resources, and markets. So we can expect the governments of these countries to be under intense pressure to accede to the will of the advanced capitalist countries (New-Liberal or not) and to crack down on dissent.

Thurow might not see this as a major problem. He argues that natural resources are declining in importance in international trade and that Third World countries are now too poor to be much of a market. He has no illusions about capitalism saving the Third World,[62] but he might be inclined to argue that First World governments will be less concerned to stamp out Third World insurgency movements now than they used to be. I suppose this must count as a gain for overall liberty, but the fact

---

[60] See Sakai (1990) for a debunking of the myth "that Japanese industry is made up of a handful of powerful giants with factories spanning the nation and workers forming an army of loyal employees who are cared for until retirement by a paternalistic corporation" (p. 39). Sakai's point is not that the "myth" is wholly false, but that it is only half true. See also Aoki (1990).

[61] For a comparison of Japanese and U.S. advertising, see Kline (1988).

[62] "In the twentieth century the rich man's club let in only one new industrial member – Japan. It would not be a great surprise if no new members were to join during the twenty-first century" (Thurow, 1992, p. 218). Thurow predicts increasingly hard times for much of the Third World (pp. 207–9).

remains that New-Liberal multinationals will continue to perceive their Third World investments as vital interests.

Equality. Thurow is quick to deplore the exorbitant income gap separating the average worker in a U.S. firm from top management.[63] He also deplores the race and gender wage gaps among fully employed workers, urging that society set itself the equity goal of "a distribution of earnings for everyone that is no more unequal than that which now exists for fully employed white males."[64] New Liberalism also wants low interest rates, which, among other things, will reduce property income.

New Liberalism is vague about the details of how these egalitarian goals will be achieved. They are not in principle impossible, but it must be said that their attainment does not seem likely. One can imagine a combination of monetary and tax policies that conceivably could bring down executive take-home pay and cut significantly into property income. One can also see the obstacles. If interest rates are low, how do we ensure sufficient savings? Raising the consumption tax still higher (the theoretical answer) might not be politically feasible. And how do we enforce a sharply graduated tax, given that those most adversely affected will be those with the most wealth and power? It is extremely difficult to tax away inequalities that derive from socially sanctioned entitlements. If, on the one hand, we permit property income, but, on the other hand, we try to tax it away, it will be difficult to avoid acute resentment – and a political mobilization to reduce those taxes. This problem, notice, will not exist for Economic Democracy, because Economic Democracy will generate its investment fund by taxing enterprise assets, not personal incomes, and will have eliminated property income altogether.

Democracy. Clearly, New Liberalism will not be as democratic as Economic Democracy. Workers will have participation rights, but they will not elect their managers. Control over management, under New Liberalism, will reside with the financial institution that has controlling interest in the firm. Democratic input into industrial policy will also be limited. Which technologies and industries are to be supported and which are to be phased out will be the decisions of government and industry experts.

Thurow is candid about this. A successful economy cannot be run by an "oligarchy" whose members are concerned only about their own narrow self-interests, but it can and should be run by an "establish-

---

[63] "In 1990 American CEOs were making 119 times as much as the average worker. Japanese CEOs had a better record in the 1980s (productivity had grown three times as fast), yet they earned only 18 times as much as their average worker" (Thurow, 1992, p. 138).

[64] Thurow (1980, p. 201). He sees this to be about 5 : 1, deriving the figure from the ratio of top-quintile average to bottom-quintile average.

ment" – well-connected rich people who go to the same schools, marry each other, and so forth, but who are responsible enough to link their own destinies with the overall well-being of the country at large.[65]

No doubt he would argue that if a society guarantees civil liberties, has a free press, holds regular and honest elections, keeps inequalities within bounds, and allows workers some real participation, that is about as close to democracy as we can hope to come. There is room in such a system for a responsible establishment. A society fortunate enough to have one will have as much democracy as is feasible, and prosperity besides.

As we have seen, Economic Democracy can do better than that.[66]

Workplace autonomy. The comparison here is obvious. New Liberalism advances further in this direction than does Laissez Faire or Fair Capitalism, but it does not go all the way.

Kind of growth. A major difficulty for free-market growth is environmental degradation. It is a basic feature of New Liberalism that economic growth not be left to the free market. With the government so deeply involved in the economy, New Liberalism would seem to be particularly well suited to impose the necessary restrictions. Thurow addresses this issue explicitly, placing the environment first on his list of "festering problems."[67] He advocates effluent taxes, a very high tax on gasoline, and international cooperation.

These measures are certainly to the good, but they do not address what we have identified as a fundamental problem with capitalism: the ability of firms, by threatening to relocate, to pit one region or country against another so as to avoid or reduce regulation. This problem will remain acute under New Liberalism. It will not exist for Economic Democracy, because worker-managed firms will not relocate, and because capital in Economic Democracy will flow to communities as a matter of right.

Rate of growth. Neither Laissez Faire nor Fair Capitalism allows for a considered, conscious choice as to how much the society should save and invest. New Liberalism makes much a choice: The government will decide whether or not the citizenry are saving enough; if they are not, consumer credit will be restricted, and the consumption tax raised.

---

[65] Thurow (1992, p. 266).

[66] I suggested in the introductory section of this chapter that this antidemocratic sentiment may not be essential to New Liberalism. Be that as it may, there is no reason to think that New Liberalism will be more democratic than Fair Capitalism, and Fair Capitalism, as we have seen, is not as democratic as Economic Democracy.

[67] Thurow (1992, pp. 219–29). See also Thurow (1980, ch. 5).

This attempt to gain conscious control over a crucial determinant of economic well-being would seem to be desirable – so long as we can be confident that the rate of growth sought after will indeed be what the citizens do (or should) want.[68] But here we have a problem. New Liberalism, like all forms of capitalism, must grow to remain stable. Both the political establishment and the capitalist class will have a vested interest in growth, an interest not necessarily shared by the population at large. Of course, if the choice is either growth or recession, the citizenry doubtless will prefer growth. But that is the choice under capitalism (New Liberalism included), not under Economic Democracy. Under Economic Democracy there will also be the option of slowing down growth, of trading consumption for leisure or for more meaningful work. Economic Democracy can aim for a more stable level of consumption, in harmony with ecological constraints. Such a goal is beyond the reach of New Liberalism.

Stability. Here we have a major advance over Laissez Faire and Fair Capitalism. As we have seen, under Laissez Faire one can only hope that savers will save enough, that these savings will be invested appropriately, and that consumers will buy the new products. Fair Capitalism will let the government intervene to stimulate demand if the invisible hand falters, but it will not address what we have seen to be the sine qua non of "Golden Age" growth: a steady increase in productivity. New Liberalism confronts this problem directly.

Indeed, New Liberalism has proposed government policies for dealing with each of the elements we identified in Chapter 4 as necessary for stability. A consumption tax will encourage savers to save. Low interest rates will encourage investment. Industrial policy will channel investment into productivity-enhancing endeavors. As for consumer demand, if enough industries are oriented toward the international market, domestic demand need not be a problem; if it does become a problem, then consumer credit can be loosened, and/or the consumption tax can be cut.

The system is not foolproof. If industry and government guess wrong about which technologies to support, or if world demand slumps, then instability might well ensue. But then no system is foolproof. Are there any reasons for thinking that Economic Democracy is better situated than New Liberalism with respect to stability?

Let me note a reason for saying yes, and then a major objection. The reason was invoked earlier. Economic Democracy will not need to grow.

---

[68] A value issue interjects itself here, but not in such a way as to affect the overall evaluation. If democracy is given independent weight, a discrepancy between what is decided and what the citizens prefer counts against the system. If democracy is valued only insofar as it enhances the well-being of society, at issue is what the citizenry should prefer. Either case poses a difficulty for New Liberalism.

It will be stable without growth. There will be no class in Economic Democracy whose legitimacy will depend upon growth. New Liberalism, like all forms of capitalism, will be structured to grow, will need to grow, and will be unstable without growth.

This brings us to major objection that a New Liberal might level against Economic Democracy, an objection perhaps powerful enough to override all the advantages thus far toted up for Economic Democracy: "New Liberalism is indeed structured to grow – and to compete on the international market. It is, in fact, better structured in this regard than Economic Democracy. An Economic Democracy in a world of New-Liberal capitalism will so suffer by comparison that it cannot help but be politically unstable – so unstable as to lack all credibility as a viable alternative to capitalism."

It is time to confront the issue of international trade and international competition. It has been demonstrated that New Liberalism suffers in comparison with Economic Democracy on almost all of the nine counts, but a large, perhaps overriding, issue remains. Can Economic Democracy compete with New Liberalism (or, for that matter, with Laissez Faire or Fair Capitalism) in the world market? If not, then what? Might an Economic Democracy disconnect from the world market and go it alone? Must we place our hopes in a world revolution that will institute Economic Democracies everywhere and all at once? On the face of it, neither of these choices looks promising.

Let us think first about the question of competition. The most significant structural differences between Economic Democracy and New Liberalism concern the internal structure of the firm and the generation and allocation of investment funds. Which will be more efficient, a fully democratic workplace or one that is merely participatory? Which will be more effective at generating funds for investment, taxation of enterprise assets or combining the lure of dividends and interest with consumption regulation? There are no grounds, so far as I can see, for judging the New-Liberal features superior.

As to the allocation of investment funds, we observe that Economic Democracy would seem to be as well situated as New Liberalism to pursue an industrial policy. In both cases, decisions can be made to direct a portion of the investment fund into those areas of research and development that are deemed most promising, as well as to encourage, via financial incentives, certain industries to embark on certain projects. In both cases, the judgments of the firms themselves will be decisive. Under Economic Democracy, firms still will have to pay taxes on their "encouragement grants," albeit at a lower rate; under New Liberalism, firms will have to put up part of the money themselves. There would seem to be no a priori reason for thinking one method superior to the other.

There remains one large difference between the two systems that would seem to be relevant to our overall assessment. As we have seen, the growth imperative will be much stronger under New Liberalism than under Economic Democracy. Successful New-Liberal firms will grow large and will battle aggressively for increased market share at home and abroad. Worker-managed firms will remain smaller and will be less aggressive in expanding sales. How significant is this difference?

It is important to recognize that size is not a guarantee of efficiency. General Motors is vastly larger than its Japanese competitors, but it does not outperform them. The megamerger in 1984 of the third and fourth largest steel producers in the United States led to bankruptcy two years later, whereas such "minimill" producers as Nucor and Chaparral (also U.S. firms) have been spectacularly successful. In Germany and Italy the small and medium-size firms, "because of their stellar performance ... are coming to be viewed as a model for the industrial future of Europe – east and west alike."[69] Smaller firms often are more innovative and more flexible than large firms, and less burdened with layer upon layer of white-collar hierarchy that seem to impede rather than promote productivity.[70]

Still, there is reason for concern. Those aggressive and efficient Japanese automakers are by no means small. And those small, flexible European firms (the capitalist ones, if not the cooperatives) will expand rapidly if conditions are right. Is it not likely that a firm structured and motivated to grow will outperform, head-to-head on the world market, a firm content with its market share? I am not sure about likelihood here, but the possibility must be entertained. It might well be true that an Economic Democracy would not have as many firms aggressively and successfully competing in the world market as one would find under New Liberalism (or, for that matter, under Fair Capitalism or Laissez Faire).

This possibility raises a series of fundamental questions: Why compete on the world market? Why play the game at all? Why not delink, opt out of the game? Or play by different rules?

Let us approach these questions by returning to Laissez Faire and one of its central tenets, thus far undiscussed: the desirability of free trade.[71] The laissez-faire approach argues for completely free trade – no tariffs or

---

[69] See Adams and Brock (1992, p. 5) on the steel merger (see p. 7 for the quotation). See Adams and Brock (1986) and Piore and Sabel (1984) for many more examples.

[70] "Within each industry, much of the productivity problem [in the United States] can be traced to rapidly rising white collar bureaucracies" (Thurow, 1992, p. 168).

[71] Support for free trade has been by no means confined to classical liberalism. Until quite recently the one settled dogma of mainstream economics was the desirability of free trade. On no other issue (save the undesirability of socialism) was there such universal agreement.

quotas – and for floating (i.e., market-determined) exchange rates among currencies.[72] A surprising corollary of the neoclassical argument is that "free trade in one country" is desirable (i.e., it pays for a country to adopt free trade unilaterally). As Friedman puts it, "we would be benefitted from dispensing with tariffs even if other countries did not. We would, of course, be benefitted even more if they reduced theirs, but our bene-fiting does not require that they reduce theirs. Self-interests coincide and do not conflict."[73] His recommendation:

> We could say to the rest of the world: We believe in freedom and intend to practice it. No one can force you to be free. That is your business. But we can offer you full co-operation on equal terms to all. Our markets are open to you. Sell here what you can and wish to. Use the proceeds to buy what you wish. In this way co-operation among individuals can be world wide yet free.[74]

It is often objected that such free trade would jeopardize domestic high-wage industries, but Friedman disagrees. He argues that differences in wage levels (or productivity) are completely irrelevant, so long as the exchange rate is market-determined.

This influential argument, at once simple and subtle, is as follows: Suppose Japan and the United States produce the same goods with the same technology, but Japanese real wages are lower. Could not Japanese goods be priced lower than American goods, and would they not, if unrestricted, flood the U.S. markets, forcing U.S. manufacturers to lower their wages or go out of business? Friedman says no.

For Japanese goods to be "cheaper" in terms relevant to an American consumer, they must be cheaper in dollars. Real costs are irrelevant. What matters is the exchange rate between dollars and yen, for Japanese businesses pay their workers in yen, and so Japanese businesses that sell in the United States must be able to convert their dollars into yen. If they have dollars to exchange for yen (from the goods sold in the United States), then they will look for people who want to exchange yen for dollars. In the absence of government interference, supply and demand will establish an exchange rate.

---

[72] During the heyday of Keynesianism, international finance was run according to the Bretton Woods accords, a dollar-and-gold system based on fixed exchange rates. This proved to be unworkable and was abandoned in the early 1970s, to be replaced by the current system of floating exchange rates. Almost all mainstream economists, conserva-tive and liberal alike, supported the change.

[73] Friedman (1962, p. 73). He acknowledges that "there are conceivable exceptions to these statements, but, they are theoretical curiosities, not relevant practical possibilities."

[74] Friedman (1962, p. 74). Lest one think this view idiosyncratic, here is Samuelson and Nordhaus (1985, p. 864): "As we have seen, a tariff is much like an increase in transpor-tation costs. If other countries were foolish enough to let their roads go to ruin, would it pay us to chop holes in ours? Of course not. Analogously, if other countries hurt us and themselves by passing tariffs, we should not add to our own injury by passing a tariff."

Now comes the punch line: This rate cannot be such that in dollar terms all Japanese goods are indeed cheaper than the corresponding U.S. goods, for if it were, then no one would want to give up yen for dollars. Why should they? Apart from a few tourists bound for the United States, no one in Japan wants dollars. In Japan, goods must be purchased in yen. Moreover, no Japanese importer is going to make money importing American goods (for the purchase of which he would need dollars), because American goods are more expensive than Japanese goods.

In terms of supply and demand this situation is unstable. Yen are scarce (to the point of vanishing) relative to dollars. So a free-market exchange rate will adjust. One will have to pay more dollars to get yen. But this means that Japanese businesses will have to raise the dollar prices of their goods – to the point that some of their goods will no longer be competitive. Equilibrium will not be established until, at that exchange rate, the demand by Japanese for American goods is equal to the demand by Americans for Japanese goods.[75]

This argument, if sound, has a profound implication: No country can be hurt by international trade. Even if one falls behind technologically, one cannot really be hurt. Whether the lower prices at a given exchange rate are due to lower wages or to technological superiority is immaterial to the argument. A technological innovation or a lower wage rate may make certain foreign products more competitive, but the exchange rates will shift to make others less so. Individual industries must worry about international competition, but the country as a whole need not.

A corollary: Economic Democracy in one country will work. Even if worker-managed firms should turn out to be less competitive in the world market than capitalist firms, there is no cause for concern. Exchange rates will adjust to ensure that whatever the real differences in productivity, enough of the country's goods will be price-competitive abroad to offset imported foreign goods that are cheaper than those domestically produced.

It might be nice if the world in fact worked the way neoclassical theory predicts, but it does not. First there is the matter of floating exchange rates, long advocated by economists of all stripes. Recent experience has shown them to be highly volatile, highly vulnerable to speculation (given the technical capacity now available for shifting large amounts of currency in anticipation of exchange-rate fluctuations), and hence poor indicators of the underlying conditions they are supposed to reflect. "With such violent swings in exchange rates, it simply isn't possible to run efficient economies. No one knows where economic activity should be

---

[75] See Friedman (1962, pp. 71–3). Multilateral (as opposed to bilateral) trade complicates the argument, but does not alter the basic logic.

located; no one knows the cheapest source of supplies. . . . The result is a needless increase in risk and uncertainty."[76]

More serious than the uncertainty caused by currency speculation is the neoclassical assumption that resource reallocation, including labor, occurs smoothly and quickly – with no time for the Keynesian problem to arise. But of course that is not the case. When a large industry begins to lose ground to a foreign competitor, it begins laying off its work force. Demand declines; other firms suffer, first those in the immediate region, and then more broadly. There is no guarantee whatsoever that the shifts in exchange rates that make some of the nation's other products more competitive internationally will lead to a large enough increase in foreign demand to offset this decline. Unemployment may well stabilize at a higher rate than before.[77]

"New trade theory" adds another argument:[78] It pays to subsidize (and protect) those new industries in which it is important to be among the first to enter, especially if they have a high degree of technological spillover. The aircraft industry is a favorite example. The world market can sustain only a few such companies. Once these few become established, it becomes very difficult for a new company to break in. Because the high-technology research required in the aircraft industry spins off many applications outside that industry, it makes good sense for a government (or consortium of governments in the case of the European Airbus) to override free-market and free-trade considerations in promoting such an industry. New trade theory posits that a large segment of international trade is like this.[79]

New liberals often emphasize another point. The classical scenario, as sketched earlier, presumes that the demand for a nation's currency derives solely from the desire to purchase that nation's *products*. But dollars can also be used to buy a nation's *assets*. If the Japanese use their surplus dollars to purchase U.S. real estate, factories, and so forth, then the dollar

---

[76] Thurow (1985, p. 344). For this reason many economists who used to support floating rates have pulled back. "Flexible exchange rates are an area where members of the economics profession, myself included, were simply wrong" (Thurow, 1992 p. 240).

[77] In the Third World, the destruction of local industry by capitalist imports has often resulted in massive catastrophe. Marx quotes the governor-general of India on the effects of English textile imports: "The misery hardly finds parallel in the history of commerce. The bones of the cotton-weavers are bleaching the plains of India." Marx comments: "No doubt, in turning them out of this 'temporal' world, the machinery caused them no more than a 'temporary inconvenience'" (Marx, 1967, p. 432).

[78] MIT's Paul Krugman is a leading exponent, along with Avinash Dixit from Princeton, Elhanan Helpman from Tel Aviv, and James Brander and Barbara Spencer of the University of British Columbia. See the edited collection (Krugman, 1986) and also Krugman (1990c).

[79] "Conventional trade theory views world trade as taking place entirely in goods like wheat; new trade theory sees it as being largely in goods like aircraft" (Krugman 1990c, p. 1).

can remain high vis-à-vis the yen even if U.S. goods are not selling in Japan. That is to say, a productivity deficit can translate into the gradual acquisition of a nation's assets by the more productive country.[80]

Let me offer a final consideration, one that is obvious, but rarely given its due by mainstream economists, for whom "the more trade the better" is virtually axiomatic.[81] A country that orients a large portion of its economic activity to the world market is vulnerable to developments over which it has no control. A country that exports much will import much (unless it is using its surplus to buy up assets abroad). It becomes dependent on those imports. This, of course, is commonly noted, but the threat is seen to be economic blackmail, by the Organization of Petroleum Exporting Countries (OPEC) or whomever – a greatly exaggerated concern. Free-trade advocates have been correct to point out the extreme difficulty that an international cartel faces in keeping its members from breaking ranks. (Oil prices now, adjusted for inflation, are below what they were at the time of the first OPEC oil shock in 1973.) One can assume that, in general, given technological advances, the prices of imported goods will come down over time, not go up. The real problem is not with imports, but with exports. Technological change in the industries producing the goods a country imports may be good, but not technological change in a country's export industries – not if the innovations are by one's competitors. Here is where the bite of international competition comes in. If one's export industries cease to be competitive (and protectionism offers no protection here), then one cannot import as much. To the extent that the economy has become addicted to imports, dislocation (and a declining standard of living) will follow.

I have offered four distinct arguments (in addition to noting the volatility of floating exchange rates – a decidedly secondary issue) intended to call into question the desirability of free trade. New Liberalism would doubtless agree with the first three (the Keynesian, aircraft, and assets objections).[82] One of the hallmarks of New Liberalism is its

---

[80] To a strict neoclassicist this is unimportant, because all owners are presumed to be identical profit-maximizing individuals. In reality, it does seem to matter to a democratic citizenry whether or not the owners of the nation's assets are citizens of that nation. (The neoclassical assumption that ownership does not matter seems less intuitively obvious to economists today than it did when it was Americans who were buying up large parts of the rest of the world.)

[81] See the chapters on international trade by Samuelson and Nordhaus (1985). Although some difficulties with completely free trade are acknowledged (notably the Keynesian problem), the text as a whole is a joyous celebration of John Stuart Mill's remark (which they use as a chapter epigraph): "The benefit of international trade – a more efficient employment of the productive forces of the world" (p. 831).

[82] It would be wary of the last, with its suggestion that less trade is better than more. New Liberalism aspires to be a "world-class economy" (one of Thurow's favorite expressions) that can take on all comers in international competition.

contention that trade should not be free. Trade, it is said, should be *managed*.[83]

To opt for managed trade is by no means to opt out of international competition, but it is a strong rejection of the laissez-faire approach characteristic of both classical and Keynesian liberalism. Thurow claims that this is already well under way in much of the world: "Industry after industry – steel, shipbuilding, cars, consumer electronics – is withdrawn from real international trade and becomes a 'managed' industry with formal or informal quotas or other government marketing arrangements."[84] A country need not abandon free trade altogether, he argues, but it should be prepared to invoke a policy of "general reciprocity" if its trade imbalance with another country becomes too severe.[85]

We are now in position to sketch a trade policy for Economic Democracy and compare its effectiveness with that of New Liberalism. Clearly, there is no need for Economic Democracy to delink completely from the international economy. It can allow its currency to be fully convertible. It can follow whatever rules the international community agrees upon, either freely floating exchange rates or some modification devised to curb rapid fluctuations.[86] The uncertainty caused by a market-determined exchange rate will hurt an Economic Democracy no more and no less than it hurts a capitalist economy.

Like New Liberalism, it, too, can opt for managed trade, as opposed to free trade. Economic Democracy may want to be even more "protectionist" than New Liberalism (and hence, *eo ipso*, than classical or Keynesian liberalism). Despite the outcry among economists and purveyors of

---

[83] Krugman is reluctant to embrace "managed trade," although he concedes that unless other countries are prohibited by international treaty from adopting strategic trade policies, the United States may have to follow suit (Krugman, 1990b, pp. 108–13).

[84] Thurow (1985, p. 335).

[85] Thurow (1985, pp. 362–3) proposes the following mechanism: The government of country A examines world trade patterns to determine the size of the imbalance it can afford to sustain with country B, then announces to B that it cannot export to A any more than the sum of what it imports from A plus the allowable imbalance. To enforce this decree, the government requires that all imports from B must be licensed. These licenses (which are not product-specific) are auctioned off each quarter. This arrangement ensures that the trade imbalance will not become severe, and it encourages those with a positive balance to open their markets more fully. See also Prestowitz (1988) for another strong advocacy of managed trade. To the argument that with this sort of arrangement countries would bog down in endless bilateral negotiations, Prestowitz (who participated on behalf of the Reagan administration in key negotiations with the Japanese) replies that "we are already so bogged down – except that now the talks are so rancorous as to be all but unmanageable" (p. 325).

[86] Thurow (1985, pp. 354–5) proposes a system of "crawling pegs": market fluctuations being confined within a fairly narrow band, the band itself being adjusted every six months or so depending on inflation, productivity, and trade surpluses and deficits.

conventional wisdom, protectionist measures are not all that bad. Krugman reveals another of the profession's "dirty little secrets":

> Just how expensive is protectionism? The answer is a little embarrassing, because standard estimates of the costs of protection are actually very low. America is a case in point. While much U.S. trade takes place with few obstacles, we have several major protectionist measures, restricting imports of autos, steel and textiles in particular. The combined costs of these major restrictions to the U.S. economy, however, are usually estimated at less than three-quarters of 1 percent of U.S. national income.[87]

Krugman offers a hypothetical scenario from which he produces an even more startling estimate. Suppose an international trade war broke out that cut international trade in half. That would cost the world economy about 2.5 percent of its income, "not a trivial sum – but it is a long way from a Depression."[88] The "terrible scourge" of protectionism, like that of inflation, turns out to be mostly (class-based) hype.

There is one sort of protectionist measure that would make eminent sense under Economic Democracy. A tariff should be imposed on imported goods coming from countries with lower real wages, to bring their prices up to what they would be if real wages were equal. Friedman to the contrary notwithstanding, low wages do give a country a competitive edge (at least in the short run), and they do pit workers in different countries against one another in a mutually destructive way.[89]

In comparing Economic Democracy with New Liberalism on the issue of international trade, we see that there are many similarities. Both will have workplace organizations that should foster a flexible, skilled, and motivated work force. Both will have removed major investment decisions from the control of blind market forces, and hence they can target funds (if so desired) to "sunrise" industries and away, gradually, from declining sectors. Neither is committed to free trade, and so these industries can be protected from international competition in the early stages.

New Liberalism does seem to possess the advantage of having firms that are geared to grow, to compete aggressively for steadily larger market shares in the international arena. But against that we might set a very different consideration. A striking difference between an

---

[87] Krugman (1990b, p. 104).   [88] Ibid., p. 105.

[89] This proposal will disturb many of the Left, who see this as hurting workers in poor countries to protect those in rich countries. On this I would make two points: First, low wages rarely benefit Third World workers in the long run, because the profits made this way tend to go into the pockets of the elite, and low wages reduce the incentive to introduce more-productive technology. Second, to offset the disadvantage to workers in poor countries that this tariff would impose, the collected tariff could be remanded to the countries from which it was collected, earmarked (why not?) for the development of worker cooperatives.

Economic Democracy and a capitalist economy is the absence from the former of cross-border capital flows. Worker-managed firms will not set up subsidiaries abroad, nor can they use a portion of their profits to buy into foreign firms. The tax-generated investment fund will stay at home also. There will be no capital outflow in Economic Democracy.[90] Neither will there be capital inflow. The capital assets of society will be the collective property of the nation. They will not be for sale. A capitalist from abroad cannot buy up, or even into, a worker-managed enterprise.

Without these capital flows, one of the most serious problems with international competition disappears. A capitalist country that lags in productivity faces the prospect of losing its assets to foreign owners. The invisible hand can finance a trade deficit by asset sales. Not so under Economic Democracy. Under Economic Democracy a trade deficit should lead to an exchange-rate adjustment (just as Friedman has argued) that will correct the imbalance by making imported goods more expensive. If, for whatever reason, the exchange rates do not adjust properly, the matter can be addressed in New-Liberal fashion by bilateral negotiation.

The fact of the matter is that a country so structured that capital does not cross its boundaries has far more control of its economic destiny than does a capitalist country. It can integrate itself into the world economy without being as vulnerable as a capitalist country. It can, if it so desires, cut back its dependence on international trade in a controlled and rational manner.[91] This has at least one consequence that seems to me quite important.

If we think about it, it should strike us as exceedingly strange that in a world beset by such real problems as decaying cities, mass poverty, and environmental degradation, the citizens of the advanced capitalist countries should be so obsessed with competing with one another. It is bizarre to be so worried about who is ahead in high-definition television, or telecommunications or computers and software, or the new materials sciences, or biotechnology, or microelectronics. And yet, in a capitalist country one must worry. If one's firms are not internationally competitive,

[90] Recall that profits, after taxes and depreciation set-asides, are to be returned to the workers. Investment by a home-country firm in a firm abroad would have to be of public funds supplied by a community bank. Such grants might occasionally be made (perhaps to enable a firm to acquire access to certain technology), but such cases presumably would be rare.

[91] Although the volume of international trade has increased substantially over the past couple of decades, it should not be assumed that there is anything inevitable about this trend. Less and less trade is in raw materials, foodstuffs, and other country-specific products; more and more is in manufactured goods that can in fact be produced anywhere. Indeed, the newest technologies would seem to offer more, not less, scope for relative self-sufficiency. See Block (1990, p. 19).

one does not simply advance more slowly than others; one's economy (and the quality of life it affords) deteriorates. The American "rustbelt" has not merely failed to keep up; it is far worse living there now than it was twenty or thirty years ago.[92]

There is something deeply irrational – one is tempted to say insane – about a world economy so structured as to require that the best and brightest people in its most advanced sectors, and massive amounts of resources as well, be devoted to improving things that hardly need improving, when the planet has such obvious and desperate needs.[93]

It is one of the great merits of an Economic Democracy that it can, if it so chooses, opt out of such madness, or at least greatly reduce the pressure it feels from such forces, and begin to foster a more human relationship to the world. In an Economic Democracy, workers can begin restructuring their workplaces to make them more interesting. They can begin choosing leisure over consumption, so as to brake the harried pace of everyday life. Citizens can begin redesigning their towns and cities to make them ecologically friendly. They can aid poorer countries without worrying that workers there will one day compete fiercely for their jobs. It does not seem unreasonable to expect that a more generous spirit will flourish. Neither Laissez Faire nor Fair Capitalism nor New Liberalism can offer such a vision. The structures of Economic Democracy will not guarantee such an outcome, but they can allow it as a rational hope.

[92] Thurow, for all his acuity, seems not to have grasped this point. In what is surely the silliest remark in his recent book, he asserts that the productivity slowdown in the United States would be critical even in the absence of foreign competition, for "Americans would want to know why it was taking more than twice as long to double their standard of living" (Thurow, 1992, p. 166). He seems not to understand that the mass discontent is a result not of living standards that are not doubling fast enough but of living standards that are in decline.

[93] There is also something deeply disturbing about the tendency now so prevalent among economists, even liberal economists, to give up on so much of humanity. Here is Thurow on sub-Saharan Africa: "If God gave it to you and made you its economic dictator, the only smart move would be to give it back to Him" (Thurow, 1992, p. 216). This I guess, is supposed to be amusing. It doubtless draws a chuckle on the business-luncheon circuit.

7. Transitions

Let me suppose that the reader has been persuaded: Economic Democracy is economically viable and is vastly preferable to any form of capitalism. What is to be done? How do we get from here to there? Is it *possible* to get from here to there?

This last question is, of course, crucial, for if the answer is no, then one must wonder about the point of the extended exercise we have just been through. To be sure, there is the intellectual satisfaction that comes from understanding a complicated argument, as well as the moral satisfaction of knowing that those passionate/dispassionate, clever/not-so-clever, so-often-smug defenders of capitalism are wrong. The Left, for all its mistakes and reversals, turns out to be correct on the central normative issue: Capitalism is not morally defensible. But this is thin satisfaction if we are forced to concede that Economic Democracy, for all its merits, will never be. This is not a concession I am prepared to make.

Plato's answer to the transition question is well known: Either philosophers become kings in their countries or kings become philosophers.[1] Marx, wholly impatient with such "idealism," spoke instead of "tendencies working with iron necessity toward inevitable results."[2] But for us, neither of these responses will do. The cataclysms of this century have made us wary of both philosopher-kings and claims of historical inevitability.

It would be presumptuous, to put it mildly, to propose a definite answer as to how to get from here to there, but it does not follow that nothing can be said. An obvious first point one might make is that it matters what "here" we are thinking of when speculating about getting "there." So let us begin by framing the question in terms of the First, Second, and Third worlds, allowing, of course, that there are major differences within each of these categories. How might we get to Economic Democracy from an advanced capitalist society, from an industrialized society that is (or was) Communist, from one of the poor countries on the periphery of the advanced capitalist core? I shall not pretend to answer these questions definitively, but let me propose some scenarios. They will necessarily be schematic, but it is a useful exercise, I think, to imagine broad possibilities.

---

[1] Plato, *The Republic*, Book V. Plato added, pessimistically, that neither eventuality seemed likely.
[2] Marx (1967, p. 8).

From advanced capitalism

Although the likelihood of an abrupt transition from advanced capitalism to Economic Democracy is remote indeed, it is not so difficult to envisage how such a transition *could* take place. Suppose a socialist government came to power, with sufficient popular support to pass and enforce whatever laws it wanted. Four laws would fairly well do the trick:[3]

1. Henceforth, all income entitlements based on property are null and void. That is to say, companies will cease paying dividends to their stockholders; neither companies nor individuals will pay any more interest on their loans; all rental payments will stop.
2. Henceforth, all private enterprises employing more than x people (where x is a small number) are to be managed by those who work there, one person, one vote, however they see fit. The only restriction is that the value of the capital stock must be kept intact.
3. Henceforth, all banks will belong to the communities in which they are located. All bank employees will now be paid from general tax revenues.
4. Henceforth, all enterprises must pay a use tax on the value of their capital assets.

Of course, things are not quite so simple. Various subsidiary adjustments would have to be made. Home mortgages, residential rentals, and consumer loans would have to be treated separately. Provisions would have to be made for those whose pensions and retirement benefits are tied to portfolio income. To avoid alienating the millions of small stockholders and bondholders, compensation might be given for holdings of up to a specified sum.[4] Banks would have to be restructured to reflect their new role in an economy without interest.

The important thing to notice is that the day after the "revolution" most people could continue doing exactly what they were doing before. Little economic dislocation need occur. People would still go to work; their managers would still be there (only now democratically accountable). Producers would still produce and continue selling their products to other enterprises or consumers. Apart from a sudden surge in unemployment on Wall Street and in other financial districts, not much need

[3] The reader will notice that these laws would seem to have, prima facie, considerable immediate appeal to a large constituency. It is not difficult to understand why the capitalist class worries about "demagogic" politics in a democracy and has set up so many institutional barriers to keep radical proposals from receiving widespread attention or a fair hearing.

[4] Given the concentration of wealth under capitalism, this figure need not be too high. In the United States, for example, "if one leaves aside homes and real estate, the top 2 percent of all families are found to own 54 percent of all net financial assets (stocks, bonds, pension funds and so on), the top 10 percent to own 86 percent, and the bottom 55 percent to have zero or negative financial assets" (Thurow, 1987, p. 32).

change immediately.[5] The real changes would occur more gradually, as workers began to exercise their newly acquired rights at the workplace, and communities began to exercise their newly acquired control over investment priorities.

I shall not pursue this scenario further, because, after all, such a revolution is nowhere near at hand, nor even on the horizon. It is a possible scenario, but not a likely one. Let us look at the matter, instead, from a different point of view. Let us consider what changes are going on right now, or are near at hand, or might be sensibly pursued today by a mass-based political party. One of the great virtues of viewing Economic Democracy as the goal of the socialist project is that it allows us to see how a great many seemingly disparate struggles and reform proposals might fit together into a coherent movement.

To give the analysis sufficient concreteness, let us confine our attention to the United States. Because one of the three fundamental features of Economic Democracy, the market, is already in existence, let us think about the other two: workplace democracy and social control of investment. Let us take the first one. What efforts might be undertaken that would push in the direction of democratizing the workplace?

First, there is the task of setting up producer cooperatives, either from scratch or as buy-outs. It is estimated that there are now about one thousand democratically organized workplaces in the United States (about three thousand if we include small retail and service co-ops).[6] Clearly there is much room for expansion here. In Italy there are well over twenty thousand producer cooperatives, many of them large, and many support structures as well.[7] In the United States there are various organizations now committed to developing a cooperative sector, but this effort is still small.[8]

---

[5] To the charge that this is grossly unfair, it could be pointed out that past (capitalist-dominated) governments have had no qualms about engineering recessions – thus throwing millions out of work – so as to discipline labor and preserve property incomes threatened by inflation. Our socialist government is, in effect, engineering a stock- and bond-market collapse. We may presume that this government will be more generous with unemployment benefits and job retraining than its capitalist counterpart.

[6] Krimerman and Lindenfeld (1992, p. 5). These authors use the term "democratically organized workplaces" to include both enterprises structured legally as cooperatives and democratically run employee stock-ownership plans (ESOPs). (More on ESOPs later.)

[7] See Earle (1986). The Italian cooperators gain political clout by being grouped into three large associations, each associated with a political party. They also benefit from a law requiring the government to add 3 lire to every 1 lira put up by workers laid off in the private sector who join or set up a co-op (Earle, 1986, p. 133). Needless to say, producer cooperatives in the United States would benefit from such a law.

[8] See Krimerman and Lindenfeld (1992) for an optimistic assessment, based on increasing union involvement, increased linkages among cooperatives, and the rise of such support groups as PACE in Philadelphia, the ICA group in Boston, Co-op America, the Federation for Industrial Retention and Renewal, etc.

Second, there are the efforts under way to make capitalist enterprises more participatory. The "Quality of Work Life" programs of the early 1970s have been given a boost by the seeming success of the "Japanese model" when transplanted to the United States. There is much talk these days about the "team concept." There are many experiments under way. Even those in the labor movement who are highly (and rightly) suspicious of many elements of these experiments generally acknowledge that *something* must be done about the traditional mode of shop-floor organization and labor–management relations. More and more are inclined to argue that

> the union movement can take advantage of the fact that management has put these ideas on the agenda. We can begin a discussion of our own vision of a humanized workplace.... The labor movement may not be able to win many of its goals right now, but if we can clearly identify them, we can try to move towards our goals, not away from them.[9]

The fight for a humanized workplace should include pressure for genuine participation, for skill upgrading, for more flexible work schedules (including "personal days" for community and family commitments, modeled on jury-duty release time), for on-site day-care and health-care provisions, and much more.[10]

A third factor, a sine qua non for any serious move toward Economic Democracy, must be revitalization of the labor movement itself. Despite the fact that organized labor has often opposed participatory and cooperative programs (on the grounds that these might undermine class solidarity and/or the effectiveness of the traditional union structures), it is impossible to imagine workers being able to push through participatory (and other) reforms that will seriously restrict the rights of capital unless they are organized. As everyone knows, the union movement in the United States has been in a state of free-fall since the early 1980s. Union membership is now less than half of what it was in the immediate post–World War II period, now barely 16 percent of the work force.[11] This trend must be reversed.

Here the struggle to reform U.S. labor law becomes central. One can take heart from the fact that unions have been battered before and have come back. Membership had plummeted from a high of 5 million members in 1920 (17.5 percent of the nonagricultural labor force) to 3 million in

---

[9] Parker and Slaughter (1988, p. 31). Parker and Slaughter offer a detailed, critical analysis of unions and the team concept, with specific reference to the auto industry. See the various contributions to the Krimerman and Lindenfeld book (1992) for a similar debate within the union movement with respect to ESOPs and worker buy-outs.

[10] See Parker and Slaughter (1988, ch. 4).

[11] *World Almanac 1992*, p. 180. By way of comparison, in Sweden, 85 percent of all blue-collar workers belong to one of twenty-four national unions; 75 percent of all white-collar workers belong to one of twenty national unions (Carson, 1990, p. 534).

1933 (10.6 percent), but then, facilitated by the new laws that accompanied the New Deal, union membership edged up to 3.7 million in 1935, exploded to 7.3 million two years later, and then doubled again over the next decade.[12] It took the Taft-Hartley legislation of 1947 to stop labor in its tracks and to provide the legal underpinning for the employer counteroffensive that remains in full swing today. The struggle to regain for U.S. workers in the private sector the right to organize (which, for all practical purposes, has been rescinded)[13] is a fundamental component of the struggle for Economic Democracy – as is, I might add, the struggle for genuine democracy *within* unions.

If a revitalized labor movement is essential to democratizing the workplace, it is equally essential to the other component of the overall movement toward Economic Democracy, namely, social control of investment. Without a strong labor movement, it is difficult to imagine winning many of the legislative battles that will bear on this issue.

Our model suggests three components of the struggle for social control of investment: attempts to eliminate property income as the source of the investment fund and to replace it with taxation; attempts to compel capital to come to, and stay within, communities; attempts to force investment decision-makers to give weight to democratically determined nonmarket priorities.

As to the first, an important element is the New-Liberal proposal to adopt a monetary policy that will keep interest rates low. Democratizing the Federal Reserve likely would help here. A more politically sensitive guardian of the money supply would find it difficult to serve the interests of capital so unabashedly as the current arrangement allows.[14] (As a side benefit, low interest rates could substantially reduce the burden on taxpayers occasioned by the national debt. Notice that refinancing the debt at an interest rate that is 50 percent less will have the same effect as paying off half of the principal. It astonishes me that this point is never raised in polite company, even by Perotian debt-o-phobes.)

---

[12] This account is derived from Series D8, D951, and D952, U.S. Department of Commerce, Bureau of the Census (1975).

[13] Labor lawyer Thomas Geoghegan (1991, p. 52) puts the matter succinctly: "When people ask me, 'Why can't labor organize the way it did in the thirties?' the answer is simple: everything we did then is now illegal." He makes a compelling case for the proposition that "nothing, no law, no civil rights act would radicalize this country more, democratize it more, and also revive the Democratic Party, than to make this one tiny change in the law: to let people join unions if they like, freely and without coercion, without threat of being fired.... The most shocking thing about this issue is: no one even knows it is one" (Geoghegan, 1991, p. 276).

[14] See Greider (1987) for an exposé of the class-based nature of Federal Reserve policies and a defense of democratization. In the late 1970s and early 1980s, "one interest group, almost alone, understood its place in the debate – the bondholders, the commercial bankers, the 400,000 financial professionals of Wall Street and their customers, the investors. They were like an ever-present chorus, scolding the Fed, applauding it, demanding that their interests be served by the government before all others" (Greider, 1987, p. 701).

If the interest rate is too low to serve as a sufficient enticement to save, the government should intervene. If low interest rates result in a savings shortfall, this should be made up by taxing capital assets.[15] Such taxation would have the double effect of generating funds for investment and reducing the inflationary tendency of low interest rates. It would also set in place a mechanism that could (and, as we know from our model, should) play an increasing role in the economy.

As to keeping capital in communities, plant-closing legislation is an obvious first step. Plants should be required to give notification and severance pay. Communities should raise the cost of capital flight. Clearly, standards need to be set at the national level, so that new capital will not avoid communities that impose tough conditions. Federal legislation to hamper international capital flight would also be desirable.

Communities should also attempt, whenever feasible, to broker worker buy-outs of companies. Recent employee stock-ownership plans (ESOP) legislation makes this more feasible than it used to be, because leveraged buy-outs are now possible (i.e., workers can set up a trust that will borrow the buy-out funds, using as collateral the earning potential of the firm itself).[16]

It is also desirable that communities set up their own (publicly owned) banks, committed to making loans to local businesses. When private banks fail (as they have been doing in record numbers recently), the federal government should not simply protect the depositors (i.e., absorb the debt with taxpayer money) and then sell the banks (along with their assets) at fire-sale prices. The government should retain ownership, and then turn them over to the local communities. An aide to Representative Bernard Sanders makes a simple proposal that presumably (in a truly democratic society) would have broad appeal:

If the taxpayer is ultimately paying to bail out the banks, shouldn't the taxpayer end up owning not just the bad debts, but the banks themselves. . . . Each bank could then become a community bank, capitalized with the solid assets that remain after the bailout. Such community reinvestment banks could have as their charge the rebuilding and reindustrialization of America. They would be required to limit their loans to three areas: underwriting local and state government efforts to rebuild infrastructure, financing for building low and moderate income housing, and providing loans to new businesses that will create jobs and to

---

[15] Our model of Economic Democracy underscores the importance of making a transition to this kind of tax. One could instead argue (as the New Liberals do) for a consumption tax, or (as more traditional liberals and many leftists do) for a sharply graduated income tax, but a capital-assets tax is more appropriate in light of the final goal, and it might even be more feasible politically.

[16] For an analysis of the role that employee stock-ownership plans might play in moving to a democratic economy, see Ellerman (1990, ch. 5–7). See also Blasi and Kruse (1991) and the interview with Blasi in Krimerman and Lindenfeld (1992, pp. 188–90). A central example here is Weirton Steel.

existing businesses – small and large – that will invest money in local expansion and create significant new employment.[17]

The positive project of bringing capital to communities (as contrasted with the negative task of keeping it from fleeing) would be powerfully advanced by enforcing a law already on the books, or, better still, by passing (and enforcing) the law as it was proposed before it was rendered toothless by conservative and "moderate" forces. The Humphrey-Hawkins Act of 1978 committed the federal government to a "full-employment" policy, but the key provision, which would have made the federal government the employer of last resort, was excised, thus stripping the government of any real capacity to realize the goals and targets mandated by the act.

If the government were really committed to full employment, it would have to contravene market forces and channel capital to where the unemployed workers are. It would have to offer incentives to businesses to increase employment. It would have to provide communities with funds for serious public-works projects. Such a program would be self-financing to a degree, because welfare expenses would be reduced, along with the indirect costs linked to poverty (police protection, prisons, health care for the indigent, etc.). If more funds should be needed, a small capital-assets tax would be the ideal solution – tax-generated funds earmarked exclusively for community investment.

In making employment an explicit goal of investment policy, market criteria would be demoted from their position of absolute primacy. This would also be the effect of environmental legislation and of various New-Liberal proposals for industrial policy. In all these cases, political criteria supplement (though they need not, and should not, entirely replace) market criteria.

Perhaps the most controversial reform proposals suggested by our analysis of Economic Democracy relate to international trade. We should strive for less, not more. We should try to restrict the flow of capital across national boundaries. We should not blanch at the charge of "protectionism."

A fundamental goal of a progressive trade policy should be to block international wage competition. From the point of view of the international working class, this is a beggar-thy-neighbor strategy that pits worker against worker. It seems wholly reasonable to impose on imports coming from country X a tariff that would raise the costs of those items to what they would be if the workers of country X were paid wages comparable

---

[17] Gutman (1992, pp. 36–7). One should not assume that because the private bank failed, its public reincarnation would also go under. The recent wave of bank failures in the United States has been due in no small part to the speculative frenzy of the deregulated 1980s. Reregulation – of private banks as well as public ones – is clearly necessary.

to our own. Such a provision would shield American workers from low-wage competition from abroad both by protecting our existing enterprises and by greatly reducing the incentives for U.S. manufacturers to move their plants abroad. Similar tariffs should be imposed when environmental restrictions are too low in country X. The goal should be "fair" trade, not "free" trade – messy and complicated though the former may be.[18]

To the nearly unanimous outcry to be expected from professional economists, we might respond with Krugman's estimate: If world trade were cut in half, the world's income would decline by 2.5 percent.[19] In exchange for a slight decline in consumption, millions of workers would gain in job security, and the nation as whole in economic independence and stability.[20] To be sure, protectionist policies involve the risk of abuse (above all, of allowing companies to postpone modernization), but this risk must be set against the near certainties of wage rollbacks and capital flight if free trade is the order of the day.

A couple of comments are in order at this juncture. I have sketched a series of reforms that might be viewed as components of a movement toward Economic Democracy. I should point out that none of these is wholly nonproblematic. Workers in cooperatives may develop "enterprise consciousness" rather than "class consciousness."[21] Participatory schemes may turn out to be little more than attempts by management to undermine unions to get more work from their work force at less cost. A labor movement can be bureaucratic, nondemocratic. Government efforts to direct investment, create jobs, and protect industries from unfair competition can be inept, and sometimes corrupt. It would be naive to pretend that such problems cannot arise. But it is an ideological reflex to presume that the laissez-faire approach would be better. Laissez Faire is

[18] "To make an open economy work, everyone must feel that they have an equal chance to win – what is known as 'a level playing field' in America; 'reciprocity' in Europe; or 'equal opportunity, not equal outcomes,' in Japan. But if the economic game is to be seen as fair, there must be broadly similar taxes, regulations, and private modes of operation" (Thurow, 1992, p. 64). Thurow makes this point for trade among advanced capitalist nations, but he fails to extend it to the Third World.

[19] Krugman (1990b, p. 105). If the costs of protectionism are so mild, why are economists so adamantly against it? Krugman recalls Paul Samuelson's remark that comparative advantage is one of the few ideas in economics that is true without being obvious (Krugman, 1990b, p. 106). I rather prefer Marx's observation: "If the Free Traders cannot understand how one nation can grow rich at the expense of another, we need not wonder, since these same gentlemen also refuse to understand how in the same country one class can enrich itself at the expense of another" (Marx and Engels, 1976, pp. 464–5).

[20] Workers in export-oriented industries would suffer, but many endeavors now unprofitable because of low-wage competition would become profitable again, allowing for employment opportunities. If protectionist measures are introduced gradually, the adjustment process need not be too painful – certainly less so than the adjustment process associated with the current deindustrialization.

[21] See Krimerman and Lindenfeld (1992, p. 158).

scarcely immune from incompetence and corruption. I take this to be obvious now, post-Reagan, post-Thatcher.

It would also be naive to think that a reform agenda such as I have proposed would be easy to implement. Such reforms will be bitterly opposed by very powerful, very wealthy interests. Although these reforms may not seem to be terribly radical, appearances here are deceptive. The proposed reforms encroach importantly on the rights of capital; they strike at its root. So they will be resisted strenuously. It does not follow that they cannot succeed, but success will not come easy.

Suppose we succeed in passing legislation to implement these reforms. We are still a long way from socialism. What we have is something not so different from Thurovian New Liberalism or Swedish Social Democracy – still capitalism, if capitalism with a more human face. Is there any plan one might propose for getting the rest of the way there? There is always the improbable scenario that opened this chapter, but let me suggest another possibility for bridging the gap that remains.

It is important to realize that two institutions that have been historically linked, private property and wage labor, are conceptually and practically distinct. It is theoretically possible to abolish one without abolishing the other. Indeed, the Soviet model did precisely that – abolished private ownership of the means of production, but not wage labor. It is less often realized that the opposite move can be made. Consider: It is perfectly possible to abolish wage labor without touching private property, because property ownership does not, in and of itself, entail the right to hire laborers (any more than it carries with it the right to purchase slaves). Wage labor could be prohibited by a simple law, such as the constitutional amendment Vanek proposed to the government of Malta:

Wherever and whenever two or more people work together in a common enterprise, it is they and only they who appropriate the results of their labors, whether the positive (products) or the negative (costs or liabilities), and who control and manage democratically on the basis of equality of vote the activities of their enterprise. These workers may or may not be owners of the capital assets with which they work, but in any event such ownership does not impart any rights of control over the firm.[22]

I am not proposing a leap from the reforms we have discussed to this law. Such a leap seems too long. But it is important to realize that the struggle to democratize the workplace is a struggle in the direction indicated by this law.

Let us suppose that major advances continue to be made in this direction, to the point that workers have considerable job security, as well as the right to inspect their company's records, the right to have representation

[22] Vanek (1990, p. 203, n. 5).

on the board of directors, and the right to be consulted about work arrangements, investment decisions, and other major policy matters. Let us suppose that these rights have been written into law.[23] Having advanced thus against wage labor, how might we now move against private ownership?

A famous answer to this question was provided by Sweden's Rudolph Meidner in the mid-1970s. He proposed that 20 percent of the before-tax profits of each firm employing more than 500 people be put into a union-controlled fund and used to purchase stock in that company. It was calculated that after twenty years, Swedish labor would own most of Swedish industry.[24]

The Meidner plan was supported by the labor movement, but bitterly opposed by business interests, and it was never implemented. The Social Democratic Party, which had governed Sweden since the Great Depression, was voted out of office in 1976, shortly after the plan had been proposed. Although returned to power in 1982, the Social Democratic Party has moved to the right and, suitably chastened, has ceased to push for such a transformation to socialism.[25]

Let me suggest an alternative scenario, derived from keeping in view our model of Economic Democracy. The basic idea is simple: Begin by (1) shifting from a corporate income tax to a capital-assets tax and (2) legislating profit sharing. Then gradually (or abruptly) increase the mandated share of profits that go to the workers of a firm. This, coupled with a monetary policy of low interest rates, will sharply reduce the share of the national income going to the capitalist class. To the extent that this reduction cuts into the supply of investment capital, increase the capital-assets tax.

Now consider: There are only two real reasons for wanting to own productive property: control and income. In modern capitalist societies,

[23] Lest the U.S. reader think this utopian, I hasten to point out that Swedish workers enjoy all these rights. Board representation came in 1972; the Security of Employment Act was passed in 1974. The 1976 Industrial Democracy Law enables unions, mainly at the local level, to negotiate the entire range of managerial decision-making prerogatives within any unionized company. Also important: The 1980 Law on Equality Between Men and Women forbids all forms of sex discrimination on the job. See Carson (1990, pp. 551–6).

[24] It should perhaps be pointed out, because so many Americans seem to believe otherwise, that Sweden is a capitalist country. A 1981 study showed that just over 1 percent of all households owned 75 percent of all individually held stock in the country, whereas 80 percent held none at all (Carson, 1990, p. 557).

[25] On the decline and fall of Scandinavian Social Democracy, see Moene and Wallerstein (1992). I do not mean to suggest that business opposition to the Meidner plan was the only reason that Swedish Social Democracy faltered. More important, it would seem, are the economic difficulties Sweden has encountered in recent years with capital flight and low-wage foreign competition. Sweden's economy is heavily dependent on foreign trade, exporting more than 40 percent of its industrial production.

control of enterprises by individual capitalists has long been in decline, with effective control shifting from stockholders toward management.[26] The reforms just discussed would erode capitalist control further, shifting it toward the workers in the firm. The proposed reforms would cut capitalist income too. Insofar as the government is well placed to counter an "investment strike," it need not fear that disenchantment on the part of capitalists will throw the country into recession.

The limiting case, of course, is for the rate of interest to fall to zero and the portion of profits going to workers to rise to 100 percent, with the capital-assets tax then supplying all the funds for new investment. This is Economic Democracy. Technically, the capitalists would still own the enterprises, but that "ownership" would confer neither control nor income rights. The stocks themselves could be sold – but who would buy them?

One other factor is worth considering, given our focus on the United States. A striking characteristic of contemporary U.S. capitalism is its private provision of pensions. Social-security benefits are insufficient for most workers, and so unions and companies set up pension plans for employees. These pension funds involve huge sums of money, much of which is invested in the stock market.[27]

This is an odd arrangement that leaves many workers quite vulnerable. "Prudent" management of the funds is required by law (the Employee Retirement Income Security Act of 1974), but prudence is not always exercised, nor is prudence always enough.[28] Why not pass a law that would allow workers to turn over their pension fund to the Social Security Administration (or some other government agency) in return for *guaranteed benefits*? This would have the effect of improving retirement security for all, and it would give the government ownership of a substantial share of the nation's productive wealth. The government would be entitled (as is any shareholder) to the dividends on the acquired stock, so the program would be more or less self-financing. In addition, the government would then have voting rights that could be exercised on behalf of the workers in the enterprise, and they would be if the right sort of government (i.e., Left sort of government) were in power. If it acquired sufficient control, it could ally with worker members on the

---

[26] This thesis was given its classical formulation by Berle and Means (1932), and was argued forcefully by Galbraith (1967). It is not clear to me that control has shifted away from capitalists *as a class*. Stupendous salaries, profit sharing, stock options, etc., ensure that the interests of upper management do not diverge significantly from those of the owners. But it seems beyond dispute that few individual stockholders have much control over the companies in which they own stock.

[27] According to Banks (1992, p. 122), union-negotiated pension funds now contain some $1.3 trillion in assets.

[28] For some pension stories, see Geoghegan (1991, pp. 149–54).

board of directors to institute democracy in the workplace and to increase to the maximum the share of profits going to workers.

I have sketched two possible transitions, one abrupt, one gradual, from here to there – from an advanced capitalist society to Economic Democracy. The first strikes me as highly implausible. I do not see the second one as inevitable, nor would it be an easy accomplishment, even under the best of circumstances. A powerful, committed, intelligent political movement would be necessary for a successful challenge to a ruling class as deeply entrenched as is the capitalist class in an advanced capitalist society. But it seems to me possible – this fulfillment of Keynes's dream ("euthanasia of the rentier"), Galbraith's dream ("euthanasia of the stockholder"), even Marx's ("expropriation of the expropriators").[29]

From command socialism

Prior to 1989, Communist parties controlled the governments of seventeen countries: the Soviet Union, China, Cambodia, Vietnam, Laos, North Korea, Cuba, Yugoslavia, Albania, Mongolia, Hungary, Bulgaria, Romania, Poland, Czechoslovakia, the German Democratic Republic, and Afghanistan. Virtually all of those governments had initially structured their economies according to some variation of what is usually called "the Soviet model" or, more generically, the "command" economy.

Conceptually, the model is simple: All means of production are nationalized. A government planning board assumes control of the entire economy, setting prices and wages and specifying for each enterprise quantitative and qualitative output quotas, the inputs and technologies to be used, and the labor to be employed. Enterprise managers, appointed by the state, are charged with executing the plan. In theory, all economic mystification dissolves, because the overall patterns of production and consumption are now consciously determined. The invisible hand of the market is replaced by the visible hand of the state.

Almost everyone now agrees that this model – which for more than half a century was synonymous in most people's minds with "socialism" – is deeply flawed.[30] By 1989, no Communist country fit the model exactly. Some had deviated quite far from it. In thinking about a transition from one of these countries to Economic Democracy, however, the command-economy model is the essential point of departure.

Of course, few people today are thinking about a transition from a command economy to Economic Democracy. In Eastern Europe and the

---

[29] Keynes (1936, p. 376); Galbraith (1973a, p. 261); Marx (1967, p. 763).
[30] A systematic critique will be provided in the next chapter.

countries formerly part of the Soviet Union the economic analyses and reform proposals emanating from the political and intellectual leadership are concerned with making the transition to a market economy, where "market economy" is understood (as it is in the West) to be synonymous with capitalism.

Let me be candid in my assessment. The conceptual confusion inherent in identifying all market economies with capitalism is symptomatic of deeper problems. I think that much of the economic restructuring now under way throughout Eastern Europe and the former Soviet Union is wrongheaded and reprehensible, deriving from ignorance, Western pressure, and the self-interest/self-deception of state policymakers and their intellectual cohorts. The "reforms" currently are generating much human suffering, and will generate much more.[31] They may well lead to an undermining of political democracy in the region. They most certainly will not work out as promised. I state this as a categorical prediction.

I shall not attempt here a systematic elaboration of this summary critique, but a few observations may not be out of place. First, it is easy enough to understand that Eastern European intellectuals and policymakers would find the free-market/privatization ideology alluring. Indeed, this ideology was all the rage throughout much of the world during the 1980s, not only in the United States and Britain (whence it had arisen) but also in New Zealand, Latin America, parts of Western Europe, and elsewhere. The U.S. economy had recovered more rapidly than had the economies of Western Europe from the deep recession of the early 1980s and was still in the midst of the longest "peacetime" expansion in our history.[32] Never mind that this expansion had little to do with a free market or privatization. From afar, the results doubtless looked good. They looked particularly good, one can assume, to intellectuals and functionaries who could imagine themselves becoming corporate executives, young entrepreneurs, or highly paid professionals – groups whose members did indeed benefit from the "Reagan revolution."

Perhaps even more significant than ignorance and bad faith was the major pressure applied by the West to ensure that certain reforms would be made and others would not. Not only did Western economists swarm to advise, but a specific strategy was set in place at the 1987 summit of the "group of seven" in Venice to thwart Gorbachev's dream of rebuilding the Soviet economy along noncapitalist lines, a strategy that employed

---

[31] Thurow (1992, pp. 87–8) notes that "in Poland's economy 1990 average family incomes were 40 percent below the peak attained under communism.... In 1990 and 1991 GDPs fell 16 percent in Poland, Czechoslovakia, Hungary, Romania and Bulgaria, with industrial production plunging 28 percent."

[32] I put this widely used term in quotation marks because this "peacetime" expansion was fueled by one of the largest military buildups in human history.

such heavy artillery as high tariffs on imports from the Soviet Union, severe restrictions on exports, promises of debt relief and foreign aid, and so forth. This sorry tale has yet to be fully told.[33]

Because it is so rarely mentioned in mainstream discussions of Eastern Europe, let me here underscore what should be an obvious point: It cannot be assumed that the interests of the advanced capitalist countries are coincident with the interests of the inhabitants of the formerly Communist world. So-called reforms that allow Western companies easy access to raw materials, markets, and cheap labor, and easy repatriation of profits (e.g., currency convertibility, unregulated prices, privatization), may well "work" from the point of view of Western capital and a local comprador class, but at the same time lead to the immiserization of great masses of people. Economic "miracles" of the Brazilian or Chilean variety are common enough in late capitalism. Various countries in Eastern Europe may be ripe for such restructuring, although it should be stressed that implementing such reforms has been incompatible, historically, with political democracy.[34]

It is difficult not to regard current developments without a sense of dismay. There are better ways in which they could proceed. Such is my contention. If the basic argument of this book is correct, then it would seem that Economic Democracy, not capitalism, should be the vision shaping the proposals put forth by the reformers of Eastern Europe and the former Soviet Union. That has not been the case.

But what if it had been? Or what if, in the near future, it should be? How might one envisage a transition from a command economy to Economic Democracy?[35] In fact, that transition is easy enough to sketch, at least in broad outline. In all likelihood it would be easier to implement than the perhaps impossible project now being attempted: creating, de novo, capitalist institutions, capitalist values, and a capitalist class.[36]

---

[33] See Gowan (1990) for an excellent beginning.

[34] Eastern European economists and their Western advisors are not unaware of this. Here is the advice that Harvard fellow Boris Rumer (1991, p. 22) is offering: "The 'creeping marketization' under way in the U.S.S.R. has need of political order and financial stability. The capitalized *nomenklatura* needs an authoritarian leadership that would at the same time implement a liberal policy toward private entrepreneurs. It desperately needs Western investment and a favorable climate for attracting that investment." The model being advocated is often referred to (chillingly) as the "Chilean model."

[35] What follows should be taken as indicative only, not as a hard-and-fast prescription. When Economic Democracy is the regulative ideal, the reforms suggested will differ substantially from those suggested when capitalism is the goal, but in either case the reforms must be tailored to the specific conditions of particular countries.

[36] Thurow (1992, p. 109) reproduces a letter from a Russian friend, who writes, "I spent the last few months, along with some of my colleagues, in preparing the background materials for policy decisions on the transition to a regulated market economy. When the time for action came it turned out that neither the economy nor public opinion is ready for it. It appears to be easier to build communism rather than return to capitalism."

The obvious first step would be to implement workplace democracy. Because all enterprises are owned by the state (or at least were, prior to "privatization," which has not, in fact, progressed very far anywhere), a simple legislative decree would suffice.[37] But workplace democracy in and of itself is not enough. Workplace democracy gives control of an enterprise to its workers, but unless this control is complemented by structures that will motivate workers to exercise this control responsibly, workplace democracy will not solve the economic problem. Indeed, it may exacerbate it. For example, if workers are allowed to elect their managers, but no other reforms are implemented, then these managers may well come under increasing pressure to lobby the authorities for higher wages and to ease off on workplace discipline. Such measures can easily translate into lower, not higher, productivity.

To ensure that workers are motivated to elect competent managers, workers' incomes must be tied to the overall performance of the firm. That is to say, incomes should go up when sales go up or costs go down, which is to say that the enterprise must operate in a market environment.

It should be noted, however, that this market need not be "free," in the sense that prices are determined by supply and demand. Virtually all command economies are characterized by shortages relative to effective demand; people have money to spend, but little to buy. (This is in stark contrast to capitalist economies, which are characterized by surplus capacity relative to effective demand.) So when prices are decontrolled in a command economy, prices soar. To be sure, waiting lines disappear, but so do personal savings.[38] Worse still, the resulting uncertainty makes long-range planning by the government and by individual firms almost impossible; vast opportunities for speculation and corruption draw off productive talent; monopolistic industries (the norm in command economies, because it is easier to plan when the number of firms is small) are free to exploit their market power. In short, the resulting incentive structures are highly nonoptimal. The fairy-tale promise that free markets will lead swiftly to enhanced productivity is a cruel deception.

---

[37] Such laws were in fact passed in various countries during the *perestroika* period. In Hungary, in 1985, such a law was passed, but political authorities retained informal veto power; see Kornai in Nee and Stark (1989, p. 40). In the Soviet Union, such a law was passed in 1987, only to be rescinded in 1990 (Panitch and Gindin, 1991, p. 19). In all cases, managers have been hostile to workplace democracy, as have been, virtually without exception, all mainstream Western advisors. Jeffrey Sachs (1991, p. 28) is typical in bemoaning the fact that "throughout Eastern Europe the enterprises are not subject to any effective corporate governance, other than an unhealthy kind that sometimes emanates from the workers' councils within each firm."

[38] Thurow (1992, p. 88) cites the joke current in former Communist countries: "In communism your pockets are full of money, but there is nothing to buy. In capitalism the stores are full, but you have no money in your pockets."

It would make far more sense to keep the price-control mechanisms of a command economy in place and to readjust prices gradually. The goal, of course, is to bring prices into line with real costs. Controls should be lifted only after prices have been rationalized and after the economy has become sufficiently competitive.

It is important to underscore the point that it is possible to have a market economy that is not "free" with respect to prices. The key feature of a market economy is a firm's right to produce what it wishes to produce, to sell to whomever will buy, to purchase its inputs from whatever sources it can find. These freedoms are compatible with controlled prices. These are the freedoms most essential to making a worker-managed enterprise a responsible economic agent. In such a market, incomes will depend on sales, and so enterprises must satisfy consumers; incomes go up if costs go down, and so enterprises are motivated to produce efficiently.[39] Without market incentives, workplace democracy cannot be expected to accomplish much (if anything) in the way of enhancing productivity.

Markets need not be "free" to play their required role in enhancing an economy's performance, nor need they embrace more than goods and services. It is a fundamental thesis of this book that capital generation and allocation should not be left to the market. In this area, a command economy must create new institutions: a network of community banks to distribute the investment fund. It must also impose a new tax: the tax on capital assets that will serve as the source of this fund.

Here we run into a difficulty. How does one value the capital assets upon which the tax will be based? Neither book value nor replacement value would make much sense. Book value was determined under a system of prices that may have had little relation to real costs. To tax a firm based on replacement value would be to presume that the existing plant was efficiently designed. (Why should workers at an enterprise bear the cost of capital expenses that may have been wasteful?) Here Vanek offers an elegant solution. He argues for a "fair" evaluation:[40] Assign a value to the firm's assets that would allow the firm's workers the incomes they had received previously. That is, assign the assets a

---

[39] Economists will be quick to point out that any form of price control leads to some sort of inefficiency. If firms cannot raise prices, they will not offer improved items that cost more. If they cannot price-compete, they will not pass cost reductions on to consumers. Against these considerations, three points may be made: (1) Any reasonable system of price controls allows for adjustments. (2) The allocative inefficiencies associated with prices deviating from perfect-competition prices are not likely to be large. (3) The alternative – moving abruptly from controlled to decontrolled prices – entails massive social costs and few discernible benefits.

[40] Vanek (1990, pp. 190ff.). The transition program I am elaborating is similar to Vanek's overall proposal, although it differs in some details.

value F, so that $W = S - C - RF$, where W is the previous wage bill, S is last year's sales, C is last year's input costs, and R is the tax rate on assets.[41] Such evaluations, if properly done, will ensure that no one is made worse off in making the transition to a market economy.[42]

Workers are now free to reorganize their facility, to apply for investment grants, and so forth. If they make good decisions, their incomes will go up; if they make bad decisions, their incomes will suffer. Henceforth they are responsible for their economic destiny.

It will be noted that for some firms, these asset valuations may be negative. At the given prices, sales may not be sufficient to allow them to meet their previous wage bill, even without an assets tax. In effect, they require a subsidy. This is to be expected. The subsidy should be paid. It would make little sense from the perspective of society as a whole to simply throw these people out of work – as will be done if the firms are "privatized" in accordance with capitalist dogma.[43] To their credit, command economies succeeded in eliminating overt unemployment. That gain should not be lightly rescinded. To be sure, full employment removed the disciplinary stick of "the sack" and often led to large inefficiencies, but the transition to an efficient socialism need not and should not reinstitute one of capitalism's most serious defects.[44]

The Vanek solution faces one potentially serious obstacle. What if it is not possible to ensure that incomes do not fall? What if so many firms require subsidies that there is not enough left in the investment fund to allow for the new investments that are deemed necessary? To take the extreme case (which is, after all, the popular impression in the West), what if none of the firms in a command economy are efficient enough to survive without subsidy?

---

[41] Computations of sales and costs are to be made using the reformed prices.

[42] Other standards of fairness could be invoked, and probably should be if previous wages were egregiously unfair. From the point of view of practical politics, however, reform strategies probably will be most successful if they can be designed so as to avoid making any firm worse off than before. As Stark points out, this has been the Chinese strategy of recent years (Nee and Stark, 1989, p. 354).

[43] From a strict cash-flow point of view, it makes sense to subsidize the low-income enterprise by at least as much as the society would have to pay in unemployment benefits. If we take into account the less quantifiable ill effects of unemployment, the subsidy could go higher. It also makes sense to make below-rate investment grants available to such enterprises, so that they can upgrade their facilities. A time limit probably should be placed on subsidies, however, so that workers will be motivated to retool and restructure.

[44] The reader will recall from Chapter 3 that this is an *efficiency defect*. Capitalist accounting procedures tend to obscure this fact. Suppose we have two societies, each with 100 workers. In the first, 10 are unemployed, the remaining 90 producing a GNP of $180,000. In the second, all are employed, producing a GNP of $190,000. Standard capitalist accounting procedures would place worker productivity in the first at $20,000 per worker (because unemployed workers are not counted), whereas it would be only $19,000 in the second, thus giving the impression that the former is "more efficient" than the latter, when in fact the latter (with the income suitably distributed) is Pareto-superior.

We need to distinguish here the real problem from the pseudoproblem. We need to ask, efficient as compared with what? In much current discussion the implied standard is the internationally competitive firm in a capitalist society. To say that a firm is inefficient by this standard is to say that it will be unable to compete in the international market.

But that is not the relevant standard. It may be true that all the firms in country X are inefficient when measured against the standard of current international competitiveness. It does not follow that all the firms in X would require a subsidy to stay in business. After all, almost no enterprise in the United States circa 1950 would be able to compete today in the international market. It does not follow that the firms at that time required subsidies. To be sure, the firms of 1950 could not compete now in international markets with the firms of the 1990s, but they could certainly produce goods and services sufficient to provide the citizenry with an adequate (indeed, an enviable) standard of living.

Much the same can be said about the countries of Eastern Europe. Their economies experienced difficulties prior to 1989, but they were not poor countries, not by international standards. They clearly had the human and material resources to provide their citizens with an adequate standard of living. Their technologies were (usually) inferior to the best in the West, but Eastern European firms did not have to compete with Western firms (any more than American firms of the 1950s had to compete in the world market of the 1990s). The Communist trading bloc was largely independent of the West.

It is important to realize that the Eastern European economies were not in crisis because their technologies were inferior to those of the West. The technologies often enough *were* inferior, but that, in and of itself, need not have produced a crisis.

Why, then, was there a crisis? The most obvious explanation, which seems to me correct, is that the economic crises of Communist Eastern Europe derived from a "motivational crisis," which derived from a "legitimacy" crisis.[45] Various economic and political difficulties undermined the legitimacy of existing governments. As a result, *work discipline* crumbled. Recall the popular saying of the day: "They pretend to pay us, and we pretend to work." Economic difficulties escalated into crises when workers lost confidence in their governments.

That loss of confidence was not without reason. The economic structures that had industrialized those nations proved unable to deliver on consumer goods. Massive amounts of investment funds, funds generated internally as well as Western loans, had been and were being squandered.

---

[45] I am borrowing these terms from Habermas (1973). The theoretical framework he has developed to understand capitalist crises turns out to be exceedingly useful in making sense of the upheavals in the Communist world.

The gap between living standards in Eastern and Western Europe, which had been closing, began widening. These phenomena led to increased worker alienation, which translated into a reduction of work effort, and that provoked the economic crises.

If this account is correct, then the worry that all the firms in a command economy are likely to be so inefficient as to require subsidies is a pseudoproblem – *unless*, of course, the economies are opened to international competition. And that, of course, is what Western advisors are advising.

If this Western pressure is resisted, then the inefficiency problem becomes tractable.[46] It does not follow that the transition to Economic Democracy can be accomplished without pain. Some reduction in living standards may be necessary. To the extent that an economy has been propped up by foreign loans, and to the extent that infrastructure investment has been sacrificed to consumption, some reduction in current consumption will be necessary to make the transition to a healthy economy. That is to say, it may not be possible to evaluate the capital assets of the country so as to generate sufficient investment funds and at the same time maintain real incomes at their previous levels.

The theoretical solution to this problem is clear enough. If the valuations are such that at tax rate R all firms will maintain their prior incomes, but this rate is too low to generate sufficient funds for new investment, then the valuations can be revised upward so that all incomes will be reduced by X percent. The investment pool thus will be increased, and the burden will be shared fairly.[47]

The structural transition to Economic Democracy is now complete. Workplaces have been turned over to their workers, who must pay an assets tax for their use. The proceeds from this tax form the investment fund, which is distributed to the network of community banks. These banks can now dispense grants to firms that request them in accordance with profitability, employment creation, and other democratically determined criteria. Firms, though not yet free to set prices, are otherwise free to buy, produce, and sell as they see fit, and to apply for investment grants. They must now bear the full consequences of these decisions.

One final point is worth noting. It is often remarked that the psychological disposition fostered by a command economy may block the transition to a more viable economy. Such claims usually are made by

[46] What is being advocated here is not autarchy. As we have seen, Economic Democracy calls for neither autarchy nor free trade, but for managed trade. What is important is that a country's economic des iny not become tied *too tightly* to international competition.

[47] Note: The initial asset valuations should be adjusted, not the tax rate. Raising R would force those workers who happened to work in plants with higher-than-average capital intensity to bear a disproportionate share of the social burden.

those bemoaning the difficulty of making the transition to capitalism. It is said that individuals are too passive, that workers do not want to give up their job security, that the entrepreneurial spirit is lacking. Thurow reports that former Soviet factory managers "have no clear grasp of capitalism's cut and thrust. They refer constantly to cooperation. The idea of competition makes them acutely uncomfortable."[48]

Insofar as attitudes about economic security and fairness stand in the way of the reckless reforms now being pushed, a socialist can only applaud. But at the same time, one must acknowledge that certain skills currently in short supply must be fostered, and certain attitudes must be held in check, if Economic Democracy is to succeed. The desire for economic security, for example, is important and laudable, but this desire should not be satisfied by reducing the hard budget constraint on firms. That is to say, a community bank must say "no" to a firm requesting an investment grant if that grant is to be used simply to subsidize an unprofitable operation. If a firm cannot stay in business without a subsidy (beyond the initial evaluation of its capital assets), and cannot come up with a feasible reorganization plan, then it must be allowed to go under.

At the same time, communities must encourage the development of entrepreneurial skills; banks must make funds available to those willing and able to develop new enterprises. It might be necessary to offer special financial incentives that seem at variance with the egalitarian ethos of socialism. Decisions to do so may be made democratically at the national, regional, or local level.[49] Care should be taken not to undermine people's basic sense of fairness; at the same time, it should be acknowledged that entrepreneurial talent is an important asset that needs to be cultivated.

From neocolonial underdevelopment

The countries of the Third World (which, if ranked on the basis of geographic area or population, would constitute the First World) are so many and diverse that it seems presumptuous to make general statements about them, let alone recommendations. At the same time, it is wrong to think that nothing has been learned from the large numbers of "experiments" that have been undertaken, particularly over the past half century. The wretched of the earth have been restless. There have been many and varied attempts, some originating from within these societies, and some from without, at breaking out of the cycle of deep poverty and degradation that still grips so much of humanity.

To be sure, there is almost nothing one can say about the Third World

[48] Thurow (1992, p. 97).
[49] The reader will recall the analysis of inequality in Chapter 5: Such incentives do not augur the return of capitalism.

that is not controversial.[50] Deep ideological rifts separate the participants in the various debates. Conceptual difficulties abound. Data are disputed. Feelings of superiority/inferiority, rage/guilt, hope/despair boil beneath the surface in even the seemingly disinterested scientific analyses. There is, after all, much at stake. Millions of people die each year of hunger and preventable diseases.[51] Riots, rebellions, and guerrilla movements have become permanent features of the landscape. Counterinsurgency operations are conducted with scarcely imaginable ferocity.

To ask about the relevance of Economic Democracy to the Third World is to raise a question too complicated to answer adequately in the compass of a section such as this, but the question is too important to go unremarked. In what follows I shall not pretend to offer a definitive answer, but let me at least set out some of the issues, take some positions, sketch some arguments, and point to some evidence.

Before speculating on the transition to Economic Democracy in a Third World setting, we must ask a more basic, more important, question. The central argument of this book purports to show that Economic Democracy will be superior to capitalism on both economic and ethical grounds. The setting for the comparison thus far has been societies as technically advanced as the United States. But what about the Third World? Is Economic Democracy an appropriate model for a Third World country seeking to address its fundamental problems?

The question is not a simple one. For starters, we must ask, appropriate to whom? In accordance with the interests of whom? What may be appropriate for the class or group in power may not be appropriate for the majority of the population. What may be appropriate for a majority may not be appropriate for the poorest segments. What may be appropriate for the poor may not be appropriate to the international lending agencies that hold so many countries hostage.

---

[50] The term "Third World" is itself a case in point. It is seen by some as denigrating the earth's majority. It is seen by others as too politically charged. The term apparently was invented by the French demographer Alfred Sauvy as analogous to the term "Third Estate" (a concept dating from the French Revolution, referring to everybody not belonging to the nobility or clergy) and was intended to designate countries distinct from the industrialized capitalist countries and the industrialized socialist countries (Chaliand, 1987, p. 197). It gained wide currency following the 1955 Bandung Conference in Indonesia, at which leaders of the Asian and African countries began using the term self-referentially. I prefer the term to the antiseptic initials LDC (for lesser-developed country), more commonly used today in academic circles and international publications, because "Third World" carries with it the connotation of previous colonial domination, which was in fact the common experience of almost all the nations in question.

[51] In 1987 the Nordic Conference on Environment and Development estimated that 500 million men, women, and children suffer from chronic malnutrition or famine and that each year some 40 million die from hunger and hunger-related diseases. This is "equivalent to more than 300 jumbo jet crashes per day with no survivors, almost half of the passengers being children." Cited by Drèze and Sen (1989, p. 36).

We must also ask about "fundamental problems." What are they? What values underlie this determination? Are reforms that address certain problems consistent with reforms that address others? We must also ask about constraints: material-resource constraints, educational and skill constraints, internal political constraints (i.e., the configuration and balance of class forces), external political constraints. (Bluntly stated: How much can be done without triggering countermeasures by the United States or other advanced capitalist countries?)

To render the complex question more manageable, let us make some simplifying assumptions. Let us assume that the question is being asked by a movement or party or new government that is committed to fundamental social change, and let us assume that it is in basic agreement with the values set out in the preceding chapters. Let us assume that the arguments of those chapters have been persuasive in the case of advanced capitalism and thus have established a strong prima facie case for the superiority of Economic Democracy over capitalism in the Third World. The question then becomes, Are the problems and constraints facing Third World countries sufficiently different from those of advanced capitalism to overturn this case?[52]

Two problems would seem to be more urgent in the Third World than in the advanced industrial societies. First, there is the matter of satisfying the basic needs of all the population, where "basic needs" comprise food, clothing, shelter, education, and health care. To be sure, not all advanced capitalist societies satisfy these needs, but it is clear that they could. Many have.[53] The matter is far more pressing in the Third World. Second, economic development is more vital to the Third World than to the First World. Development must be "rational" (i.e., in accordance with the values we have assumed and with environmental constraints), but it is wrong to think that the people of the Third World should be (or will be) content with bare subsistence when their neighbors to the north have so much more.[54]

If we set aside for now the matter of internal and external political

---

[52] The essential comparison here, as before, is between Economic Democracy and capitalism. But as we shall see, a comparison with command socialism must also be considered, because the case for command socialism is considerably stronger in a Third World context than it is for an advanced industrial society.

[53] Not the United States, where, as everyone knows, hunger and homelessness affect large numbers. See Harvard School of Public Health (1985) and Dreier and Appelbaum (1991).

[54] One facet of "rational development" deserves special mention. The values of material well-being, leisure, etc., must be fostered for women as well as for men. Marta Fuentes has provocatively declared that "development is bad for women!" Cited by Frank (1992, p. 135). This judgment is doubtless correct with respect to a great many development schemes that have been attempted in the Third World. See Shiva (1989) for numerous examples. But it is also correct to say that poverty is bad for women – and that it is disproportionately bad for women in many parts of the world. See Drèze and Sen (1989, pp. 50–9) for grim statistics on the "missing women" of South and West Asia, North Africa, and China.

constraints (because these are more appropriately considered in the con-text of transition), our question becomes the following: Is Economic De-mocracy a viable model for a Third World country seeking both to satisfy the basic needs of all its people and to engage in rational development?

Let us begin with basic needs. Consider the question of hunger and those diseases related to malnourishment that take such a toll on chil-dren and the elderly. Can Economic Democracy solve this problem? Can it be solved at all? Are there not simply too many mouths to feed in too many countries to even hope for a general solution? Jean Drèze and Amartya Sen, in one of the most sophisticated and carefully researched treatises on the topic to date, offer the following assessment:

Hunger is not a new affliction. Recurrent famines as well as endemic undernour-ishment have been persistent features of history. Life has been short and hard in much of the world most of the time. . . . Hunger is, however, intolerable in the modern world in a way it could not have been in the past. This is so not so much because it is more intense, but because widespread hunger is so unnecessary and unwarranted in the modern world. The enormous expansion of productive power that has taken place over the past few centuries has made it, perhaps for the first time, possible to guarantee adequate food for all.[55]

The fact is, we know that it would be possible to eliminate hunger in the modern world. We know this not only because we know that we have the productive capacity to do so[56] but also because some quite poor countries have in fact eliminated hunger and provided adequately for other basic needs. The most dramatic success by far has occurred in China, home to more than a billion people. Within three decades of its 1949 revolution, China, though still exceedingly poor by international standards, had cut its infant mortality dramatically, had increased adult literacy substantially, and had extended the life expectancy of its popu-lation from about forty years of age to nearly seventy.

The comparison with India highlights the magnitude of the Chinese accomplishment. Indian independence preceded the Chinese Revolution by two years. At that time, hunger in both countries was widespread; life expectancy, illiteracy, and infant mortality were at comparable levels. But by 1980, life expectancy in India was only in the middle to high fifties; the mortality among children under age five was three times higher than in China, and adult literacy was a third lower.[57]

---

[55] Drèze and Sen (1989, p. 3). [56] See Goldemberg et al. (1987).
[57] See Drèze and Sen (1989, ch. 11). Development during that period was not smooth in China. Against its remarkable overall record must be set what may have been the worst famine in human history, the terrible hunger of 1958–61 that followed the debacle of "The Great Leap Forward," during which time some 16–30 million people lost their lives. For a wrenching account of how that traumatic period was experienced in one village, see Friedman, Pickowicz, and Selden (1991, ch. 9 and 10). But even that horror must be put in perspective. Drèze and Sen calculate that "every eight years or so more people die

China is not the only poor country that has been able to feed all its people. Cuba has also been outstanding in meeting basic needs. Its infant mortality is one of the lowest in the Third World, less than half that of China.[58] Even during the "special period" occasioned by the collapse of its Comecon trading partners and the tightened U.S. embargo, Cuba has managed to provide everyone with adequate food, health care, and education.[59]

There are other success stories. Sri Lanka has recorded scores as good as those of China on such social indicators as life expectancy, infant morality, and literacy, while having a comparable per capita income.[60] The state of Kerala in India, poorer than most Indian states, also ranks with China in its social indicators.[61] Costa Rica and Jamaica have infant mortalities, life expectancies, and literacy rates comparable to Cuba's.[62]

We know from the empirical record that it is possible for Third World countries to make great strides in reducing the hunger, disease, and illiteracy so often associated with poverty. We also know how it has been done. In all cases the state has had to intervene in the economy.[63] A country wanting to address the problem of hunger cannot rely on the free market. Sen makes the point vividly in the case of Sri Lanka:

Had Sri Lanka been a typical developing country, trying to achieve its high level of life expectancy not through direct public action, but primarily through growth, then it would have taken Sri Lanka – depending on assumptions – somewhere between 58 and 152 years to get where it already now happens to be.[64]

in India because of its higher regular death rate than died in China in the gigantic famine of 1958–61. India seems to manage to fill its cupboard with more skeletons every eight years than China put there in its years of shame" (Drèze and Sen, 1989, pp. 214–15).

[58] Now at sixteen deaths per thousand (which was the U.S. rate only seventeen years ago), Cuba's rate is not only far better than those in most of the Third World but also better than the current rate for African-Americans in the United States. See *Statistical Abstracts of the United States, 1991*, p. 62; *World Almanac 1992*, pp. 752, 939.

[59] I write this in the summer of 1992, having just spent two weeks in Cuba.

[60] See Drèze and Sen (1989, pp. 227–9). Sri Lanka's excellent record doubtless has deteriorated in recent years, given the savage ethnic strife that has engulfed the country since 1983.

[61] See Franke and Chasin (1989) for a detailed exposition of this remarkable accomplishment. See Franke and Chasin (1991) for a more concise account. It should be noted that in dramatic contrast to the rest of India, there are more women than men in Kerala – indicating far less gender bias in access to basic necessities.

[62] See Drèze and Sen (1989, pp. 240–9). China, Cuba, Costa Rica, and Jamaica are four of the top six Third World countries, ranked in terms of percentage reduction in under-age-five mortality for the period 1960–85, the index that the United Nations considers the best single indicator of basic-needs satisfaction. See the list compiled by Drèze and Sen (1989, p. 184). It should be noted that in recent years Costa Rica and Jamaica have been forced by the International Monetary Fund, as a condition for aid, to cut back heavily on their health and welfare expenditures, so subsequent statistics may not be as good.

[63] Two countries might seem to be counterexamples to this claim: Chile and South Korea, both of which are on the Drèze-Sen list cited in the preceding footnote. But as Drèze and Sen show (1989, pp. 229–39, 293–7), their good performances on social indicators cannot be attributed to the workings of the free market.

[64] Sen (1984, p. 496).

In all the successful cases, the state has had to make health care and education widely available. The state has had to ensure that vulnerable groups not go hungry.

If we think about enabling structures, it is clear that in comparison with capitalism, socialist economies of the traditional type possess two clear advantages in accomplishing the task of meeting basic needs. Because there is no distinction between the public and private spheres, funds for health and education are not so dependent on the general state of the economy. Under capitalism, an economic downturn translates at once into a decrease in public revenue, thus triggering demands for budget cuts. In a command economy, an economic slowdown does not generate a fiscal crisis, for the government can always print money to pay wages, including the wages of teachers and health-care workers. The economic slowdown translates, instead, into shortages of capital equipment and consumer goods, but rarely (because these areas are so labor-intensive) into cutbacks in health care or education.[65]

The second major advantage is the result of two policies: full employment and controlled prices. These ensure that virtually every family will have an above-subsistence regular income. No one will be in a position of being too poor to obtain food. Even in an economic crisis, people are rarely laid off, and if they are they continue to receive their wages. Shortages can develop, but because prices are controlled, shortages will generate longer waiting lines, not higher prices. When the shortages become acute, they usually are resolved by rationing, which prevents anyone from being left out.

What about Economic Democracy? It should be clear that Economic Democracy will lack certain features that give command socialism the advantages just noted. The public–private distinction will not be as acute as under capitalism, because it does not apply to the investment fund. Funds for new schools or health clinics will come from the same capital-assets tax as do funds for all other capital investments. However, the salaries of teachers and health-care workers will come from general tax revenues (taxes on income or consumption). If there is an economic contraction, these tax revenues will fall, as they do under capitalism.[66] There will be pressure to cut back.

Economic Democracy, like command socialism, is committed to full employment, so there should be fewer people economically vulnerable than under capitalism. It must be admitted, however, that this commitment

---

[65] According to Cuban economist Carlos Tablata, Cuba, during its current, quite acute economic contraction, has not closed any hospitals or day-care centers nor laid off any teachers. (Presentation to a delegation of North American philosophers, June 10, 1992.)

[66] I have argued that Economic Democracy will be more stable than capitalism, and so this problem is less likely to arise. But it certainly can happen, particularly if a country is linked significantly to the international market, which likely will be the case for most Third World countries.

may be harder to fulfill, because firms will be allowed to go bankrupt under Economic Democracy, as they almost never are under command socialism. The government under Economic Democracy will assume the role of employer of last resort, but funds for public-works jobs will come from general tax revenues. If the cooperative sector is in a slump, the public sector will be under pressure.

A third count against Economic Democracy: Prices in general will not be controlled. If shortages develop, prices will go up. Workers in industries that are not doing well may find their incomes going down as food prices rise.

If basic needs constituted the whole story, then command socialism would have a good claim to being superior to Economic Democracy as a model for Third World development. But they are not the whole story. Command socialism possesses some clear advantages relative to distribution, but there is also the matter of production. The very factors that count against Economic Democracy with respect to distribution – namely, separating the economy into a competitive cooperative sphere and a public sphere, allowing unprofitable firms to go bankrupt, allowing prices to be determined by supply and demand – are precisely the factors that will make it more efficient and productive.

There does seem to be a trade-off here. When everyone is guaranteed a job by the state, and when the state controls both wages and prices, it will be relatively easy to ensure that everyone will have access to basic commodities. Unfortunately, these features make efficient production problematic.[67]

The impasse we have reached – which, of course, is a version of the equity–efficiency trade-off so beloved by economists – is by no means intractable. The problem should be less severe under Economic Democracy than under capitalism. (The public–private split is not so wide under Economic Democracy, and the commitment to full employment is more serious.) But even under Third World capitalism, basic needs can be met provided the government has the political will and political power to implement the necessary programs. That is the important lesson to be drawn from the experiences of Sri Lanka, Kerala, Costa Rica, and Jamaica. If these states can provide decent nutrition, education, and health care for their people, surely Economic Democracy can do likewise.

It must be admitted that so long as basic needs are the essential focus, command socialism has much to recommend it. Where it runs into trouble is getting beyond those needs. It is here – the arena of rational growth – that the structures of Economic Democracy should bear the most fruit.

But is this expectation warranted? This is the crucial question. Granted, the arguments of the earlier chapters have demonstrated that the basic

[67] The arguments for this claim will be given in the next chapter.

triad of worker self-management, social control of investment, and a market for goods and services will promote efficient production and rational development in a First World setting. But do these arguments hold in a Third World context?

Let us move from what is most clear to what is less so. It seems evident that the market must play a role in an economy operating under conditions of scarcity if it wants to achieve efficient production. There may well be situations where price controls are called for, but even in such cases the enterprises should be free to buy from, and sell to, whomever they want (in the national economy, though currency controls are another matter altogether).[68] Because it can hardly be doubted that Third World enterprises need to be innovative and efficient, incentives to this end are needed. I do not see an adequate substitute for the positive and negative incentives provided by the market.

It also seems to me beyond question that social control of investment (i.e., *planning* of investment) is indispensable to rational development. For all the reasons rehearsed in Chapter 4, the market is incapable of channeling scarce investment resources properly. This is not to say that planners do not make mistakes. They often do, and the results often are disastrous, particularly when large-scale megaprojects are undertaken (frequently under the auspices of the international lending agencies). As far as possible, planning should be decentralized and should involve the participation of those in the areas receiving the funds. But planning is indispensable. The "privatize and let the free market work its magic" prescriptions of the 1980s never made sense theoretically and have proved disastrous in practice.[69]

---

[68] Our discussion of Economic Democracy in the Third World will omit a specific discussion of international trade. The conclusions of the analysis of international trade given in Chapter 6 apply with even greater force. If unrestricted trade is dangerous for an advanced industrial society trying to bring its economy under democratic control, it is even more so for an underdeveloped country. This is not a brief for autarchy. Few Third World countries can avoid engaging in significant trade. But that trade should not be "free" (i.e., unregulated by the political authorities).

[69] This summary judgment will be contested in conservative circles. One country now touted as a success is Chile, whose economy has been growing at a rate of 5 percent per year since 1986 and whose social indicators are quite respectable (Briggs, 1992). But the Chilean "miracle" must be put into context. Following the brutal overthrow of the democratically elected government of Salvador Allende in 1973, General Pinochet looked to Milton Friedman and other "Chicago boys" for advice, and he implemented much of their program. The results have been decidedly mixed. Chile has done well on the basic social indicators – but by targeting relief efforts, not by relying on the free market (Graham, 1991). At the same time, it should be noted that in 1985, twelve years after the experiment had begun, real wages were some 13 percent below what they had been when the general took over (Drèze and Sen, 1989, p. 233). During the 1980s, the Chilean per-capita income rose only 1.1 percent per year – "miraculous" only in comparison with the other regimes of Latin America, most of which had also implemented free-market reforms. See Cardoso and Helwege (1992) for a general assessment of the "lost decade" in Latin America.

As to the viability of workplace democracy, the third element of our triad, it is useful to consider separately agriculture and industry. It is important to stress that in agriculture, both family farming and democratically run cooperatives are fully compatible with Economic Democracy. Family farming is *not* capitalist agriculture. Ideally (i.e., in accordance with the theoretical model) the land should be leased from the state, but at the practical level the question of ownership is not central. Private ownership of land need not be a concern, so long as an assets tax is employed and wage labor is restricted.

Both forms of agricultural organization can be effective. Which form, or what mix of the two, is most appropriate is a question that should be settled pragmatically and may well have different answers in different countries.[70] So long as family farms and cooperatives are provided with the necessary support structures (i.e., technical advice, access to capital, decent infrastructure), there is little reason to doubt their viability.

As for workplace democracy in industry, here the evidence is less clear. Peter Abell and Nicholas Mahoney's study of small-scale industrial cooperatives in Peru, Senegal, and India found that most of them (though by no means all) failed. The primary reason, they found, was not lack of capital, but lack of effective management. They also found "an almost perfect correspondence between the success of the co-operative and what one might term its high level of solidarity, and conversely, between failure and low solidarity."[71]

These findings point to the crucial importance of education, not only in technical skills but also in cooperative values (also a lesson of Mondragon). Needless to say, lack of education is a problem in much of the Third World. Educational facilities often are in short supply, and people who have been fortunate enough to have received a good education often emigrate north. At the same time, we should remember that education is highly labor-intensive and is amenable to creative experimentation.

The lack of educated personnel does not always negate the value of cooperatives. As Abell and Mahoney observe, "one was often amazed

---

[70] It is worth noting that, contrary to what is widely believed, collective agriculture is not inherently inferior to private agriculture. There is evidence, for example, that the private farms in Yugoslavia (the bulk of the agriculture there) were significantly less efficient and less productive than the cooperative farms (Boyd, 1987). Moreover, as Robert McIntyre (1991a) has observed, "agriculture in the East is highly mechanized, basically free of stoop labor and migratory harvesting as a way of life.... Pressure to break up collectives has come either from ideologically driven reformers who assume that the logic of privatization they propose for industry and city services must apply to the countryside as well, or from individuals hoping to make short-term speculative gains from acquiring and selling off land – very few are interested in going into small-scale agricultural production themselves" (pp. 179–80). McIntyre also points out (pp. 182–3) that statistics often have been flagrantly misapplied to "prove" the inefficiencies of socialist agriculture.

[71] Abell and Mahoney (1988, pp. 365–7).

how *well* they managed, given their level of expertise and education."[72] But this lack does point to the vital importance of intensifying educational efforts and organizing cooperatives in groups with support structure (as in Mondragon, and as proposed in our model), so as to enhance their effectiveness in utilizing the skills that they have.

I have given some reasons and cited some evidence for thinking that a form of socialism featuring social control of investment, a market for goods and services, and workplace democracy is a viable model for Third World countries wanting to meet their basic needs and engage in rational development. Two important examples will provide additional (if incomplete) empirical confirmation: Yugoslavia (1950–80) and China (post-1978). Let me elaborate briefly on each and address some misgivings.

As was documented in Chapter 2, Yugoslavia, in the three decades following its break with the Soviet Union and the command-socialism model, transformed itself from a poor, overwhelmingly rural, underdeveloped country into one whose standard of living was well beyond "Third World." By 1980, Yugoslavia stood at the very top of the list of low-income and middle-income countries in per-capita GNP. Its growth rate between 1960 and 1980 was second only to South Korea's; its GNP per capita was nearly double that country's.[73]

But then, from 1980 on, the Yugoslav economy began to deteriorate. In the 1990s its social fabric was torn apart by ethnic hatred (proof positive, if proof be needed, that it is easier to destroy than to build). What happened? How does one account for success turning into such tragic failure? Let me offer, without proof, a short answer, and then elaborate on one of its components. The short answer is this: In order to compensate for the structural flaws in the economic system, the Yugoslav government borrowed heavily from Western banks. The loans were not used effectively. When the low interest rates of the "petrodollar" 1970s became the high interest rates of the Reagan 1980s, the game was up.

What were these "structural flaws" in an economy that at least roughly approximated the model proposed here? Vanek lists seven conditions necessary for an optimal self-managed economy and argues that Yugoslavia violated them all. The four most crucial:[74]

1. *Full democratic self-management of independent, accountable, and viable firms.* In Yugoslavia, most directors were in fact chosen by local politicians. Moreover, firms losing money were almost always bailed out.

---

[72] Ibid., p. 376.
[73] See Sen (1984, p. 490).
[74] Vanek (1990, pp. 180–2). His other three: absence of monopolistic tendencies, existence of support structures, and equal access to technology.

2. *Selling and buying of all goods at competitive prices.* The Yugoslav markets were badly distorted by monopolistic price fixing, arbitrary government price controls, and an unrealistic exchange rate.
3. *Free exit and entry of firms.* In Yugoslavia, failing firms were not allowed to go under, and groups of individuals who wanted to form new firms were prohibited from doing so.
4. *Hiring of capital by firms at scarcity-reflecting and equal real interest rates.* For a long period, firms paid a negative real interest rate, and so they borrowed excessively.

As we know, the institutions of Economic Democracy do not share these defects. There is reason to agree with Vanek that the real lesson to be learned from Yugoslavia is not that worker self-management does not work, but that any country "which will try that path and avoid the design imperfections [of Yugoslavia] should do exceedingly well."[75]

The Chinese experience is also relevant to the case for Economic Democracy in the Third World. By the late 1970s, China had succeeded to a remarkable degree in feeding and educating its more than 1 billion people and in providing them with basic health care. But China was still a very poor country. To break through what seemed to be a major impasse, the government of Deng Xiaoping launched in 1978 a series of reforms aimed at drastically modifying the economic, political, and social structures of Chinese society. This reform process, which is still in flux, has generated an intense debate within and outside China. The economy has been radically decentralized. Prices have been selectively decontrolled, and market relations introduced. The agricultural collectives have been disbanded and replaced by the "contract responsibility system," which gives each household a plot of land and considerable freedom to decide what to produce and how to go about it.

Many on the Left see these reforms as presaging a return to capitalism.[76] I do not agree. This judgment strikes me as quite premature. To be sure, Deng has proclaimed that "to be rich is glorious."[77] To be sure, there are now joint ventures, some genuinely capitalist enterprises (some of which are undeniably exploitative), and a stock market of sorts. But the fact remains, private ownership of the means of production is still very limited in China. The agricultural collectives have been disbanded, but the land (worked now by individual households) still belongs to the state. The large urban enterprises are virtually all state-owned. The

---

[75] Vanek (1990, p. 182).
[76] For a most forceful presentation of this case, see Hinton (1990).
[77] Nee (1989, p. 184) argues that this slogan, repeated incessantly by the media for a time, was aimed at reassuring peasants that the government really did support entrepreneurial ventures and would not suddenly reverse policies. Given Chinese history since the revolution, assurances were not unwarranted.

township enterprises typically are owned by the villages in which they are located. It is quite wrong to think that the Chinese economy has become privatized. Philip Huang's research on the Yangze Delta has led him to conclude:

Collective organizations actually thrived as never before in new sidelines and industries, even if the administrative nomenclature changed from brigade to administrative village and from commune to township. In Huayangquio and indeed in the Yangze delta area as a whole, almost all industrial enterprises and highly capitalized sidelines were still under collective auspices as the 1980s came to a close.[78]

The reforms have had a major impact. China registered an annual growth rate of 10.3 percent between 1980 and 1988, the highest in Asia.[79] The number of rural Chinese below the poverty line fell from 200 million in 1979 to 70 million in 1986, "a striking decline of which there are few parallels."[80] The production of consumer goods has grown phenomenally. Refrigerators and TV sets increased from practically zero to annual outputs of 7.5 and 25 million, respectively. As M. J. Gordon points out, "for many products considered luxuries a decade ago, China has become or will soon become the world's largest producer."[81]

One of the most significant accomplishments of the reform process has been a drastic reduction of the income gap between city and country. This reduction has been accomplished by doing what both Gandhi and Mao tried but failed to do: bring industry to the countryside. More than any other single factor, this light industrialization of rural China seems to account for the rise in agricultural productivity, the closing of the city–country income gap, and the lifting of more than 100 million people out of poverty.[82]

By no means do I want to suggest that the Chinese reforms have been unproblematic. There have been many charges of corruption, as well as many charges that infrastructure has been neglected.[83] There is even statistical evidence that life expectancy has declined somewhat and that infant mortality among girls (but not among boys) has increased

---

[78] Huang (1990, p. 220). He adds that private enterprise may have played a larger role in Fujian-Guangdong and Wenzhou, but "collective enterprises still accounted for two-thirds [of] the gross income of all rural enterprises in China in 1986." Most of the noncollective income is from household (not capitalist) enterprises.
[79] Gordon (1992, p. 56), citing World Bank figures.
[80] Drèze and Sen (1989, p. 216).
[81] Gordon (1992, p. 55).
[82] This is the basic thesis, persuasively argued, of Huang (1990). We have now, he says, a model different from that of the "Maoist conservatives" in its decontrol of the economy and different from that of the "radical reformers" who want private property and a free market. "It is, in short, a model and vision for entrepreneurial initiatives within a socialist system of ownership" (Huang, 1990, p. 286).
[83] See Hinton (1990) for some graphic examples.

sharply.[84] Public-health efforts have dropped off significantly. The "bare-foot doctors" have just about disappeared. China has by no means solved all its problems.

It should be borne in mind, however, just how enormous are the constraints within which China must operate, and how great have been its accomplishments. China is the size of the United States (without Alaska), but it has five times the population and one-third the arable land. In the space of forty years (after more than a century of foreign domination) it has been transformed from a state of abject poverty into one that is both moderately prosperous and, by international standards, extremely egalitarian. The Japanese "miracle," it seems to me, pales in comparison.

Postreform China is an experiment in market socialism. I do not think this should be denied. The Chinese leadership says that is what it is (rather than a transition to capitalism), and the evidence thus far supports that claim. The leadership also claims to be democratizing the economy. "Without democracy," says Deng Xiaoping, "there can be no socialism."[85] In the aftermath of Tiananmen Square, June 1989, this no doubt rings hollow. But the fact is that since 1978 the Chinese leadership has instituted measures purporting to enhance the operation of democracy in society at large, within the Communist Party, and also in the workplace.[86] The 1984 "Reform Decision" states that

the well-spring of vitality of the enterprise lies in the initiative, wisdom, and creativeness of its workers by hand and brain.... In restructuring the urban economy, it is imperative to handle correctly the relationship of the workers and staff to their enterprises so that they are its real masters.[87]

The evidence is mixed as to implementation. Work councils are reported to exist in 34,000 state enterprises.[88] Jeanne Wilson, however, sees genuine decentralization and less party control, but little effort at encouraging worker participation, much less workplace democracy.[89] In the country-

---

[84] See Drèze and Sen (1989, pp. 216–21). The change is quite shocking. In 1978 the rates for boys and girls were virtually identical. The mortality among girls is now twice that among boys. The change doubtless is linked to China's strict limitation on family size, coupled with its historical misogyny, but perhaps also to the family contract system and the decline of publicly provided social support.

[85] Quoted by Wilson (1987, p. 298).

[86] Ibid., pp. 299–300. See also Ware (1992a), who demonstrates that the Chinese conception of democracy differs in significant ways from the prevailing Western conception. Ware does not find in these differences a compelling justification for the Tiananmen massacre (nor do I), but his analysis is a good antidote to excessive Western cynicism about Chinese claims concerning the expansion of democracy.

[87] Wilson (1987, p. 302)

[88] Bayat (1991, p. 103), citing a figure from 1981.

[89] Wilson (1987): "Although the functions and powers delegated to the workers' congresses appear extensive on paper, a closer examination of the workers' congress regulations reveals that all resolutions and proposals passed by the workers' congress are dependent on the [appointed] factory manager for implementation" (p. 311).

side, enterprises are usually set up by the townships or villages, but they do not appear to be run democratically.[90] At least not yet. Enterprise democracy would seem to be a logical next step, fully compatible with the ideology and institutions now in place. Whether or not it is the step that will be taken (abruptly or gradually) remains to be seen.[91]

The experiences of Yugoslavia and China provide evidence (suggestive, if not wholly conclusive) that the basic institutions of Economic Democracy will be viable in a Third World context. Both countries (during the relevant periods) have employed a mixture of plan and market in a noncapitalist setting (and, to a degree, workplace democracy) and have achieved impressive results. Obviously, Economic Democracy is not a magic recipe, with success guaranteed. But given the evidence at hand, and given that the alternatives would seem to be either a form of command socialism or some form of capitalism, Economic Democracy (perhaps modified in certain details) would seem to be a goal worth pursuing.[92]

If it is agreed that Economic Democracy is a desirable, viable model for a Third World movement seeking fundamental change, the transition question now comes to the fore. How does one get from here to there? But because initial conditions are so important here, and because they vary so enormously, not much can be said beyond a few generalities. A revolution of the Chinese or Cuban type would eliminate a major problem. There can be little doubt that the landlord-capitalist class stands as a major obstacle to social reform in most parts of the Third World. It is a class that rarely hesitates to call in, or ally with, the most savage and antidemocratic elements of the local "security" forces whenever its property is threatened. But it must also be said that such a revolution likely would involve an exodus of people whose skills are needed and likely would bring on a concerted attempt by the United States (or perhaps some other advanced capitalist country) to wreck the economy of the postrevolutionary society.

Is a more peaceful road to socialism possible? None has yet been demonstrated, in either the Third World or the First. It does not follow that

---

[90] See Huang (1990, ch. 12) for an account of rural industrialization.

[91] I do not want to say that a capitalist restoration is impossible in China, although I see that as highly unlikely. I would not rule out a hybrid system, neither capitalist nor socialist nor democratic. The future of China remains very much an open question.

[92] It should be observed that there is deep pessimism these days among mainstream economists that *anything* will work in the Third World. Being mainstream, they do not take socialism seriously, but they do not see much hope for capitalism either. See Thurow (1992, ch. 6). The recent figures are indeed grim. *The Economist*, April 25, 1992, p. 48, reports that the gap between rich nations and poor has doubled over the past thirty years. The countries where the richest 20 percent of the world's population live have increased their share of the world's total income from 70.2 percent in 1960 to 82.7 percent today.

such a road is impossible. In the first section of this chapter I pointed to some struggles worth waging in an advanced capitalist country so as to move us in the direction of Economic Democracy. Similar struggles may be appropriate in many Third World countries. Many are in fact under way.[93] Others may have to be invented. We know for certain that people will continue to resist the ravages of capitalism. We know that social, political, and economic conditions are in flux. It seems not unreasonable to think that the progressive forces in the Third World, who have accomplished miracles before, may do so again.

[93] See Bayat (1991) for an excellent overview of the struggle for workers' control and self-management in the Third World today.

8. Other socialisms

There no longer exists any sound ethical or economic justification for capitalism. That is the central proposition of this book. I have laid out the argument. I hope the reader has been persuaded. I do not deny that capitalism may once have been a progressive social formation, but those days have passed. If capitalism persists, it is not because there is no viable, more desirable socialist alternative but because those who most profit from the capitalist system still have sufficient power to block the emergence of any such new order.

In making the case against capitalism, I have elaborated one such alternative and have argued at length that this form of socialism, which I have labeled Economic Democracy, is preferable to capitalism on both economic and ethical grounds. What I have not shown is that Economic Democracy is the *best* alternative. That proposition is not necessary for the main argument. If there is at least one viable alternative to capitalism that better accords with our basic values, then capitalism is no longer justified.

I happen to think that Economic Democracy *is* the best feasible alternative to capitalism in the present historical period. In this chapter, for the sake of completeness, I defend this judgment. I attempt no exhaustive treatment of the topic, but let us consider several alternative models of socialism and see how they stack up against Economic Democracy.

Command socialism

It is not exactly controversial these days (as it once was, not so long ago) to say that command socialism (i.e., the Soviet model) is deeply flawed.[1] But it is important to understand the specific nature of its defects, especially because the failure of that model is so often taken as evidence that socialism per se cannot work.

Command socialism is the economic form once *identified* with socialism: central planning by the state. A government planning board assumes control of the entire economy. It specifies quantitative and qualitative output quotas for each production unit, the inputs and technologies to

---

[1] This section is but a slight modification of my earlier critique (Schweickart, 1980), which seems to me to have well stood the test of recent events. For more exhaustive analyses, see Nove (1983, Part Two) or Kornai (1992, Part Two).

be used, the prices to be charged, and the wages to be paid.[2] All economic mystification dissolves, because human agents consciously decide what gets produced, and how, and to whom it is distributed.

Unfortunately, this model, conceptually so clear, is subject to serious practical difficulties. First, there is the sheer immensity of the task at hand. "The essential point," says Alec Nove (one of the most perceptive and persistent critics on the Left of this model's economic flaws),

is that in most instances *the centre does not know* just what it is that needs doing, in disaggregate detail, while the management in its situation *cannot* know what it is that society needs unless the centre informs it. . . . The trouble lies in the near impossibility of drafting micro-economic instruments in such a way that even the most well-meaning manager will not be misled.[3]

Consider a single example: the production of sheet steel. The planning center must specify a quota for each factory. In what units? Suppose tons are selected. Then the factory manager, who has no other information on which to base his decision, will tend to produce thick sheets, because it is more "efficient" to satisfy the quota that way. If square meters are selected instead, he will tend to produce sheets as thin as possible.[4] If the planning center wants to be more specific, detailing tons, thicknesses, various grades, and so forth, it must collect the relevant information from all the potential users in the country, aggregate it properly, and then distribute it correctly to all the enterprises producing sheet steel, an enormously complicated task fraught with many possibilities for error. All this for just one product – and the planning board must plan for all the products of society.[5]

The difficulty of collecting and disseminating the appropriate information, even when everyone is cooperating honestly and fully, is but one of the fundamental problems with central planning. Equally problematic is the *incentive structure*. Why should a manager be truthful about his factory's input needs and production capabilities? Because he will be rewarded for fulfilling (or overfulfilling) the plan, it makes sense to ask for more inputs than are needed and to understate one's capacities. The planners, of course, recognize this tendency, so they are inclined to set the target higher than what the firm says it can meet and to offer fewer

---

[2] For a more detailed exposition of how this works, see Kornai (1992, ch. 7).

[3] Nove (1977, p. 85). I consider Nove to be a Left critic, despite his recent warning to readers that "some [reviewers] have put me a good deal further to the left than I really am" Nove (1991, p. ix). That Nove is far from conservative is evident in his denunciations of Chicago economics for its "inappropriate incrementalism, misplaced marginalism, and myopic monetarism" Nove (1989, p. 108).

[4] Nove (1977, p. 94) cites a cartoon published in *Krokodil*, showing an enormous nail hanging in a large workshop: "The month's plan fulfilled," says the director, pointing to the nail. In tons, of course.

[5] Nove (1983, p. 101) observes that in the Soviet Union the number of products, fully disaggregated, was estimated as being between 10 and 12 million.

inputs than the firm says it needs. But such adjustments, rational from the point of view of the planners, serve to penalize forthright managers, thus fostering further deception and breeding cynicism.

There is also little incentive for efficient utilization of the inputs received. On the one hand, if a firm increases its efficiency by conserving inputs, it can expect fewer the following period. If it reorganizes production so as to increase its output, it can expect its quota to be raised the following period. On the other hand, if it does not produce efficiently, there are few penalties. In practice, firms in a command economy operate under a "soft budget constraint." That is to say, firms never fail. If quotas cannot be met, they will be adjusted downward.[6]

One must keep all this in perspective. For all its inefficiencies (gleefully recorded by neoclassical economists), the Soviet economy in its classical form survived for well over half a century. Command socialism worked imperfectly, but it worked. In some respects it worked better than Western capitalism. In some respects it was *more efficient* than Western capitalism. There was far less unemployment and virtually no nonrational sales persuasion. Both unemployment and nonrational sales persuasion, recall, are also efficiency defects.

Of course, one would be hard pressed to show that these efficiency gains offset the profound and deep-rooted inefficiencies noted earlier, but efficiency, after all, is but one value by which to judge an economic system, and hardly the most important one in a relatively affluent society. Judged in terms of *equality*, command socialism has tended to outperform capitalism. In the Soviet Union, for example, the ratio of the income of the top manager of an enterprise to that of an average manual worker was about 4 : 1.[7] In the United States it often exceeds 100 : 1. The provision of free health care and education, and very low cost housing, also had an equalizing effect. Even Hungarian economist Janos Kornai, now a fierce critic of all forms of socialism, concedes that "ultimately, if one considers all dimensions of material welfare in the whole of society under the classical socialist system, the inequality is less than it is under the present capitalist system."[8]

If we compare command socialism with Economic Democracy, we see at once that the latter will not be prone to the inefficiencies associated with the former. The information and incentive problems so basic to a command economy will not exist under Economic Democracy, because

---

[6] It was thought, for a while, that this efficiency problem could be resolved by instructing the firm's manager to maximize the value of the produced goods relative to the costs of labor and material inputs (all quantities valorized in terms of the given prices). But the soft budget constraint simply reappears in another guise. If a firm fails to cover its costs (as often happens), it can almost always negotiate subsidies, price adjustments, credits, or tax breaks. See Kornai (1986), the originator of the term "soft budget constraint," for details.

[7] Bergson (1984, pp. 1085–6).   [8] Kornai (1992, p. 332).

these are precisely the problems that a market economy effectively resolves. Of course, being a market economy, Economic Democracy must tolerate income inequalities.[9] As we have seen, these will be substantially less than under capitalism. Whether or not they will be less than what is likely to be the case in a command economy cannot be answered a priori. Because wages are set by the center, command socialism can, in theory, choose whatever degree of equality (or inequality) it wishes. In practice it must balance the need for material incentives against the need for ideological legitimacy and the constraints imposed by political democracy (if the society should be democratic).[10]

Suppose it could be shown that in a given situation command socialism would be more egalitarian than Economic Democracy. Its advantage on this score must be counterposed not only to its inefficiencies but also to its deficiencies with respect to other important values. The most serious objection to command socialism is not to its inefficiency (although the demoralizing effects of waste and irrationality should not be discounted) but, rather, to its problematic relationships to both liberty and democracy.

Central planning requires centralized authority, and that implies a dangerous concentration of power. The classical liberal concern for liberty is not misguided here. In a command economy the government is the sole employer, and the government appoints the managers of all enterprises, including media enterprises. One can imagine constitutional safeguards for free expression, but general considerations of human behavior (to say nothing of the historical record) raise grave doubts as to their efficacy.

Is a command economy compatible with political democracy? In theory it is. Voters elect a government that appoints the planning board. But for precisely the reasons just noted, it would seem to be exceedingly difficult in practice (whatever the formal guarantees) for people out of power to challenge a sitting government that controls all employment and all the media.[11]

If one's commitment to democracy is based on a commitment to participatory autonomy, then command socialism becomes even more problematic. This value, we know, underlies a major indictment against

[9] It may also have more difficulty with unemployment and nonrational sales persuasion, although in neither case (for reasons previously elaborated) should the problem be as severe as under capitalism.

[10] Insofar as it is nondemocratic, a command economy is compatible with considerable inequality. That was the case in the Soviet Union, although the degree of inequality there was less than in most capitalist countries. See Bergson (1984) for a careful assessment. Whether or not a command economy must be nondemocratic will be taken up later.

[11] I use the phrase "people out of power" rather than "party out of power" so as not to imply that "political democracy" is synonymous with multiparty elections. The relationship between parties and democracy is quite a separate matter (and beyond the scope of this book) from the relationship of central planning to democracy.

capitalism, namely, its failure to bring democracy to the workplace. Command socialism is also vulnerable to this charge. In fact, I would contend that it is *not possible* for a centrally planned economy to grant genuine control of enterprises to their workers instead of to appointed managers – for two reasons. First, because the planning board sets production quotas, prices, inputs, and wages, there is little real scope for worker decisions and hence little real incentive for worker involvement. If workplace democracy is to be meaningful, workers must be able to make decisions that will have real consequences (negative as well as positive) for their well-being. Enterprises under command socialism lack sufficient autonomy for this to be the case.

Second, there is the problem of discipline. What would the central planners do if an enterprise failed to comply with the plan? They could try to discipline the entire work force, but such an approach could well provoke an antagonistic, disruptive reaction. It is far more "efficient" (from the point of view of the central planners) to appoint a director and make *her* responsible. But if she is responsible for quota fulfillment and for the other details spelled out in the plan, then she cannot be accountable to her work force. The tendency toward authoritarianism here seems to me irresistible.

If we tally up the comparisons, we find that Economic Democracy will be more efficient than command socialism, as well as freer and more democratic. It may or may not be more egalitarian, but any such discrepancy, if it should favor command socialism, cannot be expected to be so large as to overturn the clear superiority of Economic Democracy on these other counts.

Technocratic market socialism

Command socialism's lack of efficiency may not be the most serious charge against it, but its glaring defects in the realm of economic performance do not make it attractive, certainly not to people living in advanced capitalist societies, nor to those who have recently broken with their Communist past.

It might be conjectured that where socialism went wrong, historically, was in trying to change things too drastically. Nothing even remotely resembling the central planning of an entire economy had ever before been attempted, so it is not altogether surprising that it did not work out.[12] If one wants to move from capitalism to socialism, perhaps a few

[12] It should be mentioned that comprehensive central planning as the economic model for socialism was not advocated by Marx, who refused to "write recipes for cookshops of the future" Marx (1967, p. 17), nor was it implemented by Lenin. It was well after Lenin's death that Stalin cut short the Soviet experiment with a capitalist–socialist mixed economy (NEP, which lasted until 1928) and began to put into place the basic institutions of command socialism.

far simpler changes could be made (simpler even than the changes envisaged under Economic Democracy), with resulting gains in both economic performance and equality. Forget about central planning, it might be urged: Why not simply nationalize all enterprises, keep the market, and instruct all corporate executives to continue as before at maximizing profits, but return the proceeds not to the owners (who will have been expropriated) but to the state, which may then either use them for investment purposes or return them as a social dividend to the citizenry?

This is the essential notion underlying what I shall call "technocratic market socialism," by which I mean any form of socialism that assigns a central role to the market, but not to worker self-management. Technocratic market socialism eschews central planning, but does not embrace workplace democracy. It need not disavow *all* planning, but (like Economic Democracy) it retains the market as the basic institution for coordinating the production and distribution of most goods and services.

The intellectual origins of this form of socialism can be traced back to the academic debates of the 1920s and 1930s that pitted (among others) Oscar Lange and Fred Taylor (proponents) against Ludwig von Mises and Friedrich Hayek (critics of all forms of socialism).[13] Two recent proponents, whose specific proposals we shall examine in this section, are the economists James Yunker and John Roemer.[14]

The fundamental problem facing technocratic market socialism is what is often called "the principal-agent problem": how to structure incentives so as to ensure that the will of the principal will be carried out by subordinate agents – in this case, how to ensure that corporate managers will indeed strive to maximize profits. In the traditional, owner-run capitalist firm, the problem does not arise, because the owner and manager are one. In a capitalist corporation, the corporate leadership is monitored by the stockholders.[15] Under technocratic market socialism, how will this monitoring be carried out?

James Yunker, who has been advocating what he calls "pragmatic

---

[13] This was discussed briefly in Chapter 3. See Lavoie (1985) for a detailed account (from the perspective of one sympathetic to von Mises and Hayek).

[14] Another proponent is Leland Stauber, a long-standing advocate of market socialism. Because his model is so similar to Yunker's, I do not give it separate treatment. (It is closer to my own model than is Yunker's in certain respects: The investment fund is generated by taxation and is allocated via community banks.) See Stauber (1977, 1987) for details.

It should be noted that there is a significant difference between contemporary proponents of technocratic market socialism and its earlier advocates. The early advocates were concerned to develop rules for enterprise managers that would ensure that the economy would *simulate* a competitive economy. Contemporary advocates want *real* competition.

[15] A large debate (which need not concern us here) has developed in recent years concerning the effectiveness of such monitoring. See Jensen (1989) and the rebuttals in the November–December 1989 issue of the *Harvard Business Review*.

market socialism" for nearly three decades, succinctly summarizes his model as follows:

The economic role of the capitalist class of establishing a profit maximization incentive among the corps of corporation executives would be taken over by a national government agency called the Bureau of Public Ownership (BPO). All property return currently received by private individuals under capitalism would, under pragmatic market socialism, be received by the BPO. The BPO would retain approximately five percent of this return to cover its administrative expenses, and the rest would be paid out to the general public in the form of a social dividend. Generally speaking, everything else would remain the same.[16]

Let me fill in some details. In essence, Yunker proposes that all income-producing financial instruments issued by large-scale, established corporations and currently owned by private individuals would be turned over to the BPO, which would (1) monitor the management of these corporations to see that they continue to operate as before, according to established principles of sound corporate management, and (2) collect all the dividends and interest to which the BPO is entitled as owner of these stocks and bonds, and then return that sum (less operating expenses) to the general public, distributing it to individuals as a social dividend.

To ensure effective monitoring, the BPO would employ several thousand BPO agents, recruited from the ranks of experienced corporate executives. Each would be assigned the role of monitoring the management of several corporations and would receive, as income, a percentage of the profits of those corporations, a percentage set high enough to make the position highly attractive. If a corporation performed poorly, the BPO agent in charge would have the power to dismiss the executive officers and hire new ones.

The point of these arrangements is to eliminate (most) property income – or rather to redistribute it – while retaining all the efficiency strengths of capitalism. The BPO agent would simply fill the role currently played by a corporation's board of directors. Because his income, like theirs, would be tied to company performance, he, like they, would have an incentive to monitor effectively. (The BPO agent himself would be monitored by the BPO central staff, which would be responsible for recruiting the agents and for collecting statistical data useful to the BPO agents.)

It should be pointed out that only large, established corporations would be subject to these arrangements. Small businesses would function as

[16] Yunker (1986a, p. 65). Yunker (1992, p. xi) tells us that the basic concept of pragmatic market socialism was developed in his undergraduate senior thesis at Fordham University in 1964–5. Since then, he has written a large number of articles and two books on the topic. What follows draws primarily on these works: Yunker (1979, 1982, 1986a,b, 1992). Yunker (1992) provides an excellent summary presentation of his work in this area to date.

before. So the BPO need not be large.[17] Also exempt would be any enterprise still being managed by its founder-owner. This would preserve the entrepreneurial incentive. One could still capitalize on a good idea and get rich.

Yunker claims two basic advantages for his model vis-à-vis capitalism: It would be more egalitarian, because property income would no longer be so concentrated,[18] and it would be more efficient, because monitoring would be more effective.[19] He argues further that with the addition of two more institutions, a National Investment Bank System (NIBS) and a National Entrepreneurial Investment Board (NEIB), it would be more dynamic in its growth.[20]

Does he have a case? Frankly, I think he does. If he does not, then, of course, Economic Democracy is unambiguously preferable to pragmatic market socialism. But he is probably right: Pragmatic market socialism should be at least as efficient as capitalism. The main question is the effectiveness of the BPO, but as Roemer has pointed out,

the current debate on the relationship of corporate control to the stock market in the United States, and the experience of Japan, where banks rather than the stock market effectively monitor corporate management and evaluate investment projects, suggest the possibility of effective monitoring of public firm management by a bureau of industrial experts employed by the government.[21]

If the overall economy were to perform as efficiently under pragmatic market socialism as under capitalism, it can scarcely be doubted that there would be a large gain in equality. The reader will recall our discussion of inequality under capitalism. The massive inequalities of contemporary capitalism are sustained by the flows of property income. Pragmatic market socialism would cut deeply into these.

One might worry that without capitalists there would be insufficient savings to finance investment. This legitimate concern is answered under pragmatic market socialism much as it is under Economic Democracy

---

[17] For the U.S. economy, Yunker (1986b) estimates that a central staff 2,000–3,000 and agents numbering 5,000–6,000 would suffice.

[18] Yunker (1982) calculates that if property income were distributed in proportion to wage and salary income, more than 90 percent of the population of the United States would receive more current income under pragmatic market socialism than they do now.

[19] See Yunker (1979). His main argument is that the diffusion of stock ownership has diminished stockholder control in most corporations to the point that management would now be more effectively monitored by a single, highly qualified agent whose income would be tightly linked to enterprise profit.

[20] Yunker (1986a, pp. 74ff.). These institutions are to supplement existing savings and investing agencies. The NIBS would make loans to businesses for physical capital; the NEIB would encourage entrepreneurial business ventures.

[21] Roemer (1990, p. 5). There is also evidence of many public firms being well run with even less monitoring than is proposed by Yunker. See Vickers and Yarrow (1991).

(though less radically): If there were a shortfall in savings, it would be made up by taxation and channeled into the economy via public investment banks (the NIBS and NEIB noted earlier).[22] These mechanisms resemble those of Economic Democracy so closely that their efficacy need not be questioned here.

I am prepared to grant that pragmatic market socialism is economically viable and more desirable than capitalism. As such, it could substitute for Economic Democracy as the comparative term in the general argument against capitalism. Its weakness vis-à-vis Economic Democracy, however, is obvious: It would have no workplace democracy. So the various strengths we have found to be associated with this feature would be missing: greater X-efficiency, more participatory autonomy, a more desirable labor–leisure trade-off, an economy whose stability is less dependent on nonrational sales persuasion and on economic growth.

There is another problem with this model, of a very different nature. It was proposed in Chapter 7 that if it is not possible to get from here to there, then there is not much to be gained in debating alternatives to capitalism (apart from certain intellectual and moral satisfactions). If the transition problem is intractable, what's the point?

Of course, it is not *logically* impossible to get from where we are to pragmatic market socialism. One can always conjure up a revolution or a massive electoral triumph that would give the government the power to institute whatever changes it wished. But if we are to avoid an appeal to such a deus ex machina, we must be able to point to real forces and tendencies pushing in the direction suggested by the model. This we can do for Economic Democracy: a growing cooperative movement, pressure to extend worker participation in production, efforts to contain the mobility of capital, to wrest it from the logic of the market and bring it under community control, and so forth. But not so for pragmatic market socialism. There is no evidence, so far as I can see (nor does Yunker claim there is), of *any* movement to nationalize our established corporations and replace stockholders with government agents.[23] Something like that may once have been the goal of social democratic movements when they still considered themselves socialist, but those days have long passed.

[22] Yunker (1986a, p. 74). Under pragmatic market socialism, taxation would merely supplement private savings. Under Economic Democracy, taxation will *replace* private savings (as the source of investment funds).

[23] Yunker (1979, p. 108, n. 46) recommends, "in the interests of both justice and political feasibility," that owners be compensated, but he says nothing about the intensity of capitalist opposition to such a proposal, nor why one should expect it to succeed in the face of such opposition. His discussion of transition (Yunker, 1992) is essentially a call for "a campaign of enlightenment against the forces of entrenched ignorance and prejudice. It would be a peaceful, unhurried, good-natured campaign based on genuinely friendly persuasion" (p. 280).

At bottom, we are looking at values. The appeal of pragmatic market socialism is to greater *efficiency* and greater material *equality*. These values also play roles in Economic Democracy, but more central is *democracy* – democracy grounded in participatory autonomy. I think that democracy touches the deeper chord. If Samuel Bowles and Herbert Gintis are right (and they make a good case) that the social history of the past several centuries can best be characterized as a series of struggles to extend democracy, then Economic Democracy, more desirable in its own right than pragmatic market socialism, is also a more realistic goal for those seeking fundamental change.[24]

In recent years, John Roemer, working with other colleagues, has turned his formidable intellectual capacities in the direction of market socialism.[25] If the transition problem is the Achilles' heel of Yunker's model, the same cannot be said so readily of Roemer's "bank-centered market socialism," which is set out explicitly as a viable alternative to the privatization schemes now all the rage in Eastern Europe.[26]

Roemer regards the agency problem as the most serious problem for market socialism. To deal with it, he proposes a structure that bears a striking resemblance to one of the features of Economic Democracy: Firms will be clustered into financial groups, at the center of which a government "main bank" will serve as their principal monitor.[27]

In Roemer's model, however, these firms will not be democratically run, nor will they be owned (in unmediated fashion) by society. Each (public) firm will be a joint-stock company.[28] These shares will be distributed among (1) the main bank, (2) the workers in the firm, and (3)

[24] Bowles and Gintis (1986, ch. 2).

[25] Roemer is best known for his 1982 treatise, *A General Theory of Exploitation and Class*, a mathematically elegant, philosophically sophisticated tour de force that transformed our understanding of Marxian exploitation. Recently he has authored (and coauthored) a number of works on market socialism. In what follows, I shall draw on Roemer (1989, 1990, 1991, 1992), Ortuño-Ortin, Roemer, and Silvestre (1990, 1991), and Bardhan and Roemer (1992). Although the basic model is clearly the product of joint research, I shall refer to it as "the Roemer model."

[26] This is so in Bardhan and Roemer (1992), although not in the other works cited. Bardhan and Roemer (1992) also present, as a variation of their model that might also be suitable as an alternative to capitalism in Eastern Europe, a "clamshell" economy involving stock vouchers for all adults. I shall not discuss that here, because the differences are not significant to the argument at hand. For the most comprehensive description and defense of Roemer's basic model, see Roemer (1991).

[27] I do not think the resemblance is wholly accidental, even though the inspirations for the two were different. This feature of Economic Democracy was derived from the experience of Mondragon; for Roemer, it came from the Japanese *keiretsu*. This form, which is also found (somewhat modified) in Germany and South Korea, is proving itself in a variety of contexts to be capable of resolving many of the problems faced by modern firms in a market economy.

[28] Public firms are those structured as described. As we shall see, there will also be some private (i.e., traditional capitalist) firms in the economy.

other firms in the group.[29] The board of directors of each company will thus be composed of representatives from each of these constituencies, and each of these constituencies will be entitled to a share of the profits.

This financial stake will have a motivational effect on each. For the workers of a given firm, their share of their firm's profits will supplement their wages and thus motivate them to work efficiently. For the member firms of the group, their share of the profits of co-member firms will supplement their other revenues and thus motivate them to monitor each other. For the main bank, its share of the profits of all the member firms, together with the interest payments it receives, will constitute its entire income. This sum will serve as tangible proof of performance, thus motivating it to keep a watchful eye on each firm in its group and to look out for the economic well-being of the group as a whole.

Because the main bank will be a *state* bank, its income (from its share holdings and loan portfolio) will be public income. This will be returned to the general public (after deducting for expenses) in accordance with a politically determined formula. Thus, each worker will receive income from four sources: her wage, a share of the profits of her own firm, a share of the profits of the other firms in her cluster, and, finally, a social dividend.

How do these arrangements solve the various agency problems of a complex economy? Each of the agents, we observe, will have multiple monitors. Workers will monitor each other (because they will share in the firm's profits), and they will be monitored by management. The firm's management will be monitored by the board of directors, which will represent the interests of the workers, the main bank, and the other firms. The bank itself will be monitored directly by the political authorities, who will have a clear quantitative index of performance (the bank's net income), and indirectly by member firms, which will provide qualitative evaluations to these authorities.[30]

There is one feature of this monitoring system that deserves special attention. The main bank will serve as the principal monitor of each firm in its group, not only because of its strategic location with respect to finance but also because of a special provision in the model: If firm A in the group does not think that firm B is maximizing profits, firm A will be entitled to sell its shares in firm B back to the main bank. If that

[29] Roemer would also allow institutions outside the group to own shares: other financial institutions, pension funds, local governments, etc. Their total holdings, however, would be small in comparison with those of the other three constituencies, and so need not concern us here. (Actually, Roemer does not specify how a firm's stock would be apportioned among the various categories. I am presuming a roughly equal distribution among the three main ones, with a small percentage reserved for outside institutions.)

[30] This last provision is not mentioned by Roemer, but it seems to me sensible and in the spirit of his model.

occurs, it will serve as a signal from an independent source that a given firm is not doing well. If several firms follow suit, the main bank itself will have to take action, for if it is forced to buy back too much stock, its own cash flow will suffer.[31]

At the first signs of significant attempts by other firms at unloading the shares of a particular firm, and usually much earlier, the main bank will take measures to prod and discipline the management, renegotiate the debt contract if necessary, orchestrate financial rescue strategies, help the firm with an interest moratorium and emergency loans, and arrange for technological assistance from affiliated firms, and for the (temporary) sale of the firm's assets (in other firms) to cover its operating losses.[32]

Several other features of Roemer's model deserve special mention. He proposes a strategy similar to Yunker's in dealing with innovation. He believes that innovation will occur in the public firms, because these firms must compete with one another, but so as to allow for additional entrepreneurial incentive, traditional capitalist firms will continue to exist. Only when they reach a certain size will they be nationalized, and then with proper compensation.

For basically the same reasons put forth in my defense of Economic Democracy, Roemer's model incorporates a second feature: investment planning. Because of positive and negative externalities and other forms of market failure, "the market unaided will not achieve a socially desirable distribution of investment."[33] He proposes that this planning be market-conforming. He argues that investment planning is best done by offering a suitable mix of discounted interest rates.[34] If, as a result of this discounting, the demand for loans is too high, the investment fund will be supplemented by taxation.

Finally, Roemer's model is for a *democratic* socialism. He envisages a multiparty political democracy. With respect to the economy, each party, at election time, will put forth a platform with two planks: a proposal for distribution of the after-tax profits of all public firms, and a proposal for

---

[31] There appears to be a lacuna in the model here. Roemer does not say *at what price* the stock is to be repurchased. Ideally, the price should be what the stock would be worth if the company were well managed – but how is that to be determined? Presumably, some sort of stock market would exist, not for private individuals, but for other institutions that could purchase company stocks. One must wonder about the efficacy of such an arrangement.

[32] Bardhan and Roemer (1992, p. 108). That is to say, it will do what main banks in Japan typically do.

[33] Roemer (1991, p. 4).

[34] A formal proof of this proposition is offered by Ortuño-Ortin et al. (1991). Because of its formality and abstractness, however, one cannot give too much weight to its practical import. In practice, investment planning as advocated for Economic Democracy, which would use a combination of quantitative allocations and (in effect) interest-rate discounts, probably would be preferable. (If so, such a mechanism could be easily incorporated into the Roemer model.)

the level and pattern of investment for the economy. (The first plank might call for equal household distribution, or equal per-capita distribution, or distribution proportional to earned income, or perhaps distribution *inversely* proportional to income.[35] The second plank would emphasize various social priorities.)

This bank-centered market socialism has been proposed as an alternative to capitalism in Eastern Europe. Against it, one might raise the objection Roemer attributes to Martin Weitzman: "Why bother with all these complicated institutional arrangements which mimic capitalism, when you can have the real thing?"[36] Roemer and Bardhan offer a three-part response. It is argued that (1) the system will be more egalitarian, and (2) it will be less plagued by capitalist investment irrationality. Then (3) the transition issue is raised *against* capitalism:

The institutions of Western capitalism, including its legal, political and economic infrastructure, evolved over a long period of time. Some of them are not easily replicable. In fact the bank-centric organization that we describe is a way of mitigating an historical handicap in capital market institutions. It is important to realize that it was the underdevelopment of capital markets in late 19th century Germany that gave rise to the present system of heavy bank involvement in the financing and management of industrial companies.[37]

As in the case of Yunker's model, it is not necessary, for our purposes, to scrutinize the claim that this model is superior to capitalism.[38] The reader will not be surprised to learn that I agree with this claim. After all, the model resembles quite closely the one I have proposed: It features democratic control of investment, a market for goods and services, enterprises grouped around public banks, and profit sharing for workers. If Economic Democracy is viable, then this bank-centered market socialism should be viable. Because most of the firms will be public, and the profits of public firms will be more or less equally distributed, it will certainly be more egalitarian than capitalism. It will also be more democratic, because the capitalist class will no longer be privileged.

Curiously – and significantly – these two values, equality and democracy, are weighted differently in Roemer's model than they are in Economic Democracy. Roemer's market socialism tends to be more egalitarian

---

[35] Roemer (1991, pp. 3–4) objects to the distribution being proportional to income (which is Yunker's favored proposal). This is primarily for ethical reasons. Specifically, such a distribution would enhance, rather than mitigate, income derived from skills and talents – the basis for what Roemer (1982, p. 212) calls "socialist exploitation." (He also cites "severe efficiency problems," but he refers to an allocational argument that I do not find to have much real-world relevance.)

[36] Bardhan and Roemer (1992, p. 102).

[37] Ibid., p. 103. They note that in Japan, also, the main-bank system originated in highly imperfect financial markets.

[38] If it is not, then Economic Democracy is clearly preferable, because Economic Democracy clearly will be superior to capitalism.

than Economic Democracy, but less democratic. This, I think, is the essential difference between the two models.

There is not much difference between the two models economically. I do not think we can say, a priori, which system would be more efficient, more innovative, or more rational in its growth. Theoretically, firms under Economic Democracy will suffer a "horizon problem" with respect to investment that firms under Roemer's model will not. This fact could count against Economic Democracy, but, as was argued in Chapter 4, the horizon problem is not likely to be significant in practice. Firms under Economic Democracy should be more X-efficient, for the well-rehearsed reasons. This counts in favor of Economic Democracy, but because the firms in Roemer's system would engage in extensive profit sharing, this difference may not be significant either. Firms under Economic Democracy should be less expansionary, for the same reasons that they are less expansionary than capitalist firms. This, we have seen, counts both plus and minus. All in all, because so much depends on individual circumstances and specific institutional supplements, I do not think we can say which of the two systems would do better at promoting general material well-being overall. I do think we can say that under most circumstances, either should do better than capitalism.

As remarked earlier, the essential difference between the two models turns on a democracy–equality trade-off. Specifically, workplace democracy is attenuated in Roemer's model in favor of greater material equality.[39] The structural reason for this difference is this: Under Economic Democracy, all of a firm's after-tax profits will be returned to the workers of that firm. In Roemer's system, these after-tax profits will be redistributed to the whole of society, presumably in the direction of greater equality. There is a price to be paid for this greater equality: *Wage labor* will be retained. Managers will not be elected by the workers, but appointed by a board of directors. These managers will hire workers for a wage.

It should be noted that even this "essential" difference will not be as great as might be imagined, and it can be made even less so. Under Roemer's model, workers will receive some portion of their firm's profit, and they will have representation on their firm's board of directors. Workers *could* be granted extensive participatory rights. They could even be allowed to elect their managers, although the board would have to

---

[39] The trade-off is not, as Roemer (1989) suggests, democratic control of the workplace versus democratic control of the social surplus: "I remain an unreconstructed Marxist in believing that democratic control of the economic surplus, and not the workplace, is the real necessity for fundamental social change" (p. 99). Under Economic Democracy, democratic control of the economic surplus will be achieved, as it will in Roemer's model, by subjecting investment to democratic planning.

retain veto power. Such changes would enhance the democratic component of bank-centered market socialism.

If Roemer's model is more democratic than it might first appear, Economic Democracy is perhaps more egalitarian. Granted, firms will keep all their after-tax profits under Economic Democracy, but the tax, recall, will be on capital assets, and this revenue will be returned to the communities on a per-capita basis. If still more equality is desired, a progressive income tax is always an option.

The fact of the matter is that although Economic Democracy and bank-centered market socialism begin quite differently – the former taking workplace democracy as its starting point, the latter the need to socialize property income – their end points are not so far apart.[40]

Marketless participatory socialism

The same proximity of end point does not obtain for the final form of socialism that we shall consider. Suppose we keep workplace democracy at center stage, but reject both central planning and the market as a means of coordinating economic activities. Suppose we agree that central planning is inherently authoritarian and that the market is inherently alienating. We shall accept planning, but not centralized planning; we do not want the market at all. What we want is an economy coordinated by *decentralized, nonauthoritarian, democratic* planning.

Democratic socialists have long dreamed this dream, but its feasibility has repeatedly been called into question, sometimes quite bluntly. Alec Nove, for example, admits to feeling increasingly ill-disposed toward those who

substitute for hard thinking the image of a post-revolutionary world in which there would be no economic problems at all (or where any problems that might arise would be handled smoothly by the "associated producers" of a world commonwealth). . . . In a complex industrial economy the interrelation between its parts can be based in principle either on freely chosen negotiated contracts (which means autonomy and a species of commodity production) or on a system of binding instructions from planning offices. *There is no third way.*[41]

Michael Albert (co-editor and co-founder of *Z* magazine) and Robin Hahnel (professor of economics at American University) refuse to concede. Their 1978 book, *Unorthodox Marxism*, put forth a proposal for exactly

---

[40] There is an important argument that could be raised against the Roemer model: To the extent that it is intended to be relevant to current *capitalist* societies (structured along American lines), the transition objection raised against Yunker also applies. The model would not have much use as an orienting guide to political praxis.

[41] Nove (1983, pp. ix–x, 44).

that, a "third way" involving neither central planning nor the market, but it was widely criticized for its lack of feasibility.[42] Recently they have tried again, this time incorporating the use of computers into their model in a big way, so as to cope with that criticism.[43] To be fair, they deserve credit for thinking through in considerable detail a model for an egalitarian, participatory nonmarket economy. But I have to say that the proposal still seems to me quite mad.

Perhaps I am being too harsh. The reader should judge. The basic idea is simple enough. Start with Robinson Crusoe, alone on an island. He must choose a "work complex" (a pattern of work that will involve activities of differing degrees of pleasure and discomfort), a "consumption proposal" (what he would like to consume), and a "production proposal," (how much time he is willing to work). From among the infinite number of possible combinations of these three choices, he must settle on a set that will be consistent; that is to say, he must choose to put in a sufficient amount of time at an appropriate set of tasks that will satisfy his desired consumption.

Suppose Friday appears, and suppose that he and Robinson are committed to both participatory democracy and equality. They can doubtless benefit by cooperating, but the cooperation must be fair. Each says what he would like to consume, and how long he is willing to work. The two negotiate this matter, subject to the proviso that their job complexes, though not necessarily identical, be "balanced" (i.e., they involve roughly the same degrees of pleasure and discomfort).[44] Robinson may want to consume a bit more than Friday, but he will work longer. They discuss these matters – talk about the good and bad effects of various forms of consumption, point out what exactly is involved in doing various kinds of work.[45] In the end they agree on a plan. Notice: neither market nor central authority.

Now, extend this model from two persons to 250 million and you have the Albert-Hahnel model of a participatory economy for the United States.

---

[42] See Schweickart (1980, pp. 217–18) for a critique.

[43] For a popular presentation of the basic model, see Albert and Hahnel (1991a). For a more technical version, see Albert and Hahnel (1991b). For a shorter account, see Albert and Hahnel (1992).

[44] "Classlessness and real rather than merely formal workplace democracy *require* that each worker has a job complex composed of comparably fulfilling responsibilities" (Albert and Hahnel, 1991a, p. 19); emphasis in original.

[45] "To guard against 'reductionist accounting' each actor needs access to a list of everything that goes into producing goods directly and indirectly, and a description of what will be gained from consuming them. This means that those who produce and consume particular goods must try to communicate the qualitative human effects that cannot be captured in quantitative indicators. This does not entail everyone writing Upton Sinclair length novels about their work and living conditions. It does mean generating concise accounts that substitute for the fact that not everyone can personally experience every circumstance" (Albert and Hahnel, 1991b, pp. 61–2).

To be sure, things get a bit more complicated, but there are computers and various "facilitation boards" to make things easier.

For example, Jane Doe will not have to discuss her consumption with *everyone*. Initially she will simply type into her computer what she would like to consume for the year. She will get back (eventually) a record of average submissions, so she can see how she stands.[46] She can change her requests, and then resubmit. It is only at the third iteration that she will go to her neighborhood "consumption council." If her consumption is above average, she must try to persuade those in attendance to accept her list. There will also be a discussion of the possibly harmful effects of certain kinds of consumption that she and her neighbors have selected. (This will be done anonymously, for the most part; names will not be attached to consumption lists that do not exceed the average.)

When the neighborhood council agrees on everything, it must take the collated totals to the ward council (representing the various neighborhoods in the ward), the members of which must also reach an agreement. (Jane may be asked to reconsider some of her choices if such an agreement hits a snag.) From there, the collated totals will go to the city federation of consumption councils, and from there to the state federation, and from there to the regional federation, and from there to the national federation. At each stage there will be debate, negotiation, reconsideration – but eventually (hopefully!) acceptance. Computers will facilitate matters, keeping all participants informed at each stage as to what the averages are, so everyone will know whether or not a ward or city or region or state is out of line.

A similar procedure, suitably modified, will arrange for all job complexes to be equally balanced and for individuals and neighborhoods and cities and states and regions to propose how much work they are willing to do, in relation to their desired consumption. Again computers will facilitate.

Of course, in the end, supply and demand must match. The final match will come about as follows: The "iteration facilitation board" will survey all the accumulated data and then propose five *feasible* plans (i.e., those in which the amount of work offered will suffice to produce the goods requested). The nation will then engage in a series of winnowing votes, until only one of the original options remains. This "comprehensive plan" will then be submitted to each unit (region, state, city, ward, neighborhood) for acceptance or rejection. Further negotiations will

---

[46] Even though there is no money in a participatory economy, indicative prices will be necessary (as Albert and Hahnel acknowledge). Otherwise, consumption averages would have no relevance to one's knowing where one's proposal stood vis-à-vis "the average." What one needs to know is not whether or not one's proposed consumption of ice cream is above or below the national average, but whether or not the value of one's *total* consumption is above or below.

ensue. "These communications within and between relevant industry and consumer units [will] go on until a plan for all units and individuals is accepted."[47]

I have already rendered my summary judgment on all this. I shall not attempt a detailed critique. A long list of objections comes immediately to mind, some of which Albert and Hahnel have addressed in their books – but many of which, even quite commonsensical ones, they have not. Let me note just a couple.

Let us start with the very first step: constructing that consumption list. Jane Doe sits at her computer and types in what she would like to consume for the year. Albert and Hahnel estimate that this will "take less than thirty hours spread over the course of three weeks. For most people it won't take as long as filling out income tax forms now."[48] They assume that she has on hand her computer printout of last year's consumption, to facilitate the process. But where does that come from? At some point, people would have to resolve to keep a daily tally, for a full year, of everything purchased. Everyone would have to keep such a list, all 250 million of us. And all these data would have to be collated and typed into the computer. Do we not have here a feasibility problem of the first order?[49]

Apart from the question of feasibility, there is the question of desirability. Even if Jane had her printout of last year's consumption, and even if it would not be any worse than figuring out her taxes, why would she want to sit down and estimate all her consumption needs and desires for the coming year? Why would she want to go to a neighborhood council to discuss her list and the lists of her neighbors? Why would that be better than simply going out and buying what she needs (assuming a fair distribution of income), and then writing articles or otherwise agitating (as is now done) if she thinks certain consumption patterns are harmful?

Let us move to the last stage of the process: the final plans presented to the voters. Albert and Hahnel are vague as to the form of each plan, but there would seem to be only two possibilities: a fully disaggregated plan, listing everyone's work complex, consumption, and production, or a plan listing aggregated inputs and outputs. Obviously, five fully disaggregated plans could not be presented to the voters. Each of these plans would have 250 million entries (one for each citizen), and each of these entries would entail not simply a number but rather a description

---

[47] Albert and Hahnel (1991a, p. 86).
[48] Ibid., p. 90. I cannot help wondering where they got that figure, and why they think it encouraging that this will be no worse than filling out income-tax forms.
[49] Quite apart from the transition issue, the feasibility problem is formidable. Every family would have to have a computer; all of them would have to work properly; every family would have to use them conscientiously, etc.

of that person's job complex, the hours to be worked, and that person's consumption. Clearly, voters could not be asked to study five such plans and choose one.

So the plans would have to be presented in highly aggregated form. But here's the rub: Even if they were presented in highly aggregate form (e.g., 100 million tons of food, 20 million articles of clothing, 10 million new houses, 6 million new cars, etc.), voters would have to understand that when they voted, they would in fact be voting for a disaggregated plan. Voters might vote, say, for 100 million tons of food, but the planners could not say to the nation's farmers, "produce 100 million tons of food." They would have to tell the wheat farmers, the cattle ranchers, the strawberry growers, and the poultry producers exactly what they were expected to produce. Supply and demand would have to match for specific goods, not just for aggregate categories. So when voters voted, *they could not possibly know what they were voting for*. Not even voters with computers.

We see here the contradiction at the heart of any form of economic planning that is supposed to be both democratic and comprehensive. Economic planning, to be comprehensive, must specify an almost unlimited number of variables. Economic planning, to be effectively democratic, must confine itself to a quite limited number of variables. Ironically, Albert and Hahnel, arch-foes of command socialism, wind up giving their planners discretionary powers almost as great as those enjoyed by the Gosplan planners of the former Soviet Union. From the mind-boggling array of data sent up, their "facilitators" would be empowered not only to select five feasible alternatives (from among millions) but also to aggregate them as they saw fit – and (presumably) to *enforce* the final selection.[50]

There is a fundamental normative defect in the Albert-Hahnel approach (distinct from feasibility considerations) involving a misapplication of the principle of participatory autonomy. The principle of participatory autonomy specifies that each person has the *right* to participate in making the rules to which she must submit and the decisions whose consequences she must hear. It does not *obligate* such participation.

Albert and Hahnel's participatory economy would not simply give people the right to participate in constructing the consumption and production plans of society; it would require that they do so: Jane Doe *must* submit her consumption plan; she *must* submit her production plan. She

[50] Albert and Hahnel are reticent about enforcement, much preferring to speak of communication, negotiation, consensus. What sanctions would be imposed on those who consumed more than the plan allowed, or worked less, or refused to accept their assigned job complexes, are left unspecified. But the fact of the matter is that once decided, this plan would have to be enforced. If it were not, the economy would be vulnerable to both alienation and economic irrationality on a massive scale.

must make conscientious revisions. She *must* get her plan approved by her neighborhood council and her work council. Otherwise, because there would be no market signals, the "facilitators" would not have an accurate sense of what people wanted and what resources were available.

Albert and Hahnel seem not to realize that participatory democracy has a *negative* side, that it, too, like the market, can be alienating. Sometimes more so. The costs are not only time and effort; there can often be bruised emotions, feelings of frustration, inadequacy, and impotent anger. The emotional *distance* that a market transaction provides is by no means an unambiguous evil.

The trick, then, in building a democratic economy, is not to substitute comprehensive democratic planning for the market, but to integrate plan and market in such a way that no more is planned than can be effectively planned, with the rest left to the market. This is necessary not only for the sake of feasibility but also to enhance the meaningfulness of democracy itself and to minimize the danger of participatory alienation. Economic Democracy attempts such an integration. The "participatory economy" does not.

9. Marxian reflections

In 1969, when I was a visiting assistant professor of mathematics at the University of Kentucky, I signed up for a free-university course offered by a young sociology instructor and a graduate student, and there I began to study Marx for the first time.[1] Of course, like everyone else, I thought I knew what Marx was about, but during my years of undergraduate and graduate education I had never actually *read* anything by Marx, certainly no more than an inoculatory paragraph or two.

Both troubled and impressed by the selections we discussed, I set aside the following summer (which, incidentally, marked my transition from mathematics to philosophy) for a careful study of Volume 1 of *Capital*. My experience was quite different from that of Sartre, who, in *Search for a Method*, recalls a similar moment: "I read *Capital* and the *German Ideology*. I found everything perfectly clear, and I understood absolutely nothing. To understand is to change, to go beyond oneself. This reading did not change me."[2]

The reading *did* change me. I was not yet ready to call myself a Marxist, but I had become persuaded of one of Marx's great truths: Capitalism, for all its undeniable accomplishments, is, in its origins, in its day-to-day operations, and at its theoretical core, a profoundly unjust economic order, rooted in exploitation. I had not known that before. Marx persuaded me then. As the reader is well aware, I remain persuaded still.

Since that transformative encounter, I have read much more of Marx, and much more widely in economics, history, and philosophy also. I have tried to understand the world, and I have tried from time to time to change it a bit. At some point (I cannot recall exactly when, because there was no conversion experience) I began thinking of myself as a Marxist. I still do. Shall I continue to do so? Does Marxism have a future? In reflecting on this latter question (an underlying motif of this final chapter) I am also reflecting on the former, that is, my own identity.

In a fundamental sense these reflections are independent of the rest of this book. As I have tried to make clear, the basic argument against

[1] Free-university courses were common features of U.S. universities in the late 1960s and early 1970s: students and faculty coming together, informally and without tuition or credit, to study subjects not treated (or treated badly) in the official curriculum.

[2] Sartre (1963, pp. 17–18).

capitalism appeals to widely held values. These are values that most Marxists share, but they are by no means peculiarly "Marxist" values. These are values common to most people of a liberal or Left persuasion, and many of them are shared by conservatives as well. In *no* way does the basic argument of this book depend on anything uniquely Marxist.

At the same time, it seems appropriate to acknowledge the great debt this book owes to Marx. The reader will have noticed that many of the subarguments of the book's grand argument have been inspired by Marx. It is, of course, quite fashionable these days to denigrate Marx and to sneer at Marxism, just as, in Marx's day, "it was the good pleasure of the peevish, arrogant, mediocre epigones who now talk large in cultured Germany to treat Hegel in the same way as the brave Moses Mendelssohn in Lessing's time treated Spinoza, i.e., as a 'dead dog.'" Marx responded by openly avowing himself "the pupil of that mighty thinker."[3] I take this opportunity to do the same regarding Marx.

I take this opportunity also to situate the project of this book with respect to two fundamental features of Marxism: its ultimate vision and its theory of history. I like to characterize Marxism as having three constitutive moments. Marxism is a critique of the present (i.e., of capitalism), a vision of the future (designated communism), and a theory of history (a theoretical account of how we got to the present that allows for extrapolation into the future). This book has concentrated on the first moment. It has attempted to fill in a large lacuna in the work of Marx by offering a concrete proposal for a feasible socialism, so as to allow for the *comparative* critique.

But it is worthwhile to investigate how Economic Democracy relates to Marx's vision of genuine *communism,* described in his early writings as

the return of man himself as a *social,* i.e., really human being, a complete and conscious return which assimilates all the wealth of previous development. Communism . . . is the *definitive* resolution of the antagonism between man and nature, and between man and man. It is the true solution of the conflict between existence and essence, between objectification and self-affirmation, between freedom and necessity, between individual and species. It is the solution to the riddle of history and knows itself to be this solution.[4]

One would be hard pressed to formulate a more extravagant claim on behalf of a social order. How does Economic Democracy relate to *that*? And how does it relate to Marx's celebrated conviction that history is moving in a direction that will ultimately bring us to this communism? Is history really moving in the direction that Marx foresaw? Is it moving according to the "laws" he purported to discern? In short, is the third

---

[3] Marx (1967, pp. 19–20).
[4] *Economic and Philosophical Manuscripts of 1844,* in Fromm (1966, p. 127); emphases in original.

moment of Marxism – Marx's "historical materialism" – still viable? Has not his theory of history been definitively falsified by reality – above all by the astonishing events of the recent past? These are the questions that this final chapter will address, not exhaustively, of course, but as they link up with the issue of Economic Democracy.[5]

Communism

I must confess, I find Marx's ultimate vision profoundly appealing: a society wherein we become conscious of our species being, our deep connection with all other human beings; a society that speaks a *human* language, a language in which an expression of *need* is not "on the one hand felt and spoken as a plea, as begging, and as humiliation, on the other hand, heard and rejected as effrontery or madness."[6] I am moved by Marx's notion that one day wealth and poverty will cease to be opposing concepts, but will reflect different aspects of a full human life, allowing us to say that "the wealthy man is one who *needs* a complex of human manifestations of life and whose own self-realization exists as an inner necessity, a *need*," while "poverty is the passive bond which leads man to experience a need for the greatest wealth, the *other* person."[7] I like the idea of our senses becoming emancipated, humanized, and our work "a free manifestation of life and an enjoyment of life."[8] I do not see why human beings should settle for less.

But what does this communism have to do with Economic Democracy? Let us reflect on one of Marx's more sober discussions, written not in his youth, but toward the end of his life, as part of a polemical battle with followers of Lassalle.[9] In his *Critique of the Gotha Program*, Marx speaks of a period of revolutionary transformation that will usher in a "first phase" of communism, which then, over time, will evolve into a "higher phase." Although Marx himself did not make these terminological designations, this first phase has come to be called, in the Marxist tradition,

---

[5] There exists a large and sophisticated literature on Marx's communism and on historical materialism, much of it written over the past two decades, and much of it inspired by G. A. Cohen's brilliant attempt to bring to bear on Marxist issues the conceptual tools of analytic philosophy (Cohen, 1978). In what follows, I cannot do justice to this literature. In contrast to my aim for the rest of this book, my intention here is to offer some considered reflections, not full-scale arguments.

[6] "Excerpt Notes of 1844," in Easton and Guddat (1967, p. 280).

[7] *Economic and Philosophical Manuscripts of 1844*, in Fromm (1966, pp. 137–8); emphases in original.

[8] Ibid., p. 281.

[9] As Ware (1992b, p. 135) points out, one should approach this text with caution, because it was written quickly and was directed to a few leaders of the Eisenachers, a group Marx and Engels supported, but who, they thought, were abandoning important principles in making an alliance with the Lassalleans.

"socialism," with "communism" reserved for the higher phase. Let us follow this convention. Thus we can say that Marx envisaged a revolutionary transformation to socialism, and then the evolution, over time, of this socialism into communism.

Suppose we identify Economic Democracy with Marx's socialism (i.e., his first phase of communism).[10] Let us speculate as to how it might evolve. In the immediate aftermath of the "period of revolutionary transformation" from capitalism to Economic Democracy, not much would change for most people insofar as their immediate circumstances were concerned.[11] Stockbrokers, financiers, and the like would be out of work, and of course capitalists would find themselves with neither income from nor control over productive property. But the vast majority would go to work at their same jobs, would still have foremen and supervisors (who, however, would be democratically accountable), and would still find their incomes tied to their own performances and to those of their enterprises.

Let us now suppose that as the effects of democracy at the workplace and democratic control of new investment make themselves felt, full employment is achieved, inequalities within firms are narrowed, and *economic growth* recedes in importance. Suppose that, more and more, technological and efficiency gains are used not to increase consumption but to make workplaces more interesting, more likely to call forth and develop people's skills and capacities. Suppose these gains are also used to institute a new "political economy of time,"[12] which is to say, shorter and more flexible working hours, sabbaticals for everyone, and increased opportunities for changing jobs and careers. Suppose, finally, that the end to the disjunction between private and public investment sources brings to an end the "private affluence, public squalor" phenomenon and is accompanied by reforms that provide free, high-quality health care, education, and retirement opportunities for everyone. Let us call this overall state of affairs, once it has progressed to the point that most people are happy with their work and no one is in poverty, the "higher form" of Economic Democracy.

I would like to make three claims about this higher form, the first two of which seem to me relatively unproblematic. First, the evolutionary dynamic just described, though not inevitable, seems eminently plausible, even likely, should Economic Democracy come to be established.

---

[10] There are textual grounds for resisting this identification, but let us set this problem aside for now. More on this later.

[11] In Chapter 7, various scenarios were suggested for the transformation from capitalism to Economic Democracy. Here I am thinking of one that is rather abrupt. (Nothing in the basic argument hangs on this supposition.)

[12] This phrase, recall, is from Sirianni (1988).

Full employment is an explicit goal of Economic Democracy. Free health care, education, and so forth, have long been planks in the socialist project. I have argued at length in earlier chapters that Economic Democracy would decrease inequality, eliminate capitalism's growth imperative, and allow for more meaningful work.

If capitalism were replaced by Economic Democracy, a developmental trajectory such as I have described would seem plausible. Moreover (this is my second claim), the end state of this process is readily imaginable.[13] There is nothing wildly utopian about this higher form of Economic Democracy, nothing that is in any sort of fundamental conflict with our technological capabilities or with human nature. There is no characteristic of the society here posited as the higher phase of Economic Democracy that cannot already be found in certain occupations or in certain firms or in certain countries. I suspect that many proponents of capitalism (most modern-liberal proponents) would envisage the terminus of *their* project as having these features. After all, full employment, greater equality, good jobs, universal access to health care, education, and social security – these are the promises (if not the accomplishments) of ordinary politics today.

My third claim is more contentious: *This higher form of Economic Democracy is what Marx means by (the higher stage of) communism*. Or rather, to put the matter a bit more cautiously, such a society accords with Marx's basic good sense as to what might be expected to develop once capitalism has been definitively superseded. Marx's "communism" is not some flamboyantly utopian vision of lions lying down with lambs, the end of *all* human discord, a society where all work is play and goods are so abundant that all of us can have whatever we want whenever we want it. To represent Marx thus is to misrepresent Marx.[14]

Be that as it may, my account of communism is at odds with the readings of almost all other interpreters of Marx, for according to my interpretation, *even under communism there will be money, a market, and a*

---

[13] I use "end state" here not to indicate something stable and fixed but merely to refer to a state of affairs some years (or decades) after the initial transformation. As should be evident from the description, there is nothing final about this end state. (It is often overlooked that Marx's "end state" also lacks finality. Notice that he calls it a *higher* form of communism not *the highest*.)

[14] I grant that the rhetoric Marx sometimes employed to articulate his vision seems to imply much more than I am suggesting (witness the quotation in the first section of this chapter), but one should be careful here. The most dramatic passages were written by Marx when he was young (in his twenties) and were not for publication. Moreover (and more importantly), to see what I have described as the higher form of Economic Democracy as somehow "insufficient" is to fail to appreciate just how immense a distance separates this state of affairs from the life prospects of the vast majority of human beings in Marx's time – and in our own.

state. Marx's communism, I claim, need not be conceived of as a moneyless, marketless, stateless society.[15]

To say that there will still exist a *state* under communism is less controversial than the other parts of my thesis, because this is partly a matter of semantics. When Marx refers to the "withering away of the state," he is using "state" in a restricted sense to mean the organs of institutionalized physical coercion: police, prisons, and the military.[16] A "stateless" society could have a democratic government that would continue to make decisions concerning (among other things) the generation and allocation of investment funds and the provision of public goods. Marx's claim that the state will wither away is really nothing more than the claim that in a democratic society where everyone has a decent job and everyone is incorporated in a significant way into the community, there will be little crime or violence.[17]

I would push somewhat farther than most commentators are willing to go and argue that the "withering away of the state" need not be interpreted to mean that there would be *no need at all* for institutionalized law enforcement under communism. One should remember that Marx was a Hegelian. Quantitative change, carried far enough, makes a qualitative difference. (A man does not have to lose *all* his hair before he is considered bald.) If the numbers and significance of police and prisons in a society are tiny as compared with those under capitalism, we may say that the society is, in the Marxian sense, "stateless."[18]

Although most Marxists and Marxologists would doubtless agree that Marx's vision of full communism does not entail a total absence of government, and some might even allow that it is compatible with the presence of a small police force and a few "correctional facilities," few would be willing to grant that under communism there might still be

---

[15] Whether or not Marx himself conceived of communism as the standard interpretation would have it is beside the point. My claim is that the higher phase of Economic Democracy resolves the same real problems with socialism (carried over from capitalism), and in essentially the same fashion, as does Marx's higher phase of communism. The evidence regarding what Marx in fact believed is far more ambiguous than one might think, given the hegemonic status of the standard interpretation. For a survey of the relevant quotations, see Moore (1980), whose analysis, however, cuts differently from mine.

[16] Lenin (1932, pp. 12ff.) emphasizes this point.

[17] I have used the formulation "democratic society" in place of the more traditional "classless society" because one of the characteristics of democracy (as defined in this work) is the absence of any "privileged group." (See Chapter 5.) Insofar as they relate to the issues under discussion here, the terms "democratic" and "classless" are essentially equivalent.

[18] Lest I be misunderstood here, I do not claim that police and prisons will always be necessary, nor that Marx thought that they would be. I find it quite plausible to imagine alternative institutions or mechanisms for maintaining social order. My point is that Marx's vision of communism is *compatible with* the existence of the more traditional means, so long as they are drastically reduced in size and scope.

money and a market.[19] Marx, after all, has written powerfully against each. Moreover, there are his explicit pronouncements in the *Critique of the Gotha Program* concerning the economy of a communist society. There Marx asserts that in the first phase of communism, distribution will be in accordance with labor (which would seem to allow for money), but that this principle will be superseded eventually by the two famous principles: "from each according to his ability, to each according to his needs."

Much has been written about what these various principles do and do not entail and how they fit together.[20] Let me take another tack and consider the intent behind the formulations. I submit that the principle that Marx ascribes to socialism, essentially "to each according to her labor," is meant to emphasize that for workers, initially, neither their conditions of work nor the incentives structures will be altered appreciably. Marx stresses that socialism, initially, "is in every respect, economically, morally and intellectually, still stamped with the birth-marks of the old society from whose womb it emerges."[21] Some things will change right away. There will no longer be the inordinate consumption of the capitalist class, nor (more important for Marx, I would suggest, because he is well aware that the bulk of capitalist income is invested, not consumed) will the economy be vulnerable to the "anarchic" cycles of boom and bust. But working conditions and work motivations will not change, not immediately.

But over time, Marx believes, both these factors will change, so that, gradually, different principles will come to characterize production and distribution. Ultimately, the famous dual maxim he inscribes on the communist banner will prevail.

Now, this dual maxim is almost always interpreted to mean that people will no longer be paid to work, but will work freely, and that they will no longer have to buy what they need, but will consume freely. I would like to suggest an alternative interpretation. The traditional interpretation as I have just set it out has each of the two principles containing two clauses. I would like to affirm the second clause of each principle, while denying the first. That is to say, I agree that under communism people will work freely and consume freely. But I deny that they will

[19] Stanley Moore (1980, pp. vii–viii) asserts that Pol Pot acted in accordance with Marx's vision when his murderous regime abolished money and the market, because "it is true that wages and markets, money and banks, have no place in a fully communist society." (Moore argues that Pol Pot was non-Marxist in trying to make the leap so abruptly to full communism.) This interpretation of full communism (and the transition to it), certainly hegemonic among Marx scholars, follows Lenin. See Lenin (1932, pp. 78ff.).

[20] See Ware (1992b) for a perspicuous account.

[21] *Critique of the Gotha Program*, in McLellan (1977, p. 568).

neither get paid for their work nor buy what they need.[22] It is not necessary to interpret "free" (fetishistically, I am tempted to say) as referring to the absence of *money*.

I submit that "to work freely" need mean nothing more than that one's *primary* motivation for working is some combination of nonpecuniary factors – such as enjoyment, a need for self-actualization, a sense of self-esteem, a desire to contribute something of value to one's community, a sense of reciprocity (others having worked to produce the things I have consumed, I should do something for others) – rather than the threat of drastically reduced consumption or the desire to consume more. To work freely need not mean that one does not get paid. To work freely means that the other reasons for working are more important than the paycheck.

Similarly, I submit that "to consume freely" need mean nothing more than that one has sufficient income so as to be free from financial anxiety. To consume freely does not mean that one never has to save up for something, or weigh certain options and make certain choices. It means to be free of serious financial worry. If one can look back over one's past (as Jonathan Freeman did in the passage quoted in Chapter 4) and say "I do not remember denying myself anything because of money, though I suppose I did," one has "consumed freely," even though one has paid for one's purchases.[23]

In essence, I have interpreted the transformation from socialism to communism, which Marx characterizes in terms of a shift in principles, as representing a shift in the general psychology of the population (related to a change in material conditions), rather than as some sort of structural transformation. This seems to me very much in the spirit of Marx, who, after all, does *not* suggest that the move from socialism to communism is a move from one mode of production to another. Quite the contrary. As we have noted, Marx does not even use two separate words to designate the two forms, but refers to them respectively as a first stage and a higher stage of *communism*.

Let us consider an objection. My identification of higher Economic Democracy with higher communism might be contested on the grounds

[22] To be more precise, I deny that the principles entail the absence of money incomes or market purchases. I am not saying that a moneyless, marketless economy is impossible; I am saying that Marx's principles of communist production and distribution are compatible an economy in which money and markets continue to exist.

[23] Freeman's assessment seems to me a sufficient, though not a necessary, condition for claiming "free consumption." Even if one can recall occasionally having had to deny oneself something for lack of money, one still can be said to have consumed freely, so long as the deprivation was not serious. The rational appeal of Marx's slogan, "to each according to need," is the prospect of a society in which no one's consumption is either conspicuously excessive or seriously restricted. As Ware (1992b, p. 146) points out, the German word that Marx employs, *Bedurfnis*, does not distinguish needs from wants; so the slogan should not be given too austere an interpretation.

that the first phase of Economic Democracy – the model we have dealt with throughout this book – cannot be identified with Marx's socialism, for he is quite clear that the first phase of communism is not a market economy. Marx states explicitly that "within the co-operative society based on common ownership of the means of production, the producers do not exchange their products; just as little does the labour employed on the products appear here as the value of these products."[24]

My brief response is twofold. First, the logic of the objection is flawed. My claim is simply that the famous dual maxim that Marx uses to characterize higher communism can also be said to characterize higher Economic Democracy. Whether or not his first stage of communism can be identified with Economic Democracy is irrelevant to this claim. Second, while I am inclined to grant that the model Marx (very briefly) sketches in his *Critique of the Gotha Program* is not that of a market economy, I do not give this fact much weight, because his intention there was not to think through in any serious sense the structure of a viable socialism. His intention, quite plainly, was to criticize a specific statement in the Gotha program, namely, that "the proceeds of labour belong with undiminished and equal right to all members of society."[25] There are two things about this statement that bothered Marx, and for good reason. The statement suggests that workers will get *much more* right away, under socialism, and that the distribution will be *equal*. Neither condition can be expected to obtain in the first stage of communism, and the latter (as Marx always insisted) is *not* the aim of communism. He could have used a model like that of Economic Democracy to make the same criticisms.[26]

Let me conclude this section with several comments. I have identified Marx's communism with what I have called the "higher form" of Economic Democracy (i.e., Economic Democracy evolved to the point where most people will work for reasons other than financial exigency, and few people will feel seriously constrained by their levels of income). This interpretation cuts through the (admittedly entertaining) debate about what to do about slackers and overconsumers under communism, for under this interpretation of communism, not *everyone all the time* need enjoy his work (or be otherwise nonpecuniarily motivated), and not *everyone all the time* need be reasonable in his desire for consumer goods. People still will have to work for their incomes, and those incomes will impose consumption constraints. My point is that when the monetary

---

[24] *Critique of the Gotha Program*, in McLellan (1977, pp. 567–8).
[25] See McLellan (1977, pp. 566ff.).
[26] Moore (1980, p. 71) observes that the model Marx proposes in the *Critique of the Gotha Program* is virtually identical with the model associated with the Ricardian socialists that Marx had severely criticized just a few years earlier. I find it difficult to believe that this model represents Marx's considered judgment as to the structure of socialism.

dimension ceases to be terribly important for most people, we will be justified in saying that we have advanced to a society of a sort qualitatively different from that which immediately succeeded capitalism, one worthy of the banner Marx gives to it: "from each according to his ability, to each according to his needs."

This interpretation also allows us to see clearly something that Marx always claimed to be the case: Communism already exists in embryo in capitalist societies. On this interpretation, if one's work is challenging, satisfying, and secure, and if one does not really have to worry about paying the rent or the credit-card bills, then one is now living as one would under communism. The point is to universalize this condition. If this can be done, we shall have a world very different from the one we live in today.

One final comment: In the preceding discussion I have emphasized the transformation in the quality of work life and the reduction in financial anxiety likely to occur in an evolving Economic Democracy, because the focus has been on the principles articulated in the *Critique of the Gotha Program*. But other changes are also to be expected. Consumption should stabilize (thus allowing for an economy that will be ecologically sustainable), leisure should increase substantially, and technical development likely will be oriented less toward ever increasing efficiency, and more toward the enhancement of worker skills and product quality.

In such a context it seems to me that many of Marx's early "utopian" characterizations of communism make realistic sense. In his "Excerpt Notes of 1844" Marx asks us to "suppose we had produced things as human beings." Then,

in my production I would have objectified my individuality and its particularity, and in the course of the activity I would have enjoyed an individual life; in viewing the object I would have experienced the individual joy of knowing my personality as an objective, sensuously perceptible, and indubitable power, [and at the same time] in your satisfaction and your use of my product I would have had the direct and conscious satisfaction that my work satisfied a human need, that it objectified human nature, and that it created an object appropriate to the need of another human being.[27]

I submit that such could well be the experience of most of us under (higher) Economic Democracy – even if we are paid for our work and pay for our consumption. Note, too, that if vacations were longer, sabbaticals more plentiful, and our ecology sound, it might really be possible for me, for significant periods of my life (and for anyone else who so desired), "to do one thing today and another tomorrow, to hunt in the morning, fish in the afternoon, rear cattle in the evening, criticize after

[27] Easton and Guddat (1967, p. 281).

dinner, just as I have a mind, without ever becoming a hunter, fisherman, shepherd or critic."[28]

Marxian paradoxes, Marxian hope

When the transition from advanced capitalism to Economic Democracy was addressed in Chapter 7, the focus was on providing an account of how the structures of capitalism might be suitably modified so as to arrive at an economy structured along the lines of our basic model. But for Marx there is a more important element to the transition question. As we have repeatedly noted, Marx says almost nothing about how the structures of capitalism might be transformed into the institutions of a viable socialism, but he has much to say about who will do the transforming, and why this agent will succeed. Indeed, he has constructed an elaborate theory to answer precisely these questions, a theory that has come to be called "historical materialism."

This component of Marxism, the attempt to construct a "scientific" theory of history from which one can deduce the eventual triumph of the working class, has long been subject to criticism, even by many who are sympathetic to Marx's critique of capitalism and who would happily embrace a genuine communism, if it were in fact to come about. It is this component of Marxism that seems to have been most decisively refuted by the crumbling of the Communist regimes in Eastern Europe and the Soviet Union.

Are there any grounds for *not* thinking that historical materialism has at long last been laid to rest? This is the question I would like to address, if somewhat obliquely, in this concluding section. It is a question that bears heavily on our assessment of the future of Marxism. It is also a question that leads us into a tangle of paradoxes. Let me elucidate three.

The first is this: The 1989 revolutions in Eastern Europe and the subsequent events in the Soviet Union, which have done so much to discredit Marxism, conform almost perfectly to the Marxian paradigm. The basic outline of Marx's theory of social transformation is well known. He presents it succinctly as follows:

At a certain stage of their development the material productive forces of society come into contradiction with existing productive relationships, or, what is but a legal expression for these, with the property relationships within which they had moved before. From forms of development of the productive forces these relationships are turned into their fetters. With the change in the economic foundation the whole vast superstructure is more or less rapidly transformed.[29]

---

[28] *The German Ideology*, in Fromm (1966, p. 206).
[29] From the "Preface to a Contribution to the Critique of Political Economy," in Fromm (1966, p. 218).

This, we observe, is exactly what happened in Eastern Europe. The Soviet economic model, command socialism, which for a time proved quite effective in mobilizing resources for rapid industrialization, ran up against its limits. We should not forget that not many years ago, Western economists were offering scenarios that would have had the Soviet Union overtaking the United States in fairly short order. Paul Samuelson, for example, in the 1973 edition of his famous textbook, showed that a plausible extrapolation of the existing trends would have the Soviet economy surpassing the U.S. economy by 1990. Samuelson also noted (at the time correctly) that

> it is a vulgar mistake to think that most people in Eastern Europe are miserable. Although it is undoubtedly true that few citizens of the West would trade their degree of economic comfort and political freedom for life in the Soviet Union, it is also true that a Soviet citizen thinks he is living in paradise in comparison with life in China or in earlier times. . . . To the eye of the traveller from impoverished Asia and Africa, the rising degree of Russian affluence must seem impressive.[30]

But the "relations of production" that worked rather well when generating growth in the basic-industry sector worked not at all well in the consumer-goods sector, nor did they prove adequate for exploiting the latest computer-based and information technologies. The relations indeed "turned into fetters" (as, I cannot resist adding, many of us on the Left had been predicting), and as these relations were being altered, events were set in motion that "more or less rapidly transformed the whole vast superstructure."

These superstructural transformations (i.e., transformations in the political and ideological realms) also conformed to the Marxian paradigm. Changes in the economy, according to Marx, shift the balance of power among the classes. A new class comes to the fore and articulates its own conception of the future; it does so in "universal" terms that mobilize vast sectors of the population. Many members of the old ruling class desert to the new cause. When the dust settles, a new order has been created – more advanced than what it replaced – but one that often leaves the masses (who are rapidly demobilized) little better off materially than they were before.

Marx developed this paradigm from his studies of the English and French revolutions, but the fit with Eastern Europe is remarkable. Consider the analysis offered by Branko Milanović, an economist with the World Bank in Washington, who, despite (or perhaps because of) his Belgrade training, has little sympathy with Marxism. In a book that appeared in 1989, just before the political upheavals, Milanović argued that the situation in Eastern Europe could best be understood as a clash

[30] Samuelson (1973, pp. 883, 881).

of three sets of interests: those of the middle-level bureaucracy, whose identities and positions were tied to the status quo; those of the "technocrats," who managed the enterprises and who resented "middle-level bureaucracy because of the system-induced dependence on them," much preferring the greater autonomy that *market reforms* would give them; and those of the workers, who tended "to prefer a devolution in the direction of *labor-management*, because their importance and power would thereby be increased."[31]

In short, Milanović saw class struggle, with middle bureaucrats seeking to preserve the status quo, technocrats pushing for market reforms, and workers wanting labor management and workplace democracy. Milanović did not foresee just how rapidly things would change, although he did cite, presciently, Tocqueville's observation that "the most dangerous moment for a bad government is when it tries to become better."[32] His skepticism about workers' interests prevailing has also been borne out.[33]

So we see that the Marxian theory has in this instance been confirmed in rather amazing detail. Relations of production conducive to rapid industrialization came into conflict with the very forces of production unleashed. The balance of power shifted from bureaucrats and party functionaries to a managerial stratum created by the industrialization process, who, by articulating their discontent in universal terms (i.e., in terms of freedom and democracy), have been able to gain the political power commensurate with their economic role. Many functionaries have joined them and are now actively positioning themselves to benefit from the "privatizing" reforms currently under way. The working class, which provided the bodies for the fateful demonstrations, have become demoralized, having been made to bear the brunt of the burgeoning unemployment that has been the main legacy of economic reform.[34]

[31] Milanović (1989, pp. 79, 63). This latter claim finds confirmation in a 1985 survey that found 87 per cent of the Polish workers wanting full self-management, a figure significantly higher than the 56 per cent favoring a greater role for the church. Cited by Norr (1987, p. 292).

[32] Milanović (1989, p. 82).

[33] For a strikingly similar analysis of the Soviet situation, see the interview with the Russian academician Leonid Gordon (1991, pp. 26–7). Like Milanović, Gordon identifies three contending forces: middle-level *nomenklatura* who favor the old system; intellectuals, technocrats, managers, and some skilled workers who want capitalism; and "about half to two-thirds of the workers and peasants" who would support "economic democracy with worker control of property." Gordon reports (with evident relief) that this latter group is unorganized and unlikely to be effective, but he does worry that "an eloquent and ardent leader like Lenin could swing them into a mass movement."

[34] According to the classical Marxian paradigm, such revolutionary developments are nevertheless progressive – moving the majority into better position than they were before to achieve genuine liberation. This conclusion also seems to me accurate. It is difficult not to feel that a historical opportunity has been missed (recall our discussion in Chapter 7), but I would not want to claim that working people are unequivocally worse off now than before. Moreover, the struggle seems far from over. Although leading elements of

It seems clear that the Marxian paradigm has been confirmed in most details – and yet discredited. This is the first paradox: a theory discredited in being confirmed. A partial resolution is provided by a second: Historical materialism *predicts* its own periodic eclipse. One of Marx's most provocative assertions – declared by Sartre (correctly, in my view) to be *"absolutely* right"[35] – is that "the ideas of the ruling class are in every epoch the ruling ideas." Marx adds that "the existence of revolutionary ideas in a particular period presupposes the existence of a revolutionary class."[36]

I take Marx to be saying that the fate of revolutionary ideas (revolutionary theory, if you will) is bound up with the fate of the class struggle. Thus one would expect the attraction of Marxism itself to ebb and flow, gaining ground during times of major grass-roots activism (the great union drives of the 1930s, say, or the antiracist and antiimperialist struggles of the 1960s), and losing ground during periods of class defeat (the consolidation of the American empire in the decade or so following World War II, or the post-1960s counteroffensive that began in the mid-1970s, roared through the 1980s, and continued into the 1990s).

It seems clear now that this latter period has indeed been one of rollback. Internationally, the great wave of successful revolutionary armed struggles throughout Asia, Africa, and Latin America, framed by the Chinese Revolution of 1949 and the Nicaraguan Revolution of 1979, has receded. Noam Chomsky and Edward Herman's assessment has proved to be correct: The United States did not *lose* the war in Vietnam.[37] Granted, we were defeated militarily, but we (largely) accomplished our more important aim: to make clear to the peoples of the Third World that no challenge to the capitalist order would be permitted to succeed.[38] Even if armed struggle is triumphant, the victors will not be able to deliver on their promises of egalitarian development. An appropriate combination of economic strangulation and high-technology, "low-intensity" warfare can wreck even the most determined revolutionary government. It would be

---

the technocratic class (and most intellectuals) are pushing hard for capitalism, serious obstacles stand in their way: There is, as yet, no deep-rooted capitalist class in these countries with long experience at manipulating the formal democratic process; the mechanisms of "privatization" are proving to be difficult to implement; the example of those who have gone farthest down the capitalist road (East Germany and Poland) is not inspiring. Small wonder that so many Eastern European technocrats and intellectuals long for "an authoritarian leadership that would at the same time implement a liberal policy toward private investment" – the recommendation, quoted earlier, of Harvard fellow and consultant to the U.S. government on the Soviet economy, Boris Rumer (1991, p. 22).

[35] Sartre (1963, p. 17).   [36] *The German Ideology*, in Fromm (1966, pp. 212–13).

[37] Chomsky and Herman (1979b, ch. 1).

[38] In this section I am writing self-consciously as a citizen of the United States; hence my use of "we" and "our" here and subsequently.

a mistake to say that among the hundreds of millions of Third World poor, all hope has been extinguished, but there can be little doubt that the rulers of the First World rest easier now. Recall Ronald Reagan's proud and often-repeated boast: "No territory was lost on *my* watch."

At home, the defeat of majority interests is perhaps less obvious, but no less real. At the end of World War II, more than one-third of the American work force was unionized. By 1992 the fraction had fallen to less than one-sixth. Inequality, stable throughout most of the postwar period, surged during the 1980s. The real after-tax income of the average family in the top 1 percent of the population rose 136 percent from 1977 to 1991, while that of the average family in the bottom 60 percent fell by 10 percent.[39] Unemployment, which averaged 4.8 percent in the 1960s, averaged 7.2 percent during the 1980s, up a full 50 percent. Average weekly earnings (in 1987 dollars) were $356 during the 1970s, but fell to $318 during the 1980s.[40] And it is hardly a secret that the once-heralded safety net is now tattered and full of holes. Hungry children, violent youth, homeless people, and beggars of all ages give our cities a feel that was once associated with Third World urban squalor. Somewhere along the line the War on Poverty turned into the War Against the Poor. Clearly the rich won.

It seems reasonable to view the past decade and a half as a time of powerful counterattack by the forces of capital against two major challenges: the proliferation of Third World revolutionary movements abroad, and what seemed to be ever increasing health, safety, environmental, and welfare measures at home. Given the success of the counteroffensive, it should be expected (if a basic contention of historical materialism is correct) that a philosophy tied theoretically to the working class and in recent practice to antiimperialist movements should find itself in crisis – which indeed it has.

This second paradox – a theory predicting its own eclipse – will be resolved, of course, if the eclipse is only (as predicted) temporary. But will that be the case? Here one cannot but feel the force of two elements of Marxism in prima facie conflict. Marxism aims at being a *scientific theory*, a theory grounded in the rational apprehension of the real, empirical world. But it is also a *philosophy of hope*. In this latter respect, Marxism is but a slight variation on a New Testament beatitude: "Blessed are the exploited," said Marx, "for they shall inherit the earth."

For Marx and most Marxists, this hope has always been thought to be a *rational* hope. Marxism's scientificity and its hope may come into

---

[39] McIntyre (1991b, p. 26).

[40] Mishel and Simon (1988, p. 51). Young families have been particularly hard hit. Edelman's figures (1992, p. 14) show that median incomes for families headed by people under age thirty declined an astonishing 25.2 percent between 1979 and 1990.

dialectical contradiction from time to time – but not permanent contradiction. But what if Marx was wrong? What if Jon Elster is right? A genuine socialist revolution (i.e., one that constitutes a genuine advance over capitalism) requires for its success both objective and subjective conditions. The human and material resources must exist that will allow for a higher, more humane manner of living, and there must exist an agent sufficiently motivated to bring an end to the existing order. This is basic Marxism. But, argues Elster (and many others), these conditions now diverge, and they will continue to do so for the foreseeable future, perhaps forever.[41] The necessary objective conditions now obtain in the advanced capitalist world, but an agent is lacking, because workers now have far more to lose than their chains. The subjective conditions obtain in the Third World, but there the resources to create a truly socialist society are lacking. If this is indeed the case, then one must choose between the scientific Marx and the utopian Marx – but so severed, Marxism ceases to be Marxism. The second paradox of Marxism devolves into real, nondialectical contradiction.

I should like to propose another reading of the current situation, more hopeful, paradoxically, because of yet another Marxian paradox, which I would state as follows: Marxism, the philosophy of revolution, has missed what is perhaps the greatest revolution of our century. It need not have missed it. This revolution is fully compatible with the core elements of Marxian theory. Yet Marxism has not been so central as one might have hoped or expected to the theory and practice of the massive, worldwide, intraclass attempt, now under way, to reverse what Engels called "the world historic defeat of the female sex." The opening decades of this century witnessed struggles, ultimately successful almost everywhere, to extend formal political rights to women. And if the past decade and a half has been a period of far more defeats than victories for the working class and for the peoples of the Third World, the same cannot be said about women. Since the late 1960s there has been, as everybody knows, an explosion of feminist theoretical work and practical activism, originating in North America, but spreading to all points. Inevitably the gains have been unevenly distributed, the effects unevenly felt; there have been setbacks as well as victories, but never, it seems to me, have there been such great victories in this "longest revolution" as have occurred this century.[42]

I have asserted that Marxism missed this revolution, but one must be fair here, giving credit where it is due. Marxism has been, from its

---

[41] See Elster (1986, pp. 54–63).

[42] I do not mean to minimize the recent "backlash" against feminism – see Faludi (1991) for examples – but I think the overall assessment stands.

inception, committed to the theoretical equality of the sexes. Marxist philosophers, looking back over their favorite texts, do not have to cringe the way most other philosophers do.[43] It is also true that important theoretical currents in contemporary feminism have been deeply influenced by Marx.[44]

The practical record of Marxism has not been so bad either, in comparison with those of other political regimes. Women received the right to vote in Russia before they did in the United States. Women in the former East Germany – many to their great shock – now face a loss of benefits they had long taken for granted.[45] It was the Communists in China who banned the practice of foot-binding, and the Marxist regime in Afghanistan that insisted on greater equality for women (a key factor in provoking the fundamentalist uprising, supported by the West, that has now succeeded). I do not mean to imply that Marxist regimes eliminated male dominance – far from it. Nor do I claim that women have always been better off under Marxian regimes than under comparable non-Marxist ones. I do claim, however, that the comparative record is not bad.[46]

Be that as it may, the fact remains that Marxism has scarcely embraced feminism with open arms. Despite the fact that Marxism not only is theoretically compatible with feminism but also (I would argue) is profeminist at its core, there is considerable tension (and sometimes open hostility) between Marxists and feminists. It is worth asking why.

This is not an easy question to answer, not because so few possibilities come to mind but because so many do – from searing personal encounters to wide-ranging theoretical critiques, particularly of Marxism by feminists, but also conversely. Let me be modest here and offer what is only a partial answer, but one that has considerable bearing, it seems to me, on the future of Marxism.

Few, if any, Marxists have been able to deny the legitimacy of the feminist project. Certainly women have been oppressed – that is a basic tenet of Marxism itself. Certainly oppressed groups are right to struggle to overcome that oppression, and these struggles should be supported. The sticking point has been the conceptualization of this struggle – its relation to the *class struggle*. And an important source of this difficulty, perhaps the most important source, is the Marxian conception of

---

[43] For abundant examples of sexism in the classical texts, see Okin (1979), Shanley and Pateman (1991), or Tuana (1992).

[44] See Jaggar (1983) on Marxist feminism and socialist feminism. See also Tong (1989).

[45] See Rudolph, Appelbaum, and Maier (1990). This phenomenon is by no means confined to the former East Germany, but is widespread throughout Eastern Europe. See Simpson (1991).

[46] See Ferguson (1991, ch. 8) for a careful discussion, with much supporting evidence, of this claim.

revolution. To put the matter bluntly, it is easy for Marxists to imagine the working class making a revolution: armed insurrection, a nationwide general strike, even (conceivably) a massive electoral triumph. But how would women make a revolution? Marxists, especially male Marxists, are inclined to roll their eyes and think of *Lysistrata*.

To be sure, Marxists will grant that a successful working-class revolution must involve large numbers of women and that their specific demands must be acknowledged, but it is difficult for most Marxists to see how feminism per se can contribute much to the seizure of power, apart from serving as a mobilizing tool to bring women into the *real* struggle – the "father of all battles," if you will.

Let me be clear: I am not saying that Marxists act in bad faith when they (we) assert that genuine liberation is impossible for women unless the working class is also liberated. That assertion, I believe, is true. Nor are we insincere when we concede (as we must) that socialism does not guarantee the end of male domination. What I am saying is that it is quite difficult for most Marxists (particularly male Marxists) to grant *equal weight* to the two struggles and hence to regard with sufficient seriousness the theoretical research and practical actions of feminists that have no obvious or immediate bearing on class. It is difficult to grant equal weight because it is difficult to see how the feminist agenda contributes to the Revolution (capital *R*).

Let me introduce a subsidiary paradox: Most adherents to the philosophy of revolution, that is, Marxists (those in advanced capitalist societies, but many in the Third World as well), do not much believe in the Revolution anymore. Those revolutions made in the name of Marx have often disappointed our hopes. The electoral route – exemplified by the Eurocommunism of the 1970s – seems to have come to nothing. Some Marxists still cling to the big-bang theory: One of these days, the thousand and one "crises" we read about every day in the newspapers – budget deficit, Third World debt, savings-and-loan scandal, decaying infrastructure, consumer-credit overload, and (for the noneconomistic) drugs, crime, AIDS, education, health care, environment, and so forth – one of these days, these are going to coalesce into Crisis (capital C) and economic Collapse (also capital C), from the ashes of which will arise our hoped-for Socialism.

Far be it from me to claim that such a collapse is impossible. As I have argued in this book, capitalism is far from stable, and it is structurally incapable of resolving our basic social problems. But I do wish to claim that there is nothing at the Marxian core, apart from sheer hope, to assure us that from the ashes of catastrophe will arise our dream, rather than a fascist nightmare. I think almost all Marxists now know that. In our hearts we do.

So where does this leave us? The basic Marxian concept of revolution has been an impediment to a full appreciation of the world-historic revolution that is now under way, and it is a concept that Marxists do not much believe in anyway. I take it the answer is obvious, at least the formal answer: Marxism needs a different concept or theory of revolution, one that will enable us to achieve a clearer view of what is actually going on in the world. Marxism needs a new notion of radical transformation, one less affectively bound to images of armed insurrection and explosive release. Marxism's future, it seems to me, depends importantly on this.

If the formal answer to the third Marxian paradox is clear, the material answer is not. Obviously, this is not the place to present a new theory of revolution, even if I had one worked out (which I do not).[47] Let me conclude, instead, with something that seems to me relevant and important – not a new theory but a new practice. I do this with some trepidation, because leftists are regularly ridiculed for their enthusiasm for partisan struggles far from home. But it is the nature of Marxian hope to believe that emancipatory movements can be genuinely creative, capable of revealing new possibilities. Fundamental theoretical issues are not resolved abstractly. Marx was fond of quoting Goethe's Faust: "Im Anfang war die That" ("In the beginning was the Act").

Everyone knows that 1989 was the "Year of Revolution" in Eastern Europe. Not so many remember, if they were aware of it at all, that in 1989 a socialist steelworker came startlingly close to being elected president of Brazil – Brazil, a Third World country racked by staggering debt and inequality, by economic and environmental crises; Brazil, the world's ninth largest economy, the world's fourth largest food producer, a country enormously rich in resources and containing the Third World's largest industrial center. Luís Inácio Lula da Silva was the candidate of a political party formed only ten years earlier: Partido dos Trabalhadores (PT; Party of the Workers).

It is this party on which I want to reflect, because it is a most unusual party, one that brings together in interesting ways elements of Marxism (e.g., a concern for class and for organized, mass-based struggle) and elements to which feminist theory has contributed substantially (e.g., gender, pluralism, participation, nonviolence). The synthesis is far from trouble-free, but the party, in blending these elements, seems to point to a new notion of "radical transformation." It sees itself, in fact, as a "*sui generis* strategic experiment."[48]

The PT is a "workers' party" that has consciously rejected the Leninist

---

[47] An indispensable starting point must be Hal Draper's multivolume study (1978, 1981, 1986, 1989).
[48] Sader and Silverstein (1991, p. 106).

model of rigid discipline and has consciously rejected armed struggle.[49] It is a par'ⱼ that believes that "democracy, understood as the wide aggregate of citizens' rights to political participation and representation cannot be seen as a bourgeois value [for] democracy became a universal ideal when it was taken by the working class."[50] It is also a party that wants to participate in the construction of a powerful "civil society" and has deliberately structured itself to maintain organic links to the wide variety of grass-roots movements that have proliferated in Brazil. Its founding political declaration of 1979 proclaims that

the idea of the Partido dos Trabalhadores arose with the advance and reinforcement of this new and broad-based social movement which now extends from the factories to the neighborhoods, from the unions to the Basic Christian Communities, from the Cost of Living Mcvement to the Dwellers' Associations, from the student movement to the professional associations, from the movement of black people to the women's movement, as well as others, like those who struggle for the rights of indigenous peoples.[51]

This is a mass-based party comprising 1.5 million *militantes* (among them the highly influential Paulo Freire) and another 4 million active sympathizers. To be a regular member, one must belong to a grass-roots organization. The PT aims at *empowerment* of the oppressed, not merely at their mobilization on behalf of goals or leaders selected by a "central committee." Within the party are a variety of officially recognized "tendencies," some of them explicitly Marxist, many of them not. All have the right to present documents and candidates, to be discussed and voted on by the party membership.

I do not wish to suggest that this party has hit upon the magic solution for what ails the Left.[52] I do wish to underscore, though, that women are exceedingly active in the PT and that women's issues are prominently featured. As one of the PT's founders, Maria Helena Moreira Alves (professor of Latin American studies and political economy at the University of Rio de Janeiro), observes:

[49] Sader and Silverstein (1991, p. 106) claim that the party does not reject armed struggle per se, "but rather a certain type of armed struggle, which proposes an overthrow of the existing State in order to create a State-led society, and then outlaws independent social movements." In any event, the PT does not see armed struggle as part of its current effort to achieve political power.

[50] Sader and Silverstein (1991, p. 107), quoting from a PT document.

[51] Moreira Alves (1990a, p. 234). My account of Partido dos Trabalhadores derives from this article and from Moreira Alves (1990b), Sader and Silverstein (1991), and Cammack (1991).

[52] Following Lula's near-victory (which created panic among Brazil's ruling elite), the PT suffered significant congressional losses in 1990. Moreover, it is only one of several Left parties, all of which supported Lula in his runoff bid against Collor. See Sader and Silverstein (1991, ch. 7) for an account of ruling-class panic and subsequent "dirty tricks." See Cammack (1991) for a cautious assessment of the PT's future.

Women do not have a "women's committee" but permeate the PT, shape the platform on women's issues, exert considerable influence on the party, and have been elected to a variety of public offices throughout the country. The PT has already, in the brief period of its existence, elected three women as mayors of major cities [among them São Paulo, the world's third-largest city] and the first black congresswomen in Brazilian history.[53]

How does all this connect with Economic Democracy and the future of Marxism? Permit me a final reflection. Marxism at its best has drawn its strength from its involvement in the real-world struggles of the oppressed. In many places, and for extended periods, Marxism has been hegemonic in such struggles. But for a variety of reasons, both historical and philosophical, this hegemony has waned. Emancipatory struggles (such as the one in progress in Brazil) are increasingly coming to reflect structures and values to which contemporary feminism (drawing on its own concrete experience) has paid more attention than has Marxism: pluralism, participation, nonviolence, distrust of hierarchy, distrust of univocal formulas. So it seems to me that Marxism will increasingly be seen, and will increasingly see itself, not as *the* philosophy of liberation but as one component of such a philosophy. There will be other components also, each interacting dialectically with the others, enriching the others.

I think that Marxism (suitably enriched) will remain key to understanding the workings of a capitalist economy, the state, the international political and economic order; it will continue to provide insights into how "the base," sometimes subtly, sometimes not so subtly, shapes our politics and culture. Marxism will not let us ignore the issue of class, and its vision of human possibilities will continue to inspire. Curiously (still another paradox), Marxism may be less central to what has been an essential preoccupation of this book: the construction of viable countercapitalist or postcapitalist economic structures. Marxism's practical record here is largely negative, and its theory underdeveloped.

Marxism will certainly be less central to our understanding of how our sexual identities and psychological propensities are constructed, the roles these play in promoting and thwarting liberation, what we must do to break the various cycles of violence that permeate our world today (from intimate interactions to international confrontations), how we are to transform our experiences of racial and ethnic differences from hatred into enrichment,[54] and what we must do to keep our planet from dying. Other perspectives will be more important here.

So Marxism does indeed have a future – a future, I conjecture, coterminous with that of capitalism. Capitalism can neither deliver on

---

[53] Moreira Alves (1990a, p. 236). The last clause is from Moreira Alves (1990b, p. 14).

[54] Recent and ongoing events suggest that this project has become exceedingly urgent. Rethinking race, racism, ethnicity, etc., may well entail significant changes in our conception of democracy – and have far-reaching practical consequences.

its promise of freedom and self-actualization for all of humanity nor extinguish or keep safely contained the desire for freedom and self-actualization that is central to its functioning. The genie is out of the bottle.

I rather doubt, however, that Marxism will regain its hegemonic role as *the* philosophy of liberation.[55] It seems unlikely that any one theory will ever again dominate as Marxism has dominated. Nor is success likely for any movement that confines itself primarily to an economic critique, not even a critique that offers a viable alternative, such as Economic Democracy. It is becoming increasingly clear that to achieve Economic Democracy – or the liberation of women, or the end of racism, or a sustainable environment, or world peace – we shall have to aim at more than any one of these goals. To achieve anything, we must struggle for everything.

Can a movement for emancipation informed by a pluralistic philosophy of liberation such as I have suggested succeed in humanizing our species and thus fulfilling Marx's prophecy? Few Marxists still believe in inevitability. That tenet of historical materialism will have to be discarded. I remain convinced, however, that the Marxian hope is a *rational* hope. The obstacles are structural and contingent, and identifiable forces are pushing for their removal. Will these forces succeed? Maybe yes, maybe no. One can *hope* that Marx was right that "mankind always sets itself only such problems as it can solve," that "the problem itself only arises when the material conditions for its solution are already present or at least in the process of coming into being."[56]

But there are identifiable forces resisting as well – within our own psyches, to say nothing of the forces of wealth and privilege. To use the words of Walter Benjamin: "The enemy has not ceased to be victorious."[57]

[55] I am not saying that a living Marxism is incapable of incorporating the insights and advances of other perspectives, but by the same token, certain other perspectives would seem equally capable of incorporating the insights and advances of Marxism. Whether or not one thinks of oneself as a Marxist may come to have less to do with *what* one believes and more to do with the specific circumstances of one's intellectual, emotional, and political development.

[56] "Preface to a Contribution to the Critique of Political Economy," in Fromm (1966, p. 218).

[57] Benjamin (1969, p. 255).

Bibliography

Abell, Peter, and Nicholas Mahoney (1988). *Small-Scale Producer Co-operatives in Developing Countries.* Oxford University Press.

Adams, Walter, and James Brock (1986). *The Bigness Complex: Industry, Labor and Government in the American Economy.* New York: Pantheon Books.

(1992). "1980s Gigantomania Follies." *Challenge* 35(March–April):4–8.

Adler, Paul (1986). "Technology and Us." *Socialist Review* 16(January–February): 67–96.

Albert, Michael, and Robin Hahnel (1978). *Unorthodox Marxism.* Boston: South End Press.

(1991a). *Looking Forward: Participatory Economics for the Twenty-first Century.* Boston: South End Press.

(1991b). *The Political Economy of Participatory Economics.* Princeton University Press.

(1992). "Participatory Planning." *Science and Society* 56(Spring):39–59.

Alchian, Armen, and Harold Demsetz (1972). "Production, Information Costs, and Economic Organization." *American Economic Review* 62(December):777–95.

Allan, Emile Andersen, and Darrell Steffensmeier (1989). "Youth, Underemployment, and Property Crime: Differential Effects of Job Availability and Job Quality on Juvenile and Young Adult Arrest Rates." *American Sociological Review* 54(February):107–23.

Amin, Samir (1976). *Unequal Development.* New York: Monthly Review Press.

Anderson, Elizabeth (1990). "The Ethical Limitations of the Market." *Economics and Philosophy* 6:179–205.

Aoki, Masahito (1990). "A New Paradigm of Work and Organization?" in S. Marglin and J. Schor (eds.), *The Golden Age of Capitalism: Reinterpreting the Postwar Experience,* pp. 267–93. Oxford: Clarendon Press.

Archer, Dane, and Rosemary Gartner (1984). *Violence and Crime in Cross-national Perspective.* New Haven: Yale University Press.

Arnold, N. Scott (1985). "Capitalists and the Ethics of Contribution." *Canadian Journal of Philosophy* 15(March):87–102.

(1987a). "Marx and Disequilibrium in Market Socialist Relations of Production." *Economics and Philosophy* 3(April):23–48.

(1987b). "Further Thoughts on the Degeneration of Market Socialism." *Economics and Philosophy* 3(October):320–30.

(1987c). "Final Reply to Professor Schweickart." *Economics and Philosophy* 3(October):335–8.

(1990). *Marx's Radical Critique of Capitalist Society: A Reconstruction and Critical Evaluation.* Oxford University Press.

Arrow, Kenneth (1951). *Social Choice and Individual Values*. New Haven: Yale University Press.

(1962). "Economic Welfare and the Allocation of Resources for Invention," in National Bureau of Economic Research, *The Rate and Direction of Inventive Activity*, pp. 609–25. Princeton University Press.

Backman, Jules (1967). *Advertising and Competition*. New York University Press.

Balzer, Richard (1976). *Clockwork: Life in and outside an American Factory*. Garden City, N.Y.: Doubleday.

Banks, Andrew (1992). "Union Pension Fund Supports Worker Ownership," in L. Krimerman and F. Lindenfeld (eds.), *When Workers Decide: Workplace Democracy Takes Root in America*, pp. 122–6. Philadelphia: New Society Publishers.

Baran, Paul (1968). *The Political Economy of Growth*. New York: Monthly Review Press.

Baran, Paul, and Paul Sweezy (1966). *Monopoly Capital*. New York: Monthly Review Press.

Bardhan, Pranab, and John Roemer (1992). "Market Socialism: A Case for Rejuvenation." *Journal of Economic Perspectives* 6(Summer):101–16.

Barone, Enrico (1935). "The Ministry of Production in the Collectivist State," in F. Hayek (ed.), *Collectivist Economic Planning*, pp. 245–90. New York: Augustus M. Kelley.

Barro, Robert (1977). "Unanticipated Money Growth and Unemployment in the United States." *American Economic Review* 67:101–15.

Barry, Brian (1973). *The Liberal Theory of Justice*. Oxford: Clarendon Press.

Bayat, Assaf (1991). *Work, Politics and Power: An International Perspective on Workers' Control and Self-Management*. New York: Monthly Review Press.

Beazley, Ernest J. (1988). "Employee-Owned Weirton Steel Mills Public Stock Offering Later This Year." *Wall Street Journal*, June 23, p. 43.

Beckerman, Wilfred (1974). *In Defense of Economic Growth*. London: Jonathan Cape.

Beehler, Roger, David Kopp, and Bela Szabados (eds.) (1992). *On the Track of Reason: Essays in Honor of Kai Nielsen*. Boulder, Colo.: Westview Press.

Bell, Daniel, and Irving Kristol (1970). *Capitalism Today*. New York: Basic Books.

Benjamin, Walter (1969). *Illuminations*. New York: Shocken Books.

Ben-Nur, Avner (1984). "On the Stability of the Cooperative Type of Organization." *Journal of Comparative Economics* 8(September):247–60.

Bergson, Abram (1984). "Income Inequality Under Soviet Socialism." *Journal of Economic Literature* 22(September):247–60.

Berle, Adolph, and Gardiner Means (1932). *The Modern Corporation and Private Property*. New York: Macmillan.

Berman, Katrina (1982). "A Co-operative Model for Worker Management," in F. Stephens (ed.), *The Performance of Labour-managed Firms*, pp. 74–98. New York: St. Martin's Press.

Blasi, Joseph, and Douglas Kruse (1991). *The New Owners: The Mass Emergence of Employee Ownership in Public Companies and What It Means to American Business*. New York: Harper Collins Publishers.

Blinder, Alan (1987). *Hard Heads, Soft Hearts: Tough-minded Economics for a Just Society*. Reading, Mass.: Addison-Wesley.

(1989). *Macroeconomics Under Debate.* Ann Arbor: University of Michigan Press.

(ed.) (1990). *Paying for Productivity: A Look at the Evidence.* Washington, D.C.: Brookings Institution.

Block, Fred (1990). *Postindustrial Possibilities: A Critique of Economic Discourse.* Berkeley: University of California Press.

Blumberg, Paul (1969). *Industrial Democracy: The Sociology of Participation.* New York: Schocken Books.

Böhm-Bawerk, Eugen (1959). *Capital and Interest.* South Holland, Ill.: Libertarian Press.

Bonin, John, and Louis Putterman (1987). *Economies of Cooperation and the Labor-managed Economy.* New York: Harwood.

Boulding, Kenneth (1973). "The Shadow of the Stationary State," in M. Olsen and H. Landsberg (eds.), *The No-Growth Society,* pp. 89–102. New York: Norton.

(ed.) (1984). *The Economics of Human Betterment.* Albany: State University Press of New York.

Bowles, Samuel, and Herbert Gintis (1986). *Democracy and Capitalism.* New York: Basic Books.

Bowles, Samuel, David Gordon, and Thomas Weisskopf (1990). *After the Wasteland: A Democratic Economics for the Year 2000.* Armonk, N.Y.: M.E. Sharpe.

Boyd, Michael (1987). "The Performance of Private and Cooperative Socialist Organization: Postwar Yugoslav Agriculture." *Review of Economics and Statistics* 69(May):205–14.

Bradley, Keith, and Alan Gelb (1987). "Cooperative Labour Relations: Mondragon's Response to Recession." *British Journal of Industrial Relations* 25:77–97.

Braverman, Harry (1974). *Labor and Monopoly Capital: The Degradation of Work in the Twentieth Century.* New York: Monthly Review Press.

Brecher, Jeremy (1972). *Strike!* Boston: South End Press.

Brecht, Bertolt (1967). *Die Dreigroschenoper,* in *Gesammelte Werke,* Stüke 1. Frankfurt: Suhrkamp Verlag.

Brenner, Harvey (1973). *Mental Illness and the Economy.* Cambridge, Mass.: Harvard University Press.

Briggs, Jean (1992). "A Political Miracle." *Forbes* 150(May):108–11.

Brown, Lester, et al. (eds.) (1991). *State of the World 1991.* New York: Norton.

Brus, Wlodzimierz (1972). *The Market in a Socialist Economy.* London: Routledge & Kegan Paul.

Buchanan, Allen (1985). *Ethics, Efficiency and the Market.* Totowa, N.J.: Rowman & Allenheld.

Burawoy, Michael (1985). *The Politics of Production: Factory Regimes under Capitalism and Socialism.* London: Verso.

Byrne, John (1991). "The Flap over Executive Pay." *Business Week* (May 6):90–112.

Cammack, Paul (1991). "Brazil: The Long March to the New Republic." *New Left Review* (November–December):21–58.

Cardenal, Ernesto (1980). *Zero Hour and Other Documentary Poems.* New York: New Directions.

Cardoso, Eliana, and Ann Helwege (1992). "Below the Line: Poverty in Latin America." *World Development* 20:19–37.

Carleton, Don (1985). *Red Scare! Right-Wing Hysteria, Fifties Fanaticism, and Their Legacy in Texas.* Austin: Texas Monthly Press.

Carroll, Sidney (1991). "American Family Fortunes as Economic Deadweight." *Challenge: Magazine of Economic Affairs* 34(May–June):11–18.

Carson, Richard (1990). *Comparative Economic Systems.* Armonk, N.Y.: M.E. Sharpe.

Chaliand Gerard (1987). *Revolution in the Third World.* New York: Viking Press.

Chomsky, Noam (1973). *For Reasons of State.* New York: Random House.

(1985). *Turning the Tide: U.S. Intervention in Central America and the Struggle for Peace.* Boston: South End Press.

(1987). *On Power and Ideology: The Managua Lectures.* Boston: South End Press.

Chomsky, Noam, and Edward Herman (1979a). *The Washington Connection and Third World Fascism.* Boston: South End Press.

(1979b). *After the Cataclysm: Indochina and the Reconstruction of Imperial Ideology.* Boston: South End Press.

(1988). *Manufacturing Consent: The Political Economy of the Mass Media.* New York: Pantheon Books.

Christman, John (ed.) (1989). *The Inner Citadel: Essays on Individual Autonomy.* Oxford University Press.

Clark, Eric (1989). *The Want Makers: The World of Advertising: How They Make You Buy.* New York: Viking Press.

Clark, John Bates (1956). *The Distribution of Wealth.* New York: Kelley & Millman. (Originally published 1899.)

Cohen, G. A. (1977). "Robert Nozick and Wilt Chamberlain: How Patterns Preserve Liberty." *Erkentniss* 11(May):5–23.

(1978). *Karl Marx's Theory of History: A Defense.* Princeton University Press.

(1983). "More on Exploitation and the Labor Theory of Value." *Inquiry* 26:309–22.

(1989). "On the Currency of Egalitarian Justice." *Ethics* 99(July):906–44.

Comisso, Ellen (1979). *Workers' Control Under Plan and Market.* New Haven: Yale University Press.

Crozier, Michel, Samuel Huntington, and Joji Watanuki (1975). *The Crisis of Democracy: Report on the Governability of Democracies to the Trilateral Commission.* New York University Press.

Cunningham, Frank (1987). *Democratic Theory and Socialism.* Cambridge University Press.

Dahl, Robert (1989). *Democracy and Its Critics.* New Haven: Yale University Press.

Dahl, Robert A., and Charles E. Lindblom (1953). *Politics, Economics and Welfare.* New York: Harper & Brothers.

Debreau, Gerald (1959). *Theory of Value: An Axiomatic Analysis of Economic Equilibrium.* New Haven: Yale University Press.

Deutcher, Isaac (1967). *Stalin: A Political Biography.* Oxford University Press.

Djilas, Milovan (1969). *The Unperfect Society: Beyond the New Class.* New York: Harcourt Brace & World.

Dobb, Maurice (1969). *Welfare Economics and the Economics of Socialism.* Cambridge University Press.

Domar, Evesy (1966). "The Soviet Collective Farm as a Producer Cooperative." *American Economic Review* 56:734–57.

Domhoff, G. William (1983). *Who Rules America Now?: A View for the '80s.* Englewood Cliffs, N.J.: Prentice-Hall.

Dow, Gregory (1986). "Control Rights, Competitive Markets, and the Labor Management Debate." *Journal of Comparative Economics* 10:48–61.

Draper, Hal (1978, 1981, 1986, 1989). *Karl Marx's Theory of Revolution.* New York: Monthly Review Press.

Dreier, Peter, and Richard Appelbaum (1991). "America's Nightmare: Homelessness." *Challenge* 34(March–April):46–52.

Drèze, Jacques (1989). *Labour Management, Contracts and Capital Markets.* Oxford Blackwell Publisher.

Drèze, Jean, and Amartya Sen (1989). *Hunger and Public Action.* Oxford: Clarendon Press.

Drucker, Peter (1954). *The Practice of Management.* New York: Harper & Brothers.

Du Boff, Richard (1990). "Review of Chandler, *Scale and Scope.*" *Challenge* 33 (November–December):61–4.

Durning, Alan (1991). "Asking How Much Is Enough," in L. Brown et al. (eds.), *State of the World 1991*, pp. 153–69. New York: Norton.

Dworkin, Gerald (1988). *The Theory and Practice of Autonomy.* Cambridge University Press.

Dworkin, Ronald (1978). "Liberalism," in S. Hampshire (ed.), *Public and Private Morality*, pp. 113–43. Cambridge University Press.

Earle, John (1986). *The Italian Cooperative Movement.* London: Allen & Unwin.

Easterlin, Richard (1973). "Does Money Buy Happiness?" *Public Interest* 30 (Winter):3–10.

Easton, Loyd, and Kurt Guddat (eds.) (1967). *Writings of the Young Marx on Philosophy and Society.* New York: Doubleday.

Edelman, Marian Wright (1992). "Vanishing Dreams of America's Young Families." *Challenge* 35(May–June):13–19.

Edwards, Richard (1979). *Contested Terrain: The Transformation of Work in the Twentieth Century.* New York: Basic Books.

Egan, Daniel (1990). "Toward a Marxist Theory of Labor-managed Firms: Breaking the Degeneration Thesis." *Review of Radical Political Economics* 22(Winter):67–86.

Eisenberg, Philip, and Paul Lazarsfeld (1938). "The Psychological Effects of Unemployment." *Psychological Bulletin* 35(June):358–90.

Ellerman, David (1990). *The Democratic Worker-owned Firm: A New Model for the East and West.* Boston: Unwin Hyman.

Elster, Jon (1979). *Ulysses and the Sirens: Studies in Rationality and Irrationality.* Cambridge University Press.

(1986). "The Theory of Combined and Uneven Development: A Critique," in J. Roemer (ed.), *Analytical Marxism*, pp. 54–63. Cambridge University Press.

Elster, Jon, and Karl Moene (eds.) (1989). *Alternatives to Capitalism.* Cambridge University Press.

Engels, Friedrich (1935). *Socialism: Utopian and Scientific.* New York: International Publishers.

Enzenberger, Hans Magnus (1989). *Europe, Europe: Forays into a Continent.* New York: Pantheon Books.

Estrin, Saul (1982). "Yugoslavia," in F. Stephens (ed.), *The Performance of Labour-managed Firms*, pp. 33–52. New York: St. Martin's Press.

(1983). *Self-management: Economic Theory and Yugoslav Practice*. Cambridge University Press.

Estrin, Saul, and Derek Jones (1988). "Can Employee-owned Firms Survive?" Working Paper Series, Department of Economics, Hamilton College (May).

(1989). "Do Employee-owned Firms Invest Less?" Working Paper Series, Hamilton College Department of Economics (April).

Estrin, Saul, Derek Jones, and Jan Svejnar (1987). "The Productivity Effects of Worker Participation in Producer Cooperatives in Western Economies." *Journal of Comparative Economics* 11(May):40–61.

Faludi, Susan (1991). *Backlash: America's Undeclared War Against Women*. New York: Crown.

Faux, Jeff (1992). "EPI Links Economic Growth to Economic Justice." *Challenge* 35(January–February):13–22.

Feiwell, George (ed.) (1989). *Joan Robinson and Modern Economic Theory*. New York University Press.

Ferguson, Ann (1991) *Sexual Democracy: Women, Oppression, and Revolution*. Boulder, Colo.: Westview Press.

Firor, John (1990). *The Changing Atmosphere: A Global Challenge*. New Haven: Yale University Press.

Flew, Anthony (1989). *Equality in Liberty and Justice*. London: Routledge.

Form, William (1985). *Divided We Stand: Working-Class Stratification in America*. Urbana: University of Illinois Press.

Frank, Andre Gunder (1992). "Latin American Development Theories Revisited." *Latin American Perspectives* 19(Spring):125–39.

Franke, Richard, and Barbara Chasin (1989). *Kerala: Radical Reform as Development in an Indian State*. San Francisco: Institute for Food and Development.

(1991). "Kerala State: Radical Reform as Development." *Monthly Review* 42 (January):1–23.

Frankfurt, Harry (1987). "Equality as a Moral Ideal." *Ethics* 98(October):21–43.

Frantz, Roger (1988). *X-Efficiency: Theory, Evidence and Applications*. Boston: Kluwer Academic Publishers.

Fraser, Nancy (1989). "Talking About Needs: Interpretive Contests as Political Conflicts in Welfare-State Societies." *Ethics* 99(January):291–313.

Freeman, Jonathan (1978). *Happy People*. New York: Harcourt Brace Jovanovich.

Friedman, Edward, Paul Pickowicz, and Mark Selden (1991). *Chinese Village, Socialist State*. New Haven: Yale University Press.

Friedman, Milton (1953). *Essays on Positive Economics*. University of Chicago Press.

(1962). *Capitalism and Freedom*. University of Chicago Press.

(1968). "The Role of Monetary Policy." *American Economic Review* 58(March): 1–17.

Friedman, Milton, and Rose Friedman (1980). *Free to Choose*. New York: Harcourt.

Fromm, Erich (1966). *Marx's Concept of Man*. New York: Ungar.

Frye, Northrop (1967). *The Modern Century*. Oxford University Press.

Fukuyama, Francis (1992). *The End of History and the Last Man*. New York: Free Press.

Furubotyn, Eirik, and Svetozar Pejovich (1974a). "Property Rights and the Behavior of the Firm in a Socialist State: The Example of Yugoslavia," in E. Furubotyn and S. Pejovich (eds.), *The Economics of Property Rights*, pp. 227–51. Cambridge, Mass.: Ballinger.

(eds.) (1974b). *The Economics of Property Rights*. Cambridge, Mass.: Ballinger.

Galbraith, John Kenneth (1958). *The Affluent Society*. New York: New American Library.

(1967). *The New Industrial State*. Boston: Houghton Mifflin.

(1973a). *Economics and the Public Purpose*. Boston: Houghton Mifflin.

(1973b). "Power and the Useful Economist." *American Economic Review* 63(March):1–11.

Geoghegan, Thomas (1991). *Which Side Are You On?: Trying to Be for Labor When It's Flat on Its Back*. New York: Farrar, Straus & Giroux.

Gerlack, Michael (1989). "Keiretsu Organization in the Japanese Economy," in C. Johnson, L. Tyson, and J. Zysman (eds.), *Politics and Productivity: The Real Story of Why Japan Works*, pp. 141–70. Cambridge, Mass.: Ballinger.

Gershuny, Jonathan (1984). "Growth, Social Innovation and Time," in K. Boulding (ed.), *The Economics of Human Betterment*, pp. 36–57. Albany: State University Press of New York.

Gewirth, Alan (1978). *Reason and Morality*. University of Chicago Press.

Gilder, George (1981). *Wealth and Poverty*. New York: Basic Books.

Goldemberg, José, et al. (1987). *Energy for a Sustainable World*. Washington, D.C.: World Resources Institute.

Goldfield, Michael (1987). *The Decline of Organized Labor in the United States*. Chicago: University of Chicago Press.

Gordon, David (ed.) (1990). *Green Cities: Ecological Sound Approaches to Urban Space*. Montreal: Black Rose Books.

Gordon, Leonid (1991). "Soviet Prospects: 'Not Absolutely Hopeless.'" *Challenge* 34(May–June):23–31.

Gordon, M. J. (1992). "China's Path to Market Socialism." *Challenge* 35(January–February):53–6.

Gordon, Robert, Tjalling Koopmans, William Nordhaus, and Brian Skinner (1988). *Toward a New Iron Age?: Quantitative Modeling of Resource Exhaustion*. Cambridge, Mass.: Harvard University Press.

Gould, Carol (1988). *Rethinking Democracy: Freedom and Social Cooperation in Politics, Economy and Society*. Cambridge University Press.

Gowan, Peter (1990). "Western Economic Diplomacy and the New Eastern Europe." *New Left Review* (July–August):63–84.

Graham, Carol (1991). *From Emergency Employment to Social Investment: Alleviating Poverty in Chile*. Washington, D.C.: Brookings Institution.

Granick, David (1975). *Enterprise Guidance in Eastern Europe: A Comparison of Four Socialist Economies*. Princeton University Press.

Greenberg, Edward S. (1986). *Workplace Democracy: The Political Effects of Participation*. Ithaca, N.Y.: Cornell University Press.

Greenhouse, Steven (1985). "Employees Make a Go of Weirton." *New York Times*, January 6, p. 4F.

Gregory, Paul, and Robert Stuart (1990). *Soviet Economic Structure and Performance*, 4th ed. New York: Harper & Row.

Greider, William (1987). *Secrets of the Temple: How the Federal Reserve Runs the Country*. New York: Simon & Schuster.

Gui, Benedetto (1984). "Basque versus Illyrian Labor-managed Firms: The Problem of Property Rights." *Journal of Comparative Economics* 8:168–81.

Gunn, Christopher (1984). *Workers' Self-Management in the United States*. Ithaca, N.Y.: Cornell University Press.

Gutman, Huck (1992). "Failed Banks, Bailouts, and Federal Policy." *Monthly Review* 43(March):29–37.

Habermas, Jürgen (1973). *Legitimation Crisis*. Boston: Beacon Press.

Hahn, Frank (1984). *Equilibrium and Macroeconomics*. Cambridge, Mass.: MIT Press.

Halliday, Jon, and Bruce Cummings (1988). *Korea: The Unknown War*. New York: Pantheon Books.

Hammond, Peter (1989). "Some Assumptions of Contemporary Neoclassical Economic Theology," in G. Feiwell (ed.), *Joan Robinson and Modern Economic Theory*, pp. 186–257. New York University Press.

Hampshire, Stuart (ed.) (1978). *Public and Private Morality*. Cambridge University Press.

Hansen, Alvin (1938). *Full Recovery or Stagnation?* New York: Norton.

(1953). *A Guide to Keynes*. New York: McGraw-Hill.

Harasti, Miklós (1977). *A Worker in a Worker's State*. New York: Universe Books.

Harrod, Roy (1939). "An Essay in Dynamic Theory." *Economic Journal* 49:14–33.

(1958). "The Possibility of Economic Satiety," in *Problems of United States Economic Development*, Vol. 1, pp. 207–13. New York: Committee for Economic Development.

Harvard School of Public Health (1985). *Hunger in America: The Growing Epidemic*. Cambridge, Mass.: Harvard University Press.

Hashimoto, Masanori (1990). "Employment and Wage Systems in Japan and Their Implications for Productivity," in A. Blinder (ed.), *Paying for Productivity: A Look at the Evidence*, pp. 245–93. Washington, D.C.: Brookings Institution.

Haug, W. F. (1986). *Critique of Commodity Aesthetics: Appearance, Sexuality and Advertising in Capitalist Society*. Minneapolis: University of Minnesota Press.

Hausman, Daniel (1981). *Capital, Profits, and Prices: An Essay in the Philosophy of Economics*. New York: Columbia University Press.

Hayek, F. A. (ed.) (1935). *Collectivist Economic Planning*. New York: Augustus M. Kelley.

(1944). *The Road to Serfdom*. University of Chicago Press.

(1960). *The Constitution of Liberty*. London: Routledge & Kegan Paul.

(1972). *A Tiger by the Tail: The Keynesian Legacy of Inflation*. Tonbridge, Kent: Institute of Economic Affairs.

Heilbroner, Robert (1974). "The Clouded Crystal Ball." *American Economic Review* 64(May):121–4.

(1989). "The Triumph of Capitalism." *New Yorker* 64(January):98–109.

(1990). "Analysis and Vision in the History of Modern Economic Thought." *Journal of Economic Literature* 28(September):1097–114.

Heilbroner, Robert, and Lester Thurow (1984). *The Economic Problem*, 7th ed. Englewood Cliffs, N.J.: Prentice-Hall.

Hersh, Seymour (1983). *The Price of Power: Kissinger in the Nixon White House.* New York: Summit Books.

Hinton, William (1990). *The Great Reversal: The Privatization of China, 1978–1989.* New York: Monthly Review Press.

Hirsch, Fred (1976). *Social Limits to Growth.* Cambridge, Mass.: Harvard University Press.

Hirschman, A. O. (1970). *Exit, Voice and Loyalty.* Cambridge, Mass.: Harvard University Press.

(1977). *The Passions and the Interests: Political Arguments for Capitalism Before Its Triumph.* Princeton University Press.

Hirshhorn, Larry (1984). *Beyond Mechanization: Work and Technology in a Postindustrial Age.* Cambridge, Mass.: MIT Press.

Hodgson, Geoffrey (1988). *Economics and Institutions: A Manifesto for Modern Institutional Economics.* Philadelphia: University of Pennsylvania Press.

Hogan, Michael (1987). *The Marshall Plan.* Cambridge University Press.

Hollis, Martin, and Edward Nell (1975). *Rational Economic Man: A Philosophical Critique of Neoclassical Economics.* Cambridge University Press.

Horvat, Branko (1976). *The Yugoslav Economic System: The First Labor-managed Economy in the Making.* White Plains, N.Y.: International Arts and Sciences Press.

(1982). *The Political Economy of Socialism: A Marxist Social Theory.* Armonk, N.Y.: M.E. Sharpe.

(1986). "The Theory of the Worker-managed Firm Revisited." *Journal of Comparative Economics* 10:9–25.

Huang, Philip (1990). *The Peasant Family and Rural Development in the Yangze Delta: 1350–1988.* Stanford University Press.

Hunt, E. K., and Jesse Schwartz (eds.) (1972). *A Critique of Economic Theory.* Baltimore: Penguin Books.

Jackall, Robert, and Henry Levin (eds.) (1984). *Worker Cooperatives in America.* Berkeley: University of California Press.

Jaggar, Alison (1983). *Feminist Politics and Human Nature.* Totowa, N.J.: Rowman & Allanheld.

Jensen, Michael (1989). "Eclipse of the Public Corporation." *Harvard Business Review* 67(September–October):61–74.

Jensen, Michael, and William Meckling (1979). "Rights and Production Functions: An Application to Labor-managed Firms and Codetermination." *Journal of Business* 52(October):469–506.

Johnson, Chalmers (1982). *MITI and the Japanese Miracle: The Growth of Industrial Policy, 1925–1975.* Stanford University Press.

Johnson, Chalmers, Laura D'Andrea Tyson, and John Zysman (eds.) (1989). *Politics and Productivity: The Real Story of Why Japan Works.* Cambridge, Mass.: Ballinger.

Johnson, Elizabeth (1973). "John Maynard Keynes: Scientist or Politician?" in J. Robinson (ed.), *After Keynes*, pp. 11–25. New York: Barnes & Noble.

Johnson, Harry (1973). *The Theory of Income Distribution.* London: Gray-Mills.

Jones, Derek (1984). "American Producer Cooperatives and Employee-owned Firms: An Historical Perspective," in R. Jackall and H. Levin (eds.), *Worker Cooperatives in America*, pp. 536–54. Berkeley: University of California Press.

Jones, Derek, and Jan Svejnar (eds.) (1982). *Participatory and Self-managed Firms: Evaluating Economic Performance.* Lexington, Mass.: Heath.

Kahn, Alfred (1966). "The Tyranny of Small Decisions: Market Failures, Imperfections and the Limits of Economics." *Kyklos* 19:23–47.

Kalecki, Michael (1972). "Political Aspects of Full Employment," in E. Hunt and J. Schwartz (eds.), *A Critique of Economic Theory,* pp. 420–30. Baltimore: Penguin Books. (Originally published 1943.)

Kant, Immanuel (1959). *Foundations of the Metaphysics of Morals.* Indianapolis: Bobbs-Merrill.

Key, William (1973). *Subliminal Seduction.* Englewood Cliffs, N.J.: Prentice-Hall. (1976). *Media Sexploitation.* Englewood Cliffs, N.J.: Prentice-Hall.

Keynes, John Maynard (1936). *The General Theory of Employment, Interest and Money.* New York: Harcourt Brace & World.

(1963). *Essays in Persuasion.* New York: Norton.

(1971). *The Economic Consequences of Peace.* New York: Harper Torchbooks.

Keyssar, Alexander (1986). *The First Century of Unemployment in Massachusetts.* Cambridge University Press.

Kirzner, Israel (1989). *Discovery, Capitalism and Distributive Justice.* Oxford: Blackwell Publisher.

Kline, Stephen (1988). "The Theater of Consumption: On Comparing American and Japanese Advertising." *Canadian Journal of Political and Social Theory* 12(Fall):101–20.

Knight, Frank (1921). *Risk, Uncertainty and Profit.* Boston: Houghton Mifflin.

Kohn, Melvin, and Carmi Schooler (1978). "The Reciprocal Effects of the Substantive Complexity of Work and Intellectual Flexibility: A Longitudinal Assessment." *American Journal of Sociology* 84(July):24–52.

(1982). "Job Conditions and Personality: A Longitudinal Assessment of Their Reciprocal Effects." *American Journal of Sociology* 87(May):1257–86.

Kornai, Janos (1986). "The Soft Budget Constraint." *Kyklos* 39:3–30.

(1992). *The Socialist System: The Political Economy of Communism.* Princeton University Press.

Kregel, J. A., and Alfred Eichner (1975). "An Essay on Post-Keynesian Theory: A New Paradigm in Economics." *Journal of Economic Literature* 13(December):1293–314.

Krimerman, Len, and Frank Lindenfeld (eds.) (1992). *When Workers Decide: Workplace Democracy Takes Root in America.* Philadelphia: New Society Publishers.

Krugman, Paul (ed.) (1986). *Strategic Trade Policy and the New International Economics.* Cambridge, Mass.: MIT Press.

(1990a). "The Income Distribution Disparity." *Challenge* 33(July–August): 4–16.

(1990b). *The Age of Diminished Expectations: U.S. Economic Policy in the 1990s.* Cambridge, Mass.: MIT Press.

(1990c). *Rethinking International Trade.* Cambridge, Mass.: MIT Press.

Kuznets, Simon (1965). *Economic Growth and Structure.* New York: Norton.

Kwitney, Jonathan (1981). "The Great Transportation Conspiracy." *Harper's* 262(February):14–21.

Lavoie, Don (1985). *Rivalry and Central Planning.* Cambridge University Press.

Leibenstein, Harvey (1966). "Allocative Efficiency vs. X-Efficiency." *American Economic Review* 56(June):392–415.

(1976). *Beyond Economic Man: A New Foundation for Microeconomics.* Cambridge, Mass.: Harvard University Press.

(1987). *Inside the Firm: The Inefficiencies of Hierarchy.* Cambridge, Mass.: Harvard University Press.

Leisner, Thelma (1985). *Economic Statistics 1900–1983.* New York: Facts on File Publications.

Lenin, V. I. (1932). *State and Revolution.* New York: International Publishers.

Lerner, Abba (1944). *The Economics of Control.* New York: Macmillan.

Levin, Henry (1982). "Issues in Assessing the Comparative Productivity of Worker-managed and Participatory Firms in Capitalist Societies," in D. Jones and J. Svejnar (eds.), *Participatory and Self-managed Firms: Evaluating Economic Performance,* pp. 45–64. Lexington, Mass.: Heath.

(1984). "Employment and Productivity of Producer Cooperatives," in R. Jackall and H. Levin (eds.), *Worker Cooperatives in America,* pp. 16–32.

Levine, David, and Laura D'Andrea Tyson (1990). "Participation, Productivity and the Firm's Environment," in A. Blinder (ed.), *Paying for Productivity: A Look at the Evidence,* pp. 203–14. Washington, D.C.: Brookings Institution.

Lindblom, Charles (1977). *Politics and Markets.* New York: Basic Books.

Linder, Staffan (1970). *The Harried Leisure Class.* New York: Columbia University Press.

Lippincott, Benjamin (ed.) (1938). *On the Economic Theory of Socialism.* Minneapolis: University of Minnesota Press.

Lipsey, Robert E., and Irving B. Kravis (1987). *Saving and Economic Growth: Is the United States Really Falling Behind?* New York: Conference Board.

Lipsey, Robert, and Helen Stone Tice (eds.) (1989). *The Measurement of Saving, Investment and Wealth.* University of Chicago Press.

Lucas, Robert (1981). *Studies in Business-Cycle Theory.* Cambridge, Mass.: MIT Press.

(1987). *Models of Business Cycles.* Oxford: Blackwell Publisher.

Lydall, Harold. (1984). *Yugoslav Socialism: Theory and Practice.* Oxford: Clarendon Press.

(1989) *Yugoslavia in Crisis.* Oxford: Clarendon Press.

McClelland, David (1984). *Motives, Personality and Society.* New York: Praeger.

McClelland, David, and David Winter (1969). *Motivating Economic Achievement.* New York: Free Press.

Machiavelli, Niccolo (1966). *The Prince, with Selections from the Discourses.* New York: Bantam Books.

McIntyre, Robert (1991a). "Eastern European Success with Socialized Agriculture: Developmental and Sovietological Lessons." *Review of Radical Political Economics* 23(Spring–Summer):177–86.

(1991b). "Tax Inequality Caused Our Ballooning Budget Deficit." *Challenge* 34(November–December):24–33.

McLellan, David (1977). *Karl Marx: Selected Writings.* Oxford University Press.

Magaziner, Ira, and Robert Reich (1982). *Minding America's Business: The Decline and Rise of the American Economy.* New York: Random House.

Mann, Charles (1990). "The Man with All the Answers." *Atlantic Monthly* 268 (January):45–62.

Marglin, Stephen, and Juliet Schor (eds.) (1990). *The Golden Age of Capitalism: Reinterpreting the Postwar Experience.* Oxford: Clarendon Press.

Marshall, Alfred (1948). *Principles of Economics*, 8th ed. New York: Macmillan.

Marx, Karl (1967). *Capital*, Vol. 1. New York: International Publishers.

Marx, Karl, and Friedrich Engels (1948). *Communist Manifesto.* New York: International Publishers.

(1976). *Collected Works: 1845–48.* New York: International Publishers.

Meade, James (1972). "The Theory of Labour-managed Firms and Profit Sharing." *Economic Journal* 82:402–28.

(1986). *Alternative Systems of Business Organization and of Workers' Remuneration.* London: Allen & Unwin.

Meek, Christopher, and Warner Woodworth (1990). "Technical Training and Enterprise: Mondragon's Educational System and Its Implications for Other Cooperatives." *Economic and Industrial Democracy* 11:505–28.

Meyer, Herbert (1978). "Jobs and Want Ads: A Look Behind the Words." *Fortune* 20(November):88–95.

Milanović, Branko (1989). *Liberalization and Entrepreneurship: Dynamics of Reform in Socialism and Capitalism.* Armonk, N.Y.: M.E. Sharpe.

Mill, John Stuart (1958). *Considerations on Representative Government.* Indianapolis: Bobbs-Merrill.

(1965). *Principles of Political Economy (The Collected Works of John Stuart Mill,* Vol. 3). University of Toronto Press.

(1978). *On Liberty.* Indianapolis: Hackett.

Miller, David (1989). *Market, State and Community: Theoretical Foundations of Market Socialism.* Oxford: Clarendon Press.

Miller, Joanne, Carmi Schooler, Melvin Kohn, and Karen Miller (1979). "Women and Work: The Psychological Effects of Occupational Conditions." *American Journal of Sociology* 85(July):66–94.

Minsky, Hyman (1986). "Review of *The Zero-Sum Solution.*" *Challenge* 29(July–August):60–4.

Mishel, Lawrence, and Jacqueline Simon (1988). "The State of Working America." *Challenge* 31(November–December):50–1.

Miyazaki, Hajime (1984). "On Success and Dissolution of the Labour Managed Firm in a Capitalist Economy." *Journal of Political Economy* 92(October):909–31.

Mises, Ludwig von (1935). "Economic Calculation in the Socialist Commonwealth," in F. Hayek (ed.), *Collectivist Economic Planning*, pp. 87–131. New York: Augustus M. Kelley.

(1949). *Human Action: A Treatise on Economics.* London: William Hodge.

Moene, Karl, and Michael Wallerstein (1992). "The Decline of Social Democracy." Working Paper no. 255, Institute of Industrial Relations, University of California, Los Angeles.

Monsen, Joseph, Jr. (1963). *Modern American Capitalism: Ideologies and Issues.* Boston: Houghton Mifflin.

Moore, Stanley (1980). *Marx on the Choice between Socialism and Communism.* Cambridge, Mass.: Harvard University Press.

Moreira Alves, Maria Helena (1990a). "The Workers' Party of Brazil: Building Struggle from the Grassroots," in W. Tabb (ed.), *The Future of Socialism*, pp. 233–48. New York: Monthly Review Press.

(1990b). "Building Democratic Socialism: The Partido dos Trabalhadores in Brazil." *Monthly Review* 42(September):1–16.

Morishima, Michio (1982). *Why Has Japan "Succeeded"?* Cambridge University Press.

Morrison, Roy (1991). *We Build the Road as We Travel*. Philadelphia: New Society Publishers.

Mowery, David, and Nathan Rosenburg (1989). *Technology and the Pursuit of Economic Growth*. Cambridge University Press.

Nagel, Thomas (1975). "Libertarianism Without Foundations." *Yale Law Journal* 85(November):136–49.

National Bureau of Economic Research (1962). *The Rate and Direction of Inventive Activity*. Princeton University Press.

Nee, Victor (1989). "Peasant Entrepreneurship in China and the Politics of Regulation," in V. Nee and D. Stark (eds.), *Remaking the Economic Institutions of Socialism: China and Eastern Europe*, pp. 169–207. Stanford University Press.

Nee, Victor, and David Stark (eds.) (1989). *Remaking the Economic Institution of Socialism: China and Eastern Europe*. Stanford University Press.

Nichols, Theo, and Huw Beynon (1977). *Living with Capitalism: Class Relations in the Modern Factory*. London: Routledge & Kegan Paul.

Nielsen, Kai (1985). *Equality and Liberty: A Defense of Radical Egalitarianism*. Totowa, N.J.: Rowman & Allanheld.

Nobel, David (1984). *Forces of Production: A Social History of Industrial Automation*. New York: Knopf.

Nordhaus, William (1986). "Can the Share Economy Cure Our Macroeconomic Woes? Probably Not." *Journal of Comparative Economics* 10:448–53.

Norr, Henry (1987). "Self-Management and the Politics of *Solidarity*," in C. Sirriani (ed.), *Worker Participation and the Politics of Reform*, pp. 267–97. Philadelphia: Temple University Press.

Nove, Alec (1977). *The Soviet Economic System*. London: Allen & Unwin.

(1983). *The Economics of Feasible Socialism*. London: Allen & Unwin.

(1989). "The Role of Central Planning Under Capitalism and Socialism," in J. Elster and K. Moene (eds.), *Alternatives to Capitalism*, pp. 98–109. Cambridge University Press.

(1991). *The Economics of Feasible Socialism, Revisited*. London: Allen & Unwin.

Nozick, Robert (1974). *Anarchy, State and Utopia*. New York: Basic Books.

(1989). *The Examined Life: Philosophical Meditations*. New York: Simon & Schuster.

Okin, Susan (1979). *Women in Western Political Thought*. Princeton University Press.

Ollman, Bertell (1971). *Alienation: Marx's Conception of Man in Capitalist Society*. Cambridge University Press.

Olsen, Mancur, and Hans Landsberg (eds.) (1973). *The No-Growth Society*. New York: Norton.

Ortuño-Ortin, Ignacio; John Roemer; and Joachim Silvestre (1990). "Market Socialism." Department of Economics Working Paper Series, nos. 355, 356, University of California, Davis.

(1991). "Investment Planning in Market Socialism." Unpublished mimeograph (April 15).

Packard, Vance (1958). *The Hidden Persuaders*. New York: Pocket Books.

   (1960). *The Waste Makers*. New York: McKay.

Palm, Göran (1977). *The Flight from Work*. Cambridge University Press.

Panitch, Leo, and Sam Gindin (1991). "Soviet Workers: A New Beginning?" *Monthly Review* 42(April):17–35.

Parel, Anthony, and Ronald Keith (eds.) (1992). *Comparative Political Philosophy: Studies under the Upas Tree*. New Delhi: Sage.

Parker, Mike, and Jane Slaughter (1988). *Choosing Sides: Unions and the Team Concept*. Boston: South End Press.

Paul, Jeffrey (ed.) (1981). *Reading Nozick: Essays on Anarchy, State and Utopia*. Totowa, N.J.: Rowman & Littlefield.

Pen, Jan (1971). *Income Distribution: Facts, Theories, Policies*. New York: Praeger.

Peterson, Wallace (1982). *Our Overloaded Economy*. Armonk, N.Y.: M.E. Sharpe.

Phelps, E. S. (1970). "Growth and Government Intervention," in A. Sen (ed.), *Growth Economics*, pp. 496–533. Baltimore: Penguin Books.

Piore, Michael, and Charles Sabel (1984). *The Second Industrial Divide: Possibilities for Prosperity*. New York: Basic Books.

Polanyi, Karl (1970). *The Great Transformation*. Boston: Beacon Press.

Prasnikar, Janez (1980). "The Yugoslav Self-managed Firm and Its Behavior." *Economic Analysis and Worker Management* 14:1–32.

Prestowitz, Clyde (1988). *Trading Places: How We Allowed Japan to Take the Lead*. New York: Basic Books.

Prude, Jonathan (1984). "ESOP's Fable: How Workers Bought a Steel Mill in Weirton, West Virginia, and What Good It Did Them." *Socialist Review* 14(November–December):27–60.

Putterman, Louis (1982). "Some Behavioral Perspectives on the Dominance of Hierarchical over Democratic Forms of Enterprise." *Journal of Economic Behavior and Organization* 3:139–60.

Rawls, John (1971). *A Theory of Justice*. Cambridge, Mass.: Harvard University Press (Belknap Press).

   (1975). "Fairness to Goodness." *Philosophical Review* 84(October):536–54.

   (1977). "The Basic Structure as Subject." *American Philosophical Quarterly* 14(April):159–65.

   (1988). "The Priority of Right and the Ideas of the Good." *Philosophy and Public Affairs* 17(Fall):251–76.

Reese, Jennifer (1991). "The Billionaires." *Fortune* 124(September 9):42ff.

Reeves, Rosser (1961). *Reality in Advertising*. New York: Knopf.

Rescher, Nicholas (1966). *Distributive Justice*. Indianapolis: Bobbs-Merrill.

Robbins, Lionel (1932). *An Essay on the Nature and Significance of Economic Science*. New York: Macmillan.

Robinson, Joan (1966). *The Accumulation of Capital*, 2nd ed. New York: St. Martin's Press.

   (1970). "Capital Theory up to Date." *Canadian Journal of Economics* 3(May):307–17.

   (1971). *Economic Heresies: Some Old-fashioned Questions in Economic Theory*. New York: Basic Books.

(ed.) (1973). *After Keynes*. New York: Barnes & Noble.

(1976). "The Age of Growth." *Challenge* 19(May–June):4–9.

Roemer, John (1982). *A General Theory of Exploitation and Class*. Cambridge, Mass.: Harvard University Press.

(ed.) (1986). *Analytical Marxism*. Cambridge University Press.

(1989). "Visions of Capitalism and Socialism." *Socialist Review* 19(July–September):93–100.

(1990). "On Market Socialism." Unpublished mimeograph (October 1).

(1991). "The Possibility of Market Socialism." Unpublished mimeograph (January 28).

(1992). "The Morality and Efficiency of Market Socialism." *Ethics* 102:448–64.

Rorty, Richard (1992). "For a More Banal Politics." *Harper's* 284(May):16–21.

Rostow, W. W. (1960). *The Stages of Economic Growth: A Non-Communist Manifesto*. Cambridge University Press.

Rothschild, Kurt: (1986–7). "Is There a Weitzman Miracle?" *Journal of Post-Keynesian Economics* 9(Winter):198–211.

Rousseau, Jean-Jacques (1968). *The Social Contract*. Baltimore: Penguin Books.

Rudolph, Hedwig, Eileen Appelbaum, and Friederike Maier (1990). "After German Unity: A Cloudier Outlook for Women." *Challenge* 33(November–December):33–40.

Rumer, Boris (1991). "New Capitalists in the U.S.S.R." *Challenge* 34(May–June):33–40.

Runciman, W. G. (1966). *Relative Deprivation and Social Justice: A Study of Attitudes to Social Inequality in Twentieth Century England*. Berkeley: University of California Press.

Ryan, Alan (1984). *Property and Political Theory*. Oxford: Blackwell Publisher.

Ryan, Cheyney (1977). "Yours, Mine and Ours: Property Rights and Individual Liberty." *Ethics* 87(January):126–41.

Sachs, Jeffrey (1991). "Crossing the Valley of Tears in East European Reform." *Challenge* 34(September–October):26–34.

Sacks, Stephen (1983). *Self-management and Efficiency: Large Corporations in Yugoslavia*. London: Allen & Unwin.

Sader, Emir, and Ken Silverstein (1991). *Without Fear of Being Happy: Lula, the Workers' Party and Brazil*. London: Verso.

St. Clair, David (1986). *The Motorization of American Cities*. New York: Praeger.

Sakai, Kuniyasu (1990). "The Feudal World of Japanese Manufacturing." *Harvard Business Review* 67(November–December):38–49.

Samuelson, Paul (1965). *Foundations of Economic Analysis*. New York: Atheneum.

(1973). *Economics*, 9th ed. New York: McGraw-Hill.

(1980). *Economics*, 11th ed. New York: McGraw-Hill.

Samuelson, Paul, and William Nordhaus (1985). *Economics*, 12th ed. New York: McGraw-Hill.

Sarti, Roland (1971). *Fascism and the Industrial Leadership in Italy, 1919–1940*. Berkeley: University of California Press.

Sartre, Jean-Paul (1963). *Search for a Method*. New York: Random House.

Scanlon, Thomas (1976). "Nozick on Rights, Liberty and Property." *Philosophy and Public Affairs* 6(Fall):3–23.

Schlesinger, Stephen, and Stephen Kinzer (1983). *Bitter Fruit: The Untold Story of the American Coup in Guatemala*. New York: Doubleday.

Schmitz, David (1988). *The United States and Fascist Italy: 1922–1940*. Chapel Hill: University of North Carolina Press.

Schneider, Kenneth (1971). *Autokind vs. Mankind: An Analysis of Tyranny, a Proposal for Rebellion, a Plan for Reconstruction*. New York: Schocken Books.

Schor, Juliet (1991). *The Overworked American: The Unexpected Decline of Leisure*. New York: Basic Books.

Schudson, Michael (1984). *Advertising, the Uneasy Persuasion: Its Dubious Impact on American Society*. New York: Basic Books.

Schumacher, E. F. (1973). *Small Is Beautiful: Economics as if People Mattered*. New York: Harper & Row.

Schumpeter, Joseph (1962). *Capitalism, Socialism and Democracy*. New York: Harper Torchbooks.

Schwartz, Adina (1982). "Meaningful Work." *Ethics* 92(July):634–46.

Schweickart, David (1980). *Capitalism or Worker Control?: An Ethical and Economic Appraisal*. New York: Praeger.

(1987a). "Market Socialist Capitalist Roaders." *Economics and Philosophy* 3 (October):308–19.

(1987b). "More on Market Socialist Capitalist Roaders: A Reply to Arnold." *Economics and Philosophy* 3(October):335–8.

(1988). "Reflections on Anti-Marx Marxism: Elster on Functionalism and the Labor Theory of Value." *Praxis International* 8(April):109–22.

(1989). "On the Exploitation of Cotton, Corn and Labor," in R. Ware and K. Nielsen (eds.), *Analyzing Marx: New Essays on Analytical Marxism*, pp. 281–98. University of Calgary Press.

Scitovsky, Tibor (1954). "Two Concepts of External Economies." *Journal of Political Economy* 62(April):143–51.

(1971). *Welfare and Competition*, rev. ed. Homewood, Ill.: Irwin.

(1976). *The Joyless Economy*. Oxford University Press.

Sellers, Patricia (1991). "The Billionairesses." *Fortune* 124(September 9):52–8.

Sen, Amartya K. (1961). "On Optimizing the Rate of Savings." *Economic Journal* 71(September):479–95.

(ed.) (1970). *Growth Economics*. Baltimore: Penguin Books.

(1984). *Resources, Values and Development*. Cambridge, Mass.: Harvard University Press.

Serrin, William (1986). "Success Story in Steel Town: Sharing Profits." *New York Times*, March 15, p. 1.

Shaiken, Harley (1985). *Work Transformed: Automation and Labor in the Computer Age*. New York: Holt, Rinehart & Winston.

Shanley, Mary Lyndon, and Carole Pateman (eds.) (1991). *Feminist Interpretations and Political Theory*. University Park: Pennsylvania State University Press.

Sheppard, Harold, and Neil Herrick (1972). *Where Have All the Robots Gone? Worker Dissatisfaction in the 70's*. New York: Macmillan.

Shiva, Vandana (1989). *Staying Alive: Women, Ecology and Development*. London: Zed Books.

Silk, Leonard, and David Vogel (1976). *Ethics and Profits: The Crisis of Confidence in American Business.* New York: Simon & Schuster.

Simon, Julian (1970). *Issues in the Economics of Advertising.* Urbana: University of Illinois Press.

Simpson, Peggy (1991). "No Liberation for Women: Eastern Europe Turns Back the Clock." *The Progressive* 55(February):20–4.

Sirianni, Carmen (ed.) (1987). *Worker Participation and the Politics of Reform.* Philadelphia: Temple University Press.

—— (1988). "Self-Management of Time: A Democratic Alternative." *Socialist Review* 18(October–December):5–56.

Sloterdijk, Peter (1987). *Critique of Cynical Reason.* Minneapolis: University of Minnesota Press.

Smith, Adam (1976). *An Inquiry into the Nature and Causes of the Wealth of Nations,* 2 vols. Indianapolis: Liberty Classics.

Solow, Robert (1968). "The Truth Further Refined: A Comment on Marris." *The Public Interest* 11(Spring):47–52.

—— (1970). "Science and Ideology," in D. Bell and I. Kristol (eds.), *Capitalism Today,* pp. 94–107. New York: Basic Books.

—— (1973). "Is the End of the World at Hand?" *Challenge* 16(March–April):39–50.

—— (1980). "On Theories of Unemployment." *American Economic Review* 10(March): 1–11.

—— (1988). "Growth Theory and After." *American Economic Review* 78(June):307–17.

Stauber, Leland (1977). "A Proposal for a Democratic Market Economy." *Journal of Comparative Economics* 1(September):235–58.

—— (1987). *A New Program for Democratic Socialism: Lessons from the Market-Planning Experience in Austria.* Carbondale, Ill.: Four Willows Press.

Stephens, Frank (ed.) (1982). *The Performance of Labour-managed Firms.* New York: St. Martin's Press.

Stretton, Hugh (1976). *Capitalism, Socialism and the Environment.* Cambridge University Press.

Sweezy, Paul (1942). *The Theory of Capitalist Development.* New York: Monthly Review Press.

Tabb, William (ed.) (1990). *The Future of Socialism.* New York: Monthly Review Press.

Taylor, Frederick Winslow (1947). *Scientific Management.* New York: Harper & Brothers.

Terkel, Studs (1975). *Working.* New York: Avon Books.

Thomas, Hendrick (1982). "The Performance of the Mondragon Cooperatives in Spain," in D. Jones and J. Svejnar (eds.), *Participatory and Self-managed Firms: Evaluating Economic Performance,* pp. 129–52. Lexington, Mass.: Heath.

Thomas, Henk, and Chris Logan (1982). *Mondragon: An Economic Analysis.* London: Allen & Unwin.

Thurow, Lester C. (1980). *The Zero-Sum Society: Distribution and the Possibilities for Economic Change.* New York: Basic Books.

—— (1983). *Dangerous Currents: The State of Economics.* New York: Random House.

—— (1985). *The Zero-Sum Solution: An Economic and Political Agenda for the 80's.* New York: Simon & Schuster.

(1987). "A Surge in Inequality." *Scientific American* 256(May):30–7.

(1992). *Head to Head: The Coming Economic Battle Among Japan, Europe, and America.* New York: Morrow.

Tietenberg, T. H. (1990). "The Poverty Connection to Environmental Policy." *Challenge* 33(September–October):26–32.

Tong, Rosemarie (1989). *Feminist Theory: A Comprehensive Introduction.* Boulder, Colo.: Westview Press.

Tuana, Nancy (1992). *Women and the History of Philosophy.* New York: Paragon House.

Turner, Henry, Jr. (1969). "Big Business and the Rise of Hitler." *American Historical Review* 75(October):56–70.

Tyson, Laura D'Andrea (1980). *The Yugoslav Economic System and Its Performance in the 1970s.* Berkeley: University of California Institute of International Studies.

U.S. Department of Health, Education, and Welfare (1973). *Work in America.* Cambridge, Mass.: MIT Press.

Useem, Michael (1984). *The Inner Circle: Large Corporations and the Rise of Business Political Activity in the U.S. and U.K.* Oxford University Press.

Vanek, Jaroslav (1970). *The General Theory of Labor-managed Market Economies.* Ithaca, N.Y.: Cornell University Press.

(1971). *The Participatory Economy.* Ithaca, N.Y.: Cornell University Press.

(1977). *The Labor-managed Economy.* Ithaca, N.Y.: Cornell University Press.

(1989). *Crisis and Reform: East and West.* Ithaca, N.Y.: author.

(1990). "On the Transition from Centrally Planned to Democratic Socialist Economies." *Economic and Industrial Democracy* 11(May):179–203.

Vickers, John, and George Yarrow (1991). "Economic Perspectives on Privatization." *Journal of Economic Perspectives* 5(Spring):111–32.

Wachtel, Paul (1983). *The Poverty of Affluence: A Psychological Portrait of the American Way of Life.* New York: Free Press.

Walzer, Michael (1980). *Radical Principles: Reflections of an Unreconstructed Democrat.* New York: Basic Books.

Ward, Benjamin (1958). "Market Syndicalism." *American Economic Review* 48:566–89.

Ware, Robert (1992a). "What Good Is Democracy?: The Alternatives in China and the West," in A. Parel and R. Keith (eds.), *Comparative Political Philosophy: Studies under the Upas Tree,* pp. 115–40. New Delhi: Sage.

(1992b). "Marx on Some Phases of Communism," in R. Beehler, D. Kopp, and B. Szabados (eds.), *On the Track of Reason: Essays in Honor of Kai Nielsen,* pp. 135–53. Boulder, Colo.: Westview Press.

Ware, Robert, and Kai Nielsen (eds.) (1989). *Analyzing Marx: New Essays on Analytical Marxism.* University of Calgary Press.

Weitzman, Martin (1985). *The Share Economy: Conquering Stagflation.* Cambridge, Mass.: Harvard University Press.

Whyte, William Foote, and Kathleen King Whyte (1988). *Making Mondragon: The Growth and Dynamics of the Worker Cooperative Complex.* Ithaca, N.Y.: Cornell University Press.

Wild, Rolf (1978). *Management by Compulsion.* Boston: Houghton Mifflin.

Wiles, Peter (1974). *Distribution East and West*. Amsterdam: North Holland.

Wilson, Jeanne (1987). "The Institution of Democratic Reforms in the Chinese Enterprise since 1978," in C. Sirianni (ed.), *Worker Participation and the Politics of Reform*, pp. 298–328. Philadelphia: Temple University Press.

World Commission on Environment and Development (1987). *Our Common Future*. Oxford University Press.

Yunker, James (1979). "The Microefficiency Argument for Socialism Revisited." *Journal of Economic Issues* 13(March):73–112.

(1982). "The People's Capitalism Thesis: A Skeptical Evaluation." *Association for Comparative Economic Studies Bulletin* 24(Winter):1–47.

(1986a). "A Market Socialist Critique of Capitalism's Dynamic Performance." *Journal of Economic Issues* 20(March):63–86.

(1986b). "Would Democracy Survive Under Market Socialism?" *Polity* 18 (Summer):678–95.

(1992). *Socialism Revised and Modernized: The Case for Pragmatic Market Socialism*. New York: Praeger.

Zimbalist, Andrew, and Claes Brundeius (1989). *The Cuban Economy: Measurement and Analysis of Socialist Performance*. Baltimore: Johns Hopkins University Press.

Zuboff, Shoshana (1988). *In the Age of the Smart Machine: The Future of Work and Power*. New York: Basic Books.

Index

About the Book and Author

Capitalism is hegemonic today not because it is the best we fallible humans can do but because it supports, and is supported by, special interests of immense power. This book argues that Economic Democracy, a competitive economy of democratically run enterprises that replaces capitalist financial markets with more suitable institutions, will be more efficient than capitalism, more rational in its growth, more democratic, more egalitarian, and less alienating.

Against Capitalism is an ambitious book, drawing on philosophical analysis, economic theory, and considerable empirical evidence to advance its controversial thesis. It examines both conservative and liberal forms of capitalism; it compares Economic Democracy to other models of socialism; and it considers the transition to Economic Democracy from advanced capitalist societies, from economies built on the Soviet model, and from conditions of underdevelopment. The book concludes with some unconventional reflections on historical materialism, ideal communism, and the future of Marxism.

David Schweickart is professor of philosophy at Loyola University of Chicago. He holds doctorate degrees in both mathematics and philosophy. He is author of *Capitalism or Worker Control? An Ethical and Economic Appraisal* and of numerous articles published in both philosophical and economic journals.